MECCAN TRADE
AND THE RISE OF ISLAM

MECCAN TRADE

AND THE RISE OF ISLAM

PATRICIA CRONE

GORGIAS PRESS
2004

First Gorgias Press Edition, 2004.

ISBN 1-59333-102-9

GORGIAS PRESS
46 Orris Ave., Piscataway, NJ 08854 USA
www.gorgiaspress.com

Printed and bound in the United States of America.

CONTENTS

PREFACE

This book owes its existence to the fact that lecturers in early Islamic history are supposed to know something about Meccan trade even if it does not happen to interest them much. I should thus like to thank the students of Islamic subjects at Oxford for forcing me to get into the subject, and also for gracefully putting up with an exasperated teacher thereafter. If, much effort notwithstanding, the sense of exasperation still shows through in this book, all I can say is that I would not have written it without it. Further, I should like to thank Adrian Brockett, Michael Cook, Gerald Hawting, Martin Hinds, and Fritz Zimmermann for reading and commenting on drafts in various stages of completion. I am also indebted to Professor A.F.L. Beeston for assistance on south Arabian matters, to Professor J. Baines for speedy and helpful replies to Egyptological queries, to F. N. Hepper of the Royal Botanic Gardens at Kew for his views on a botanical problem, and to Professor M. G. Morony for a reaction to the typescript which gave me ample warning of the potential unpopularity of its contents.

P C

PART I

THE SPICES OF ARABY

I

INTRODUCTION

Every first-year student knows that Mecca at the time of the Prophet was the centre of a far-flung trading empire, which plays a role of some importance in all orthodox accounts of the rise of Islam. Indeed, the international trade of the Meccans has achieved such fame that not only first-year students, but also professional Islamicists have come to consider documentation to be quite superfluous. Thus Montgomery Watt, whose well-known interpretation of Muḥammad's life centres on the impact of commercial wealth on the social and moral order in Mecca, devotes less than a page of his two-volume work to a discussion of the commerce from which the wealth in question supposedly derived; and with references he dispenses altogether.[1] But what do we actually know about Meccan trade? The groundwork on the subject was done by Lammens, a notoriously unreliable scholar whose name is rarely mentioned in the secondary literature without some expression of caution or disapproval, but whose conclusions would nonetheless appear to have been accepted by Watt.[2] More recently, various aspects of the question have been taken up and richly documented by Kister.[3] Kister's work is apparently held to corroborate the picture drawn up by Lammens; there is, at least, no appreciable difference between the portraits of Meccan trade presented by Watt on the basis of Lammens, by Shaban on the basis of Kister, and by Donner on the basis of both.[4] But, in fact, neither

[1] W. M. Watt, *Muhammad at Mecca*, p. 3.

[2] H. Lammens, *La Mecque à la veille de l'hégire*; *id.*, "La république marchande de la Mecque vers l'an 600 de notre ère"; cf. also *id.*, *La cité arabe de Ṭāif à la veille de l'hégire*. That Lammens is the source behind Watt's presentation is clear both from considerations of content and from the fact that he is the only authority mentioned there. Lammens is reproved for having been too sure about the details of financial operations in Mecca, but his conclusion that the operations in question were of considerable complexity is accepted (Watt, *Muhammad at Mecca*, p. 3).

[3] See in particular M. J. Kister, "Mecca and Tamīm (Aspects of Their Relations)"; and *id.*, "Some Reports Concerning Mecca from Jāhiliyya to Islam."

[4] M. A. Shaban, *Islamic History, A New Interpretation*, pp. 2 ff; that this presentation is based on the work of Kister is stated at p. 2n. F. M. Donner, "Mecca's Food Supplies and

Lammens nor Kister provides support for the conventional account, the former because his work collapses on inspection of his footnotes, the latter because his impeccable footnotes undermine our basic assumptions concerning the nature of the trade. What follows is evidence to the effect that Meccan trade is nothing if not a problem.

The conventional account of Meccan trade begs one simple question: what commodity or commodities enabled the inhabitants of so unpromising a site to engage in commerce on so large a scale? That the trading empire grew up in an unexpected place is clear, if not always clearly brought out. There have, of course, been commercial centres in Arabia that developed in areas of comparable barrenness, notably Aden. But Aden and other coastal cities of south Arabia all owed their existence to the sea, as Muqaddasī noted, whereas Mecca was an inland town.[5] It did

Muhammad's Boycott"; the reader is referred to the works of Lammens and Kister at p. 250n.

[5] Muḥammad b. Aḥmad al-Muqaddasī, *Descriptio imperii moslemici*, pp. 85 (Aden), 95 (coastal cities in general). There is something of a parallel to Mecca in pre-Islamic Shabwa, an inland city in a barren environment, which was also a cult centre and a centre of trade

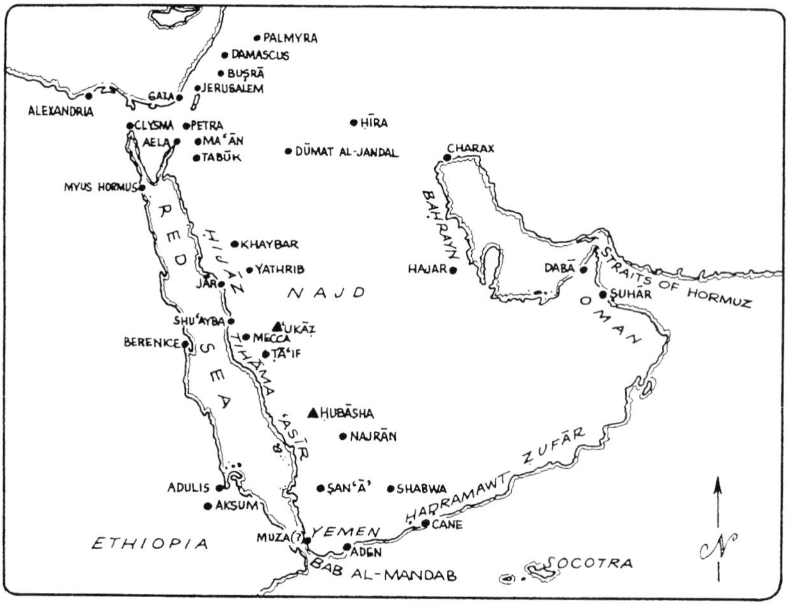

have a little port, Shuʿayba,[6] and the Koran speaks at length about the miraculous navigability of the sea.[7] The sources are agreed that the Meccans traded with Ethiopia, and there is even an isolated tradition which asserts that they used to engage in maritime trade with Rūm.[8] But the Meccans had no timber[9] and no ships;[10] they made no use of their port when blockaded by Muḥammad,[11] and neither Shuʿayba nor the sea receives much attention in the tradition.

Centres of caravan trade, on the other hand, have usually been located

---

(cf. *EI*², *s.v.* Ḥaḍramawt [Beeston]). But the rulers of Shabwa had the good fortune to control the frankincense-producing areas of Arabia so that they could decree more or less at will where they wished the frankincense to be collected (a point to which I shall return). There was nothing comparable in the vicinity of, or under the control of, Mecca.

6 Not Jār, as Donner says ("Mecca's Food Supplies," p. 254). Jār was the port of Medina, Shuʿayba being that of Mecca until it was replaced by Jedda in the caliphate of ʿUthmān (cf. *EI*², *s.vv.* Djār, Djudda; cf. also G. R. Hawting, "The Origin of Jedda and the Problem of al-Shuʿayba."

7 Forty times, according to S. Fraenkel, *Die aramäischen Fremdwörter im arabischen*, p. 211. This is odd, as Barthold points out, for there is no record of Muḥammad having travelled by sea, or even of having gone close to it, and the descriptions are very vivid (W. W. Barthold, "Der Koran und das Meer").

8 Aḥmad Ibn Ḥanbal, *al-ʿIlal*, I, 244, no. 1,410 (first noted by Kister, "Some Reports," p. 93). Compare the tradition in Sulaymān b. Aḥmad al-Ṭabarānī, *al-Muʿjam al-ṣaghīr*, I, 113, according to which the Companions of the Prophet used to engage in maritime trade with Syria (also first noted by Kister).

9 When Quraysh rebuilt the Kaʿba shortly before the *hijra*, the timber for its roof came from a Greek ship which had been wrecked at Shuʿayba (thus Muḥammad b. ʿAbdallāh al-Azraqī, *Kitāb akhbār Makka*, pp. 104 f., 107; Muḥammad Ibn Saʿd, *al-Ṭabaqāt al-kubrā*, I, 145; Yāqūt b. ʿAbdallāh, *Kitāb Muʿjam al-buldān*, III, 301, *s.v.* Shuʿayba; Aḥmad b. ʿAlī Ibn Ḥajar al-ʿAsqalānī, *Kitāb al-iṣāba fī tamyīz al-ṣaḥāba*, I, 141, no. 580, *s.v.* Bāqūm. The parallel version anachronistically has the ship stranded at Jedda (ʿAbd al-Malik Ibn Hishām, *Das Leben Muhammed's nach Muhammed Ibn Ishâk*, p. 122; Muḥammad b. Jarīr al-Ṭabarī, *Taʾrīkh al-rusul waʾl-mulūk*, ser. I, p. 1,135). A more elaborate version has it that the ship was carrying building material such as wood, marble, and iron for the rebuilding of an Ethiopian church destroyed by the Persians (Ismāʿīl b. ʿUmar Ibn Kathīr, *al-Bidāya waʾl-nihāya*, II, 301, citing the *Maghāzī* of Saʿīd b. Yaḥyā al-Umawī; similarly ʿAlī b. al-Ḥusayn al-Masʿūdī, *Kitāb murūj al-dhahab*, IV, 126 f.) Cf. also [M.] Gaudefroy-Demombynes, *Le pèlerinage à la Mekke*, pp. 33 f.

10 The *muhājirūn* who went to Ethiopia travelled in ships belonging to some obviously foreign merchants; Quraysh pursued them, but had to stop on reaching the coast (Ṭabarī, *Taʾrīkh*, ser. I, pp. 1,181 f.; Ibn Saʿd, *Ṭabaqāt*, I, 204).

11 "Avoid the coast and take the Iraq route," as a Qurashī advised when the route to Syria was blocked (Muḥammad b. ʿUmar al-Wāqidī, *Kitāb al-maghāzī*, I, 197). This point has been made several times before, first probably by Lammens (*Mecque*, p. 381).

in less hostile environments and within closer proximity to their customers than was Mecca; witness Minaean Dedan, Roman Palmyra, and Ibn Rashīd's Ḥā'il. By way of compensation, Mecca is frequently credited with the advantage of having been located at the crossroads of all the major trade routes in Arabia,[12] or at least with having been a natural halt on the so-called incense route from south Arabia to Syria.[13] But as Bulliet points out, these claims are quite wrong. Mecca is tucked away at the edge of the peninsula: "only by the most tortured map reading can it be described as a natural crossroads between a north-south route and an east-west one."[14] And the fact that it is more or less equidistant from south Arabia and Syria does not suffice to make it a natural halt on the incense route. In the first place, the caravans which travelled along this route stopped at least sixty-five times on the way; they were under no constraint to stop at Mecca merely because it happened to be located roughly midway. "On a journey of some two months duration the concept of a halfway point as a natural resting place is rather strained."[15] In the second place, barren places do not make natural halts wherever they may be located, and least of all when they are found at a short distance from famously green environments. Why should caravans have made a steep descent to the barren valley of Mecca when they could have stopped at Ṭā'if? Mecca did, of course, have both a well and a sanctu-

[12] This idea goes back to Lammens (*Mecque*, p. 118; "République," pp. 26, 51), and has since been repeated by Watt, *Muhammad at Mecca*, p. 3; Shaban, *Islamic History*, 1, 6; M. Rodinson, *Mohammed*, p. 39; P. K. Hitti, *Capital Cities of Arab Islam*, p. 7; I. Shahid (Kawar), "The Arabs in the Peace Treaty of A.D. 561," p. 192.

[13] This idea also goes back to Lammens (cf. "République," p. 51, where it is one of the most important halts on this route; *Mecque*, p. 118, where it is probably such a halt). It was cautiously accepted by B. Lewis, *The Arabs in History*, p. 34, and wholeheartedly by Hitti, *Capital Cities*, p. 5.

[14] R. W. Bulliet, *The Camel and the Wheel*, p. 105 and n40 thereto. Lammens adduced Balādhurī's version of the Ḥudaybiyya agreement in favour of his view. In this agreement, safety is granted to people travelling (from Medina) to Mecca on *ḥajj* or *ʿumra*, or on their way to Ṭā'if or the Yemen, as well as to people travelling (from Mecca) to Medina on their way to Syria and the east (Aḥmad b. Yaḥyā al-Balādhurī, *Kitāb futūḥ al-buldān*, p. 36; *id.*, *Ansāb al-ashrāf*, 1, 351. Other versions of the treaty lack such a clause, cf. *EI*², *s.v.* al-Ḥudaybiya and the references given there). This certainly suggests that people might go via Mecca to the Yemen; but it is from Medina, not Mecca, that they are envisaged as going to Syria and Iraq. (Lammens frequently adduced information about Medina as valid for Mecca, as well.)

[15] Bulliet, *Camel and the Wheel*, p. 105.

ary, but so did Ṭā'if, which had food supplies, too. In the third place, it would appear that Mecca was not located on the incense route at all. Going from south Arabia to Syria via Mecca would have meant a detour from the natural route, as both Müller and Groom have pointed out; and Groom estimates that the incense route must have bypassed Mecca by some one-hundred miles.[16] Mecca, in other words, was not just distant and barren; it was off the beaten track, as well. "The only reason for Mecca to grow into a great trading center," according to Bulliet, "was that it was able somehow to force the trade under its control."[17] It is certainly hard to think of any other. But what trade? What commodity was available in Arabia that could be transported at such a distance, through such an inhospitable environment, and still be sold at a profit large enough to support the growth of a city in a peripheral site bereft of natural resources? In Diocletian's Rome it was cheaper to ship wheat from Alexandria to Rome at a distance of some 1,250 miles than to transport it fifty miles by land.[18] The distance from Najrān to Gaza was roughly 1,250 miles, not counting the detour to Mecca.[19] "A caravan takes a month to go to Syria and a month to return," as the Meccans objected when Muḥammad claimed to have visited Jerusalem by night.[20] Whatever the Meccans sold, their goods must have been rare, much coveted, reasonably light, and exceedingly expensive.

One can read a great many accounts of Meccan trade without being initiated into the secret of what the Meccans traded in, but most Islamicists clearly envisage them as selling incense, spices, and other exotic goods. "By the end of the sixth century A.D. they had gained control of most of the trade from the Yemen to Syria—an important route by which the West got Indian luxury goods as well as South Arabian frankincense," as Watt informs us.[21] Mecca was "a transfer-point in the long-

[16] W. W. Müller, *Weihrauch*, col. 723; N. Groom, *Frankincense and Myrrh*, p. 193. In W. C. Brice, ed., *An Historical Atlas of Islam*, pp. 14 f., 19, the incense route still goes via Mecca.

[17] Bulliet, *Camel and the Wheel*, p. 105.

[18] A.H.M. Jones, "The Economic Life of the Towns of the Roman Empire," p. 164; compare N. Steensgaard, *Carracks, Caravans and Companies*, p. 40.

[19] See the helpful list of distances, in both miles and days' journey, in Groom, *Frankincense*, p. 213.

[20] Ibn Hishām, *Leben*, p. 264.

[21] Watt, *Muhammad at Mecca*, p. 3; similarly *id.*, *Muhammad, Prophet and Statesman*, p. 1; *id.*, "Ḳuraysh" in *EI*².

distance trade network between India, Africa and the Mediterranean," as we are told in the more recent statement by Donner. Similar statements are commonplace in the secondary literature.[22] Incense, spices, slaves, silk, and so forth would indeed fit the bill. The source for all this, however, is Lammens, and on turning to Kister one finds the Meccans engaged in a trade of a considerably humbler kind. The international trade of the Meccans here rests on articles such as leather and clothing, which the Meccans, moreover, advertise as being *cheap*. There is no incense, nor any other spices, in the work of Kister, and the same is true of that of Sprenger, who likewise identified the chief article of export as leather.[23] Clearly, something is amiss. Did the Meccans really trade in incense, spices, and other luxury goods? If not, could they have founded a commercial empire of international dimensions on the basis of leather goods and clothing? The answer to both questions would appear to be no, and it is for this reason that Meccan trade is a problem.

Why do Islamicists find it so easy to believe that the Meccans traded in incense, spices, and the like? Presumably because Arabia is indelibly associated with this kind of goods in the mind of every educated person. Besides, what other significant articles were available in Arabia for the Meccans to export? Because the classical spice trade of Arabia is so famous, practically every account of Meccan trade tends to be cast in its image; or in other words, Meccan trade tends to be described on the basis of stereotypes. The stereotypes in question may be summarized as follows.

Already in the third millennium B.C. the south Arabians traded in incense, later also in foreign goods; indeed, the very earliest commercial and cultural contacts between the Mediterranean and the lands around

[22] Donner, "Mecca's Food Supplies," p. 250. See, for example, H.A.R. Gibb, *Islam*, pp. 17, 26; B. Aswad, "Social and Ecological Aspects in the Origin of the Islamic State," p. 426; Hitti, *Capital Cities*, p. 7; Shahid, "Arabs in the Peace Treaty," pp. 190 ff.; cf. *id.*, "Two Qur'ānic Sūras: *al-Fīl* and *Qurayš*," p. 436 (I am grateful to Dr. G. M. Hinds for drawing my attention to this article); I. M. Lapidus, "The Arab Conquests and the Formation of Islamic Society," p. 60; Groom, *Frankincense*, p. 162.

[23] Kister, "Mecca and Tamīm," p. 116. A. Sprenger, *Das Leben und die Lehre des Moḥammad*, III, 94 f.

the Indian ocean were established via the overland incense route.[24] In any case, there is no doubt that the trade was fully developed by about 900 B.C., when the Queen of Sheba visited Solomon and when the Arabs assuredly controlled the sea route to India;[25] and they certainly supplied Egypt with Indian spices, fabrics, and precious stones about this time.[26] They also supplied ancient Iraq, for Assyrian policy vis-à-vis Arabia was dictated by concern for the security of the incense route,[27] though some are of the opinion that the trade between Babylonia and India only fell into Arab hands on the Achaemenid conquest of Iraq.[28] At all events, they soon offered their customers all the products of India, the Far East, and tropical Africa from Abyssinia to Madagascar.[29] They were a curious people in that they sailed to Africa and India, but transported their goods by caravan on reaching their native shores: this was because their boats, though adequate for long-distance journeys, were too primitive for navigation in the Red Sea and, apparently, also the Persian Gulf.[30] But they were perfectly capable of keeping the Indians out of the Red Sea, and it is because they guarded their commercial monop-

[24] C. Rathjens, "Die alten Welthandelstrassen und die Offenbarungsreligionen," pp. 115, 122.

[25] H. von Wissmann, *Die Mauer der Sabäerhauptstadt Maryab*, p. 1; R. Le Baron Bowen, "Ancient Trade Routes in South Arabia," p. 35. A similar view seems to be implied in G. L. Harding, *Archaeology in the Aden Protectorates*, p. 5. It is not clear whether the spices which the Queen of Sheba throws at the feet of Solomon in Rathjens, "Welthandelstrassen," p. 122, are envisaged as both Arabian and Indian. Müller certainly does not commit himself to such a view, though he cautiously accepts her as evidence of the existence of the south Arabian incense trade (*Weihrauch*, col. 745).

[26] W. H. Schoff, tr., *The Periplus of the Erythraean Sea*, p. 3. (References by translator and page are to Schoff's comments, those by title and paragraph to the translation.)

[27] T. W. Rosmarin, "Aribi und Arabien in den babylonisch-assyrischen Quellen," pp. 2, 7, 22; A. van den Branden, *Histoire de Thamoud*, p. 6.

[28] Thus J. Kennedy, "The Early Commerce of Babylon with India," p. 271.

[29] Rathjens, "Welthandelstrassen," p. 122.

[30] Thus B. Doe, *Southern Arabia*, p. 50; Rathjens, "Welthandelstrassen," p. 115, both with reference to the Red Sea only. Kennedy, "Early Commerce," pp. 248 f., implies that they were equally incapable of navigation in the Persian Gulf. But Doe assumes that the primitive boats of the Gerrheans were good enough for navigation in the Persian Gulf (*Southern Arabia*, p. 50), and Schoff assumes that those of the south Arabians were good enough for navigation in the Red Sea, too (Schoff, *Periplus*, p. 3), which makes the use of the overland route even odder.

oly with such jealousy that we are so ill-informed about this early trade.[31] We can, however, rest assured that all the bustling commerce described by Pliny (d. 79 A.D.) and the *Periplus* (probably about 50 A.D.) was part of the normal scene in ancient Saba some nine hundred years before.[32] We can also rest assured that it was part of the normal scene some five hundred years later. The south Arabian hold on the India trade somehow survived the establishment of direct commercial contact between India and the Greco-Roman world, so that when in due course south Arabia declined, the Meccans took over the task of satisfying the enormous Roman demand for luxury goods.[33] The Meccans used the same overland route; indeed, it was on their control of the old incense route that their commercial predominance in Arabia rested.[34] And they exported the same goods: Arabian frankincense, East African ivory and gold, Indian spices, Chinese silk, and the like.[35] It was only on the Arab conquest of the Middle East that this venerable trade came to an end, after a lifespan of some fifteen hundred or twenty-five hundred years.

All this, of course, is somewhat incredible; in what follows I shall devote myself to a demonstration that it is also quite untrue. The south Arabian trade in incense and spices is not nearly as old as is commonly assumed, and the goods in question were not invariably sent north by caravan: the last allusion to the overland route dates from the first (or, as some would have it, early second) century A.D., and the transit trade would appear to have been maritime from the start. Neither the incense

[31] Schoff, *Periplus*, pp. 88 f.; E. H. Warmington, *The Commerce between the Roman Empire and India*, pp. 11, 13. Cf. below, Ch. 2 n105.

[32] On the date of the *Periplus*, see now M. G. Raschke, "New Studies in Roman Commerce with the East," pp. 663 ff. with full references to the huge literature on the question. For Saba, see G. W. van Beek, "The Land of Sheba," p. 48; cf. also *id.*, "Frankincense and Myrrh in Ancient South Arabia," p. 146.

[33] Schoff, *Periplus*, p. 6; H. Hasan, *A History of Persian Navigation*, p. 48; Donner, "Mecca's Food Supplies," p. 250.

[34] Watt, *Muhammad at Mecca*, p. 3; Shahid, "Two Qur'ānic Sūras," p. 436. Similarly R. Paret, "Les villes de Syrie du sud et les routes commerciales d'Arabie à la fin du vi[e] siècle," pp. 441 f.; R. Simon, "Ḥums et īlāf, ou commerce sans guerre," p. 222 (though Simon's work is in other respects a refreshing attempt to go beyond hackneyed truths).

[35] Detailed documentation will be given in Chapter 3; but compare for example Doe, *Southern Arabia*, p. 52 (with reference to the sixth and fifth centuries B.C.) and Donner, "Mecca's Food Supplies," pp. 250, 254 (with reference to the sixth and early seventh centuries A.D.).

trade nor the transit trade survived long enough for the Meccans to inherit them, and there was no such thing as a Meccan trade in incense, spices, and foreign luxury goods. At least, the Islamic tradition is quite unaware that the Meccans are supposed to have handled this type of goods, and the Greeks to whom they are supposed to have sold them had never even heard of Mecca. Meccan trade there was, if we trust the Islamic tradition. But the trade described in this tradition bears little resemblance to that known from Lammens, Watt, or their various followers.

2

THE CLASSICAL SPICE TRADE

The purpose of this chapter is to correct various misconceptions about the classical spice trade that have influenced the standard account of Meccan trade; and two of its findings (the collapse of the incense trade, the foreign penetration of Arabia) are of direct relevance to the subject of this book. The reader without interest in the classical background can go straight to part II, provided that he or she is willing to refer back to the pages singled out as relevant in the notes to parts II and III.

The Incense Trade

The spices of Araby were spices in the classical sense of the word—that is, they composed a much wider category than they do today. They included incense, or substances that gave off a nice smell on being burnt; perfumes, ointments, and other sweet-smelling substances with which one dabbed, smeared, or sprinkled oneself or one's clothes; things that one put into food or drink to improve their taste, prolong their life, or to endow them with medicinal or magical properties; and they also included antidotes.[1] It is thanks to this usage that the spices of the Meccans turn out to be incense in Rodinson, but perfume in Margoliouth, whereas Watt's "Indian luxury goods" presumably mean condiments.[2] In what follows I shall likewise use "spices" without qualifications to mean any one or all three of these categories, distinguishing where necessary. We may begin by considering the trade in "spices" native to Arabia.

The spices of Arabia were primarily incense products, and the two most important ones were frankincense and myrrh.[3] Frankincense (Greek *li-*

[1] J. I. Miller, *The Spice Trade of the Roman Empire*, p. 2.

[2] M. Rodinson, *Islam et capitalisme*, p. 46 and the note thereto. D. S. Margoliouth, *Mohammed and the Rise of Islam*, p. 49; cf. Ṭabarī, *Ta'rīkh*, ser. 1, p. 1,162 (*ʿiṭr*). Watt, *Muhammad at Mecca*, p. 3.

[3] What follows is based on Müller, *Weihrauch*; Groom, *Frankincense*. Cf. also van Beek,

banos, libanōtos; Latin *t(h)us*; Arabic *lubān*) is a gum resin, or more precisely an oleo-gum-resin, exuded by various species of the genus *Boswellia* Roxb., of the family of Burseraceae, on incision of the bark.[4] The genus is native to Arabia, Socotra, East Africa, and India. Only two species of the genus, however, produce "true frankincense," the commodity so highly esteemed in the ancient world. These two species are *B. carteri* Birdw. and *B. sacra* Flück (previously lumped together under the former designation),[5] and these are native only to south Arabia and East Africa. It was thus the products of south Arabian and East African trees that were coveted by Egyptians, Jews, Greeks, Romans, and Persians alike; in due course they came to be coveted even by the Indians and the Chinese. Frankincense was burnt in honour of the gods, at funerals, and in private homes. It was also used as a medicine, a spice (in our sense of the word), and, on a small scale, as an ingredient in perfume.

Myrrh (Greek *myrrha*, *smyrnalē*; Latin *myrr(h)a*; Arabic *murr*) is also an oleo-gum-resin. It is exuded by various species of *Commiphora* Jacq. (= *Balsamodendron* Kunth.), Burseraceae, the same family as that to which frankincense belongs. The common myrrh tree is *C. myrrha* (Nees) Engl., but there are also other species in Arabia, where their habitat is considerably wider than that of frankincense, and many more in Somalia. Other species are found in India, where they yield a substance known as bdellium, to which I shall come back. Myrrh was used as an incense, or as an ingredient therein, but its most important role was in the manufacture of ointments, perfumes, and medicines. It was also used in embalming.

When did the trade in south Arabian incense and myrrh begin? This question can be disposed of briefly here, since it has recently been dealt with by Groom, whose conclusions may be accepted with slight modi-

"Frankincense and Myrrh in Ancient South Arabia"; *id.*, "Frankincense and Myrrh"; H. Ogino, "Frankincense and Myrrh of Ancient South Arabia."

[4] Gums are distinguished from resins by their ability to dissolve in or absorb water. Resins are soluble in alcohol, ether, and other solvents, but not in water. Gum-resins are a mixture of the two. Oleo-gum-resins contain an essential oil, as well (F. N. Howes, *Vegetable Gums and Resins*, pp. 3, 85, 89, 149).

[5] Cf. F. N. Hepper, "Arabian and African Frankincense Trees," pp. 67 f.; Groom, *Frankincense*, ch. 6.

fications.[6] The answer would seem to be not earlier than the seventh century B.C., for reasons that may be summarized as follows.

It may well be that the ancient Egyptians imported myrrh and frankincense from Punt as early as the third millennium B.C., and Punt may well have been the name of not only the African, but also the Arabian side of the Red Sea.[7] It is, however, most unlikely that the ancient Egyptians sailed beyond Bāb al-Mandab, let alone all the way to Ẓufār, the only or major frankincense-producing region of Arabia;[8] and the association of Punt with ivory, ebony, giraffes, grass huts, and the like certainly suggests that the Egyptians obtained their aromatics in East Africa. From an Arabian point of view, the ancient Egyptian evidence can thus be dismissed.

Thereafter there is no evidence until the Queen of Sheba, who presented Solomon with spices of an unidentified kind about 900 B.C. This queen does not, however, prove that a trade in South Arabian spices already existed, because she is most plausibly seen as a north Arabian ruler.[9] In the first place, the Sabaeans are a north Arabian people in the Assyrian records, as well as in some Biblical and classical accounts; and the traditional explanation that these Sabaeans were a trading colony from the south is implausible in view of the fact that they appear as a warlike people in the Assyrian records and as raiders who carry off Job's flocks in the Bible.[10] In the second place, queens are well attested for north Arabian tribes in the Assyrian records,[11] whereas none is attested for south Arabia at any time; indeed, there is no independent evidence for monarchic institutions at all in south Arabia as early as 900 B.C. In the third place, the unidentified spices that the Queen of Sheba presented to Solomon could just as well have come from north Arabia as

[6] Groom dates the beginning of the trade to the sixth century B.C., which must be about a century too late (*Frankincense*, ch. 2).

[7] Cf. Müller, *Weihrauch*, cols. 739 ff.

[8] Cf. C. A. Nallino, "L'Égypte avait elle des relations directes avec l'Arabie méridionale avant l'âge des Ptolémées?"; Müller, *Weihrauch*, cols. 740 f.

[9] The first to argue this was Philby, though his work was not published till long after his death (H. St. John Philby, *The Queen of Sheba*, ch. 1). The same conclusion was reached by A. K. Irvine, "The Arabs and Ethiopians," p. 299, and, independently of Irvine, by Groom, *Frankincense*, ch. 3 (the most detailed discussion).

[10] Rosmarin, "Aribi und Arabien," pp. 9 f., 14; Job 1:14 f.; Strabo, *Geography*, XVI, 4:21.

[11] Cf. Rosmarin, "Aribi und Arabien," pp. 29 ff., *s.vv.* Adia, Bâz/ṣlu, Japa', Samsi, Telchunu, and Zabibê.

from the south. Numerous incense products and other aromatics were available in north Arabia, Palestine, and elsewhere. It was such local products, not south Arabian imports, which the Ishmaelites of Gilead sold in Egypt, and there is nothing in the Biblical account to suggest that those with which the Queen of Sheba regaled her host came from any further afield.[12] The Biblical record thus takes us no further back than the seventh century B.C., the date generally accepted by Biblical scholars for the Israelite adoption of the use of frankincense and other incense products in the cult.[13]

As regards the Assyrian records, they frequently mention spices among the commodities paid by various Arabian rulers as tribute to the Assyrian kings in the eighth and seventh centuries B.C.[14] But these would again appear to have been north Arabian products, for frankincense is not attested in Mesopotamia until several centuries later and the commonly mentioned *murru* was a local plant, not an imported resin.[15] There is nothing in the Assyrian evidence to suggest a date earlier than the seventh century B.C. for the beginning of the trade.

[12] For the spices of the Ishmaelites of Gilead, see Genesis 37:25, and below, ch. 3, no. 4 (on *lōṭ*, mistranslated as "myrrh" in the authorized version) and no. 10 (on *ṣᵉrî*, "balm"). Apart from these two commodities they carried *nᵉk'ōt*, "spicery," which has been identified as the gum of *Astragalus gummifer* Labill., a Palestinian shrub (cf. H. N. Moldenke and A. L. Moldenke, *Plants of the Bible*, pp. 51 f.). Just as the Queen of Sheba presents Solomon with spices in the Bible, so a king of Sheba, clearly a northerner, pays tribute in spices (and precious stones) in the Assyrian records (cf. Rosmarin, "Aribi und Arabien," p. 14). Bulliet's proposed link between the spread of camel domestication and the incense trade is weakened by his assumption that spices sold by Arabs necessarily came from the south (*Camel and the Wheel*, pp. 67, 78).

[13] Cf. M. Haran, "The Uses of Incense in the Ancient Israelite Ritual," pp. 118 ff.

[14] The relevant passages are translated by Rosmarin, "Aribi und Arabien," pp. 8 ff., 14 ff.

[15] Frankincense is first mentioned in a medical recipe dating from the late Babylonian period, that is, not long before the Persian conquest, and Herodotus is the first to mention its use as an incense there (Müller, *Weihrauch*, col. 742). *Murru* is frequently mentioned, but not in connection with the tribute payments of the Arabs. Its physical appearance was well known; it had seeds and was used, among other things, in tanning. In principle the "myrrh-scented oil" known to the Assyrians could have been a south Arabian product, but since it figures among the gifts sent by Tushratta of Mitanni (and never in an Arabian context), this is in fact most unlikely to have been the case: "myrrh-scented" is a misleading translation (cf. *The Assyrian Dictionary of the Oriental Institute*, *s.v.* murru. Judging from this dictionary, the spices mentioned by name in connection with the tribute payments of the Arabs have not been identified).

That leaves us with the archaeological evidence. Of such there is not much, and what there is does not suggest an earlier date, either. The south Arabian clay stamp found at Bethel certainly does not prove that the trade already existed by the ninth century B.C., partly because there is a case for the view that it only came to Bethel in modern times,[16] and partly because, even if this is not the case, the stamp itself is completely undatable.[17] The south Arabian potsherds that have been found at ʿAqaba are now said to date from the sixth century B.C.;[18] the south Arabian

[16] Cf. G. W. van Beek and A. Jamme, "An Inscribed South Arabian Clay Stamp from Bethel"; A. Jamme and G. W. van Beek, "The South Arabian Clay Stamp from Bethel Again." In the first article the authors announced the discovery of a south Arabian clay stamp at Bethel; in the second they informed their readers that they had found an exact replica of this stamp in the form of a squeeze in the Glaser collection. They concluded that they had found two stamps made by the same workman: this, in their view, would suffice to explain why the two stamps had even been broken in the same place. Yadin, however, concluded that the stamp from which the squeeze in the Glaser collection had been made (and which had since disappeared) was the very stamp that had turned up at Bethel (Y. Yadin, "An Inscribed South-Arabian Clay Stamp from Bethel?"). Two rejoinders were written (G. W. van Beek and A. Jamme, "The Authenticity of the Bethel Stamp Seal"; J. L. Kelso, "A Reply to Yadin's Article on the Finding of the Bethel Stamp"), and there has been one attempt to prove that the two stamps, though similar, are not completely identical (P. Boneschi, "L'antique inscription sud-arabe d'un supposé cachet provenant de Beytīn (Béthel)." But it must be conceded that the coincidence is odd, and a hypothesis has since been proposed concerning how the Glaser stamp could have come to be buried at Bethel (R. L. Cleveland, "More on the South Arabian Clay Stamp Found at Beitîn."

[17] It was found in undatable debris outside the city wall; or more precisely, the debris ranged from the iron age to the Byzantine period (Jamme and van Beek, "Clay Stamp from Bethel Again," p. 16). It was dated to the ninth century B.C. on the ground that it must have been connected with the incense trade, which in turn must have been connected with the temple at Bethel; this temple only existed from 922 to 722 B.C., and it is conjectured that it imported most of its frankincense in the earlier part of this period (the authors take no account of the fact that the Israelites are not supposed to have made ritual use of incense at this stage). The date of the stamp thus rests on the assumption that the incense trade already existed in the ninth century B.C., a fact that does not prevent the authors from adducing the stamp as proof of this assumption (cf. van Beek and Jamme, "Clay Stamp from Bethel," p. 16). Palaeography is also invoked in favour of this date, but not convincingly (cf. Boneschi, "L'antique inscription," pp. 162 f., and the following note).

[18] Cf. N. Glueck, "The First Campaign at Tell el-Kheleifeh," p. 16 (discovery *in situ* of a large broken jar inscribed with two letters of a south Arabian script, dated to the eighth century B.C. on the basis of stratigraphy); G. Ryckmans, "Un fragment de jarre avec caractères minéens de Tell El-Kheleyfeh" (date accepted, script identified as Minaean); N. Glueck, "Tell el-Kheleifeh Inscriptions," pp. 236 f. (Ryckmans reported to have

tripod that may have been found in Iraq only dates from the sixth to fourth centuries B.C.;[19] and the same is true of other finds suggestive of trade between south Arabia and Mesopotamia. In short, the belief that the incense trade between south Arabia and the Fertile Crescent is of immense antiquity does not have much evidence in its favour.

By the seventh century B.C., however, the trade must have begun. This is clear partly from the Biblical record and partly from the fact that both frankincense and myrrh were known under their Semitic names even in distant Greece by about 600 B.C., when they are attested in the poetry of Sappho.[20] The archaeological evidence sets in about the sixth century B.C., as has been seen, and the trade becomes increasingly attested thereafter.[21] The trade may thus be said to be of a venerable age even if it is not as old as civilisation itself.

How were the incense products transported? It is a plausible contention that the earliest trade was by land. But leaving aside the obvious point that maritime expeditions to Punt on the part of the ancient Egyptians do not testify to the existence of an overland route, as has in all seriousness been argued,[22] the fact that the earliest trade was by land in no way

changed the date to the sixth century B.C.; another ostracon, possibly Minaean, dating from the seventh or sixth century B.C. discovered); *id.*, *The Other Side of the Jordan*, pp. 128, 132 (sixth-century date accepted, though the script resembles that of inscriptions dated to the fourth century B.C.); W. F. Albright, "The Chaldaean Inscription in Proto-Arabic Script," pp. 43 f. (Glueck's eighth-century date not queried, but the script possibly proto-Dedanite, under no circumstances Minaean); Müller, *Weihrauch*, col. 745 (it is probably Sabaean). Cf. also P. Boneschi, "Les monogrammes sud-arabes de la grande jarre de *Tell El-Ḫeleyfeh* (Ezion-Geber)" (where the jar still dates from the eighth or seventh century B.C.).

19 Cf. T. C. Mitchell, "A South Arabian Tripod Offering Saucer Said To Be from Ur," p. 113.

20 See the passages adduced by Müller, *Weihrauch*, col. 708.

21 The Biblical passages mentioning frankincense are listed by Moldenke and Moldenke, *Plants of the Bible*, pp. 56 f.; it is common in the Prophets, from about 600 B.C. onward. In the fifth century B.C. it was used by the Jews of Elephantine (A. Cowley, ed. and tr., *Aramaic Papyri of the Fifth Century B.C.*, nos. 30:25; 31:21; 33:11). On the Greek side it is attested in the poetry of Pindar (*fl. c.* 490 B.C.) and Melanippides (*fl. c.* 450?), and of course in Herodotus (*fl. c.* 450) (cf. H. G. Liddell and R. Scott, *A Greek-English Lexicon*, *s.v.* libanos).

22 Rathjens, "Welthandelstrassen," p. 122 and the note thereto.

means that all Arabian aromatics continued to be transported largely or wholly in this fashion until the very end of the trade;[23] as will be seen, the evidence suggests the contrary.

We do not hear anything about the overland route until the Hellenistic period. According to Hieronymus of Cardia (historian of the period 323-272 B.C.), who is cited by Diodorus Siculus, a fair number of Nabataeans were "accustomed to bring down to the sea [the Mediterranean] frankincense and myrrh and the most valuable kinds of spices, which they procure from those who convey them from what is called Arabia Eudaemon." Given the date of this statement, the goods in question were presumably conveyed to the Nabataeans by the overland route, though the text does not explicitly say so.[24] A more explicit account is given by Eratosthenes (*c.* 275-194 B.C.), who is cited by Strabo. According to him, frankincense, myrrh, and other Arabian aromatics from the Ḥaḍramawt and Qatabān were bartered to merchants who took seventy days to get from Ailana (that is, Ayla) to Minaia, whereas the Gabaioi, whoever they may have been,[25] got to the Ḥaḍramawt in forty days.[26] The overland route is alluded to again by Artemidorus (about 100 B.C.), who is also cited by Strabo and who, after an account of the lazy and easygoing life of the (southern) Sabaeans, tells us that "those who live close to one another receive in continuous succession the loads of aromatics and deliver them to their neighbours, as far as Syria and Mesopotamia"; in the course of so doing they are supposed to have become so drowsy, thanks to the sweet odours, that they had to inhale various other substances in order to stay awake.[27] A more matter-of-fact account is given by Juba (*c.* 50 B.C.–19 A.D.), who is cited by Pliny. All frankincense, according to him, had to go to Sobota, that is, Shabwa, the Ḥaḍramī capital: "the king has made it a capital offense for camels so laden

[23] *Pace* Le Baron Bowen, "Ancient Trade Routes," p. 35; Groom, *Frankincense*, p. 153.

[24] Diodorus Siculus, *Bibliotheca Historica*, XIX, 94: 5. On his source, see J. Hornblower, *Hieronymus of Cardia*. If this had been a statement by Diodorus himself, one would have taken it to mean that the Nabataeans received their goods at the northern end of the Red Sea and conveyed them from there to the Mediterranean.

[25] For an attractive solution to this problem, see A.F.L. Beeston, "Some Observations on Greek and Latin Data Relating to South Arabia," pp. 7 f.; cf. *id.*, "Pliny's Gebbanitae."

[26] Strabo, *Geography*, XVI, 4:4.

[27] *Ibid.*, XVI, 4:19. As noted by Groom, *Frankincense*, p. 243 n29, this does not appear to go back to Agatharchides.

to turn aside from the high road." From Shabwa it could only be sent on by the Gebbanitae, whose capital was Thomna, that is, the site known inscriptionally as *Tmn'*, the capital of Qatabān.[28] From here the caravans proceeded to Gaza, the journey being divided into sixty-five stages with halts for camels. Taxes were paid to the Ḥaḍramī kings in Shabwa and to the Qatabānī kings in Thomna, but a host of priests, secretaries, guards, and attendants also had to have their cut, so that the expenses reached 688 denarii per camel even before Roman import duties were paid.[29] Pliny alludes to the overland route again in a passage on inland towns to which the south Arabians "bring down their perfumes for export," and he also knew that frankincense was transported through Minaean territory "along one narrow track."[30] In the *Periplus*, too, we are informed that "all the frankincense produced in the country [the Ḥaḍramawt] is brought by camels to that place [Shabwa] to be stored," presumably for transport overland.[31] But this is the sum total of our literary evidence on the overland route.

The evidence is noteworthy in two respects. First, it mentions only Arabian goods, primarily Ḥaḍramī frankincense: no Indian spices, Chinese silk, or East African ivory are being transported by caravan to Syria here (unless one wishes to read them into Hieronymus' unidentified spices). Second, there is no mention of the overland route after Pliny and/or the *Periplus* (depending on one's views on the date of the latter). The overland route, in short, would appear to have been of restricted use in terms of both products carried and period of time.

I shall come back to the absence of foreign imports from the overland route in the next section. As regards the Arabian goods carried, Eratosthenes identifies them as coming from the Ḥaḍramawt and Qatabān (Khatramōtis, Kittabania). They similarly come from the Ḥaḍramawt and Qatabān (Sobbotha, Thomna) in Juba. The *Periplus* only mentions the Ḥaḍramawt, possibly because this state had by then absorbed its Qatabānī neighbour.[32] At all events, the Sabaeans (here and in what fol-

[28] Cf. *EI*[2], *s.v.* Ḳatabān (Beeston). The Gebbanitae are unlikely to have been Qatabānīs (cf. Beeston, "Pliny's Gebbanitae"), but Pliny, or his source, clearly took them to be rulers of the Qatabānī capital.

[29] Pliny, *Natural History*, XII, 63 ff.

[30] *Ibid.*, VI, 154; XII, 54.

[31] *Periplus*, §27.

[32] Cf. W. F. Albright, "The Chronology of Ancient South Arabia in the Light of the

lows those of the southern kind) are only mentioned in connection with Artemidorus' drowsy caravaneers and Pliny's list of inland towns to which aromatics were sent for export. Further, the goods carried are frankincense, myrrh, and other aromatics in Hieronymus and Eratosthenes, but only frankincense in Pliny and the *Periplus*; and the latter two sources explicitly inform us that the route via Shabwa was fixed by the Ḥaḍramī kings. What this suggests is that the overland route was always associated particularly with the Ḥaḍramawt (with or without its Qatabānī neighbour), not with the Sabaeans; and this makes sense, given that the Ḥaḍramawt was the only source of Arabian frankincense, or at least the only one of any importance, thanks to its control of Ẓufār.[33] The Ḥaḍramī kings were free to favour any route they wished, and by the time of Pliny and the *Periplus* it would seem that Ḥaḍramī frankincense (and apparently Ḥaḍramī frankincense alone) came north by caravan for the simple reason that the rulers of the Ḥaḍramawt decreed that this be so.[34]

First Campaign of Excavation in Qataban," pp. 9 f. (Qatabān fell about 50 B.C.); Müller, *Weihrauch*, col. 726 (about A.D. 25). A much later date is proposed by J. Pirenne, *Le royaume sud-arabe de Qatabân et sa datation* (A.D. 250); and according to Beeston, all one can say for sure is that Qatabān ceases to be mentioned in the inscriptional material by the fourth century A.D. (*EI*², *s.v.* Ḳatabān).

[33] For the view that the frankincense-bearing area of ancient Arabia was the same as today, that is, Ẓufār, see van Beek, "Frankincense and Myrrh," p. 72; *id.*, "Frankincense and Myrrh in Ancient South Arabia," pp. 141 f.; *id.*, "Ancient Frankincense-Producing Areas." According to Groom, *Frankincense*, pp. 112 ff., and J. Pirenne, "The Incense Port of Moscha (Khor Rori) in Dhofar," pp. 91 ff., it grew considerably further to the west in the past than it does today, and both have a good case. But Groom leaves the preeminence of Ẓufār unshaken, and neither claims that it grew extensively to the west of the Ḥaḍramawt.

[34] *Pace* Müller and Groom. Müller conjectures that it was the Minaeans who kept the overland route going, the destruction of their kingdom in the first century B.C. being the cause of its decline (*Weihrauch*, col. 725). But this explanation does not account for the strong interest displayed in it by the Ḥaḍramī kings, or for the continued use of the route into the first century A.D. (although this can be queried, as will be seen). Groom, on the other hand, suggests that the overland route survived because the harvest cycle was such that the incense trade and the India trade could not be combined (*Frankincense*, pp. 143 ff.). That they could not be combined may well be true; but on the one hand, one would have expected the incense trade to have become maritime even before the Greeks began to sail to India; and on the other hand, the Greeks were quite willing to sail to south Arabia for the purchase of incense alone after the India trade had got going (cf. below, n49). This explanation is thus also unsatisfactory.

Why should they have favoured the overland route? As will be seen, the south Arabians were already capable of sailing in the Red Sea in the second century B.C., and for purposes of taxation the Ḥaḍramī kings could just as well have decreed that all frankincense must go through coastal Cane: later sultans of the area were to rule that all frankincense must go through coastal Ẓufār.[35] The sea route may well have been hazardous, but then the overland trek from south Arabia to Syria was not easy, either. Caravan journeys in Arabia were arduous undertakings even in much later times, as every pilgrim knew, and the pirates with which the Red Sea was frequently infested always had their terrestrial counterparts.[36] Sailing from Cane (*Qn'*, the Ḥaḍramī port) to Berenice took only thirty days,[37] whereas it took the caravaneers sixty-five, seventy, or, according to an alternative interpretation, 120 to 130 days to get from Shabwa to Syria.[38] And the heart of every merchant must have bled at the expenditure of 688 denarii per camel on travel costs alone. In short, the overland route would seem to have owed its survival to the interests of kings rather than those of merchants. And if the Ḥaḍramī rulers enforced the use of the overland route, it was presumably because they were inland rulers allied to inland tribes, and because they did not want their goods to pass through straits controlled by their Sabaean rivals.

But the point is that by the second century B.C. their Sabaean rivals had discovered a rival source of frankincense. According to Agathar-

[35] Cf. Yāqūt, *Buldān*, III, 577, *s.v.* Ẓafār: "they gather it and carry it to Ẓafār, where the ruler takes his share. They cannot carry it elsewhere under any circumstances, and if he hears of someone who has carried it to some other town, he kills him."

[36] "And strangely to say, of these innumerable tribes an equal part are engaged in trade or live by brigandage" (Pliny, *Natural History*, VI, 162). It is not impossible that the overland route was sometimas safer than the sea route; but in view of the duration and cost of the overland route, it seems unlikely that merchants would choose whichever happened to be the more secure at the time (as suggested by Van Beek, "Frankincense and Myrrh in Ancient South Arabia," p. 148). The existence of pirates in the Red Sea is attested in both Pliny (*Natural History*, VI, 101) and the *Periplus* (§ 20), but both passages also show that pirates did not dissuade merchants from sailing, though they did make them take the precaution of manning their ships with archers, as described in Pliny.

[37] Pliny, *Natural History*, VI, 104. *Qn'* is modern Ḥisn al-Ghurāb, or more precisely a site on the isthmus connecting Ḥiṣn al-Ghurāb with the mainland (cf. A.F.L. Beeston, review of W. B. Huntingford, p. 356).

[38] Cf. Beeston, "Some Observations," pp. 8 f.

chides (*c.* 130 B.C.), the Sabaeans made use of rafts and leather boats for the transport of their goods;[39] and though he does not say from where to where, Artemidorus (*c.* 100 B.C.) took him to mean "from Ethiopia to Arabia." In Ethiopia (both in the modern sense and that of East Africa in general) large quantities of frankincense and myrrh were to be found, as the ancient Egyptians would appear to have discovered; and Artemidorus thus also knew the Sabaeans to be trading in aromatics of "both the local kind and that from Ethiopia."[40] By the first century A.D., African frankincense was as least as important as the Arabian variety, while African myrrh had already acquired priority.[41] By the sixth century, African frankincense was the only variety a merchant such as Cosmas saw fit to mention. It still dominates the market today.[42] In short, the Sabaean discovery drastically undermined the monopoly of the Ḥaḍramī suppliers.

The Sabaeans did not, of course, hand over their frankincense to the Ḥaḍramīs for transport overland via Shabwa.[43] The question is whether they sent it by land at all. Artemidorus' drowsy caravaneers certainly suggest that they did, as does Pliny's list of inland towns to which aromatics were sent, if less conclusively;[44] and Agatharchides' statement

[39] Agatharchides, § 101, in Photius, *Bibliothèque*, VII (previously edited with a Latin translation by C. Müller, *Geographi Graeci Minores*, I). For an annotated German translation, see D. Woelk, *Agatharchides von Knidos über das Rote Meer*. There is an alternative French translation of §§ 97-103 in Pirenne, *Qatabân*, pp. 82 ff., an English translation of §§ 86-103 by J. S. Hutchinson in Groom, *Frankincense*, pp. 68 ff., and an English translation of passages relating to the East African coast in G.W.B. Huntingford, tr., *The Periplus of the Erythraean Sea*, pp. 177 ff.

[40] Artemidorus in Strabo, *Geography*, XVI, 4, 19.

[41] *Periplus*, §§8-12 (also translated in Groom, *Frankincense*, pp. 138 ff.); Dioscorides, *De Materia Medica*, I, 64 = J. Goodyer, tr., *The Greek Herbal of Dioscorides*, ed. R. T. Gunther, I, 77.

[42] Cosmas Indicopleustes, *Topographie chrétienne*, II, 49; cf. II, 64. Groom, *Frankincense*, p. 135 (roughly two-thirds of the frankincense handled by Aden in 1875 came from Somali ports); Müller, *Weihrauch*, col. 730 (in 1972 about three-fifths of the world demand was met by Ethiopia).

[43] As Groom unthinkingly assumes (*Frankincense*, p. 147).

[44] Cf. above, nn27, 30. Artemidorus' caravaneers are mentioned in the middle of an account of the Sabaeans. Pliny is talking of the south Arabians at large, but he also says that it is the Sabaeans who are the best known of all Arabian tribes "because of their frankincense." B. Doe suggests that "Saba did not officially participate in the aromatics trade" ("The *WD'B* Formula and the Incense Trade," p. 41), but the Sabaeans are associated

that they made use of rafts and leather boats presumably means no more than what Artemidorus took it to mean, that is, between Africa and Arabia.[45] But Agatharchides also tells us that the Minaeans, Gerrheans, and others would unload their cargoes at an island opposite the Nabataean coast; or at least, this is what he appears to be saying.[46] In other words, Agatharchides suggests that though the Sabaeans themselves may have confined their maritime activities to crossings of the Red Sea, their distributors in the north had already taken to maritime transport by the second century B.C.[47] By the first century B.C., at any rate, there is no

with the incense trade time and again in the classical sources (cf. Müller, *Weihrauch*, cols. 711, 725); conceivably, the absence of the *wd'b* formula could be invoked in favour of the view that they did not trade much by land.

45 Artemidorus in Strabo, *Geography*, XVI, 4:19. Cf. also *ibid.*, XVI, 4:4, where Eratosthenes mentions islands in the Red Sea that were used for the transport of merchandise "from one continent to the other."

46 Agatharchides, § 87; also cited by Diodorus Siculus, *Bibliotheca*, III, 42:5; and by Artemidorus in Strabo, *Geography*, XVI, 4:18. We are told that near the island of Phocae (corrupted to "a place called Nēssa" in Photius' excerpt) there is a promontory that extends to Petra and Palestine, and that the Minaeans, Gerrheans, and others bring down their cargoes to this (island or Palestine). The most natural reading of *eis gar tautēn* (in Diodorus; *eis hēn* in Photius and Artemidorus) is that it refers to the island, partly because it is the island, not Palestine, that Agatharchides wishes to give information about, and partly because he is not sure that his information is correct; he would hardly have found it necessary to add "as they say" (*hōs logos*, in both Photius and Diodorus) if he had been talking about the arrival of caravans in Palestine. Moreover, both *phortion* (load, especially that of a ship) and *katagō* (to go down, especially to the coast, from sea to land, or to bring a ship into harbour) suggest that the transport was maritime. In Woelk's translation this interpretation is explicit, and Müller reads the passage similarly (*Weihrauch*, col. 730; but the cargoes are here unloaded at the promontory, which is grammatically impossible, the promontory being neuter). The island in question was probably Tiran (Woelk, *Agatharchides*, p. 212).

47 As distributors of Ḥaḍramī frankincense, the Gerrheans had to some extent taken to maritime transport in the Persian Gulf, too, about this time. They probably collected their frankincense by land (whatever route they may have taken), but on their return to Gerrha they would transport it by raft to Babylon and sail up the Euphrates (Aristobulus in Strabo, *Geography*, XVI, 3:3, where the apparent contradiction is easily resolved along these lines). As regards the Minaeans, Rhodokanakis would have it that a Minaean who shipped myrrh and calamus to Egypt is attested in the Gizeh inscription of 264 B.C. (N. Rhodokanakis, "Die Sarkophaginschrift von Gizeh"). But as Beeston points out, Rhodokanakis' rendering of the inscription makes a most implausible text for a sarcophagus. The linen cloth of the crucial line was either "of his *ksy*," that is, of his mummy wrapping, or else "for his *sy*," that is, for his ship in the sense of funerary barge: either way the inscription fails to mention a ship on which the deceased transported his aromatics to Egypt (A.F.L.

longer any doubt that maritime transport had come to be the norm. Thus Strabo informs us that Arabian aromatics were unloaded at Leukē Kōmē, a Nabataean port and emporium to which, he says, camel traders could travel from Petra and back in perfect safety and ease, though "at the present time" they were more often unloaded at Myus Hormus on the Egyptian side of the Red Sea; either way, it was only from these ports that the goods were transported overland, be it to Alexandria, Rhinocolura, or elsewhere.[48] Strabo, an associate of Aelius Gallus, knew of the overland route from his literary sources, but of its existence in his own time he seems to be quite unaware. By the first century A.D., Greek and Roman traders were collecting their own aromatics in Muza, a Yemeni port which, according to Pliny, was visited exclusively by merchants specializing in such aromatics, not by those on their way to India.[49] And about the same time (if we accept the traditional date of the *Periplus*) they had also come to import frankincense and myrrh directly from East African ports.[50] In short, by the first century A.D. the Yemeni incense trade had come to be wholly maritime. Indeed, the Nabataeans may have been driven to piracy by circumstances related to this very fact.[51]

It is hard to believe that the overland route survived this competition for long. In fact, it is arguable that the Ḥaḍramī incense trade had also

---

Beeston, "Two South-Arabian Inscriptions: Some Suggestions," pp. 59 ff.; *id.*, personal communication).

[48] Strabo, *Geography*, XVI, 4:23 f. (in connection with the expedition of Aelius Gallus). Strabo's statement is too circumstantial and too obviously based on contemporary rather than literary information for it to be rejected, as it is by Groom (*Frankincense*, pp. 207 f.; Groom did not notice the passage in Agatharchides cited above, n46, nor apparently the passage by Pliny cited in the following note).

[49] Pliny, *Natural History*, VI, 104.

[50] *Periplus*, §§7 ff.

[51] Cf. G. W. Bowersock, *Roman Arabia*, p. 21. The new traffic by sea was not in itself contrary to Nabataean interests: as long as the goods were unloaded at Leukē Kōmē, it was the Nabataeans who would transport them from there to Gaza via Petra. But as seen already, Strabo explicitly states that goods were more commonly unloaded at the Egyptian side of the Red Sea in his days; and the *Periplus* confirms that Leukē Kōmē had lost importance by the first century A.D. (above, n48; below, n55). Bowersock may thus well be right that it was the new maritime trade which caused the decline of the Petra-Gaza road (if it did decline then, cf. the literature cited by Bowersock, *ibid.*). He may also be right that this is what drove the Nabataeans to piracy, though the fact that Diodorus' account probably goes back to Agatharchides makes the phenomenon a little too early for comfort.

come to be maritime by the first century A.D., though this cannot be proved. Pliny, after all, derived his information on the overland route from Juba, who derived his from literary sources, in his turn—a chain that takes us well back into the first century B.C.[52] And the allusion to this route in the *Periplus* could easily have been cribbed from an earlier merchants' guide. It is certainly not very consistent to tell us first that all frankincense must go via Shabwa and next that frankincense was also exported from Cane, the Ḥaḍramī port, unless we are to take it that the exports from Cane were destined for Ommana and India alone.[53] But this is not of major importance in the present context. What matters here is that there is no reference to the overland route in the classical literature after (Juba in) Pliny and the *Periplus*, a work composed about 50 A.D. according to some, in the early second century according to others, and in the third century according to a few. And by the end of the third century A.D. the Ḥaḍramī kings who enforced the use of this route had lost their autonomy to the Sabaeans.[54]

There is nothing to suggest that the trade ever ceased to be maritime thereafter. Trajan (98-117) linked Clysma (Qulzum) to the Nile by canal and built roads between Aela (Ayla), Petra, Bostra, and Damascus, and these two ports definitively ousted Berenice and Leuke Kome.[55] Qulzum and Ayla appear as centres of Red Sea shipping in the Islamic tradition, too.[56] In the Yemen, Muza was eclipsed by Aden, the famous Eudaemon Arabia which, according to a controversial statement in the

[52] Cf. Raschke, "New Studies," p. 661. (But the well-known idea that he used the work of a Uranius who flourished in the first century B.C. is refuted at pp. 837 f.).

[53] *Periplus*, §§ 27 f.; cf. §36, where Ommana (probably on the Arabian side of the Gulf, cf. Beeston, review of Huntingford, p. 357, and possibly identifiable with Ṣuḥār, cf. Müller, *Weihrauch*, col. 728) receives frankincense from Cane, and §39, where frankincense is exported to Barbaricon in India, presumably from Cane. Groom harmonizes by assuming that frankincense could only be exported by sea by special permission (*Frankincense*, p. 153).

[54] *EI*², *s.v.* Ḥaḍramawt; W. W. Müller, "Das Ende des antiken Königreichs Ḥaḍramaut, die Sabäische Inschrift Schreyer-Geukens = Iryani 32," pp. 231, 249.

[55] G. F. Hourani, *Arab Seafaring in the Indian Ocean in Ancient and Early Medieval Times*, p. 34. Leukē Kōmē was still of minor importance in the days of the *Periplus* (cf. §19, where it is a market town for small vessels sent there from Arabia).

[56] The Byzantine ship that was stranded at Shuʿayba was on its way from Qulzum to Ethiopia, according to Masʿūdī (cf. above, ch. 1 n9). When Ayla surrendered to the Prophet, its inhabitants, including the Yemenis who were there, were granted freedom to travel by sea (below, p. 44).

Periplus, had been destroyed by "Caesar," but which had regained its former importance by the fourth century A.D.[57] The termini thus changed in the later empire, but not the mode of transport itself. It is not clear why some scholars believe the overland route to have continued into the fourth century A.D., or even later,[58] or why Islamicists generally assume it to have retained its importance until the time of Mecca's rise to commercial prominence, or to have recovered it by then. Insofar as the Islamic tradition remembers anything about the pre-Islamic incense trade, it remembers it as sea-borne.[59]

The incense trade that the Islamic tradition remembers as sea-borne was undoubtedly a trade conducted primarily with the non-Roman world. Thus Persia is still on the list of importers of African frankincense in Cosmas, who wrote in the sixth century A.D.; China is known to have imported both Arabian and African frankincense, partly via India and partly directly, until at least the thirteenth century A.D.; and India has continued to import it until today.[60] In the Greco-Roman world,

[57] *Periplus*, ed. H. Frisk, §26 (Schoff emends "Caesar" to "Charibael"); discussed by Pirenne, *Qatabân*, pp. 180 f. Cf. Philostorgius, *Kirchengeschichte*, III, 4 = E. Walford, tr., *The Ecclesiastical History of Philostorgius*, pp. 444 f., where Constantius asks for permission to build churches for the Romans who come to south Arabia by sea: one was built at Adanē, where everybody coming from the Roman empire lands in order to trade. (I do not know on what authority it is claimed that Aden later lost its importance to the Red Sea ports of Ahwāb and Ghulāfiqa: *EI*², *s.v.* ʿAdan.).

[58] See Groom, *Frankincense*, pp. 153, 162 (until the collapse of the Greco-Roman empire in the fourth century A.D.); Le Baron Bowen, "Ancient Trade Routes," p. 35 (implies much the same); Doe, *Southern Arabia*, p. 30 (until shortly before the rise of Islam); cf. also van Beek, "Frankincense and Myrrh in Ancient South Arabia," p. 148, where the evidence shows that both land and sea routes were used in *all* periods. According to Irvine, "The Arabs and Ethiopians," p. 301, by contrast, the overland route had already declined on the advent of the Christian era; similarly J. Ryckmans, *L'institution monarchique en Arabie méridionale avant l'Islam*, p. 331.

[59] The Ḥaḍramī port of Shiḥr traded in frankincense (*kundur*) and myrrh in pre-Islamic times (Aḥmad b. Muḥammad al-Marzūqī, *Kitāb al-azmina wa'l-amkina*, II, 163 f.). Aden was tithed by the Persian Abnā' and *ṭīb* was carried from there to other regions (Aḥmad b. Abī Yaʿqūb al-Yaʿqūbī, *Ta'rīkh*, I, 314). It is, however, likely that the *ṭīb* from Aden was manufactured perfume rather than raw materials, cf. below, ch. 4, p. 95.

[60] Cosmas, *Topographie*, II, 49; Müller, *Weihrauch*, cols. 721, 728; Groom, *Frankincense*, p. 135.

however, Arabian aromatics soon lost the importance which they had enjoyed in the days of Pliny.

There is general agreement that the Roman market failed to survive Christianization,[61] though the spread of Christianity does not in itself suffice to explain the decline of the trade. The early Christians certainly condemned incense-burning as idolatrous; but they soon adopted the use of incense for a variety of purposes themselves, and by the fifth or sixth century, incense-burning had come to be part of the Christian cult.[62] In terms of Christian doctrine, the market could thus have picked up again at the very time of Mecca's rise to commercial prominence. Yet it did not. The point is that Christianity had contributed, along with numerous other factors, to an irreversible change of life style in the Greco-Roman world. The classical incense trade had thrived on ostentatious behaviour by men and gods alike, a behavioural pattern that was alien to the Christians. The Christian God came to terms with incense, but in principle he continued to have no need of it, and he scarcely consumed 1,000 talents a year after the fashion of Bel.[63] Similarly, frankincense was burnt at the funeral of Justinian, but the quantity burnt was hardly greater than the annual production of Arabia, as was that which Nero saw fit to burn at the funeral of Poppaea.[64] As the grandiose squandering of incense products by the Greco-Roman elite, imitated by whoever could afford it, came to an end, frankincense ceased to be the classical equivalent of wine and cigarettes, the indispensable luxuries of everyday life.[65] The use of incense is attested for both the eastern Roman empire and the West right into the Middle Ages in connection with funerals,

[61] Thus G. Hourani, "Did Roman Commercial Competition Ruin South Arabia?" pp. 294 f.; R. Le Baron Bowen, "Irrigation in Ancient Qatabân (Beiḥân)," p. 85; Bulliet, *Camel and the Wheel*, p. 104; Groom, *Frankincense*, p. 162; Müller, *Weihrauch*, col. 746 (there is, however, no evidence that the demand had decreased in Persia, as Müller seems to imply).

[62] E.G.C.F. Atchley, *A History of the Use of Incense in Divine Worship*, pp. 81 ff.; Müller, *Weihrauch*, cols. 761 ff.; G.W.H. Lampe, ed., *Patristic Greek Lexicon*, pp. 656 f.

[63] "It is not that the Lord hath need at all of incense" (W. Riedel and W. E. Crum, eds. and trs., *The Canons of Athanasius of Alexandria*, p. 58 = 68, where the burning of incense [*bakhūr*] is part of the cult). If the attribution of this work to Athanasius, a fourth-century patriarch, were genuine, this would be one of the first attestations of incense-burning as an element in Christian worship; but the attribution is undoubtedly false. For Bel, see Herodotus, *History*, I, 183.

[64] Müller, *Weihrauch*, col. 764 (Corippus); Pliny, *Natural History*, XII, 83.

[65] Cf. Müller, *Weihrauch*, col. 733, on daily purchases of frankincense.

processions, and rituals of various kinds.[66] Yet by the sixth century, a merchant such as Cosmas no longer knew or saw fit to mention that the Byzantines imported the commodity.[67] Some clearly must have been imported for the uses mentioned, as well as for the manufacture of medicines,[68] and frankincense still figures (together with myrrh) in the tenth-century *Book of the Eparch*.[69] But the quantity imported is unlikely to have been large, and in the period of relevance to us it would seem to have come largely or wholly from East Africa.[70] Cosmas apparently did not even know that frankincense was produced in south Arabia; at least it is only as an East African product that he mentions it. Zacharias Rhetor, his contemporary, also thought of it as Ethiopian.[71] And the land that had invariably conjured up incense and spices to classical authors from Herodotus to Lucian merely suggested tribal politics, missionary activities, and Christian martyrs to authors such as Philostorgious, Pro-

[66] Cf. Atchley, *Use of Incense*, part II. Incense (*besmā*) was burnt at reliquaries of saints, on feast days, and in connection with healing in Christian Mesopotamia (cf. A. Palmer, "Sources for the Early History of Qartmin Abbey with Special Reference to the Period A.D. 400-800," *passim*). The burning of incense after meals is also well attested for the post-classical period (cf. L. Y. Rahmani, "Palestinian Incense Burners of the Sixth to Eighth Centuries C.E.," p. 122, for the Jewish evidence; below, ch. 4, n35, for attestation of the same custom in pre-Islamic Arabia; M. Aga-Oglu, "About a Type of Islamic Incense Burner," p. 28, for the same custom under the ʿAbbāsids).

[67] Cosmas, *Topographie*, II, 49 (frankincense comes from East Africa and is exported from there to south Arabia, Persia, and India).

[68] Cf. Müller, *Weihrauch*, col. 722. Both frankincense and myrrh figure prominently in E.A.W. Budge, ed. and tr., *Syrian Anatomy, Pathology and Therapeutics, or "The Book of Medicines,"* index.

[69] J. Nicole, tr., *Le livre du préfet*, (reprinted together with the Greek text, Freshfield's English translation, and other works in *The Book of the Eparch*), X, 1.

[70] The church used a variety of incense products and references to incense-burning are not necessarily references to the use of frankincense (see Atchley, *Use of Incense*, p. 272n, on the Copts; compare also the absence of myrrh and frankincense from the ingredients attested for the eighth-century monastery of Corbie in F. Kennett, *History of Perfume*, p. 91).

[71] See above, n67; this point was also noted by Müller, *Weihrauch*, col. 729, and by S. Smith, "Events in Arabia in the 6th Century A.D.," p. 426. Zacharias Rhetor, *Historia Ecclesiastica*, II, 206 = 139. In the *Book of the Eparch*, where myrrh and frankincense are mentioned together with musk, nard, cinnamon, aloe-wood and other sweet-smelling things, we are told that all these products are imported from the land of the Chaldees, Trebizond, and elsewhere (Nicole, *Livre*, X, 2), so presumably the Byzantines had come to depend on Muslim middlemen by then.

copius, and the majority of Syriac churchmen.[72] Sixth-century Corippus thought of incense as Sabaean; Jacob of Sarug (d. 521) found it appropriate to compare the faith of the Yemeni Christians with the sweet smell of the spices, incense, and aromatics sent "from your region here to us"; and Jacob of Edessa (d. 708) identified Saba as the homeland of myrrh, frankincense, and other spices associated with Arabia in antiquity.[73] But such resonances of the past are fairly rare in the texts, and to those devoid of classical learning, Arab traders conjured up the very opposite of pleasant smells. "Normally the Ishmaelites only carry hides and naphtha," a third-century rabbi observed, surprised by the association of Ishmaelites and aromatics in Genesis 37:25; it was by way of exception that God let Joseph be saved by people with sacks full of sweet-smelling things.[74] Long before the rise of Mecca to commercial prominence, Arabian frankincense and related products had ceased to be of economic consequence in the Greco-Roman world.

To summarize, the Yemeni incense trade had become wholly maritime by the first century A.D., and the Ḥaḍramī incense trade must have followed suit shortly thereafter. By the third century A.D., the Greco-Roman market had begun to collapse, never to recover. By the time of Mecca's rise to prominence, there was no overland incense trade for Quraysh to take over, and no Roman market for them to exploit.

[72] Philostorgius, *Kirchengeschichte*, III, 4, has nothing to say about Arabian incense products, though he mentions both cinnamon and cassia in connection with Ethiopia (III, 6). Procopius, *History of the Wars*, books I and II, especially I, 19 f. Cf. A. Moberg, *The Book of the Himyarites*; and I. Shahid, *The Martyrs of Najrân*. We are told that one martyr was buried in linen and aromatics (Shahid, *Martyrs*, p. x = 48), but there is no sense in these works that we are in incense land.

[73] Atchley, *Use of Incense*, pp. 101 f. R. Schröter, ed. and tr., "Trostschreiben Jacob's von Sarug an die himjaritischen Christen," p. 369 = 385 f.; the translation notwithstanding, there is no balsam in the text. Jacob of Edessa, *Hexaemeron*, p. 138 = 115 (I owe this reference to M. A. Cook); cf. A. Hjelt, "Pflanzennamen aus dem Hexaëmeron von Jacob's von Edessa," I, 573, 576 f.

[74] S. Krauss, "Talmudische Nachrichten über Arabien," pp. 335 f., with other attestations of Arabs as traders in camel hides and evil-smelling pine tar (*ʿiṭrān*). (Lammens also knew of a pre-Islamic trade in *qaṭirān*, misrepresented as an aromatic, but the passages to which he refers relate to the period of ʿAbd al-Malik; cf. Lammens, *Ṭāif*, pp. 225 f.; *id.*, *Le berceau de l'Islam*, p. 92.)

The Transit Trade

We may now turn to the role of the Arabs in the eastern trade, and once more we may start with the beginnings. Did the Arabs have maritime contacts with India long before such contacts were established between India and the rest of the western world (including Mesopotamia)? As will be seen, there is no reliable evidence in favour of this view.

Regular commercial contacts by sea between India and the western world are not attested until the first century A.D., and this is scarcely surprising. Where the Mediterranean world was united by a sea, India and the Near East were separated by one. The coasts on the way were barren, uninhabited, difficult of access due to coral reefs, rocks, and mountain chains, lacking in natural harbours, and generally devoid of timber. Exceptional patches notwithstanding, it was not a coastline that encouraged cabotage, the leisurely trundling from port to port that soon gave the inhabitants of the Mediterranean the feeling of being frogs around a pond.[75] "The sea is vast and great," as Mesopotamian soldiers told a Chinese ambassador in 97 A.D., ". . . it is for this reason that those who go to sea take with them a supply of three years' provisions. There is something in the sea which is apt to make a man homesick, and several have thus lost their lives."[76] Regular contacts thus depended on the ability to cross the ocean at mid-sea, a feat that reduced the duration of the journey to some two months, or even less. This was possible by the time of the Chinese ambassador, who was duly informed that if the winds were good, the journey would be short. But it had only become possible thanks to deliberate experiments and explorations, and the breakthrough owed much to expertise acquired in the Mediterranean. Briefly, the history of these experiments may be summarized as follows.

Contacts between Mesopotamia and India (Harappa) are attested for the third millennium B.C., and in view of the fact that there was Babylonian navigation in the Persian Gulf at the time, these contacts may have been maritime. But if they were, they were not kept up, and subsequently even navigation in the Persian Gulf would appear to have con-

[75] M. A. Cook, "Economic Developments," p. 221.

[76] F. Hirth, *China and the Roman Orient*, p. 39; cited in Hourani, *Seafaring*, p. 16.

tracted.[77] In the Assyrian period the inhabitants of the Persian Gulf demonstrated some capacity for navigation in local waters in the course of a revolt against Sennacherib (705-681 B.C.); but inasmuch as Sennacherib reacted by importing Mediterranean sailors for both the construction and the navigation of the ships he needed to suppress the rebels, little maritime expertise would seem to have been available in Mesopotamia.[78] Some scholars place the inception (or resumption) of maritime contacts between Mesopotamia and India in the neo-Babylonian period (626-539 B.C.);[79] but though maritime activities are certainly attested for this period,[80] the evidence for maritime contacts with India at this time is spurious, be it archaeological,[81] philological,[82] or other.[83] Under the

[77] A. L. Oppenheim, "The Seafaring Merchants of Ur." For numerous further references, see Raschke, "New Studies," p. 941 n1170.

[78] Hourani, *Seafaring*, p. 10.

[79] Kennedy, "Early Commerce," pp. 266 ff.

[80] Listed by Hourani, *Seafaring*, p. 10n.

[81] Thus we are told that logs of Indian teak have been found in the temple of the moon god at Muqayr and in the palace of Nebuchadnezzar at Birs Nimrud, both dating from the sixth century B.C., and logs could hardly have been transported by land (H. G. Rawlinson, *Intercourse between India and the Western World from the Earliest Time to the Fall of Rome*, p. 3; cf. R. K. Mookerji, *Indian Shipping*, pp. 60 f). But Taylor, who discovered the logs at Muqayr, merely reported that they were "apparently teak," and the logs have since disappeared. The beam at Birs Nimrud, on the other hand, was identified as Indian cedar, "a kind of teak," by Rassam, who thought that Taylor's logs were probably the same. But the only reason given by Rassam for this identification is that Indian cedar does not rot so fast as that from Lebanon (Kennedy, "Early Commerce," pp. 266 f. and the notes thereto, with reference to J. E. Taylor, "Notes on the Ruins of Muqeyer," p. 264, and a letter from H. Rassam).

[82] Thus Kennedy infers the existence of an early sea trade from his belief that rice and peacocks were known to the Greeks under their Indian names in the fifth century B.C., and that peacocks and sandalwood were similarly known in Palestine at the time of the compilers of I Kings and II Chronicles (who credited Solomon with having imported something usually identified as such), cf. Kennedy, "Early Commerce," pp. 268 f. But Sophocles (c. 460 B.C.) does not mention rice, only an *orindēs artos* which his glossators took to be made of rice (cf. Liddell and Scott, *Greek-English Lexicon*, *s.v.*). Aristophanes (*c.* 420 B.C.) does mention peacocks; but whatever the origin of these peacocks, they were not known by an Indian name. Greek *taos* is not derived from Tamil *togei* or *tokei* via Persian *ṭāwūs* (a false etymology adopted even by Liddell and Scott), for the Pahlavi word was **frashēmurv* (H. W. Bailey, *Zoroastrian Problems in the Ninth-century Books*, p. xv). Persian *ṭāwūs* is simply a transcription of the Arabic word for peacock, and the Arabic word in its turn is simply a transcription of Greek *taōs*, presumably via Aramaic or Syriac (cf. M. Jastrow, *A Dictionary of the Targumim, the Talmud Babli and Yerushalmi, and the Midrashic Literature*, I,

Achaemenids and Alexander, however, Mediterranean sailors once more came to be employed in eastern waters, and it was then that things began to happen. Both Darius and Alexander sent Greeks to explore the Indus; Alexander employed Phoenicians for the development of shipping in the Persian Gulf; and he also sent a fleet down the Gulf with orders to circumnavigate Arabia, which it failed to do, though a fleet despatched by Darius from Egypt had succeeded in reaching the Gulf.[84] Herodotus has it that Darius "subdued the Indians and made regular use of this sea"; an early Jātaka story, sometimes dated to about 400 B.C., refers to merchants sailing to Bāveru, presumably Babylon, for the sale of peacocks; and there is some evidence for ships coasting from India to the straits of Hormuz in the Hellenistic period.[85] But it is not until the first century A.D. that there is good attestation for regular contacts between India and the ports on the Persian Gulf.[86]

As regards the Red Sea, it is now generally agreed that the Punt of the ancient Egyptians was located no further away than the Somali coast opposite Arabia, for all that it may have included the Arabian side as

---

522; R. Payne Smith, *Thesaurus Syriacus*, I, col. 1444). For the sandalwood and peacocks supposedly imported by Solomon, see below, n89.

[83] Thus Kennedy adduces the sutra of Baudhāyana, which prohibits travel by sea, while admitting that the Brahmans of the north habitually engage in this and other reprehensible practices, as evidence of early Indian sea trade with the West ("Early Commerce," p. 269; similarly Mookerji, *Indian Shipping*, pp. 41 f.). But though the sutra is pre-Christian, it does not necessarily date from the seventh century B.C., and there is no indication of where the reprehensible sea journeys went. The first evidence of contact with the West in the Indian tradition is the *Bāveru Jātaka* (below, n85), dated by Kennedy to about 400 B.C.; cf. the sober discussion in A. L. Basham, "Notes on Seafaring in Ancient India," pp. 60 ff., 67 f.

[84] Pauly-Wissova, *Realencyclopädie*, *s.vv.* Skylax, 2, Nearchos, 3; Arrian, *Anabasis Alexandri*, VII, 7 f. 19, 20; G. Posener, *La première domination perse en Égypte*, pp. 48 ff.; Raschke, "New Studies," p. 655.

[85] Herodotus, *Histories*, IV, 44. E. B. Cowell and others, trs., *The Jātaka*, III, 83 f. (no. 339). W. W. Tarn, *The Greeks in Bactria and India*, pp. 260 f. Note also that according to Theophrastus (d. about 285 B.C.), fragrant plants are partly from India, "whence they are sent by sea" (Theophrastus, *Enquiry into Plants*, IX, 7:2).

[86] Cf. the story of the Chinese ambassador (above, n76). When Trajan came to Charax on the Persian Gulf in 116 A.D., he saw a ship leave for India (Dio Cassius, *Roman History*, LXVIII, 29). And by then both Apologos (Ubulla) and Ommana (Ṣuhār?, cf. above, n53) were in regular commercial contact with Barygaza in northern India (*Periplus*, §§ 35 f.).

well.[87] Solomon, who enrolled Phoenician help for his maritime enterprises, may have found his gold in ʿAsīr,[88] but the view that his fleets reached India is unconvincing.[89] The first attestation of sailing beyond Bāb al-Mandab comes from the seventh century B.C., when Neko, the Egyptian king, despatched a Phoenician fleet with orders to circumnavigate Africa, which it claimed to have done, though Herodotus did not believe it.[90] Later, Darius displayed considerable interest in the Red Sea route to the Persian Gulf and beyond.[91] But the Ptolemies concentrated

[87] See the survey in Müller, *Weihrauch*, cols. 739 ff.

[88] As argued by H. von Wissmann, "Ōphīr und Ḥawīla"; cf. also G. Ryckmans, "Ophir," where the various possibilities are discussed with further references.

[89] There are three relevant passages. We are told that the navy of Hiram brought gold, *'almuggîm* trees, and precious stones to Solomon from Ophir (I Kings 10:11), that Solomon had a navy of Tarshish together with Hiram, which brought in gold, silver, ivory, apes, and peacocks every three years (I Kings 10:22), and that Solomon's ships went to Tarshish together with Hiram's servants, bringing back gold, silver, ivory, apes, and peacocks (II Chronicles 9:8). Proponents of the view that Solomon reached India treat the Ophir and Tarshish fleets as identical, adduce the Septuagint, which renders Ophir as Zophera (that is, Supara in India), and explain the Hebrew words for ape, ivory, and peacock as loanwords from Sanskrit and Tamil. But the two fleets were not necessarily identical, their joint association with Hiram notwithstanding, and the goods brought from Ophir are not suggestive of India: gold and precious stones were not exclusively Indian commodities, and *'almuggîm* trees could be anything, though scarcely sandalwood (a fragrant wood), given that Solomon made pillars of them (I Kings 10:12). The fact that the Septuagint renders Ophir as Zophera merely proves that Supara had come to be known by the time the translation was made.

The goods brought in by the Tarshish fleet are certainly more suggestive of India. But for one thing, the sailors ought to have returned with loanwords from either Sanskrit *or* Tamil, not both. For another, the loanwords ought to have been exclusive to Hebrew. Yet Hebrew *qôp*, supposedly borrowed from Sanskrit *kapi*, "monkey," is also found in ancient Egyptian as *qwf*, *qjf*, *qfw*, in Akkadian as *uqupu*, and in Greek as *kēpos*; it may even be attested in Sumerian (cf. Oppenheim, "Seafaring Merchants," p. 12n). There were, after all, monkeys in Egypt, North Africa, Spain, and possibly elsewhere. Similarly, *šenhabbîm*, "ivory," is supposed to be related to Sanskrit *ibha*. But if so, we also have to suppose that the ancient Egyptians borrowed their word for elephants and ivory (*'bw*) from Sanskrit (as does Rawlinson, *India and the Western World*, p. 13); and the idea that the ancient Egyptians sailed to India to learn the word for an animal found in East Africa is clearly absurd. As for *tukkiyyîm*, "peacocks," supposedly derived from a supposed Tamil word such as *togei* or *tokei*, it is not clear that they were peacocks at all.

[90] Herodotus, *Histories*, IV, 42.

[91] Cf. Posener, *Première domination*, pp. 180 f.

their efforts on the African side of the Red Sea, their main interest being elephants, and there is no evidence for Greeks sailing to India, or for that matter Indians to Egypt, under the Ptolemies until about 120 B.C.[92] About this time, however, the Greeks began to coast to India,[93] and soon thereafter (though how soon is disputed), they worked out how to make use of the monsoons for mid-sea crosings, a feat traditionally credited to a certain Hippalus.[94] Of Ptolemaic coins in India there are few or none, but by the first century A.D. both coins and literary evidence show the maritime trade between India and the Greco-Roman world to have acquired major importance.[95]

What, then, is the evidence for contacts between Arabia and India before this date? The Indian tradition has nothing to say on the subject.[96] With regard to the possibility of Arabs sailing to India, the claim that the Sabaeans had founded colonies in India before or by the Hellenistic period rests on a misunderstanding of Agatharchides.[97] It may well be

[92] It was about 120 B.C. that Eudoxus of Cyzicus coasted to India, guided by an Indian who had been picked up wildly off course in the Red Sea as the sole survivor of his crew (Poseidonius in Strabo, *Geography*, II, 3:4). The story implies that nobody had sailed from Egypt to India, or the other way round, before. It is true that an Indian is said to have given thanks for a safe journey in Pan's temple at Edfu in the third or second century B.C.; but the date of the inscription is uncertain, and the man may not have been an Indian at all: Sophōn Indos is an emendation of an otherwise meaningless word (Tarn, *Greeks in Bactria*, p. 370; H. Kortenbeutel, *Der ägyptische Süd- und Osthandel in der Politik der Ptolemäer und römischen Kaiser*, pp. 49 f.).

[93] Cf. *Periplus*, § 57.

[94] The stages and dates of this discovery are discussed by Tarn, *Greeks in Bactria*, pp. 366 ff.; Warmington, *Commerce*, pp. 43 ff.; Raschke, "New Studies," pp. 660 ff. Hippalus is the name of a wind in Pliny (*Natural History*, VI, 100), his first appearance as a person being in the *Periplus*, § 57.

[95] Raschke, "New Studies," p. 663 and n1,321 thereto. Warmington, *Commerce*, p. 39.

[96] Cf. Basham, "Notes." There is plenty of conjecture, but no further evidence in the uncritical work by Mookerji, *Indian Shipping*.

[97] Cf. J. W. McCrindle, tr., *The Commerce and Navigation of the Erythraean Sea*, p. 86n, according to whom Agatharchides mentions a city, probably Aden, whence "the Sabaeans sent out colonies or factories into India, and where the fleets from Persis, Karmania and the Indus arrived." But Agatharchides mentions no city in the passage referred to, only islands (*nēsoi de eudaimōnes*, not *eudaimōn Arabia*), and he says nothing about colonists *going* from there: "in these islands it is possible to see merchant vessels at anchor. Most come from the place where Alexander established anchorage on the Indus river. A considerable number (*sc.* of colonists, not fleets) come from Persia, Carmania and all around" (Agatharchides, § 103, translated by Hutchinson in Groom, *Frankincense*, p. 72). The reference is

possible to sail to India in leather boats and rafts, the only type of vessels attested for the Arabs in the Hellenistic period,[98] but one can hardly found a regular trade on such means of transport, and Arabs sailing to India are first mentioned in the *Periplus*, that is, (probably) in the first century A.D.[99] As regards the possibility of Indians sailing to Arabia, the Islamic tradition states that the Indians of Socotra were there when the Greeks arrived in the time of Alexander. But, in fact, the Greeks do not seem to have come to Socotra until the first century B.C.[100] By then there were clearly Indians there, but how long they had been there we do not know: the Sanskrit name of the island offers no clue to the date of their arrival.[101] The first evidence for commercial contacts between India and

---

usually taken to be to Socotra. McCrindle's claim was repeated by E. Glaser, *Skizze der Geschichte und Geographie Arabiens von den ältesten Zeiten bis zum Propheten Muhammad*, II, 10, and more recently by Doe, *Southern Arabia*, p. 55.

[98] Cf. Agatharchides on the Sabaeans (above, p. 22); Aristobulos on the Gerrheans (above, n47), and the rafts at Cane and Ommana in *Periplus*, §§27, 36. Cf. also Pliny, *Natural History*, XII, 87 (East African rafts). The discussion between G. F. Hourani, "Ancient South Arabian Voyages to India—Rejoinder to G. W. van Beek," and G. W. van Beek, "Pre-Islamic South Arabian Shipping in the Indian Ocean—a Surrejoinder," does not offer any help in the present context since it is based on the view that "South Arabian participation in early trade on the Indian Ocean . . . is accepted by all scholars who are concerned with this region" (van Beek).

[99] *Periplus*, §§ 27, 54, cf. § 57. For a typical example of the way in which these passages get handled, see van Beek, "Frankincense and Myrrh in Ancient South Arabia," p. 146: "while none of these references specifically states that these contacts originated in early times, the picture as a whole is one of highly developed Arab merchant fleets and well-established commercial relations which probably have a long tradition behind them."

[100] Masʿūdī, *Murūj*, III, 36; Yāqūt, *Buldān*, III, 102, *s.v.* Suquṭrā. According to Cosmas (*Topographie*, III, 65), they were sent there by the Ptolemies. If so, it must have been toward the end of the Ptolemaic period that they were sent, for Agatharchides (d. about 130 B.C.) did not know of a Greek presence there. As far as he was concerned, it was colonized by merchants who came mainly from "the place where Alexander established anchorage on the Indus river," though some also came from "Persia, Carmania and all around" (§ 103, cited above, n97). For Agatharchides, then, the colonists were Indians and Persians. But the Greeks could well have arrived in the first century B.C., and they were certainly there by the time of the *Periplus* (§30).

[101] For the first attestation of the Indian presence, see the preceding note. (The Indian who was picked up off course in the Red Sea about 120 B.C. had perhaps also been on his way to Socotra, cf. above, n92). As for the name of the island, Greek Dioscoridēs (Dioscorida) and Arabic Suquṭrā are believed both to be corruptions of Sanskrit Dvīpa Sukhatara or Sukhatara Dvīpa, "Blessed Isle" (cf. Basham, "Notes," p. 63; *id.*, *The Wonder That was India*, p. 230n; compare above, n97, where Agatharchides speaks of Socotra [and other

Arabia is Agatharchides' statement that the Gerrheans and Sabaeans acted as "the warehouse for everything in Asia and Europe which goes under the name of distinction" in Ptolemaic Syria, that is, between 301 and 198 B.C., together with the statement in the *Periplus* that Eudaemon Arabia, the Sabaean port, served as an entrepôt for goods from India and Egypt before the establishment of direct maritime contacts between these two countries, that is, before 120 B.C. at the earliest, the first century A.D. at the latest.[102] It is clear from these statements that the Arabs played a role in the eastern trade as early as the third century B.C., but there is no direct evidence for such a role before this time.

There is, however, one important piece of indirect evidence (in addition to some that carries no weight whatever).[103] Long before the Hellenistic period the Arabs traded in cinnamon and cassia (an inferior form of cinnamon), and these products are generally assumed to have come from India, or even further east. If so, the Arabs must have had contacts with India (or the Far East) by the seventh century B.C., and it is with reference to the cinnamon trade that an early date for their contacts with India is generally advocated.[104] The trouble with this argument is that nobody in the classical world held cinnamon and cassia to be Indian or Far Eastern products. The consensus was first that they came from Ara-

---

islands?] as "blessed isles," and Philostorgius, *Kirchengeschichte*, III, 4, where Socotra seems to reappear as Dibous). Presumably it was the colonists from the Indus who brought it with them, so *pace* Kennedy, "Early Commerce," p. 257, it is not in the least odd that the name is Sanskrit rather than Tamil (and Kennedy's suggestion that the Sanskrit name is a rendering of Greek *eudaimōn Arabia* is unconvincing). But the fact that the Indian colonists came from the place where Alexander had established anchorage does not, of course, imply that they only started immigrating when, or after, this anchorage had been established. The date of their arrival thus remains unknown.

[102] Agatharchides, § 102; *Periplus*, §26.

[103] Such as the flourishing conditions of the Minaeans and Sabaeans in the first millennium B.C., or their later nautical activities (cf. Hourani, *Seafaring*, p. 11). There is no archaeological evidence, though some have thought otherwise, cf. Raschke, "New Studies," p. 654 (Raschke's work is a superb attack on fanciful notions and regurgitated truths on the classical side of the fence).

[104] Van Beek, "Frankincense and Myrrh," p. 80 (where cinnamon from Ceylon is imported as early as the fifteenth century B.C.!); Doe, *Southern Arabia*, p. 55; cf. W. Tarn and G. T. Griffiths, *Hellenistic Civilisation*, p. 244 (where the Arabian associations of cinnamon are identified as the only evidence for Arab trade with India as late as the third century B.C.). The same argument is implied, if not always spelled out, in the works cited in the following note.

bia, and later that they came from East Africa. It is for this reason that the Arabs are invariably said in the secondary literature to have hidden the true origin of their spices, enveloping their trade in such a shroud of mystery that no evidence of their contact with India remains.[105] But this explanation is unsatisfactory, for reasons which I have set out in detail in Appendix 1 and which may be summarized as follows. First, the Greeks continued to assert that cinnamon and cassia came from East Africa until at least the sixth century A.D., that is, they stuck to their delusion long after the Arabs had ceased to act as middlemen in the trade. Second, the ancient Egyptians would seem to have suffered from the same delusion: the idea of cinnamon and cassia as East African products was thus current before the Arabs can possibly have begun to act as middlemen. Third, classical descriptions of the plants involved conclusively establish both that the plants in question belonged to a genus quite different from that of *Cinnamomum*, and that they belonged to the area in which the sources place them. Finally, Muslim authors confirm that East African cinnamon was different from that imported from China. In other words, the cinnamon and cassia known to antiquity were products native to Arabia and East Africa, on a par with the frankincense and myrrh with which they are associated in the earliest attestations; they were not the products known under these names today. The same is true of calamus, another product that has been misidentified as an eastern spice, with the same implications for the question of Arab contacts with India (though in this case the implications do not seem to have been noticed). The evidence on calamus is to be found in Appendix 2. If the conclusions reached in the appendices are accepted (and they have been reached by many others before), there is no reason to credit the Arabs with contacts with India until the third century B.C., when the direct evidence begins.

We may now turn to the question of whether the overland route was ever used for the transport of Indian and other eastern goods from south Arabia to Syria and Egypt. If it is granted that cinnamon and cassia were

[105] Cf. R. Sigismund, *Die Aromata in ihrer Bedeutung für Religion, Sitten, Gebräuche, Handel und Geographie des Alterthums bis zu den ersten Jahrhunderten unserer Zeitrechnung*, p. 95; Schoff, *Periplus*, pp. 3 f.; van Beek, "Frankincense and Myrrh in Ancient South Arabia," p. 147; Hitti, *Capital Cities*, p. 6; Warmington, *Commerce*, pp. 185 ff.

local products, there is no evidence to suggest that it was. As has been seen, the classical accounts of the overland route describe it as used for the transport of Arabian aromatics alone; all fail to mention foreign spices. On the transit trade we have only the two testimonia which, in their turn, fail to mention the overland route. Thus Agatharchides merely says that no people seems to be wealthier than the Sabaeans and Gerrheans, who act as the warehouse for (or "profit from") everything from Asia and Europe of distinction, and who have made Ptolemy's Syria rich in gold, procuring markets for the Phoenicians (or the Phoenicians procuring markets for them). A wildly exaggerated account of their wealth follows, but there is no reference to modes of transport.[106] As regards the Sabaeans, however, the *Periplus* passage offers some illumination. According to this, the Sabaean port of Eudaemon Arabia (usually identified as Aden) "was called Eudaemon, because in the early days of the city when the voyage was not yet made from India and Egypt, and when they did not yet dare sail from Egypt to the ports across this ocean, but all came together at this place, it received the cargoes (*phortous*) from both countries, just as Alexandria now receives the things brought from both abroad and from Egypt."[107] The natural reading of this passage is that sailors from India and Egypt used to converge at Aden, whereas nowadays the maritime commerce between India and Egypt is direct. This agrees with Strabo's observation that in the past not twenty Greek or Roman ships dared go beyond Bāb al-Mandab, whereas nowadays whole fleets leave for India.[108] In both passages the contrast is between sailing to south Arabia and sailing all the way to India, not between a maritime and an overland route. Given the date of the *Periplus*, we cannot, of course, be sure that the eastern trade of south Arabia was wholly maritime as early as the period referred to by Agatharchides. But if it was not maritime from the start, it clearly soon became so.

That leaves us with the Gerrheans, who also participated in this

[106] Agatharchides, § 102. For the various translations to which one might have recourse, see above, n39. There seems to be general agreement that Hourani's rendering of this passage (*Seafaring*, p. 21) is inaccurate.

[107] *Periplus*, § 26. The translation is Schoff's. The alternative rendering by Huntingford, *Periplus*, does not alter the meaning.

[108] Strabo, *Geography*, XVII, 1:13; cf. II, 5:12.

trade, according to Agatharchides. Unlike the Sabaeans, they probably did not have independent access to Indian goods. The ships that coasted from India to the Persian Gulf in the Hellenistic period seem to have put in at Hormuz, not at Gerrha, which was not much of a port; and when the Gerrheans bought their freedom from Antiochus in 205 B.C., their tribute consisted of myrrh, frankincense, and silver, not of Indian spices or other foreign commodities.[109] That they sailed to India themselves is unlikely, given that the only shipping attested for them was by raft.[110] In all likelihood, then, they bought their spices at Hormuz, where the cargoes from India were unloaded for transhipment, or at Charax at the head of the Gulf, where they were unloaded again, or at Selucia on the Tigris, where the overland and maritime routes from India converged. They distributed their goods not only in Mesopotamia, but also (if Agatharchides is right) in Syria. They may have done so by transporting them across the desert to Syria, using the route on which Palmyra was later to flourish; but in fact they also seem to have bought aromatics (including Indian ones?) in south Arabia for sale in Syria, for Agatharchides enumerates them among the people who unloaded their aromatics at the island opposite the Nabatean coast.[111] Either way, their goods only travelled by land from the Gulf or the Nabataean coast, not all the way from south Arabia to Syria.

Who, then, did make use of the overland route from south Arabia for the transport of eastern goods before the establishment of direct maritime contacts between India and the west? Insofar as we can tell, nobody did, or nobody did for long.[112]

[109] Tarn, *Greeks in Bactria*, appendix 12; Pauly-Wisova, *Realencyclopädie*, *s.v.* Gerrha; Polybius, *The Histories*, XIII, 9.

[110] Cf. above, n47.

[111] Above, n46. This passage suggests that the Gerrheans operated not only from Gerrha, but also quite independently of it. (This differs from Beeston, "Some Observations," p. 7, who sees them as carrying the aromatics in question, identified as Indian products, across the peninsula from the Gulf: if they unloaded the aromatics on an island in the Red Sea, this interpretation is impossible.) Tarn's question of how the Gerrheans withstood the competition of Hormuz is beside the point in that the Gerrheans were distributors, not importers, that is, there was no competition between them and Hormuz at all.

[112] *Pace* Raschke, "New Studies," p. 657. Raschke does not distinguish between Arabian and foreign goods, but the Ptolemaic official stationed at Gaza with the title of *ho epi tēs libanōtikēs* was clearly concerned largely or wholly with Arabian spices. It is quite pos-

What was the subsequent development? From the first century A.D., not only the inhabitants of Mesopotamia, but also the Greeks and the Romans sailed directly to India, and soon also to Ceylon. The numismatic evidence indicates the trade to have been at its liveliest in the first two centuries A.D. By the end of the third century A.D., it had declined, and though it was partially revived in the fourth, it petered out thereafter.[113] There is some literary evidence for Greek traders in the East relating to the fourth and (possibly) fifth centuries,[114] and Cosmas was not the only Greek to visit Ceylon in the sixth.[115] But even so, it is clear that direct contacts had become infrequent. By the sixth century, it was the Ethiopians who conducted most of the eastern trade of the Byzantines, India and Ethiopia becoming increasingly confused in the sources.[116] The last

---

sible that the aromatics mentioned by Agatharchides in the passage discussed in the preceding note included foreign spices, but then the mode of transport envisaged seems to be maritime.

[113] R.E.M. Wheeler, "Roman Contact with India, Pakistan and Afghanistan," pp. 371 ff. According to Miller, there is numismatic evidence for trade with the Greco-Roman world in Ceylon until the fifth century, in south India until the sixth (*Spice Trade*, pp. 159, 218). But Miller gives no reference, and the most recent work on the subject disagrees (Raschke, "New Studies," p. 1068, n1,744).

[114] In the mid-fourth century, Frumentius was captured by Ethiopians on his return from India. He converted them and became the first bishop of Axum (Rufinus of Aquileia, *Historia Ecclesiastica*, I, 9, in J. P. Migne, *Patrologia Graeco-Latina*, XXI, cols. 478 ff). A certain scholasticus from Thebes set out for Ceylon about the same time (though a fifth-century date has also been advocated). He was captured somewhere in the east and remained captive for six years (J. Desanges, "D'Axoum à l'Assam, aux portes de la Chine: le voyage du 'scholasticus de Thèbes' [entre 360 et 500 après J.-C.].") The story of the scholasticus was told by Palladius about 420 (though the authorship of this letter has also been queried). Palladius himself set out for India, accompanied by Moses, bishop of Adulis, but he only managed to reach its outskirts. This has been taken to mean that he got no further than the outskirts of Ethiopia (thus most recently B. Berg, "The Letter of Palladius on India," pp. 7 f.; cf. also Desanges, "D'Axoum à Assam," p. 628n).

[115] He had heard of another Greek who had been there some thirty-five years before himself (*Topographie*, XI, 17). Compare also A. Scher and others, eds. and trs., "Histoire Nestorienne" in *Patrologia Orientalis*, VII, 160 f., where a ship returning from India with a precious cargo belonging to Greek traders is pillaged by Persian *marzubāns* in the reign of Khusraw I (531-578); whether the ship was manned by Greeks or Ethiopians is not, however, stated.

[116] Cf. Hourani, *Seafaring*, p. 39.

reference to ships returning from India before the Arab conquest dates from about 570, but whether it was from India or Ethiopia that they returned one cannot tell.[117] What does all this mean to us?

The significance of the subsequent development is threefold. First, the Arabs lost their role in the eastern trade, initially to the Greeks and subsequently to the Ethiopians. Naturally, they did not altogether cease to matter in this trade. In the Syrian desert, Palmyra thrived on the transport of exotic goods from the Persian Gulf to Syria; even the Islamic tradition remembers the existence of this route.[118] And in south Arabia, Greek ships continued to call at a number of ports for servicing and provisioning. There were Arabs in Alexandria in the first century A.D., as well as in India, and later also in Ceylon.[119] And in the sixth century, when it was uncommon for the Greeks to make the round trip to the east themselves, the south Arabians may conceivably have participated in the transport of eastern goods from Ceylon to Aden together with the Ethiopians, though this is pure conjecture. Even so, the Arabs were never to regain the predominance that the Gerrheans and Sabaeans had enjoyed in the exchange of goods between India and the Mediterranean world in the Hellenistic period, or rather not until they conquered the Middle East; and it is hard to believe that south Arabia did not suffer from the change.[120] Quite apart from its loss of predominance, such commercial roles as remained were increasingly taken over by ports on the African side of the Red Sea. Greek travellers to India invariably called at one or more ports on the African side, but it was possible to sail directly from the Horn of Africa to Ceylon, cutting out south Arabia altogether.[121] Both African myrrh and frankincense had eclipsed the Arabian varieties long before, and the same is true of African cin-

[117] C. Milani, ed. and tr., *Itinerarium Antonini Placentini*, pp. 212 f. = 257 (40:2).

[118] Thus the story of the downfall of Zabbā' (Zenobia) takes it for granted that caravans loaded with perfumes, luxury goods, and merchandise of all sorts used to cross the Syrian desert (Philby, *Queen of Sheba*, pp. 88, 105).

[119] Warmington, *Commerce*, p. 76; *Periplus*, §§ 32, 54, cf. § 57; the Sa-bo merchants mentioned by Fa-hien in Ceylon in 414 are usually taken to be Sabaeans (J. Legge, tr., *An Account by the Chinese Monk Fâ-Hien of His Travels in India and Ceylon [A. D. 399-414]*, p. 104).

[120] "Of Arab navigation we hear nothing at all" (Hourani, *Seafaring*, p. 40, with reference to this century). Cf. Hourani, "Did Roman Commercial Competition Ruin South Arabia?" (where the answer is no).

[121] Tarn, *Greeks in Bactria*, p. 368.

namon and cassia.[122] The south Arabian role in the exchange of goods between Byzantium and the east is conjectural, but that of the Ethiopians is well attested; and Adulis was certainly far better known as an emporium to the Greeks than was Aden.[123]

All this helps to explain why south Arabia was in due course to fall under the political domination of the Ethiopians, first in the fourth century and next in 525 (to adopt the traditional dates).[124] But the point to note is that the commercial decline of south Arabia had begun long before the Ethiopian conquests. The fact that south Arabia lost its autonomy does not mean that there was a commercial role for the Meccans to inherit: here, as in the case of the incense trade, Islamicists envisage them as taking over something which had in fact long ceased to exist. And one is astonished to learn that by about 600 A.D., Mecca had acquired "something like a *monopoly* of the trade between the Indian Ocean and East Africa on the one hand and the Mediterranean on the other."[125] How, one wonders, did a minor tribe of a minor city in the desert manage to clear the seas of Ethiopians, taking over even the trade between Ethiopia itself and the Byzantine world? The Ethiopians, who flourished on the eastern and African trade with Byzantium, would have found the claim more than a little surprising.

The second point of significance to us is that if the overland route had not been used for the transport of eastern goods even in the Hellenistic period, *a fortiori* it was not going to be used now. Cosmas informs us that eastern goods were commonly sent from Ceylon to Aden and Adulis, evidently for transport to the north.[126] It is not usually assumed that those which arrived at Adulis were sent on by caravan, and there is no reason to think that those which arrived at Aden were destined for this form of transport, either. The journey through the desert would have lasted two, three, or even four times as long as that from Ceylon to Arabia itself. The idea that the overland route suddenly acquired, or, as

[122] Cf. Appendix 1.

[123] Cf. Hourani, *Seafaring*, pp. 42 f. And note that just as it was with a bishop of Adulis that Palladius had set out for India (above, n114), so it was with people of Adulis that Cosmas' predecessor in Ceylon had set out for the east (above, n115). It was also in Adulis that Abraha's Byzantine master was conducting his maritime trade (below, n134).

[124] Ryckmans, *Institution monarchique*, pp. 306 ff., 320 ff.

[125] *EI*², *s.v.* Ḳuraysh (Watt); similarly Gibb, *Islam*, p. 17; Rodinson, *Mohammed*, p. 40. The italics are mine.

[126] Cosmas, *Topographie*, XI, 15.

most would have it, resumed importance in the trade between India and the west in the centuries before the rise of Islam goes back to Lammens, who claimed that on the one hand the wars between Byzantium and Persia disrupted the route from the Persian Gulf to Syria, and on the other hand people in antiquity disliked sailing, being afraid, in Lammens' terminology, of "liquid roads."[127] If so, what other route was available? This argument has been widely repeated in the secondary literature, with such substitutes for the fear of liquid roads as one can find. There is complete agreement that the Red Sea route was "apparently not much used,"[128] be it because it "remained outside Byzantine control,"[129] or because "Egypt too was in a state of disorder and no longer offered an alternative route through . . . the Red Sea,"[130] or because of factors which, as one scholar notes, are "not easily documented."[131] But in what sense was the Red Sea route apparently not much used? Shipping in the Red Sea was important enough for the Byzantines to maintain a customhouse at Iotabe, as we are told with reference to 473 A.D., when the island was seized by an Arab adventurer.[132] Some time before 500 the Byzantines recaptured Iotabe, thus giving "Roman merchants once again the opportunity to inhabit the island and to fetch cargoes from the Indians (*sc.* Ethiopians?) and bring in the tribute appointed by the emperor."[133] Of Abraha (*fl. c.* 540) we are told by Procopius that he began

[127] Lammens, "République," pp. 23 f.; *id.*, *Mecque*, pp. 108 f., 116 f.

[128] Watt, *Muhammad at Mecca*, p. 12. Watt refers his reader to Hourani's work, but gives no reason for his own position.

[129] Paret, "Les Villes de Syrie du Sud," p. 411; similarly Lapidus, "Arab Conquests," p. 60; Shahid, "Arabs in the Peace Treaty," pp. 184 ff.

[130] Lewis, *Arabs in History*, p. 33.

[131] Aswad, "Aspects," p. 422.

[132] A. A. Vasiliev, "Notes on Some Episodes Concerning the Relations between the Arabs and the Byzantine Empire from the Fourth to the Sixth Century," p. 313. The adventurer, Amorcesos = Imr' al-Qays, was not a Persian, as stated in the text, but an Arab who had previously been under Persian suzerainty, as stated in the note. Even so, the mere fact that he was called Imr' al-Qays scarcely suffices to make it probable that he was a descendant of the king of that name, as Smith, "Events in Arabia," p. 444, would have it. The island of Iotabe is generally identified as Tiran, the same island (probably) as that at which Minaeans and others used to unload their goods.

[133] Theophanes, *Chronographia*, anno mundi 5990; the translation is that of S. Smith, "Events in Arabia," p. 443 (but this statement does not testify to state-supported merchants: all Theophanes is saying is that the merchants could trade again and the state get its custom duties).

his career as a slave "of a Roman citizen who was engaged in the business of shipping in the city of Adulis in Ethiopia," a city in which, as Cosmas says, "we do trade, we merchants from Alexandria and Aela."[134] There were Byzantine traders in the Yemen at the time of Dhū Nuwās,[135] and Yemeni traders in Aela at the time of its surrender to Muḥammad: Yemeni and local inhabitants alike were granted freedom to travel by both land and sea.[136] Greek ships returning from India (*sc.* Ethiopia?) to Aela are mentioned about 570 A.D.[137] And both Byzantine and Ethiopian shipping in the Red Sea are attested in the Islamic tradition.[138]

The fact of the matter is that, just as there is no evidence for Indian goods travelling along the overland route in the Hellenistic period, so there is none for Indian goods travelling along this route in the centuries before the rise of Islam. The only reason why the overland route is believed to have mattered in the transit trade is that we need an explanation for the commercial success of Mecca: "much trade, however, still passed

[134] Procopius, *Wars*, I, 20, 4 (and note that Procopius gives a long account of navigation in the Red Sea, discussed by Smith, "Events in Arabia," pp. 428 f.); Cosmas, *Topographie*, II, 54, cf. 56 (Menas, another Egyptian merchant there). Note also the description of Ayla as a port from which one goes to India in Theodoretus, "In Divini Jeremiae Prophetiam Interpretatio," in J. P. Migne, *Patrologia Graeco-Latina*, LXXXI, col. 736.

[135] Malalas, *Chronographia*, p. 433; Theophanes, *Chronographia*, anno mundi 6035; Pseudo-Dionysius in N. Pigulewskaja, *Byzans auf den Wegen nach Indien*, pp. 325 f.

[136] Ibn Hishām, *Leben*, p. 902. The treaty is reproduced elsewhere, too.

[137] Cf. above, n117. The ships are described as returning with aromatics to Abila / Abela/ Ahela, a place in Arabia near Sinai.

[138] The ships belonging to unidentified merchants, which carried the Muhājirūn to Ethiopia, were presumably either Ethiopian or Byzantine (cf. above, ch. 1 n10). The Muhājirūn returned in ships provided by the Najāshī (Ibn Hishām, *Leben*, pp. 781, 783, cf. p. 223; Ṭabarī, *Ta'rīkh*, ser. 1, p. 1,571; Ibn Sa'd, *Ṭabaqāt*, I, 208), and Ethiopian ships are mentioned elsewhere, too; Ṭabarī, *Ta'rīkh*, ser. 1, p. 1,570. A Byzantine ship stranded at Shu'ayba (cf. the references given above, ch. 1 n9). It was a trading ship according to Ibn Isḥāq (it belonged to a man *min tujjār al-Rūm*), Azraqī (all the passengers were allowed to sell their goods in Mecca), and Ibn Ḥajar (Bāqūm, an important passenger, was a Rūmī trading with [Bāb] al-Mandab). According to others, the ship was carrying building materials for a church in Ethiopia, an elaboration of the idea that the timber from the ship was used for the rebuilding of the Ka'ba, and many identify Bāqūm as a carpenter, even when the ship is a trading ship (in Ibn Isḥāq the carpenter resides in Mecca and is a Copt like Bāqūm, a name usually, though not invariably, taken to reproduce "Pachomius," see Hawting, "Origin of Jedda," p. 319n). But trading ship or otherwise, it is clearly envisaged in most versions as going from the northern end of the Red Sea (Qulzum according to Mas'ūdī) to somewhere in Ethiopia.

up the west coast route," as Watt observes, "if we may judge from the continued prosperity of Mecca."[139] Just as there was no south Arabian India trade, so there was no overland spice route for the Meccans to take over.

The third point of significance to us is that the opening up of direct maritime relations between India and the western world made Arabia vulnerable to imperialism. Arabia was now encircled by routes over which the empires were liable sooner or later to attempt to establish direct control. No such attempts were made by the Parthians or their Roman contemporaries: it was rumours of south Arabian wealth, not concern for the passage to India, which prompted Augustus' despatch of Aelius Gallus.[140] But as the loosely knit empires of the first two centuries A.D. gave way to the Sāsānid and Byzantine super powers, Near Eastern politics came to be increasingly polarized, and even commercial rivalry now came to be invested with a political and ideological fervour that was felt all the way from the Syrian desert to Ceylon. In the Syrian desert the caravan cities of the past disappeared for good. Palmyra fell after its spectacular revolt in 273, Hatra some time before 363;[141] and the states that replaced them, Ghassān and Ḥīra, were political buffers designed to cope with border tension rather than with trade. Meanwhile, the merchants *en route* to India turned missionaries. A Roman traveller captured on his return from India converted the Ethiopians to Christianity in the fourth century A.D.;[142] a Yemeni merchant who frequented both Constantinople and Ḥīra is reputed to have spread Christianity among the Yemenis in the fifth century A.D.;[143] Syrian traders proselytized for Christianity in pre-Islamic Medina;[144] and Persian traders spread Nestorian Christianity all the way from Arabia to India, Ceylon, and beyond.[145] Even in Ceylon, Byzantine and Persian traders would argue the

[139] Watt, *Muhammad at Mecca*, p. 13.

[140] Strabo, *Geography*, XVI, 4:22 (Augustus expected "either to deal with wealthy friends or to master wealthy enemies").

[141] For the date, see *EI*², *s.v.* al-Ḥaḍr.

[142] See above, n114.

[143] Scher and others, "Histoire Nestorienne," *Patrologica Orientalis*, V, 330 f.; cf. J. Spencer Trimingham, *Christianity among the Arabs in Pre-Islamic Times*, 294 f.

[144] See below, ch. 6, n35.

[145] There was a church of Persian Nestorians in Socotra in the sixth century, as well as in Calliana, Male, and Ceylon (Cosmas, *Topographie*, III, 65). Abraham of Kashkar and Bar Sahde, Nestorian monks of the sixth and seventh centuries, both went to India on business

merits of their respective sovereigns, egged on by imperial effigies on coins that earlier merchants had taken to symbolize no more than money.[146] In the second century B.C., Agatharchides had been of the opinion that if the south Arabians "had not had their dwellings at such a distance . . . foreign administrators would soon have become the masters of such a prize."[147] By the third century A.D., the Arabs were no longer credited with fabulous wealth, nor were their dwellings located at such a distance, and their coasts had acquired much too much strategic importance to be left alone.

By far the most concerted attempt to bring Arabia under control was made by the Sāsānids. Ardashīr I (226-241) subjected the Gulf even before his formal accession, founded numerous cities on both sides, and turned the Azd of Oman into sailors. Shāpūr I (241-272) formally incorporated Oman into his domains.[148] Shāpūr II (309-379) made a punitive expedition to Arabia that took him through Baḥrayn, Hajar, and the Yamāma to the vicinity of Yathrib, and up through the Syrian desert.[149] And at some unidentified stage the Sāsānids crossed into the Najd, presumably for purposes of tribal control, discovered silver there, and proceeded to settle a colony and engage in building activities of which there may be archaeological remains.[150] The Persian Gulf was overwhelm-

(A. Mingana, "The Early Spread of Christianity in India," p. 455). There are Christian Pahlavi inscriptions in India from the seventh or eighth century onwards (A. C. Burnell, "On Some Pahlavî Inscriptions in South India"). The Nestorians may, in fact, have reached both China and Southeast Asia by sea before the fall of the Sāsānids (see B. E. Colless, "Persian Merchants and Missionaries in Medieval Malaya").

[146] Cosmas, *Topographie*, XI, 17 ff.

[147] Agatharchides, § 102.

[148] Cf. Hasan, *Persian Navigation*, pp. 59 ff.; Hourani, *Seafaring*, pp. 36 ff.; D. Whitehouse and A. Williamson, "Sasanian Maritime Trade," esp. pp. 31 f.; A Christensen, *L'Iran sous les Sassanides*, p. 87; Yāqūt, *Buldān*, IV, 522, *s.v.* Muzūn; A. Maricq, ed. and tr., " 'Res Gestae divi Saporis,' " p. 307 = 306; cf. p. 337.

[149] Ṭabarī, *Ta'rīkh*, ser. I, pp. 838 f.; cf. T. Nöldeke, tr., *Geschichte der Perser und Araber zur Zeit der Sasaniden*, p. 56. *Pace* Hasan, *Persian Navigation*, p. 64, and Whitehouse and Williamson, "Sasanian Maritime Trade," p. 32, the text does not say that Shāpūr reached Yathrib itself.

[150] Hasan b. Aḥmad al-Hamdānī, *Ṣifat Jazīrat al-ʿarab*, I, 149; *id.*, *Kitāb al-jawharatayn*, p. 143 = 142; the passage has also been translated by D. M. Dunlop, "Sources of Gold and Silver according to al-Hamdānī," p. 40: Shamām is a large village in the Najd formerly inhabited by a thousand/thousands of Magians (thousands in the *Ṣifa*), who had two fire-temples; it had a silver and copper mine, but is now in ruins. Cf. H. St. J. B. Philby, *The Heart of Arabia*, II, 84.

ingly Christian from the Tigris to Oman, and there was a church of Nestorian Christians in Socotra.[151] But there was also a diaspora of Zoroastrians in the Gulf, as well as in Najd,[152] and apparently even some Zoroastrian converts.[153] There would seem to have been a sizable Indian colony in southern Iraq,[154] and there were also Indian pirates in the Gulf.[155]

The Byzantines responded to all this mainly through the agency of the Ethiopians. As early as the fourth century A.D., as mentioned before, the Ethiopians had invaded south Arabia, presumably with a view to establishing control of both sides of the straits.[156] In the sixth century, Justinian encouraged the Ethiopians to buy silk for him, while at the same time he encouraged the Ḥimyarites to make war on the Persians.[157]

[151] Trimingham, *Christianity among the Arabs*, pp. 279 ff.; cf. also pp. 278 f., on Christianity in the Yamāma. See above, n145.

[152] Balādhurī, *Futūḥ*, pp. 78, 80 f., 85 (Baḥrayn); Ṭabarī, *Ta'rīkh*, ser. 1, p. 1,686 (Oman); above, n150 (Najd).

[153] Thus Aqra' b. Ḥābis, Abū'l-Sud b. Hassān, Zurāra b. 'Udus, and his son, according to 'Abdallāh b. Muslim Ibn Qutayba, *al-Ma'ārif*, p. 266; cf. also *EI*², *s.v.* Ḥādjib b. Zurāra; and G. Monnot, "L'Histoire des religions en Islam, Ibn al-Kalbī et Rāzī," p. 29, where other Tamīmī Zoroastrians are cited from Ibn al-Kalbī's unpublished *Mathālib al-'arab*.

[154] It is well known that Muslim sources speak of the head of the Persian Gulf as *arḍ al-Hind*, "the land of India / the Indians" (cf. the references given by J. C. Wilkinson, "Arab-Persian Land Relationships in Late Sasānid Oman," p. 41), an expression that is usually taken to mean no more than that this was a place with close relations with India. But non-Muslim sources speak about the same area as "the land of the Indians" or "India" in what appears to be a completely literal vein. Bēth Hendwāyē is enumerated as on a par with Bēth Ḥuzāyē, Beth Ṭayyayē, and so forth in O. Braun, tr., *Ausgewählte Akten persischer Märtyrer*, p. 275, and it is a place between Damascus and Fars in S. Brock, "A Syriac Life of John of Dailam," p. 166. In Malalas, *Chronographia*, p. 434, cf. 435, an Arab phylarch withdraws from Palestine to *ta Indika*, where he meets Mundhir, the chief of the Persian Saracens. And Sebeos speaks of Indians bordering on the great desert, enumerating India as a place near Asorestan (Sebeos [attrib.], *Histoire d'Héraclius*, pp. 130, 148 f.). The implication is that there was a substantial Indian population there, though there is not much sign of one after the Muslim conquest.

[155] Cf. Ṭabarī, *Ta'rīkh*, ser. 1, p. 2,023 (the ruler of *farj al-Hind*, that is, the head of the Persian Gulf, used to fight against the Arabs by land and against the Indians by sea; C. J. Lyall, ed. and tr., *The Mufaḍḍalīyāt*, no. XLI, 9: Lukayz, a branch of 'Abd al-Qays, hold the coast, but flee "if there should come danger from India's threatening mien"). In Marco Polo's time the centre of Indian piracy in this area was Socotra (Basham, "Notes on Seafaring," p. 63).

[156] Cf. above, n124.

[157] Procopius, *Wars*, I, 20, 9 ff.; discussed by Smith, "Events in Arabia," p. 427.

And when the Ethiopians invaded south Arabia again in or about 525, it was undoubtedly with Byzantine backing.[158] The Persians reacted, reluctantly at first, by conquering the Yemen for themselves.[159] Here, too, they found silver and proceeded to settle a colony. They also opened up an overland route, apparently, for the transport of silver from south and central Arabia to Iraq.[160]

By about 570, the Sāsānids thus had military colonies in Baḥrayn, Oman, and the Yemen,[161] as well as commercial colonies in both the Yemen and the Najd.[162] With the exception of Shiḥr, the successor of classical Cane in the Ḥaḍramawt, they controlled all the major Arabian ports, that is Aden, Ṣuhār, and Dabā;[163] and it was to Dabā in Oman,

[158] As the Islamic tradition claims (cf. Nöldeke, *Geschichte*, pp. 189 f.).

[159] Cf. Nöldeke, *Geschichte*, pp. 220 ff.

[160] Hamdānī, *Jawharatayn*, pp. 143, 145, 147 = 142, 144, 146; Dunlop, "Sources of Gold and Silver," pp. 41 f. Hamdānī gives the names of several of the families who made up the "Persians of the Mine" at al-Raḍrāḍ, and who survived into the Islamic period. As for the route, it was known as *ṭarīq al-Raḍrāḍ*. It is described in detail in Yūsuf b. Yaʿqūb Ibn al-Mujāwir, *Descriptio Arabiae Meridionalis*, II, 214 f. Both Hamdānī and Ibn al-Mujāwir have it run from the Yemen to Basra, but presumably it went to Ctesiphon via Ḥīra in pre-Islamic times (cf. below, n167). One might have questioned its Sāsānid origins if the first Persian governor of the Yemen had not despatched his tribute (including silver) by caravan (cf. below, ch. 4 n7).

[161] Baḥrayn was ruled by a *marzubān* who resided at Hajar and by Mundhir b. Sāwā (or Sāwī), an Arab client king of Tamīm (though he is sometimes described as an ʿAbdī), cf. Balādhurī, *Futūḥ*, p. 78; W. Caskel, *Ǧamharat an-nasab, das genealogische Werk des Hišām Ibn Muḥammad al-Kalbī*, II, *s.v.* al-Mundir b. Sāwī. In the days of Khusraw I both wine and prostitutes were imported for the colonists at Hajar (Ṭabarī, *Ta'rīkh*, ser. 1, p. 986). Baḥrayn was still part of *mamlakat al-furs* at the time of the Prophet (Balādhurī, *loc. cit.*). Cf. also R. N. Frye, "Bahrain under the Sasanians."

Oman, too, was ruled by a Persian governor in collaboration with an Arab client king, Julandā b. al-Mustakbir (frequently Mustanīr) al-Azdī and his descendants, and the Persians used Oman as a place of exile (Wilkinson, "Arab-Persian Land Relationships," p. 41; cf. also A. Abu Ezzah, "The Political Situation in Eastern Arabia at the Advent of Islam," pp. 54 ff.; Caskel, *Ǧambara*, II, *s.v.* Ǧulandā b. al-Mustakīr [*sic*]).

In the Yemen a Persian governor ruled in collaboration with a Ḥimyarī puppet king, Sayf b. Dhī Yazan, who had been enthroned on the conquest. The governor arrived with some 1,800 troops, later reinforced with another 4,000, and the Yemen was also used as a dumping ground for unwanted elements: a large part of the original troops were prisoners (Nöldeke, *Geschichte*, pp. 223 ff.; cf. *EI*², *s.v.* Abnā', II).

[162] See above, nn150, 160.

[163] Muḥammad Ibn Ḥabīb, *Kitāb al-muḥabbar*, pp. 265 f.; cf. the parallel version in Yaʿqūbī, *Ta'rīkh*, 313 f.: Ṣuhār and Dabā were both tithed by the Julandid client king of Oman, whereas Aden was tithed by the Abnā', the Persian colonists there.

we are told, that the merchants of "Sind, Hind, China, East, and West" would come.[164] Even Arabic poetry remembers something of the eastern trade in the Gulf.[165] The settlements of the Persians were protected by a string of client kings and other protégés, whose influence stretched from Ḥīra through central and eastern Arabia to the Yemen,[166] and who serviced the silver route, the only overland route of importance to anyone outside Arabia at the time.[167] And though in principle their authority stopped short of the Ḥijāz,[168] the Persians would seem to have made their impact felt even there. Thus Shāpūr, as mentioned already, is said to have campaigned in the vicinity of Yathrib, and both Yathrib and Tihāma (presumably including Mecca) are said to have had a Persian governor at some stage.[169] There is even supposed to have been Manichae-

[164] Ibn Ḥabīb, *Muḥabbar*, p. 265.

[165] Cf. G. Jacob, *Altarabisches Beduinenleben*, p. 149.

[166] For the Lakhmids of Ḥīra, see G. Rothstein, *Die Dynastie der Lahmiden in al-Ḥīra*; M. J. Kister, "al-Ḥīra." For the client kings of Baḥrayn, Oman, and the Yemen, see above, n161. We also hear of a certain Laqīṭ b. Mālik Dhū Tāj in Oman at the time of the Prophet, possibly another Sāsānid protégé (cf. Abu Ezzah, "Political Situation," p. 55 and n23a thereto). In the Yamāma they made use of Hawdha b. ʿAlī al-Ḥanafī (cf. Caskel, *Ǧamhara*, II, *s.v.*, where there is not, however, any indication of the chronological problems that this figure poses).

[167] See Abū'l-Faraj ʿAlī b. Ḥusayn al-Iṣbahānī, *Kitāb al-aghānī*, XVII, 319 f., from Ḥammād al-Rāwiya: when Kisrā wanted to send a caravan to his governor in the Yemen, he sent it under escort to Nuʿmān in Ḥīra; from Ḥīra it would be sent on, escorted by people supplied by Nuʿmān; on reaching (the Yamāma) it would pass to Hawdha b. ʿAlī, who would take it to the limits of Ḥanafī territory, where Saʿd (of Tamīm) would take over in return for payment, escorting it to the Yemen. This is clearly an account of arrangements along the *ṭarīq al-Raḍrāḍ*.

[168] Cf. Ṭabarī, *Ta'rīkh*, ser. I, p. 958, where Mundhir b. al-Nuʿmān, a Lakhmid (Mundhir III, according to Smith, "Events in Arabia," p. 442) is appointed to the area between Oman, Baḥrayn, and the Yamāma on the one hand and Ṭā'if and the rest of the Ḥijāz on the other.

[169] The passage is reproduced almost identically by Yāqūt, *Buldān*, IV, 460, *s.v.* al-Madīna, and ʿUbaydallāh b. ʿAbdallāh Ibn Khurdādhbih, *Kitāb al-masālik wa'l-mamālik*, p. 128 = 98: Medina and Tihāma were subject to a governor who was subordinated to the *marzubān* of Zāra (Yāqūt) or the *marzubān al-bādiya* (Ibn Khurdādhbih), and who would collect taxes; this was in the days when the Jews were kings, so that the Arabs in Medina would pay taxes first to Kisrā and next to Qurayẓa and Naḍīr. The evidence is poetry which is elsewhere adduced in a quite different context (cf. the discussion in Kister, "Ḥīra," pp. 145 ff., and note especially the different construction in Ṭabarī, *Ta'rīkh*, ser. I, p. 2,042). If there ever was such a governor, the most plausible period would be that of the Persian occupation of Syria, when a *marzubān al-bādiya* might well have been ap-

ism and/or Mazdakism (*zandaqa*) in Mecca.[170] Indeed, some of the votive offerings found by Quraysh in the Zamzam are supposed to have been placed there by Persian kings.[171] Only in the Ḥaḍramawt would it appear that the Persians failed to make their presence felt.

Where in all this, one wonders, is there room for the commercial and political supremacy of Mecca against the background of which Muḥammad is usually said to have enacted his career? What trade in Arabian spices was left for the Meccans to take over? What trade in eastern products could they possibly have wrested from Persians, Ethiopians, and Greeks? Where in an Arabia so "confined between Persia and Rome," as Qatāda put it,[172] was there room for the creation of a far-flung "Meccan commonwealth"? It does not make sense. I shall begin by demonstrating, item by item, that the Qurashī trade in incense, spices, and related luxury goods is a fiction.

---

pointed (but not, of course, from Zāra, which is simply a different reading). This is also a period in which there was Persian collaboration with Jews.

[170] The Meccans picked it up from the Christians (*sic*) of Ḥīra (Muḥammad Ibn Ḥabīb, *Kitāb al-munammaq*, p. 488; *id.*, *Muḥabbar*, p. 161, where the reference might be to Manichaeism), or it was imposed on the Arabs at the order of Kavādh himself (Kister, "Ḥīra," p. 145, where the reference is evidently to Mazdakism).

[171] ʿAbd al-Raḥmān b. ʿAbdallāh al-Suhaylī, *Kitāb al-rawḍ al-unuf*, I, 97; cf. Gaudefroy-Demombynes, *Pèlerinage*, p. 73.

[172] Qatāda in explanation of "remember when you were few and abased" (Qur'ān, 8:26), cited by Kister, "Ḥīra," p. 143.

3

"MECCAN SPICE TRADE"

Arabian Spices

The number of Arabian spices imported by the Greco-Roman world at the height of the trade was surprisingly large, yet by the sixth century hardly any remained on the market. Six of them had gone out of fashion, disappeared altogether, or come to be supplied from within the Greco-Roman world (frankincense, myrrh, cancamum, tarum, ladanum, sweet rush). Two may well have continued to be imported, but if so, undoubtedly by sea (aloe, cinnabar). Another two were now obtained exclusively from East Africa (cinnamon/ cassia, calamus). Two products believed by modern scholars to have been exported by the Arabs probably never entered the trade (Arabian as opposed to Judean balsam, senna). One is of problematic identity, and another two cannot be identified at all (bdellium, cardamomum, comacum). Not one is associated with Meccan trade in the sources. Readers who are willing to take this on trust can proceed to the next chapter. For those who are not, I shall deal with the spices in the above order.

1. Frankincense

As has been seen already, frankincense had ceased to be of economic consequence in the Greco-Roman world long before the rise of Mecca. In fact, it would seem to have gone out of fashion even in Arabia itself, insofar as it had ever been popular there.[1] There are no references to the use of frankincense in pre-Islamic or early Islamic poetry.[2] The incense

[1] "Frankincense is no more of Arabia Felix, and yet the perfume is sovereign in the esteem of all Arabians. The most is brought now in the pilgrimage from the Malay Islands to Mecca" (C. M. Doughty, *Travels in Arabia Deserta*, I, 137). It has been suggested that even in antiquity the Arabs preferred foreign aromatics to their own (W. W. Müller, "Notes on the Use of Frankincense in South Arabia," p. 126), and the dearth of references to frankincense in the pre-Islamic inscriptions (discussed *ibid.*) is certainly striking.

[2] No examples are adduced in the *Wörterbuch der klassischen arabischen Sprache*, *s.vv.* lubān and kundur, or in Müller's *Weihrauch*, a superbly well-documented work. The *Lisān* only adduces one passage in which *lubān* could be taken to mean frankincense; the reference is

which was burnt at the pre-Islamic Kaʿba[3] and other sanctuaries[4] could have been *lubān*; but it is not identified as such, and there is nothing to suggest that the product was highly esteemed after the conquests. Muslim geographers knew it as a product native (according to some, exclusive) to south Arabia;[5] some knew it from the Bible;[6] and druggists, herbalists, and doctors knew it from the classical tradition.[7] But references to the sale and use of *lubān* (or *kundur*) are rare.[8] As regards the Meccans,

to a tree rather than its product, and the tree in question is explained as a *ṣanawbar*, "stone pine" (Muḥammad b. Mukarrim Ibn Manẓūr, *Lisān al-ʿarab*, XVII, 260, *s.v.* lbn, on Imr' al-Qays' *labā ʿunuqun ka-suḥūqi'l-lubāni* and variants). The other attestations of *lubān* adduced there do not refer to frankincense, be it in the sense of tree or resin, and the same is true of those collected by the Poetry Concordance of the Hebrew University (I am grateful to Professor M. J. Kister and Z. Cohen for letting me have them). The *lubnā* adduced by J. H. Mordtmann and D. H. Müller, *Sabäische Denkmäler*, p. 82, is not frankincense, but storax (Müller, "Notes on the Use," p. 126; Jacob, *Beduinenleben*, p. 15), a foreign product imported by the Arabs even in the days of Pliny (*Natural History*, XII, 81).

3 Cf. Azraqī, *Makka*, pp. 105 f.; Ibn Hishām, *Leben*, p. 430.

4 Wāqidī, *Magbāzī*, III, 972 (*ṭīb*, gold and silver were deposited in the cave of Allāt, the Thaqafī idol).

5 It is one of the four things which Aṣmaʿī is said to have believed exclusive to south Arabia (Abu Ḥanīfa al-Dīnawarī, *The Book of Plants, Part of the Monograph Section*, no. 377; ʿAbd al-Malik b. Muḥammad al-Thaʿālibī, *The Laṭā' if al-maʿārif*, p. 123). It grew in the mountains of Shiḥr ʿUmān, not on the coast (Abū Ḥanīfa al-Dīnawarī, *Le dictionnaire botanique (de sīn à yā')*, no. 971, cf. also no. 979). It came from Shiḥr and Mahra territory, and it was exported via Oman and Aden (Muqaddasī, *Descriptio*, pp. 87, 97n, 98; V. Minorsky (tr.), *Ḥudūd al-ʿālam*, p. 148), and it was a well-known Arabian export (ʿAmr b. Baḥr al-Jāḥiẓ (attrib.), *Kitāb al-tabaṣṣur bi'l-tijāra*, p. 35 = C. Pellat, tr., "Ǧāḥiẓiana, I. Le *Kitāb al-tabaṣṣur bi'l-tijāra* attribué à Ǧāḥiẓ," §15. Pellat's explanation of *kundur* in the glossary, p. 163, should be ignored). For further references, see *Wörterbuch*, *s.vv.* lubān, kundur.

6 Ṭabarī, *Taʾrīkh*, ser. 1, pp. 729, 740 (Jesus was presented with gold, *murr*, and *lubān*).

7 The bulk of the references in the *Wörterbuch*, *s.vv.* lubān and kundur, are to such sources, many of which are also cited in Müller, *Weihrauch*, *passim*.

8 The caliph Hishām's feeble-minded mother chewed *kundur* and made figures (*tamāthīl*) of it (Ṭabarī, *Ta'rīkh*, ser. 2, p. 1,466; compare Müller, "Notes on the Use," pp. 130 f., on frankincense as a chewing gum for women and children today). The Ismāʿīlī missionaries would travel in the guise of itinerant traders carrying pepper, aromatic plants, spindles, mirrors, frankincense, and the like (W. Ivanow, *Ismaili Traditions Concerning the Rise of the Fatimids*, pp. 158 f.; and note that here too it is the sort of thing that women and children like). An Antiochene who used to sell *lubān* appears in Muḥammad b. Ṭāhir Ibn al-Qaysarānī, *Kitāb al-ansāb al-muttafiqa*, p. 131. And frankincense is also an article of commerce in the Geniza documents (S. D. Goitein, *A Mediterranean Society*, I, 154).

one Qurashī could be turned into a dealer in frankincense by recourse to textual emendation of a variant,[9] but this seems to be the best that one can do for the theory that the Meccans exported frankincense to the Greco-Roman world.

The belief that the Meccans traded in frankincense rests on a methodology akin to the invocation of ghosts. Lammens invented it by crediting the Meccans with the trade described by Pliny, the *Periplus* and other classical sources, and later Islamicists have followed suit; Rodinson refers to Pliny in a discussion of Qurashī trade; Donner adduces the *Periplus* as a source on south Arabian incense production in the time of Muḥammad; and Spuler regards the fact that Pliny's incense route probably bypassed Mecca, though not Medina, as evidence that not only Mecca, but above all Medina thrived on the export of frankincense on the eve of Islam.[10] But although it is undoubtedly important to use early non-Muslim sources for our reconstruction of the rise of Islam, it does appear extreme to use those which were written half a millennium or so before the event.

2. *Myrrh*

The history of myrrh is similar to that of frankincense. Once an exclusively Arabian product, it had come to be imported as much or more from East Africa by the time of the *Periplus.*[11] Unlike frankincense, though, it was not condemned by the Christians, Jesus himself having been embalmed with it, and it continued to be used for this purpose in the period of interest to us.[12] Even so, it seems to have lost importance

[9] According to the fatuous list of "professions of the *ashrāf*" in Ibn Qutayba, *Maʿārif*, p. 249, Abū Ṭālib used to sell perfume, or perhaps *al-burr*. In the parallel version given by Aḥmad b. ʿUmar Ibn Rusta, *Kitāb al-aʿlāq al-nafīsa*, p. 215, he sold perfume, or maybe *laban*. *Laban* could be emended to *lubān* on the ground that it goes better with perfume; but it is, of course, more easily explained as a misreading of *al-burr*.

[10] Lammens, *Mecque*, pp. 296 ff.; Rodinson, *Islam et capitalisme*, pp. 46, 260; Donner, "Mecca's Food Supplies," p. 253; B. Spuler, review of Müller, *Weihrauch*, p. 339 (I am grateful to Dr. F. W. Zimmermann for drawing my attention to this review). Note also how Birkeland adduces Strabo and Pliny in elucidation of the Meccan trade supposedly reflected in the Qur'ān (H. Birkeland, *The Lord Guideth: Studies on Primitive Islam*, p. 122).

[11] Cf. *Periplus*, §§7 f, 10, 24.

[12] When Tertullian (d. about 240) says that the Christians use more Sabaean merchandise in burying their dead than do the pagans in the worship of their deities, he does not, according to Atchley, mean that the Christians had already come to burn incense at their

in the Greco-Roman world, though not in India and China.[13] Cosmas does not mention it, and attestations in Arabic literature are rare.[14] The medieval lexicographers knew it as a medicine comparable to bitter aloe, with which some held it to be identical.[15]

3. Cancamum and tarum

Cancamum and tarum have been identified by classicists as gum benjamin and aloe-wood, respectively, both products of the Far East.[16] In fact, however, as south Arabianists have long been aware, both were derived from trees native to south Arabia and East Africa.[17]

According to Dioscorides, *kankamon* was the resin of an Arabian tree resembling myrrh.[18] According to Pliny and the *Periplus*, it came from East Africa; Pliny adds that it was imported together with *tarum*, a word that does not occur elsewhere.[19] Muslim authors disagree among themselves regarding the exact relationship between *kamkām* and *ḍarw* (or *ḍirw*), identifying now the one and now the other as a tree, a resin, or some other product of a tree.[20] In modern south Arabia *ḍaru* is a tree and

funerals, but rather that they used Arabian aromatics, including myrrh, in embalming. Atchley adduces numerous examples from both the Greek and the Latin world (*Use of Incense*, pp. 104 ff.). Jesus is wound in linen cloth with myrrh and aloe "as the manner of the Jews is to bury" in John 19:39 f.

[13] Cf. B. Laufer, *Sino-Iranica*, pp. 460 f. (I am grateful to Prof. S. Shaked for reminding me of this work).

[14] Myrrh was known to Muqaddasī, Hamdānī, and Nuwayrī (all three adduced in A. Grohmann, *Südarabien als Wirtschaftsgebiet*, I, 150 f.). Ṭabarī knew that Jesus had been presented with not only frankincense, but also myrrh (above, n6). And the *Wörterbuch* will no doubt have numerous references to the medical and herbalist literature when in due course it reaches *mīm*; but this information will be derived largely from the classical tradition.

[15] E. W. Lane, *An Arabic-English Lexicon*, *s.v. murr*. The confusion seems to go back to Dīnawarī, cf. his *Dictionnaire botanique*, no. 1,011.

[16] Miller, *Spice Trade*, pp. 36, 38 f., 66, 108 f. Rackam similarly renders them as gum benjamin and aloe-wood in his translation of Pliny. The source behind the confusion is presumably Ibn Sīnā (cf. Grohmann, *Südarabien*, I, 114 f.).

[17] Cf. Mordtmann and Müller, *Denkmäler*, pp. 81 ff.

[18] Dioscorides, *Materia Medica*, I, 24/23.

[19] Pliny, *Natural History* XII, 98; *Periplus*, §8 (*kankamon*, translated as "Indian copal" by Schoff).

[20] Cf. Grohmann, *Südarabien*, I, 114 f.; and the references given in *Wörterbuch*, *s.v.* "kamkām."

kamkām its resin, and this agrees with the information in Dīnawarī.[21] But both the bark(?) and the resin of this tree must have been used as incense products in antiquity, for *kmkm* and *ḍrw* are attested together on Sabaean incense bowls,[22] and it was clearly incense products of some kind that Pliny knew as *cancamum* and *tarum*. Diocorides explicitly states that *kankamon* was used as a perfume, and *ḍrw*, moreover, is the same word as Hebrew *ṣᵒrî*, "balm" (of Gilead).[23]

Ḍarw is generally identified as *Pistacia lentiscus*, L., the word designating both the tree and its bark.[24] *P. lentiscus* is the mastic tree, which has also been proposed in connection with Hebrew *ṣᵒrî* and *kamkām* was the resin of this tree.[25] Varieties of *P. lentiscus* are, in fact, attested for both south Arabia and former British Somaliland.[26] The products were still exported from south Arabia in medieval Muslim times,[27] but they were evidently never of much importance in the Greco-Roman world.

[21] Groom, *Frankincense*, p. 142; Dīnawarī, *Monograph Section*, nos. 380 f., 816; *id.*, *Dictionnaire*, nos. 648, 968.

[22] Mordtmann and Müller, *Denkmäler*, p. 81 (Prideaux, no. 1). *Ḍrw* is also attested without *kmkm* on such bowls, cf. *ibid.*; Grohmann, *Südarabien*, I, 116; G. Ryckmans, "Inscriptions sub-arabes (troisième série)," pp. 176 f.

[23] Dioscorides, *Materia Medica*, I, 24/23; Mordtmann and Müller, *Denkmäler*, p. 83.

[24] Thus Lewin in Abū Ḥanīfa al-Dīnawarī, *The Book of Plants (aliph to zāʾ)*, glossary, p. 43; Grohmann, *Südarabien*, I, 114, 119; Groom, *Frankincense*, p. 142. (*Ḍarw* also means sage, cf. Lewin, *loc. cit.*)

[25] See below, no. 10. Grohmann, *Südarabien*, I, 115. According to the *Wörterbuch*, *s.v. kamkām*, it is the resin of the terebinth, that is, *P. terebinthus*, the turpentine tree that has also been proposed in identification of the Hebrew balm; but here for once the *Wörterbuch* must be wrong. It is true that *P. terebinthus* is said to grow in south Arabia and to yield a resin similar to frankincense (thus Grohmann, *Südarabien*, I, 114; but Dīnawarī, *Monograph Section*, no. 816, had not been able to confirm that it grew in Arabia at all). But the name of the terebinth is *buṭm*, not *ḍarw* or *ḍirw*, the only alternative name being *ḥabbat al-khaḍrāʾ*; and Dīnawarī explicitly states that the *buṭm* resembles the *ḍarw* without being identical with it (*loc. cit.*). In antiquity, terebinth resin came from Syria (Theophrastus, *Plants*, IX, 2: 2 and *passim*), or from Syria, Judea, Arabia Petraea, Cyprus, and elsewhere, but not from the Yemen (Dioscorides, *Materia Medica*, I, 71/91; cf. also Moldenke and Moldenke, *Plants of the Bible*, p. 178).

[26] Howes, *Vegetable Gums and Resins*, p. 138. It is common throughout the Mediterranean. For a picture, see W. Walker, *All the Plants of the Bible*, p. 129 (not a scholarly work).

[27] Jawharī in Mordtmann and Müller, *Denkmäler*, p. 83; Yāqūt, *Buldān*, III, 470, *s.v.* Ḍarwa; Muḥammad b. Aḥmad al-Khwārizmī, *Kitāb mafātīḥ al-ʿulūm*, p. 172 (all reproducing the same passage).

4. Ladanum

Ladanum is an oleo-resin exuded by several species of the rock-rose *Cistus*, L., Cistaceae, which is still used in perfumery.[28] Herodotus believed that it was only produced in south Arabia, where it owed its production to the grazing habits of goats (an idea which is by no means as silly as it sounds). In Pliny's time it was held by some to be the exclusive product of the Nabataeans, who similarly combed it from the beards of their goats.[29] But the rock-rose is common throughout the Mediterranean and its hinterland.[30] It was probably a product of the rock-rose which the Ishmaelites from Gilead sold under the name of *lōṭ* in Egypt[31] and which the Assyrians received as tribute from the west under the name of *ladinnu*;[32] and the production of ladanum soon ceased to be an Arabian monopoly, if it ever was one. By the first century A.D., Cypriot, Libyan, and other ladanum competed with the Arabian variety, which was no longer so highly esteemed.[33] In modern times the production has centred on Crete.[34] Neither the *Periplus* nor Cosmas mentions ladanum, and in Arabia itself it would also appear to have lost importance. Herodotus explicitly says that *ladanon* is an Arabic word (or at least an Arabic pronunciation, as against his own *lēdanon*), and *ldn* is attested on south Arabian incense bowls.[35] But Dīnawarī believed *lādhin* not to be an Ara-

[28] Howes, *Vegetable Gums and Resins*, p. 158; J.C.T. Uphof, *Dictionary of Economic Plants*, *s.v.* Cistus ladaniferus.

[29] Herodotus, *History*, III, 112. Nowadays ladanum is collected by drawing a bunch of leather thongs or woven material over the bushes, a method attested already in Dioscorides (*Materia Medica*, I, 97/128). But it is said still to be collected from the beards of goats who have browsed among these bushes in some places (Howes, *Vegetables Gums and Resins*, p. 158; Sigismund, *Aromata*, p. 21; Moldenke and Moldenke, *Plants of the Bible*, p. 77). Pliny, *Natural History*, XII, 73.

[30] It is one of the shrubs that were formerly subdominants in the woodland of the Mediterranean and that now survive in the maquis (N. Polunin, *Introduction to Plant Geography*, p. 355).

[31] Suggested by I. Löw, *Aramäische Pflanzennamen*, p. 127, and, in greater detail, by *id.*, *Die Flora der Juden*, I, 361 ff. The identification is now generally accepted, cf. Moldenke and Moldenke, *Plants of the Bible*, p. 77. For a pretty picture, see Walker, *All the Plants*, p. 139.

[32] *Assyrian Dictionary*, *s.v.*

[33] Pliny, *Natural History*, XII, 74 ff.; Dioscorides, *Materia Medica*, I, 97/128.

[34] Sigismund, *Aromata*, p. 21.

[35] Herodotus, *History*, III, 112; Grohmann, *Südarabien*, I, 116, 118.

bian product at all; and what other Muslim authors have to say about *lādhin* or *lādin* is derived from the classical tradition.[36]

5. *Sweet Rush*

Readers of Miller's *Spice Trade* may be surprised to find sweet rush listed as an Arabian rather than an Indian spice, but for this there is full justification.[37] Sweet rush (Greek *skhoinos euōdes*, Latin *junçus odoratus*, Arabic *idhkhir*)[38] is generally identified as a species of *Cymbopogon*, Spreng. (= *Andropogon*, L.) of the family of Gramineae or grasses. Most species of *Cymbopogon* are aromatic, and the classical authors would seem to have known more than one variety; but what one might call "true sweet rush" is held to have been *C. schoenanthus*, (L.) Spreng., a plant currently in danger of extinction by reclassification as *C. olivieri*, (Boiss.) Bor.[39] Now *pace* Miller, both *C. schoenanthus* (and/or *olivieri*) and other species of *Cymbopogon* are common in the Middle East,[40] and *C. schoenanthus* still grows

[36] Dīnawarī, *Dictionnaire*, no. 977, where *lādhin* is identified as the product of *marzanjūsh* (marjoram), which does not grow wild *bi-arḍ al-ʿarab*, though it does elsewhere; *Wörterbuch*, *s.v.* lādhin; Grohmann, *Südarabien*, I, 118n.

[37] Cf. Miller, *Spice Trade*, pp. 94 ff. Miller's book is thoroughly unreliable in both botanical and other respects; it is hard not to agree with the verdict of Raschke, "New Studies," p. 650.

[38] For the equivalence of these terms, see Löw, *Pflanzennamen*, p. 168; *id.*, *Flora der Juden*, I, 694 f.

[39] Uphof, *Dictionary*, *s.v.*; similarly Miller, *Spice Trade*, p. 94. Bor began by reclassifying the *C. schoenanthus* of India, Afghanistan, and Iraq as *C. olivieri* (Boiss.) Bor; the true *C. schoenanthus*, he held, was attested only for Arabia, Jordan, Egypt, and North Africa, though it was likely also to turn up in Iraq (N. L. Bor in K. H. Rechinger, *Flora of Lowland Iraq*, p. 39; *id.*, *Gramineae* [= C. C. Townsend, E. Guest, and A. al-Rawi, eds., *Flora of Iraq*, IX], pp. 552 f.). It was duly discovered there by A. al-Rawi, *Wild Plants of Iraq with Their Distribution*, p. 39; similarly *id.* and H. L. Chakravarty, *Medicinal Plants of Iraq*, p. 34. But since Bor still regarded it as awaiting discovery in Iraq in his publication of 1968, this can presumably be discounted. By 1970 Bor had eliminated the species from Iran, as well (N. L. Bor, *Gramineaea* [= K. H. Rechinger, ed., *Flora Iranica*, no. 70], pp. 541 ff.). Maybe he would wish also to eliminate it from Arabia (cf. below, n 41) and North Africa (cf. P. Quezel and S. Santa, *Nouvelle Flore de l'Algérie*, I, 86; P. Ozenda, *Flore du Sahara*, p. 157), thus reducing it to an ideal type. But it does not make much difference in the present context: reclassification notwithstanding, the plant continues to be known locally as *idhkhir* (*adhkhar* in North Africa) and to yield an essential oil.

[40] It had a distribution from Morocco to Sind before reclassification (N. L. Bor, *The Grasses of Burma, Ceylon, India and Pakistan*, p. 131; compare also Uphof, *Dictionary*, *s.v.* Cymbopogon schoenanthus).

widely in Arabia.[41] Its English name is camel grass, not ginger grass, and there is no evidence that the Greeks and Romans ever imported it from India. The classical authors identify sweet rush as Lebanese, Syrian, Nabataean, Arabian, Babylonian, African, and Libyan.[42] Naturally, they could be referring to local species which had to be supplemented with foreign imports, or to locally manufactured ointments made from an imported commodity, while the absence of sweet rush from the extant tariffs could be taken to mean that it was imported duty-free.[43] But why make all these assumptions? There is not a single explicit or implicit statement to the effect that the commodity came from further east than Iraq;[44] and the Arab lexicographers who identified *idhkhir* as a well-known plant used, among other things, for the roofing of houses and the manufacture of perfume evidently did not have an Indian plant in mind.[45] Sweet rush is a plant that Quraysh could well have exported. It grows in the vicinity of Mecca, and indeed in the *ḥaram* itself, this being one of the plants which the Prophet allowed to be cut there.[46] The reason why he allowed it to be cut, however, is that the Meccans needed

[41] D. F. Vesey-Fitzgerald, "The Vegetation of Central and Eastern Arabia," p. 780; *id.*, "The Vegetation of the Red Sea Coast North of Jedda, Saudi Arabia," pp. 553, 556; *id.*, "Vegetation of the Red Sea Coast South of Jedda, Saudi Arabia," p. 480. Cf. also E. Blatter, *Flora Arabica (Records of the Botanical Survey of India*, VIII, pp. 483 f. (*Andropogon = Cymbopogon caesius* and *jwarancusa*).

[42] Theophrastus, *Plants*, IX, 7: 1 (from a marsh beyond the Lebanon); Pliny, *Natural History*, XII, 104 (the same) and XXI, 120 (from Nabataea, Babylonia and Africa); Dioscorides, *Materia Medica*, I, 17/16 (from Nabataea, Arabia, Libya, the Arabian type being sometimes known as Babylonian; Diodorus Siculus, *Bibliotheca*, II, 49;2(Arabia Felix). Ginger grass is *C. martini*, not *schoenanthus*, cf. A. F. Hill, *Economic Botany*, p. 529.

[43] Cf. Miller, *Spice Trade*, p. 96. Miller notes its cheapness, but not its absence from the tariffs.

[44] The fact that Pliny concludes his discussion of sweet rush with the remark "now we leave the countries facing the ocean to return to those which encircle our own sea" (*Natural History*, XII, 107) has no bearing on the question, as Miller would have it (*Spice Trade*, p. 96), since sweet rush has been discussed by way of digression. It is precisely in this passage that Pliny describes sweet rush as growing in the Lebanon, some seventeen miles from the Mediterranean.

[45] Lane, *Lexicon*, *s.v.* (there is, of course, no question of deriving "the *izkhir* of Arab traders" from Greek *skhoinos*, as Miller suggests [*Spice Trade*, p. 95]).

[46] Vesey-Fitzgerald, "Vegetation of the Red Sea Coast South of Jedda," p. 480; Balādhurī, *Futūḥ*, p. 11; Azraqī, *Makka*, p. 131; Ibn Hishām, *Leben*, p. 414 (a poetic attestation); Gaudefroy-Demombynes, *Pèlerinage*, pp. 8 f.

it for the thatching of their houses, for the graves of their dead, and for unspecified use by smiths and goldsmiths,[47] not that they wanted to sell it in Syria; and the one occasion on which we see a Qurashī load his camels with *idhkhir* (in Medina after the *hijra*), the customers were local goldsmiths.[48] Elsewhere we learn that *idhkhir* would be exchanged for *ḥamḍ* in Mecca, *ḥamḍ* being plants much liked by camels.[49] The idea that Quraysh were suppliers of *idhkhir* to the perfume manufacturers of Alexandria is quite alien to the sources.

6. Aloe (medicine)

Greek *aloē* is the name of two quite different products, a bitter medicine and a fragrant wood—a source of much confusion. Bitter aloe, or aloes (the latter an English plural, not a Greek or Latin form) is the inspissated juice of several species of *Aloe*, L., Liliaceae. Classical Muslim authors were familiar only or mainly with the species that is native to Socotra, *A. perryi* Baker.[50] This plant has tall serrated leaves that ressemble "the sheathes of knives," and from which the Socotrans extract a juice containing aloin, a purgative. The juice is left to dry in leather bags and subsequently sold as a medicine known in classical Arabic as *ṣabir* (or *ṣabr*, *ṣabāra*).[51] It is still a recognized source of aloin in modern pharmacy, though it has been eclipsed by rival products from South Africa, Zanzibar, and Curaçao.[52]

Bitter aloe does not appear ever to have been transported overland together with frankincense. Theophrastus does not mention it, though he was well informed about frankincense and myrrh, and it was never to be

[47] Aḥmad b. al-Ḥusayn al-Bayhaqī, *al-Sunan al-kubrā*, v, 195; Balādhurī, *Futūḥ*, pp. 42 f., 45 (cleansing [*ṭubūr*] rather than roofing [*ẓubūr*] of houses).

[48] Muslim b. Ḥajjāj, *al-Ṣaḥīḥ*, XIII, 143 ff. (*kitāb al-ashriba*, nos. 1-3), where ʿAlī wants to sell *idhkhir* in order to pay for his wedding feast.

[49] *Aghānī*, XIII, 13.

[50] Cf. I. B. Balfour, *Botany of Socotra*, pp. 291 f.; Dīnawarī, *Monograph Section*, nos. 376, 390; *id.*, *Dictionnaire*, no. 611; Masʿūdī, *Murūj*, III, 36; Yāqūt, *Buldān*, III, 1024 f., *s.v.* Suquṭrā; Grohmann, *Südarabien*, I, 162 f.

[51] Dīnawarī, *Monograph Section*, no. 390; *id.*, *Dictionnaire*, no. 611; Lane, *Lexicon*, *s.v.* ṣabir (citing Dīnawarī). For a picture of the plant (though of a slightly different species), see Walker, *All the Plants*, p. 17.

[52] *The British Pharmaceutical Codex*, pp. 89 ff. The collection of aloe in Socotra was reported to be haphazard in the late nineteenth century, and much supposedly Socotran aloe is believed to have come from East Africa (Grohmann, *Südarabien*, I, 164; *Codex*, p. 91).

identified as "Sabaean."[53] It is first attested in John 19:39 in connection with the burial of Jesus, and next in Celsus (*fl.* about 20 A.D.).[54] It reappears soon thereafter in Dioscorides. In the *Periplus* it is explicitly said to be exported from Cane, the Ḥaḍramī port; according to Marzūqī, it was purchased in pre-Islamic times at *qabr Hūd* near Shiḥr in the Ḥaḍramawt by traders who arrived by both sea and land; and several centuries later Muqaddasī described the trade as maritime.[55] Given that Marzūqī is talking about trade in Arabia itself, it may thus be assumed that the export trade was always maritime.

7. *Cinnabar*

Like aloe, cinnabar (Greek *kinnabari*, Latin *cinnabaris*) is the name of two quite different substances. Both have been used as a red dye, but one is mineral and the other vegetable. Mineral cinnabar is mercuric sulphide, which yields the colour known as vermilion, and with which we are not concerned here. Vegetable cinnabar (or "dragon's blood") is a resin obtained from various plants, notably *Dracaena* (spp.), Liliaceae, which has been used both as a dye and as a medicine.[56] Pliny asserts that the two were confused even by doctors in his own time, with unfortunate results for patients.[57]

According to the *Periplus*, vegetable cinnabar was produced in Socotra.[58] The plant referred to is *D. cinnabari* Balf., which is endemic in Socotra and which still produced some vegetable cinnabar in the nine-

[53] Compare also a late author such as Jacob of Edessa, *Hexaemeron*, pp. 138 f. = 115 f., where incense is said to come from the region of the Sabaeans, whereas no comparable claim is made for aloe (known to Jacob under both its Greek and its Arabic name).

[54] Celsus, *De Medicina*, I, 3: 26, where it is recommended as a purgative. It is mentioned again *ibid.*, V, 1; V, 20: 2; VI, 6: 5 f. and 24; VI, 7: 2C, frequently together with myrrh. *Pace* the translator, there is nothing to indicate that the aloe of these passages should be understood as aloe-wood, or, in other words, as a substance different from that mentioned in the first passage; cf. appendix 3.

[55] Dioscorides, *Materia Medica*, III, 22/25; *Periplus*, §28 (mistaken for aloe-wood in Huntingford's translation, see the glossary at p. 132); Marzūqī, *Azmina*, II, 164; Muqaddasī, *Descriptio*, p. 97. Incidentally, both Masʿūdī and Yāqūt have it that it was for the sake of aloe that the Greeks settled in Socotra (see above, ch. 2 n100).

[56] Cf. Liddel and Scott, *Lexicon*, *s.v.* kinnabari; Howes, *Vegetable Gums and Resins*, pp. 139 f. Vegetable cinnabar has also been used in the varnishing of violins.

[57] Pliny, *Natural History*, XXXIII, 116.

[58] *Periplus*, §30.

teenth century.[59] The Indian colonists in Socotra would seem to have participated in the industry, for Socotran cinnabar is labelled "Indian" in both classical and Muslim sources, and the Arabic name of the substance, *dam al-akhawayn* or "the blood of the two brothers," sounds like a reference to an Indian story about the origins of cinnabar which was also known to classical authors such as Pliny.[60] At all events, there is nothing to suggest that it came north by land together with frankincense. Presumably it was marketed in the same way as aloe, that is, via Cane to Ommana and from there to the head of the Persian Gulf for transport overland to Syria.[61] There is, at all events, no reference to Greeks buying cinnabar in Socotra and Cane themselves.[62] But however it may have been marketed, the product is never associated with Meccan trade.

8. Cinnamon and Cassia

These two products have been relegated to Appendix 1. Here it suffices to say that they ceased to be associated with Arabia in the first century A.D., and that they were still imported from East Africa in the time of Cosmas.

9. Calamus

For the identification of calamus as a Middle Eastern rather than an Indian plant, the reader is referred to Appendix 2. It was still imported by the Byzantines in the sixth century A.D., but they imported it from East

59 Balfour, *Botany of Socotra*, pp. 293 f.; cf. also Grohmann, *Südarabien*, I, 119 f.

60 Pliny, *Natural History*, XXXIII, 116; *Periplus*, § 30; Dīnawarī in Grohmann, *Südarabien*, I, 120. In India, we are told, dragons were in the habit of draining elephants of their blood, being addicted to it; but having done so, they would be crushed under the weight of the dying animal, thus spilling both their own blood and that of their victim ("brother") on the ground (Pliny, *Natural History*, VIII, 32 ff. cf. XXX, 116). For the Arabic name, see Lane, *Lexicon*, *s.v.* dam; Dīnawarī, *Plants*, no. 380; Grohmann, *Südarabien*, I, 120. The name of *edah* given by Balfour, *Socotra*, p. 293, is also attested in the classical literature, cf. Dīnawarī, *Monograph Section*, no. 376; Yāqūt, *Buldān*, III, 102, *s.v.* Suquṭrā (*al-ayda'*).

61 Socotra was a dependency of the Ḥaḍramawt, so the natural port was Cane, and Cane traded with Ommana (*Periplus*, §§ 27, 31). In Dīnawarī's time, aloe was sent to Ṣuḥār (with which Ommana has been identified by some), and it also passed through Oman in the time of Muqaddasī (Dīnawarī, *Monograph Section*, no. 376; Muqaddasī, *Descriptio*, p. 97).

62 The *Periplus* only mentions tortoise shells among the goods that ships returning from India would pick up at Socotra (§ 31).

Africa, not from Arabia, and it is never mentioned in connection with Meccan trade.

10. Balsam

In the Old Testament, one hears of a balm (*ṣᵉrī*) which Ishmaelites from Gilead in Transjordan sold in Egypt, and which Jacob's sons likewise brought with them to Egypt. Jeremiah knew this "balm of Gilead" as a medicinal substance.[63]

In Greek and Latin works, and later also in Arabic sources, one hears of a famous balsam tree (Greek *(opo)balsamon*, Latin *(opo)balsamum*; Arabic *balasān*), which once grew exclusively in two royal gardens in Judea,[64] but which had also been planted elsewhere in Syria by Pliny's time, and which had been transplanted to Egypt by the time of Dioscorides.[65] It is possible, through not very likely, that it still grew in Syria in the ninth century A.D.;[66] in Egypt, however, it survived down to 1615.[67] It yielded an extremely expensive perfume,[68] which was used by the Monophysites as an ingredient in their Myron until the thirteenth century A.D., and which was also appreciated by Muslims on festive occasions; occasionally, it even passed into the hands of Christians in the

[63] Genesis 37:25; 43:11. Jeremiah 8:22; cf. also Ezekiel 27:17.

[64] Theophrastus, *Plants*, IX, 6: 1; Pliny, *Natural History*, XII, 111; Strabo, *Geography*, XVI, 2: 41; Josephus, *Jewish Antiquities*, IX, 7; XIV, 54; XV, 96; *id.*, *The Jewish War*, I, 138; IV, 469; Diodorus Siculus, *Bibliotheca*, II, 48: 9; Sigismund, *Aromata*, pp. 15 f.

[65] "It is now cultivated by the treasury authorities and was never more plentiful" (Pliny, *Natural History*, XII, 113). Dioscorides, *Materia Medica*, I, 19 (in the note)/18. According to Sigismund, *Aromata*, p. 15, it was transplanted to Egypt under Vespasian.

[66] Cf. Laufer, *Sino-Iranica*, pp. 429, 432. Laufer's evidence for Syria is a Chinese report that does not seem to be confirmed by any local source. According to Jacob of Edessa and Moses Bar Kepha, balsam was Egyptian (Jacob of Edessa, *Hexaemeron*, p. 138 = 115; cf. also A. Vööbus, *Syrische Kanonessammlungen*, Ia, 214n; W. Strothmann, ed. and tr., *Moses Bar Kepha, Myron-Weihe*, p. 52 = 53). It was exclusively Egyptian, according to Jāḥiẓ (*Tijāra*, p. 32 = §13, cf. p. 35 = §15) and several authors cited by Bīrūnī (Muḥammad b. Aḥmad al-Bīrūnī, *al-Biruni's Book on Pharmacy and Materia Medica*, pp. 93 f.; = 73 ff.) and ʿAbd al-Laṭīf al-Baghdādī, as well as in the view of ʿAbd al-Laṭīf himself (*Kitāb al-ifāda wa'l-iʿtibar*, translated as *The Eastern Key*, pp. 40 ff). Both Bīrūnī and ʿAbd al-Laṭīf knew that it had once grown in Syria, but only on the basis of classical sources.

[67] Laufer, *Sino-Iranica*, p. 433.

[68] Cf. Theophrastus, *Plants*, IX, 7: 3; Pliny, *Natural History*, XII, 111, 123; Ibn Samajūn in ʿAbd al-Laṭīf, *Key*, p. 44 = 45 (presumably copied from Dioscorides, cited below, n 70).

West.[69] The resin also served as a medicine, again extremely expensive.[70]

In Arabia there is a species of *Commiphora* which is known in Arabic as *bashām*. Its habitat extends from south Arabia to Mecca, and it also grows in Somalia.[71] In Greek this tree was also known as *balsamon*.[72] It yields a gum of no great value.

The relationship between these three products has been a source of much confusion.[73] In fact they had little or nothing to do with each other.

That the Biblical balm cannot have been a product of the Arabian *Commiphora* is now generally agreed. The Ishmaelites in question came from Gilead, not from Mecca, and other Biblical passages make it clear that their balm was native to Palestine. Modern identifications of the plant or plants in question vary, but they do not usually include species of *Commiphora*.[74]

The relationship between Judean balsam and Arabian *bashām* is more

[69] S. Brock, "Jacob of Edessa's Discourse on the Myron," p. 20; M. M. Ahsan, *Social Life under the Abbasids*, p. 288; Egyptian balsam appears in the sixth-century *Liber Pontificalis* (Atchley, *Use of Incense*, p. 141).

[70] Diodorus Siculus, *Bibliotheca*, II, 48: 9; Strabo, *Geography*, XVI, 2: 41; Dioscorides, *Materia Medica*, I, 19/18 (worth twice its weight in silver); Laufer, *Sino-Iranica*, p. 429 (worth its weight in gold). It also figures as a medicine in Celsus, *De Medicina*, and Budge, *Book of Medicine*, indices (the Syriac word here is not *balsamon*, but *afursāmā*).

[71] Groom, *Frankincense*, pp. 126 f.; cf. also Vesey-Fitzgerald, "Vegetation of the Red Sea Coast South of Jedda," pp. 485 f. (*Commiphora opobalsamum*).

[72] *Balsamon* grew along the Sabaean coast, according to Agatharchides, §97; Strabo, *Geography*, XVI, 4: 19; Diodorus Siculus, *Bibliotheca*, III, 6.

[73] Thus Arabian *bashām* has been labelled *Commiphora* (or *Amyris*) *opobalsamum*, as if it were this tree which grew in Judea, and Hort duly renders *balsamon* as "Meccan balsam" in his translation of Theophrastus. The Arabian tree has also been labelled *Commiphora* (or *Amyris*) *gileadensis*, as if it were the product of this tree that the Ishmaelites from Gilead sold in Egypt, as well as *Balsamodendron gileadense*, a label that conflates all three plants (cf. Moldenke and Moldenke, *Plants of the Bible*, p. 84n; Groom, *Frankincense*, p. 126).

[74] It was one of the "best fruits in the land" (Genesis 43:11) and one of the commodities sold by Judah and the land of Israel to Tyre (Ezekiel 27:17). It is usually identified as the product of *Balanites aegyptiaca* (L.) Delile, an evergreen shrub, or *Pistacia lentiscus*, the mastic tree, or *Pistacia terebinthus*, the turpentine tree (Moldenke and Moldenke, *Plants of the Bible*, pp. 55, 84, 177 f.; Hepper in Groom, *Frankincense*, p. 249 n20; for pictures of the plants proposed, see Walker, *All the Plants*, pp. 29, 129, 221). But there are also some who take the Biblical passages to refer to a variety of products.

problematic. They certainly cannot have been identical. The sources are agreed that Judean balsam only grew in Judea, later also in Syria and Egypt, and that it only existed in a cultivated state.[75] The cultivated plant was smaller than the Arabian and Somali trees; it needed diligent watering, and its resin was quite unlike that of Arabian and Somali *bashām*. It was extremely sweet in taste, whereas that of the Arabian tree is said to be acid, that of the Somali tree bitter.[76] It was exuded in tiny droplets, and though the Arabian tree has also been said not to flow freely, more recent reports are to the contrary.[77] It was an extremely costly perfume, whereas the volatile oil of the Arabian tree is reported to evaporate quickly, leaving an insipid gum.[78] Muslim authors, moreover, confirm that *balasān* and *bashām* were two quite different plants.[79]

It is, however, possible that the Judean plant was a cultivated version of the Arabian tree. This was the opinion of Josephus and later also of ʿAbd al-Laṭīf.[80] There certainly cannot be much doubt that Greek *balsamon* (transliterated into Arabic as *balasān*) is a transcription of a Semitic, presumably Phoenician, word derived from the same root as Arabic *bashām*.[81] And long cultivation could presumably account for most of the differences between the two.[82] Nevertheless, completely different botanical identifications have also been proposed.[83]

[75] See above, nn64-66; Theophrastus, *Plants*, IX, 6: 4 ("balsam is said not to grow wild anywhere").

[76] Compare Pliny, *Natural History*, XII, 112 ff. (refuting Theophrastus, *Plants*, IX, 6: 1), 116; Groom, *Frankincense*, pp. 126, 127, 129; Theophrastus, *Plants*, IX, 6: 3; to Pliny acidity was a sign of adulteration.

[77] Pliny, *Natural History*, XII, 116 ff.; cf. ʿAbd al-Laṭīf, *Key*, pp. 42, 44 = 43, 45 (on Judean and Egyptian balsam); Schweinfurt in Löw, *Flora der Juden*, I, 300 (on the Arabian tree); Groom, *Frankincense*, p. 127.

[78] Groom, *Frankincense*, p. 127.

[79] Bīrūnī discussed *balasān* without referring to *bashām* at all, whereas ʿAbd al-Laṭīf al-Baghdādī, who described the *balasān* of Egypt on the basis of personal observation, explicity noted that it differed from Arabian *bashām* (Bīrūnī, *Pharmacy and Materia Medica*, pp. 93 f. = 73 ff.; ʿAbd al-Laṭīf, *Key*, p. 44 = 45).

[80] Josephus, *Antiquities*, VIII, 174: the Judean plant has been grown from (seedlings of the Arabian tree) presented by the Queen of Sheba to Solomon; ʿAbd al-Laṭīf, *Key*, p. 44 = 45.

[81] Cf. R. C. Steiner, *The Case for Fricative-Laterals in Proto-Semitic*, pp. 123 ff.

[82] Compare Pliny, *Natural History*, XII, 112: 117, on induced changes in the cultivated plant.

[83] Cf. Hepper in Groom, *Frankincense*, pp. 129, 250 n33.

The point that matters to us is that even if we accept that Judean balsam was a cultivated version of the Arabian tree, it was only the cultivated version that had any value in the classical world. Classical authors knew of the existence of Arabian *bashām*, yet made no reference to imports of it, and it is hard to see why they should have imported so inferior a sap. Early Muslim authors, moreover, do not associate *bashām* with resin at all. Dīnawarī knew its leaves as an ingredient in hair dyes, whereas the Meccans knew its branches as a source of toothpicks (or rather tooth-sticks).[84] And ʿAbd al-Laṭīf was under the impression that Arabian *bashām* yields no resin at all.[85] In fact, the modern Arabs and Somalis rarely bother to collect it, except, occasionally, for use as a chewing gum.[86] The view that the commercial importance of balsam in Arabia was comparable with that of frankincense and myrrh is thus unjustifiable.[87]

In this particular case, then, no trade had ever existed. The Meccans did, however, create one after the rise of Islam. The Meccan balsam tree enjoyed a vogue in the medieval Muslim world, presumably as a source of resin. It was, at all events, the resin of Arabian *bashām* which circulated in the nineteenth and early twentieth centuries under the name of "balsam of Mecca."[88] But the popularity of Meccan balsam clearly owed more to the prestige of Mecca than to the intrinsic merits of the product, for it has been reported by modern authors to have a bitter taste and to have smelled "in no way enchantingly."[89]

[84] Dīnawarī, *Monograph Section*, no. 811; Azraqī, *Makka*, p. 374; cf. Dīnawarī, *Monograph Section*, no. 853.

[85] ʿAbd al-Laṭīf, *Key*, p. 44 = 45.

[86] Groom, *Frankincense*, pp. 126 f., 130; cf. Jacob, *Beduinenleben*, p. 15.

[87] Cf. Müller, *Weihrauch*, col. 717; Miller, *Spice Trade*, p. 102; A.H.M. Jones, "Asian Trade in Antiquity," p. 4. Groom, who rightly notes that the Arabs of antiquity may not have regarded *bashām* as worth exploiting, nonetheless suggests that some *bashām* resin may have been exported under the label of myrrh (*Frankincense*, p. 131). But it is hard to believe that the connoisseurs of antiquity could have mistaken an insipid gum for an oleo-gum-resin.

[88] Cf. Lane, *Lexicon*, *s.v.* balasān (with reference to the species between the *ḥaramayn* and Yanbuʿ); Grohmann, *Südarabien*, I, 156; cf. Jacob, *Beduinenleben*, p. 15.

[89] Löw, *Flora der Juden*, I, 300 (on the taste); Sigismund, *Aromata*, p. 17 (on the smell); cf. also Groom, *Frankincense*, p. 127 (when burnt, it is said to smell like burning india rubber).

11. *Senna*

Senna is the dried leaflets of *Cassia* (spp.), Leguminosae. In modern pharmacy, in which they are used as an ingredient in laxatives, the recognized species are *C. acutifolia* Delile and *C. angustifolia* Vahl, but numerous other species endowed with both medicinal and other properties exist.[90] The genus *Cassia* has nothing to do with the cassia of classical literature, which was a form of cinnamon.[91]

"Senna" is a Europeanized version of Arabic *sanā*, Egypt and East Africa being the source of the so-called "Alexandrian senna," one of the better known commercial brands. There is, however, also senna in Arabia, where both *C. angustifolia* and other species grow wild, and senna is attested for the *ḥaram* area in early Islam.[92] By the tenth century, "Meccan senna" was famous in the Muslim world, and it is still used in modern pharmacy as a substitute for better varieties.[93] Lammens accordingly puts senna on the list of Meccan exports.[94] But his references merely go to show that senna leaves were used in the Ḥijāz, and presumably elsewhere, in early Muslim times. Their medicinal properties were known, and they were used together with henna as an ingredient in dyes, while the branches were a source of toothpicks.[95] There are no references to exports, and the commodity was not known on the Greco-Roman side.[96] As in the case of "Meccan balsam," the trade only developed after the rise of Islam.

[90] *British Pharmaceutical Codex*, pp. 94 ff. For a helpful survey of the properties of the various species, see J. M. Watt and M. G. Breyer-Brandwijk, *The Medicinal and Poisonous Plants of Southern and Eastern Africa*, pp. 566 ff.

[91] They are treated as identical in Walker, *All the Plants*, p. 48.

[92] Grohmann, *Südarabien*, I, 161; Vesey-Fitzgerald, "Vegetation of the Red Sea Coast North of Jedda," p. 553; Lewin in his glossary to Dīnawarī, *Plants*, p. 39; *British Pharmaceutical Codex*, p. 945; Azraqī, *Makka*, p. 374; Balādhurī, *Futūḥ*, p. 45.

[93] Muqaddasī, *Descriptio*, p. 98; cf. Dīnawārī, *Dictionnaire botanique*, no. 543; Löw, *Pflanzennamen*, p. 384; *British Pharmaceutical Codex*, p. 945. This is not, of course, to say that the senna which goes under this name necessarily comes from Mecca.

[94] Lammens, *Mecque*, p. 299.

[95] Dīnawārī, *Dictionnaire botanique*, no. 543 (also cited in Lane, *Lexicon*, *s.v.* sanā); Balādhurī, *Futūḥ*, p. 45.

[96] C. Martius, *Versuch einer Monographie der Sennesblätter* pp. 24 ff. It was from the Muslims that knowledge of the medicine passed to Byzantium and western Europe.

12. Bdellium

Bdellium is described in the classical literature as a gummy substance which was used in perfumery, pharmacy, and the manufacture of incense, and which was obtained from a tree native to northwest India, Persia, and Arabia.[97] It is assumed to have been identical with the substance known in Akkadian as *budulkhu* and in Biblical Hebrew as *b^edōlaḥ*.[98] Jewish and Syriac lexicographers equated Greek *bdellion* with Arabic *muql*,[99] thus identifying it as the resin of a tree usually labelled *Commiphora mukul* Engl. This tree is indeed native to India, Iran, and Arabia, and that it was the source of classical bdellium seems to be unanimously accepted.[100] Nonetheless, this can only be partly right. Pliny described bdellium as scented, and according to Dioscorides, it was "of a very sweet smell in burning."[101] But *C. mukul* is reported to yield a resin that smells badly in general or especially on being heated.[102] That it has been used medicinally is well known,[103] but it can hardly have been this product which went into the manufacture of incense and perfumes in the classical world.

The source of sweet-smelling bdellium is thus problematic. It was imported from Bactria and Media, according to Pliny, and from Barygaza in northwest India, according to the *Periplus*, which also informs us that

[97] Pliny, *Natural History*, XII, 35 f.; Dioscorides, *Materia Medica*, I, 67/80; *Periplus*, §§37, 39, 48 f. (*bdella*).

[98] Cf. *Assyrian Dictionary*, *s.v.* budulhu (where the word is assumed to be an Aramaic borrowing into neo-Babylonian); B. Meisner, "Bᵉdōlaḥ," pp. 270 f.

[99] Löw, *Pflanzennamen*, p. 359.

[100] Pauly-Wissova, *Realencyclopädie*, *s.v. myrrha*, col. 1141 (*C. roxburghiana*, the name given there, is one of the former labels of *C. mukul*); Miller, *Spice Trade*, p. 69; Uphof, *Dictionary*, *s.v.* Commiphora mukul; cf. also Löw, *Flora der Juden*, I, 304.

[101] Above, n97.

[102] Groom, *Frankincense*, p. 124; W. A. Talbot, *The Trees, Shrubs and Woody Climbers of the Bombay Presidency*, p. 69 (where the genus is still labelled *Balsamodendron* Kunth. rather than *Commiphora* Jacq.). It is true that Dīnawārī described the resin of this tree as sweet-smelling (*Dictionnaire*, no. 1,038). But the Persians were to call it "the smell of Jews" (*bū-yi jāhūdān*, cf. Bīrūnī, *Pharmacy and Materia Medica*, p. 350 = 307), so it would seem that Dīnawārī was wrong.

[103] Groom, *Frankincense*, p. 124: the Arabs and the Persians have used it as a fumigation in the cure of hemorrhoids and other complaints.

it grew on the southeastern coast of Iran.[104] But there are only two species of *Commiphora* (indeed of Burseraceae) in Iran, *C. mukul* and *C. pubescens* Stocks.; and where the resin of *C. mukul* is said to smell badly, that of *C. pubescens* is described as an inodorous and tasteless gum. Neither species can thus have been the source of scented bdellium.[105] Maybe there were more species of *Commiphora* in Iran in the past than there are today.[106] If so, it is hard to say whether the tree in question also grew in Arabia, as Pliny claims. But the problem is not of major importance to us, inasmuch as he makes no mention of imports from there.[107]

Medicinal bdellium, on the other hand, may well have been the resin of *C. mukul*, as the lexicographical equation of *bdellion* and *muql* implies. Dioscorides, who wrote on the medicinal substance, explicitly says that it was the resin of an Arabian tree, and the Septuagint's refusal to translate *bᵉdōlaḥ* by bdellion could be taken to mean that the substance was unpleasant: *bᵉdōlaḥ*, as the rabbis insisted, had nothing to do with the "bdellium of the druggists."[108] Dioscorides' claim that medicinal bdellium was of "a very sweet smell in burning" would thus seem to arise

[104] Above, n97.

[105] A. Parsa, *Flore de l'Iran*, II, 3 f. K. H. Rechinger, *Burseraceae*, pp. 1 f. (where the trees have been relabeled); Talbot, *Trees, Shrubs and Woody Climbers*, p. 170 (inodorous gum soluble in water); D. Brandis, *The Forest Flora of North-West and Central India*, p. 65 (tasteless). Curiously, this problem does not seem to have been noticed before.

[106] Thus the Phoenician traders who accompanied Alexander's army found plenty of myrrh trees to tap in Gedrosia (Arrian, *Anabasis*, VI, 22: 4). Groom takes the resin to have been bdellium rather than genuine myrrh (*Frankincense*, pp. 115 f.); but if it resembled myrrh, it can hardly have been resin of the two species of *Commiphora* attested for modern Iran. (Sigismund's conjecture [Aromata, pp. 19 f.] that some of the bdellium which reached the classical world was in fact gum benjamin, a Far Eastern product, does not solve the problem, as most bdellium was clearly a product native to Iran and northwest India.)

[107] Nor from East Africa, where several species of *Commiphora* yield scented bdellium (cf. Uphof, *Dictionary*, *s.vv.* Commiphora abyssinica, C. africana, C. erythraea, C. hildebrandtii, and C. kataf). The Biblical *bᵉdōlaḥ* is frequently assumed to have been the product of these trees (Meisner, "Bᵉdōlaḥ", pp. 270 f.; Moldenke and Moldenke, *Plants of the Bible*, pp. 81 f.); but if they contributed to the Roman market, they did so under the name of myrrh (cf. Groom, *Frankincense*, pp. 123 f.).

[108] Dioscorides, *Materia Medica*, I, 67/80; Jastrow, *Dictionary*, *s.v.* *bᵉdōlaḥ* (Genesis Rabba 2: 12). The Septuagint has *anthrax* in Genesis 2:12, and *krystallos* in Numbers 11:7. For the bdellium of the druggists, see also Celsus, *De Medicina*, and Budge, *Book of Medicine*, indices.

from confusion with the bdellium of the perfumers and incense manufacturers.[109] But it is odd that two such apparently different products came to be known by the same name, and that the distinction between the two was not explicitly made.

At all events, we may accept that there was an Arabian trade in the product. In Muslim sources, however, *muql* is not commonly mentioned, and it is not associated with Meccan trade.[110] It is true that we hear of a product known as *muql* that was exported from Dhū'l-Marwa north of Medina in medieval times,[111] but this *muql* was the fruit of the doum palm, not the resin of a *Commiphora.*[112] A contemptuous reference to the pre–Islamic Meccans describes them as mere traders who derived inviolability from their sanctuary and who would decorate themselves with *muql* on leaving it so as to make themselves recognizable to potential

[109] Dioscorides knew several kinds of bdellium, and the variety which smelt sweet in burning is described as transparent, like Pliny's, whereas that which came from India and Petra was dark.

[110] It was known to Dīnawārī, who correctly identifies medicinal *muql* as a resin resembling frankincense (*Dictionnaire*, no. 1,038); and it figures in the pharmacological literature, where it tends to be confused with the fruit of the doum palm (cf. Bīrūnī, *Pharmacy and Materia Medica*, pp. 350 f. = 307 f.; W. Schmucker, *Die pflanzliche und mineralische Materia Medica im Firdaus al-Ḥikma des Ṭabarī*, pp. 483 f.; Grohmann, *Südarabien*, 1, 155; below, n112).

[111] Muqaddasī, *Descriptio*, p. 83. The text has Marwa for Dhū'l-Marwa.

[112] *Pace* A. al-Wohaibi, *The Northern Hijaz in the Writings of the Arab Geographers, 800-1150*, pp. 159 f., and Groom, *Frankincense*, p. 124; cf. Dīnawarī, *Dictionnaire*, no. 1,038 (medicinal *muql* is the resin of a tree resembling frankincense, but *muql* is also the fruit of *dawm*, a tree like the date palm); *id.*, *Plants*, no. 376 (on the palm tree, cf. also *ibid.*, nos. 29, 53, 73, 261, 308 f.); Ibn al-Mujāwir, *Descriptio*, 1, 54; Masʿūdī, *Murūj*, 1, 61 (where it figures among the ten trees producing fruit with pits [*nawā*] which Adam brought with him from Paradise). *Dawm* is the Theban palm (cf. Lane, *Lexicon*, *s.v.*), or *Hyphaene Thebaica*, Palmaceae (cf. Uphof, *Dictionary*, *s.v.*, where the information given about the tree is somewhat unsatisfactory, apparently due to confusion between this tree and *Hyphaene coriacea*). It was described by classical authors (cf. F. Woenig, *Die Pflanzen im alten Ägypten*, p. 315). The use of the word *muql* for both the resin and the fruit produced endless confusion. Thus Bīrūnī, who correctly states that *muql* (in the sense of resin) was known as *gugul* in India, also cites authorities stating that *muql* is the fruit of *dawm*, as if the same substance were involved, with the result that *muql makkī* becomes a fruit of *dawm* imported from India! (*Pharmacy and Materia Medica*, pp. 350 f. = 307 f.). And Abū'l-Khayr reciprocates by identifying *muql makkī* as the resin of *dawm*, Mecca being supposedly the one place where a resin could be obtained from this palm tree (Löw, *Flora der Juden*, 1, 304; cf. the further confusion *ibid.*, p. 305).

attackers.[113] For all we know, they may also have used the leaves of this tree for the manufacture of mats, spears, and camel sacks.[114] But that still leaves the question of what the camel sacks contained.

13. Cardamomum

Classical authors knew of two spices which resembled each other and which were known as *amomum* and *cardamomum*: of these two, *cardamomum* was to be found in Arabia.[115] The spices in question have been identified as different forms of cardamom. Thus *amomum* is supposed to have been the product of *Amomum subulatum* Roxb., Zingiberaceae, which yields the so-called "Nepal cardamom," whereas *cardamomum* is said to have been the product of *Elettaria cardamomum* Maton, Zingiberaceae, which yields the cardamom familiar to us. Both plants are native to India, but other species are found further east, and Miller would like some of the Greco-Roman imports to have come from Southeast Asia.[116] Neither plant, however, can have had anything to do with the product we know as cardamom today.[117]

In the first place, the plants had a distribution quite different from that of cardamom. According to Theophrastus, they came from Media, though some held them to come from India. According to Pliny, *amomum* was an Indian vine or other bush that grew in Armenia, Pontus, and Media, whereas *cardamomum* grew in both Media and Arabia. Dioscorides and others say much the same. Miller takes this to mean that *amomum* came by the overland route from India, whereas *cardamomum* came by sea via Arabia.[118] But it is hard to believe that the sources would identify a plant as native to the Pontus or Armenia simply because consignments of products derived from it might pass through there, and they would scarcely have been able to describe its physical appearance if this were the case. The commodities are not mentioned by the *Periplus*

[113] Jāḥiẓ, *Tria Opuscula*, p. 63. I shall come back to this claim in ch. 8.

[114] Cf. Dīnawarī, *Plants*, no. 376.

[115] Cf. the testimonia in Sigismund, *Aromata*, p. 36; Miller, *Spice Trade*, pp. 37 f., 67 f., 71 ff.

[116] Miller, *Spice Trade*, pp. 37 f., 67 f., 71 ff.; cf. also Warmington, *Commerce*, pp. 184 f.; Uphof, *Dictionary*, under the names in question.

[117] H. N. Ridley, *Spices*, p. 326.

[118] Theophrastus, *Plants*, IX, 7: 2; Pliny, *Natural History*, XII, 48 ff.; Dioscorides, *Materia Medica*, I, 6/5 and 15/14; Miller, *Spice Trade*, p. 68 (on the poetic evidence); 69, 73.

or Cosmas, presumably because they were not purchased in India or Ceylon at all.

In the second place, the products did not look like modern cardamom. Modern cardamom is in the form of seed capsules, usually light brown, containing dark brown seeds resembling peppercorns. Pliny's *amomum* consisted of leaves "gently pressed together into bundles," the best kind being that "with leaves like those of the pomegranate and devoid of wrinkles, coloured red," and adulteration was "with leaves of the pomegranate and liquid gum to make the leaves stick together and form a cluster like a bunch of grapes."[119] One certainly could not adulterate cardamom these days by gumming together leaves of any kind. As for *cardamomum*, it was the product of a similar shrub, the seeds of which were oblong; and here too it must have been the leaves rather than the seeds that were sold, for we are told that the best kind was "very green and oily."[120] We may thus take it that *amomum* and *cardamomum* were plants that grew where the sources say they grew, including, as far as *cardamomum* is concerned, Arabia. What they were is another matter, and given that they have not been identified, it is hard to trace their fate on the Muslim side. Quraysh are not, of course, said to have traded in *habb al-hān*, cardamom; nor are they said to have traded in anything resembling the leaves described by Pliny.

14. Comacum

According to Theophrastus, *kōmakon* came from Arabia. It was a fruit, or else there was a fruit called *kōmakon* and a *kōmakon* that was something else; at all events, it was used as a perfume in the choicest unguents. According to Pliny, *comacum* was a juice squeezed out of a nut which, though reminiscent of cinnamon and almost as agreeable, was extremely cheap. It was produced in Syria. On the basis of this information, Miller identifies the spice as nutmeg, the product of *Myristica fragrans* Houttuyn, Myristicaceae, and other species native to India and Southeast Asia.[121] If so, everything can be anything. Whatever *kōmakon* may have

[119] Pliny, *Natural History*, XII, 48 f. It is not clear from Dioscorides that the product was made of leaves, though it is obvious here, too, that it had nothing to do with seed capsules (cf. *Materia Medica*, I, 15/14: pale red or pale green, soft to touch and full of veins in the wood).

[120] Pliny, *Natural History*, XII, 50.

[121] Theophrastus, *Plants*, IX, 7: 2; as the editor points out, the text would seem to be

been, it was clearly a product native to the Near East that did not become sufficiently well known in the classical world for us to identify it.

Indian Spices

Contrary to what is usually imagined, the number of Indian spices associated with Arabia in the classical sources is not large. It has been inflated in the secondary literature by the misidentification of cinnamon, cassia, calamus, and sweet rush as Indian imports. The number reduces to four: nard, costum, aloe-wood, and ginger. The testimonia linking the first three with Arabia are few, their eastern origins being perfectly well known; and as for ginger, it would seem to have grown in Arabia, though the classical world cannot have imported most of its supplies from there. Not one of these spices is associated with Meccan trade. There is, however, one source which claims that Quraysh used to trade, among other things, in pepper, though pepper was never associated with Arabia in antiquity.

15. Nard

Nard or spikenard (Sanskrit *nalada*, Hebrew *nērd*, Syriac *nardīn*, Greek *nardos*, Arabic *sunbul hindī*) is a perennial plant indigenous to the Himalayan region that is now labelled *Nardostachys jatamansi* D.C. (= *Valeriana jatamansi* Jones), Valerianaceae.[122] Its rhizomes are covered in hair or spikes resembling the ears of corn (*stakhys*, *spica*), whence its name *nardostakhys* or *spica nardi*, spikenard. The rhizomes contain an essential oil that was used in the manufacture of ointments and perfumes in antiquity. The Indians and the Muslims also ascribed medicinal properties to it.[123]

Nard is first attested in the western world in the *Song of Songs*.[124] By

---

corrupt here. Pliny, *Natural History*, XII, 135; Miller, *Spice Trade*, pp. 58 ff., where the *makir* of Dioscorides and others is thrown in to play the role of mace.

[122] Uphof, *Dictionary*, *s.v.* Nardostachys jatamansi; Miller, *Spice Trade*, pp. 88 ff.

[123] Miller, *Spice Trade*, p. 91; G. Watt, *The Commercial Products of India*, p. 792; Khwārizmī, *Mafātīḥ*, p. 169 (where the root of Indian *sunbul* is listed as a medicine under the name of *dār-i shīshaghān*, elsewhere assumed to be the name of *aspalathos*, cf. Löw, *Pflanzennamen*, pp. 340 f.). For a picture of the plant, see Walker, *All the Plants*, p. 197 (where the name *nardostachys* is erroneously said to refer to the shape of the flowerets).

[124] Song of Songs 1:12; 4:13 f. According to Miller (*Spice Trade*, p. 90), nard is already

the first century A.D. it was well known that it came from India, and the *Periplus* describes it as imported directly from there.[125] In the sixth century, it was imported via Ceylon.[126] It is associated with Arabia mainly in the form of claims, current at the time of Alexander, that it grew wild in that country.[127] As has been pointed out before, the nard in question was probably a species of *Cymbopogon*, or scented grass, though there is also a species of *Cyperus* in south Arabia that the Muslims were later to identify as *sunbul ʿarabī*, "Arabian nard," in contradistinction to the genuine commodity, *sunbul hindī*.[128] There is no indication that Arabia ever played any role in the nard trade other than that of providing anchorage for India ships.[129] Arabic *sunbul* is a translation of Greek *stakhys*, presumably via Syriac, Arabic *nardīn* being a straight transliteration of Syriac; and what the Muslims have to say about the plant seems to be derived from Dioscorides.[130]

16. Costum

Costum or costus (Sanskrit *kuṣṭha*, Aramaic *qushtā*, Greek *kostos*, Arabic *qusṭ*, *kusṭ*, *qusht*, *kusht*, etc.) is a perennial herb, *Saussurea lappa* G. P. Clarke, Compositae, which grows in Kashmir and which has been used as a source of incense, perfume, and medicine in China, the classical world, and elsewhere.[131] It is first attested in Greek literature in Theophrastus. Pliny was well aware that it was an Indian plant, and accord-

attested in Akkadian *lardu*. This was proposed by E. Ebeling, "Mittelassyrische Rezepte zur Bereitung von wohlriechenden Salben," p. 137, and others, but the identification has not been endorsed by the *Assyrian Dictionary*.

[125] Pliny, *Natural History*, XII, 45; Dioscorides, *Materia Medica*, I, 7/6; both knew of other kinds of nard, too. *Periplus*, §§39, 48 f., 56, 63.

[126] Cosmas, *Topographie*, XI, 15. For Byzantine imports of nard in the tenth century, see above, ch. 2 n71.

[127] Arrian, *Anabasis*, VII, 20.2; Strabo, *Geography* XV, 1: 22; cf. *ibid.*, XVI, 4: 25.

[128] Miller, *Spice Trade*, p. 90, with reference to Gedrosian nard; aromatic species of *Cymbopogon* were also common in Arabia (cf. above, Arabian spices, no. 5). Grohmann, *Südarabien*, I, 159.

[129] *Pace* Jones, "Asian Trade," p. 4. Originally, moreover, nard would seem to have come via the overland route through Central Asia and Persia (cf. Löw, *Pflanzennamen*, pp. 368 f.).

[130] Cf. Löw, *Pflanzennamen*, pp. 368 f.; Lane, *Lexicon*, *s.v.* sunbul (listed under both *sbl* and *snbl*).

[131] Uphof, *Dictionary*, *s.v.* Saussurea lappa; Löw, *Pflanzennamen*, pp. 357 f.; *Wörterbuch*, *s.v.* kust; Lane, *Lexicon*, *s.v.* qusṭ; Miller, *Spice Trade*, pp. 84 ff.

ing to the *Periplus* it was imported directly from Barygaza and Barbaricon in northwest India. Cosmas similarly knew that it came from India, though by then it reached the western world via Ceylon.[132]

Only two classical authors associate costum with Arabia. Dioscorides spoke of Arabian, Indian, and Syrian costum, whereas Diodorus Siculus held it to be an Arabian product used not only by Greeks, but also by the Arabs themselves.[133] Dioscorides' Arabian brand presumably reflects the fact that the product passed through Arabian ports: in medieval times a brand of costum was similarly known as ẓafārī.[134] And Diodorus is right that the Arabs used it themselves, even though they did not produce it: *qsṭ* is attested on south Arabian incense bowls and later also in Prophetic traditions.[135] The Muslims knew it as an Indian product used in fumigation, pharmacy, and perfumery.[136] But they never identify it as a commodity sold by the pre-Islamic Meccans.

17. Aloe-wood

As mentioned already, Greek *aloē* is the name not only of a bitter medicine, but also of a fragrant wood. The wood in question was the heartwood of *Aquillaria agallocha* Roxb., Thymelacaceae, a tree found in India, China, and Malaysia. In English it is sometimes known as "eaglewood." Since ancient times it has been chewed as a sweetener of the breath, sprinkled over the body as a powder, mixed in ointments, perfumes, and medicines, and burnt as a fumigant of bodies, clothes, and holy places.[137]

Aloe-wood is said first to be attested in the Old Testament under the name *ʾᵃhālîm*/*ʾᵃhālôt* (always in the plural), but this identification is uncertain.[138] The first certain attestation in Greek literature comes in Dios-

[132] Theophrastus, *Plants*, IX, 7: 3; Pliny, *Natural History*, XII, 41; *Periplus*, §§ 39, 48; Cosmas, *Topographie*, XI, 15.

[133] Dioscorides, *Materia Medica*, I, 16/15. Diodorus Siculus, *Bibliotheca*, II, 49: 3.

[134] Lane, *Lexicon*, *s.v.*.

[135] Mordtmann and Müller, *Denkmäler*, p. 81; Ryckmans, "Inscription sub-arabes", p. 177. Cf. A. J. Wensinck and others, *Concordance et indices de la tradition musulmane*, *s.v.* qusṭ.

[136] Mordtmann and Müller, *Denkmäler*, p. 84; Lane, *Lexicon*, *s.v.* qusṭ. The information is dependent on Dioscorides.

[137] Uphof, *Dictionary*, *s.v.* Aguillaria agallocha; Miller, *Spice Trade*, pp. 34 ff., 65 ff. Several other species are used in similar ways, cf. the subsequent entries in Uphof. Unlike the Indians and the Arabs, the Greeks and the Romans do not appear to have used it much for fumigation.

[138] Cf. appendix 2.

corides, who calls it *agalokhon* (or *agallokhon*), presumably from Pali *agalu*, *agaḷu*, *akalu*, or *akaḷu* or Tamil *akil*. According to Dioscorides, it came from India and Arabia, so some of it must have passed through Arabian ports. In the sixth century it was imported via Ceylon.[139]

Aloe-wood, not frankincense, was *the* incense product of the pre-Islamic and early Islamic world, as indeed it would seem to have remained long thereafter.[140] It is attested under the names of *yalanjūj* and *kibā'* in pre-Islamic and later poetry.[141] *Mijmar*, usually understood as aloe-wood, is said to have been donated to the Kaʿba together with other aromatics in early Islamic times, and it was a spark from a *mijmara*, a censer usually envisaged as containing aloe-wood, that caused one of the conflagrations of the pre-Islamic Kaʿba.[142] *Mijmar* was still burnt in the Kaʿba at the time of Ibn al-Zubayr, we are told.[143] It had numerous names, *yalanjūj (alanjūj, anjūj, najūj)*, *kibā'*, *mijmar*, or simply *ʿūd* or *ʿūd hindī*, "Indian wood"; and as might be expected, it figures in Ḥadīth.[144] Even the mysterious *rand* of pre-Islamic poetry (which is also attested on south Arabian incense bowls) was held by some early Muslim scholars to have been aloe-wood; in fact, there were also some who believed costum to be aloe-wood. All in all, *bakhūr*, the general term for incense, conjured up aloe-wood unless otherwise specified.[145]

139 Dioscorides, *Materia Medica*, I, 22/21. Cosmas, *Topographie*, XI, 15.

140 Cf. the numerous references to the use of aloe-wood in Aga-Oglu, "About a Type of Islamic Incense Burner," p. 28. Aloe-wood was one of the products imported by eighth-century Ibāḍī merchants from China (T. Lewicki, "Les premiers commerçants arabes en Chine," pp. 179 f.). Numerous types of aloe-wood were known to classical and medieval authors (cf. Lewicki, *loc. cit.*; Minorsky, *Ḥudūd al-ʿālam*, pp. 86 f.; Jāḥiẓ, *Tijāra*, p. 22 = §7; ʿAbd al Malik b. Muḥammad al-Thaʿālibī, *Thimar al-qulūb*, p. 553; *id.*, *Laṭā'if*, p. 139, 146). It was a well-known article of commerce in medieval times (Goitein, *Mediterranean Society*, I, 154; S. Y. Labib, *Handelsgeschichte Ägyptens im Spätmittelalter*, pp. 3, 49, 130, 193). It was still popular in nineteenth-century Arabia (Doughty, *Travels*, I, 137; Groom, *Frankincense*, p. 121).

141 Jacob, *Beduinenleben*, p. 12; *Wörterbuch*, *s.v.* kibā'.

142 Azraqī, *Makka*, pp. 176 f. 105 f.; compare Ibn Hishām, *Leben*, p. 430.

143 Azraqī, *Makka*, p. 179.

144 Cf. Nöldeke in Löw, *Flora der Juden*, III, 414; Dīnawarī, *Monograph Section*, nos. 827 ff. (where it is also known that it was called *aluwwa*, aloe); *id.*, *Dictionnaire*, no. 1,116. Cf. Ibn Saʿd, *Ṭabaqāt*, I, 400; Ṭabarī, *Ta'rīkh*, ser. I, p. 1,571; Wensinck, *Concordance*, *s.v.* al-ʿūd al-hindī.

145 Lane, *Lexicon*, *s.v.* rand (where myrtle and bay are also proposed); cf. Mordtmann and Müller, *Denkmäler*, pp. 81 f. (the suggestion at p. 82n that *rand* is an inversion of "nard" was rejected by Grohmann, *Südarabien*, I, 158 f.). Lane, *Lexicon*, *s.v.v.*, qusṭ, bakhūr.

Aloe-wood was appreciated not only in Arabia and Byzantium, but also in Persia.[146] It was without doubt a product out of which Quraysh could have made a fortune if the Greeks, Persians, and Ethiopians had not learnt to sail. But the sources never credit Quraysh with the sale of aloe-wood, not even for consumption in the Ḥijāz.

18. Ginger

Ginger (Prakrit *siṃgavera*, Pali *siṅgivera*, Greek *zingiberi*, Aramaic and Syriac *zangebīl*, Arabic *zanjabīl*) is the rhizome of *Zingiber officinale* Roscoe, Zingiberaceae, a plant now widely cultivated throughout the tropics of the old and new worlds.[147] It is first mentioned in the classical literature in the first century A.D., though it may have been known before.[148] The Greek word is derived from middle Indian, and both Pliny and Dioscorides wrote at a time when direct maritime connections had been established between India and the Greco-Roman world. Yet neither identified the spice as Indian. According to them, it grew in Arabia and East Africa.[149]

Given that the Greeks learnt their word for ginger in India, it is not very satisfactory to explain this information with reference to the Arab propensity for hiding the true origin of their spices.[150] It is by no means implausible that ginger should have been transplanted to Arabia and East Africa, where it is known to have been cultivated in modern times,[151] and where numerous Muslim and European authors writing between the ninth and the sixteenth centuries believed it to be cultivated.[152] Moreover, the ginger Dioscorides knew of was fresh: one

[146] One of the accounts of the tribute sent by the Persian governor of the Yemen to the Persian king includes *ʿūd* among the gifts (*Aghānī*, XVII, 310).

[147] Uphof, *Dictionary*, *s.v.* Zingiber officinale; Löw, *Pflanzennamen*, pp. 138 f.; A.S.C. Ross, *Ginger, A Loan Word Study*; Miller, *Spice Trade*, pp. 53 ff.

[148] It is first attested in Celsus, *De Medicina*, V, 23: 3, but the antidote in question was composed about 80 B.C. (cf. Miller, *Spice Trade*, p. 5).

[149] Ross, *Ginger*, p. 19; the etymologies of Miller, *Spice Trade*, p. 56, can be discarded. Pliny, *Natural History*, XII, 28; Dioscorides, *Materia Medica*, II, 160/190.

[150] As does Warmington, *Commerce*, p. 184.

[151] Cf. the Chinese habit of carrying ginger plants in pots on their ships, adduced by Miller, *Spice Trade*, p. 54. Others presumably did the same. Watt and Breyer-Brandwijk, *Medicinal and Poisonous Plants*, p. 1,063 (East Africa); Miller, *Spice Trade*, p. 108n (Ethiopia); Ross, *Ginger*, p. 41 (Ethiopia and Arabia).

[152] Ross, *Ginger*, pp. 40 ff. The Muslim statements come from Dīnawarī, Ibn al-Mujā-

should choose roots without rottenness, he said, adding that because they rotted so fast, they were sometimes preserved. The claims of Pliny and Dioscorides may thus be accepted at face value.[153]

But this is not to say, of course, that the classical world imported most of its ginger from Arabia and East Africa. The etymology of *zingiberi* makes this extremely unlikely, and by the second century A.D. it was well known that ginger was available in India and Ceylon.[154] We may take it that the spice was imported primarily from India and Ceylon, but that some (notably the fresh variety) also came from Arabia and East Africa. There is, however, no suggestion in the Muslim sources that the Meccans traded in this spice, for all that the word *zanjabīl* occurs in the Qur'ān.[155]

19. Pepper

It is well known that the classical trade between India and the Greco-Roman world was a trade above all in pepper (*Piper longum*, L., Piperaceae, and *P. nigrum*, L., of the same family).[156] In the sixth century, pepper was exported from India via Ceylon to Aden and Adulis,[157] and there is no indication in the Greek sources that the Arabs played any role in this trade other than that of providing anchorage for ships in Aden.[158] Nor is there in the Islamic tradition at large. A Shīʿite commentary on

wir, and ʿAbd al-Laṭīf, and the first two are innocent of the classical tradition. Cf. also Bīrūnī, *Pharmacy and Materia Medica*, p. 207 = 169; Laufer, *Sino-Iranica*, p. 545. (Dīnawarī's information, *Monograph Section*, no. 812, is also reproduced in Lane, *Lexicon*, *s.v.* zanjabīl)

153 Similarly Miller, *Spice Trade*, pp. 107 f., though Miller also wanted ginger to have reached the classical world by the same route from Malaya to Madagascar which he proposed for cinnamon (*ibid.*, pp. 56 f.).

154 Ptolemy lists it among the products of Ceylon (*Geographia*, ed. C.F.A. Nobbe, VII, 4: 1), and Ibn Bayṭār quotes Galen as saying that it was brought from India (ʿAbdallāh b. Aḥmad Ibn Bayṭār, *al-Jāmiʿ al-kabīr*, I, 538). It is not mentioned in the *Periplus* or Cosmas.

155 "And therein shall they be given to drink a cup, mixed with *zanjabīl*" (76:17). The commentators have nothing of interest to say about this.

156 Cf. Tarn, *Greeks in Bactria*, pp. 370 ff., on the beginnings of the trade; Warmington, *Commerce*, pp. 181 ff., on its nature in classical times; Miller, *Spice Trade*, pp. 80 ff., on the trade in general; and Uphof, *Dictionary*, *s.vv.* Piper longum and Piper nigrum on the plants involved.

157 Cosmas, *Topographie*, XI, 15 f.

158 *Pace* Rodinson, *Mohammed*, p. 20.

the Qur'ān, composed about the mid-tenth century, nonetheless claims that Quraysh made a living carrying "leather, clothes, pepper, and other things which arrived by sea" from Mecca to Syria.[159] Apparently we are to take it that Indian spices unloaded at Aden were shipped to Shuʿayba for transport overland from there, a most peculiar idea. That Quraysh carried (Ḥijāzī) leather and clothing to Syria is an idea familiar from the so-called *īlāf* traditions to which I shall come back on several occasions, and it is clearly these traditions which lie behind Qummī's account. How he came to add pepper and other overseas goods is not clear, and one could, if one wished, claim that Quraysh traded in spices on the basis of this one tradition. But in so doing, one would be pitching a single and late tradition against the literature at large.

East African Goods

As has been seen already, the products of East Africa included frankincense, myrrh, cancamum, tarum, cinnamon, cassia, calamus, and ginger. That the Meccans played no role in the marketing of these goods (insofar as the Greco-Roman world continued to import them) need not be repeated. The Meccans have, however, also been credited with the export of East African ivory, gold, and slaves; and this belief is worth refuting.

20. *Ivory*

"Apart from gold-dust, Africa supplied, above all, ivory and slaves," we are informed by Lammens, with a strong intimation that Africa supplied these articles for reexport to the north.[160] What Lammens implies others take as facts: the Meccan caravans, we are told, went north "bearing spices, ivory, and gold."[161] But elsewhere Lammens is of the opinion that it was in return for their exports that the Meccans bought "the rich merchandize of India, Persia, and Africa," as well as Syrian grain and oil; or, in other words, ivory would here seem to be something the Mec-

[159] Abū'l-Ḥasan ʿAlī b. Ibrāhīm al-Qummī, *Tafsīr*, II, 444. I owe my knowledge of this passage to M. A. Cook.

[160] Lammens, *Mecque*, p. 300.

[161] Donner, "Mecca's Food Supplies," p. 254. Lammens' claim is also repeated in Hitti, *Capital Cities*, p. 7.

cans could afford to buy because they exported something else.[162] Did the Meccans, then, import ivory from East Africa for reexport to the north, or did they only do so for local consumption? In fact, there is no evidence that they did either.[163]

It is a reasonable conjecture that some East African ivory was imported by the Yemen as early as ancient times, and that the Yemenis passed on some of this ivory to other Arabs, including, in due course, the Meccans; and naturally there is ivory in Prophetic ḥadīth.[164] But it is not a reasonable assumption that first the south Arabians and next the Meccans should have imported ivory for export to the north by caravan.[165] Why should heavy tusks have been shipped to Arabia for transport through the desert? It is for good reason that all our evidence is squarely against this idea. The Mediterranean world had imported its ivory directly from East Africa (insofar as it did not get it from India) since the days of the Ptolemies, who had penetrated East Africa precisely because they wanted elephants—primarily, but not exclusively, for warfare.[166] And as regards the sixth century, we are told by Cosmas that East African tusks were exported "by boat" to Byzantium, Persia, south Arabia, and even India (by then apparently short of tusks).[167] Naturally, caravans loaded with ivory are not attested in the Islamic tradition.

[162] Lammens, "République marchande," p. 47.

[163] Lammens' evidence is instructive of his method of work. In *Mecque*, p. 204n, he adduces Pliny, *Natural History*, VI, 173, which describes a trading centre in East Africa to which ivory and other things were brought some 500 years before the rise of Mecca; T. Nöldeke, *Neue Beiträge zur semitischen Sprachwissenschaft*, p. 46, which merely states in general terms that the Meccans traded with the Ethiopians, from whom they brought slaves and other goods; and Fraenkel, *Fremdwörter*, p. 177, where it is conjectured that the king of Ḥīra bought Ethiopian ivory and slaves, as well as leather, in Arabia. The first reference is to the wrong period and the third to the wrong place, whereas that which mentions Mecca fails to mention ivory. The references in "République marchande," p. 47n, similarly fail to mention ivory, most of them being to caravans carrying foodstuffs to various places, chiefly Medina.

[164] Cf. Wensinck and others, *Concordance*, *s.v.* *'āj*.

[165] For the view that even the south Arabians exported ivory by land, see Rodinson, *Mohammed*, p. 20.

[166] Kortenbeutel, *Osthandel*, *passim*; cf. also M. P. Charlesworth, *Trade-Routes and Commerce of the Roman Empire*, pp. 58, 64. The relevant texts have been conveniently assembled and translated in Huntingford, *Periplus*, appendix 5.

[167] Cosmas, *Topographie*, XI, 23.

21. *Gold*

Lammens is, of course, right that East Africa supplied gold, but Pliny and Cosmas are agreed that it supplied it to the Ethiopians,[168] and Lammens is the only authority for the view that the Ethiopians passed it on to the Meccans. This does not rule out the possibility that the Meccans exported gold mined in Arabia itself, a possibility to which I shall come back in the next chapter.

22. *Slaves*

It is a well-known fact that the pre-Islamic Arabs, including the Meccans, had slaves, some of whom were "Ethiopians," that is, natives of East Africa.[169] There is, however, nothing to indicate that the centre of distribution for such slaves in Arabia was Mecca rather than the Yemen,[170] and even less to suggest that the Meccans exported them to the north. The Byzantines got their East African slaves directly from East Africa, insofar as they imported them at all.[171] I shall come back to

[168] Pliny, *Natural History*, VI, 173; Cosmas, *Topographie* II, 50 ff. According to N. Chittick, "East African Trade with the Orient," p. 101, the East African trade in gold did not acquire (international?) importance until the fourteenth century or later.

[169] Thus Bilāl, Waḥshī and Ṣāliḥ Shaqrān were Ethiopian freedmen of various Meccans (*EI*², *s.v.* Bilāl b. Rabāḥ; Ibn Hishām, *Leben*, p. 556; Ibn Sa'd, *Ṭabaqāt*, III, 49). The mother of 'Antara, the poet, was likewise an Ethiopian, as were those of other "ravens of the Arabs" (*Aghānī*, VIII, 237, 240). 'Abdallāh b. Abī Rabī'a, a Meccan, had a large number of Ethiopian slaves who practised all sorts of crafts (*ibid.*, I, 65), and Ibn Ḥabīb saw fit to compile a whole list of *abnā' al-Ḥabashiyyāt* in Mecca and elsewhere (*Muḥabbar*, pp. 306 ff.).

[170] No Meccan, to the best of my knowledge, is explicitly said to have purchased Ethiopian slaves in Ethiopia. 'Abdallāh b. Abī Rabī'a, the owner of numerous Ethiopian slaves mentioned in the preceding note, had presumably bought his in the Yemen; that, at least, is where he is said to have traded (*Aghānī*, I, 64). Similarly, it was from the Sarāt rather than directly from Ethiopia that Bilāl came to Mecca (Ibn Sa'd, *Ṭabaqāt*, III, 232; alternatively, he was born into slavery in Mecca, cf. *EI*², *s.v.*); and several other Ethiopian slaves seem to have come to Mecca from the same area (cf. below, ch. 5 n90). Of one black slave girl we are told that she was purchased at Ḥubāsha, a market located in Tihāma (Yāqūt, *Buldān*, II, 192 f., *s.v.*, but the story in question identifies it with the market of B. Qaynuqā' in Yathrib). Of black slaves purchased by visitors to Mecca there is no mention.

[171] Cosmas, *Topographie*, II, 64 ("most of the slaves who arrive to us come from these people, and even today one finds some in the hands of merchants there"). It is well known that slavery contracted in the later empire, not just in the west, but also in the east.

the (remote) possibility that the Meccans exported Arab slaves in the next chapter.

Other Luxury Goods

23. Silk

It is well known that in antiquity the Mediterranean world was dependent on Persia for its supply of silk, which in the sixth century reached the west partly via Central Asia and partly by sea via Ceylon. In 524-525 Justinian tried to break the Persian monopoly on the trade by encouraging the Ethiopians to buy silk directly from the Indians, not in Ceylon, as is usually assumed, but in some port adjacent to Persia, possibly Dabā, the port on which traders from India, China, east, and west are said to have converged. The attempt was a failure because the Persians always got there first and were in the habit of buying the entire cargoes.[172] Some thirty years later, the Byzantines succeeded in setting up a silk industry of their own by means of silkworms smuggled, probably, from Central Asia.[173] This did not make them self-sufficient at once, and Justin II (565-578) once more tried to circumvent the Persians, this time by negotiating with the Turks.[174]

Against this background, one is surprised to learn from Lammens and others that one reason why the Meccans did so well is that they exported silk to the Byzantines,[175] a view that has gained such currency that even the ancient south Arabians have been credited with an overland trade in silk.[176] There does not appear to be any evidence in favour of Lammens'

[172] Procopius, *Wars*, I, 20, 9 ff. Procopius explicitly says that the Persians got there first because they inhabited the adjoining country, a claim which rules out Ceylon. For Dabā, see above, ch. 2, pp. 48 f. It does not in any way follow that the Ethiopians were not interested in the eastern trade, as argued by Smith, "Events in Arabia," p. 463.

[173] Procopius, *Wars*, VIII, 17; cf. R. Hennig, "Die Einführung der Seidenraupenzucht ins Byzantinerreich."

[174] Menander Protector in Kortenbeutel, *Osthandel*, pp. 78 f.; Hennig, "Einführung," pp. 303, 310.

[175] Lammens, *Mecque*, p. 299; followed by Watt, *Muhammad, Prophet and Statesman*, p. 1; Hitti, *Capital Cities*, p. 7; Aswad, "Social and Ecological Aspects," p. 426; Donner, "Mecca's Food Supplies," p. 250, and apparently even by Bulliet, *Camel and the Wheel*, p. 295 n40.

[176] Thus Rodinson, *Mohammed*, p. 20; Doe, *Southern Arabia*, p. 52. There is not, to my

view. The Islamic tradition associates the Yemen with textiles, and there is no reason to doubt the existence of a textile industry there.[177] But what the Yemen produced was fine cotton, not silk.[178] Some silk was probably available in the Yemen, too, and silk is occasionally attested in the Ḥijāz. Thus, leaving aside Prophetic traditions for and against its use, the Kaʿba is sometimes said to have been covered in silk at various times before the rise of Islam.[179] But the fact that silk may have circulated in the Ḥijāz does not mean that the Meccans exported it to Byzantium, and it was Byzantine Syria that appeared as a source of silk to the Arabs rather than the other way round.[180] The storytellers who presented Hāshim as having founded the international trade of the Meccans by getting permission from the Byzantine emperor to sell cheap leather goods and clothing in Syria were evidently not aware that Quraysh could have supplied the one commodity that the emperor really wanted;[181] and the Byzantine emperors who tried to get silk through Ethiopians and Turks might have been surprised to learn that they were approaching the wrong barbarians. Given that the Byzantine evidence on the silk trade is perfectly well known, it is extraordinary that the Qurashī trade in this commodity has retained its credibility for so long.

What the sources do assert is that there was a trade in silk between the Yemen and ʿUkāẓ, the market near Ṭāʾif, apparently independently of

knowledge, any evidence that the ancient south Arabians sold silk to the Greeks and Romans.

177 Lammens' references, in fact, show no more than that. Thus Abū Lahab is described as wearing an *ʿadanī* cloak at Minā (Ibn Hishām, *Leben*, pp. 282, 815), and Yemeni *ḥullas* are mentioned with some frequency in passages relating to the pre-Islamic and early Islamic periods (cf. *ibid.*, pp. 229, 830; *Aghānī*, I, 259; XVIII, 125; Balādhurī, *Futūḥ*, p. 65 (on the 2,000 *ḥullas* paid in tribute by the Christians of Najrān); cf. also Jacob, *Beduinenleben*, pp. 148, 154; Marzūqī, *Azmina*, II, 163 f.). J. Baldry, *Textiles in Yemen*, pp. 7 ff. Yemeni cloth and clothes are famed in later works such as Jāḥiẓ, *Tijāra*, pp. 25 f., 35 = §§8, 15; Thaʿālibī, *Thimār*, pp. 534, 539; *id.*, *Laṭāʾif*, p. 129.

178 Baldry, *Textiles in Yemen*, p. 7.

179 Azraqī, *Makka*, p. 174; Thaʿālibī, *Laṭāʾif*, p. 42 (but according to Balādhurī, *Futūḥ*, p. 47, it was not covered in silk until the time of Yazīd I). ʿAlī is also supposed to have given the Prophet a *ḥulla* of silk (Aḥmad b. Yaḥyā al-Balādhurī, *Ansāb al-ashrāf*, II, 36 f.) and a late account of the Meccan gifts to the Najāshī has them include a *jubbat dībāj* (ʿAlī b. Burhān al-Dīn al-Ḥalabī, *al-Sīra al-ḥalabiyya*, I, 322).

180 Cf. the oracular utterance cited in *Aghānī*, XXII, 110.

181 Kister, "Mecca and Tamīm," p. 116. I shall come back to this tradition in greater detail in chapters 5 and 9.

Mecca. We are told that Nuʿmān b. al-Mundhir would send unspecified goods by caravan to ʿUkāẓ every year and buy Yemeni products, including silk, in return.[182] This is hard to believe. Even if we grant that silk was available in the Yemen in some quantity, it does not make sense that Nuʿmān should have gone to ʿUkāẓ for the purchase of a commodity that must have been available in even larger quantities, and presumably also better quality, in Iraq. He may have bought Yemeni cloth at ʿUkāẓ; but the claim that he bought silk as well was already rejected as mistaken by Fraenkel.[183]

24. *Perfume*

Many of the commodities dealt with already were used as ingredients in perfume. So were other commodities well known from the Islamic tradition, notably musk and ambergris. Both musk and ambergris appear in one version of the tribute sent by the Persian governor of the Yemen to the Persian emperor,[184] but whether there was a regular trade in these products between the Yemen and Persia is hard to say. The Byzantines also knew of musk, as is clear from Cosmas.[185] Neither product, however, is associated with Meccan trade in the sources.

There remains the question whether the Meccans traded in perfume as a finished product, and for this claim there is good evidence. I shall come back to it in the next chapter, in which I consider all the commodities with which the Meccans are associated, however tenuously, in the Muslim sources. The conclusion of the present chapter is purely negative. Quraysh did not trade in incense, spices, or other foreign luxury goods. To the extent that perfume is a spice, one could, of course, speak of a Qurashī spice trade; but there was no such thing as conventionally understood.

182 *Aghānī*, XXII, 57.

183 Fraenkel, *Fremdwörter*, p. 178. No silk is mentioned in Balādhurī's version of Nuʿmān's purchases at ʿUkāẓ, but then his version is brief (*Ansāb*, I, 100 f.).

184 *Aghānīi*, XVII, 318.

185 Cosmas, *Topographie*, XI, 15.

PART II

ARABIA WITHOUT SPICES

4

WHAT DID THE MECCANS EXPORT?

The commodities with which the sources associate Meccan trade share the feature that all are of Arabian origin. Three of those explicitly said to have been exported—silver, gold, perfume—were expensive and would help to explain the rise of Mecca if the export was large-scale. But this it was not. In fact, the Meccans cannot be said to have exported silver or gold at all. The commodity they did export on a large scale, if the tradition can be trusted, was a modest one: leather in various forms. Another three are less well attested, but of a similarly humble kind: clothing, animals, miscellaneous foodstuffs. The rest would appear to have been sold only in Arabia, insofar as the Meccans handled them at all: raisins, wine, slaves, and other things.

1. Silver

The sources are agreed that after their defeat at Badr, the Meccans tried to avoid interception at the hands of Muḥammad by travelling to Syria via the Iraq route under the guidance of a tribesman native to central or eastern Arabia. The attempt was a failure: Muḥammad's men intercepted the caravan at Qarada, a watering place in Najd.[1] The interest of this episode lies in the fact that the caravan in question is said to have carried large quantities of silver, generally said to have been in the care of Ṣafwān b. Umayya, though Ibn Isḥāq's account implies that it was being looked after by Abū Sufyān.[2] In connection with this raid, Ibn Isḥāq goes so far as to claim that silver was what the Meccans mostly traded in.[3] Sprenger accepted this claim, though he found it problem-

[1] Ibn Hishām, *Leben*, p. 547; Wāqidī, *Maghāzī*, I, 197 f.; Ibn Sa'd, *Ṭabaqāt*, II, 36; Balādhurī, *Ansāb*, I, 374; *Aghānī*, XVII, 324 f. (mostly from Wāqidī); Ya'qūbī, *Ta'rīkh*, II, 73.

[2] Abū Sufyān is the only Qurashī mentioned by name in Ibn Isḥāq's account, and he is still there in Ya'qūbī, as well as in Wāqidī's survey of the Prophet's campaigns (*Maghāzī*, I, 3; contrast the main account). But in the other versions he is ousted by Ṣafwān.

[3] *Wa-hiya 'uẓm tijāratihim*. Similarly Ibn Ḥumayd's recension of Ibn Isḥāq in Ṭabarī, *Ta'rīkh*, ser. I, p. 1,374, and that of Muḥammad b. Salama in M. Ḥamīdallāh, ed., *Sīrat Ibn Isḥāq*, no. 500.

atic; Lammens also accepted it, without noticing any problems, but since then the Qurashī silver trade seems to have been forgotten by the secondary literature.[4] It probably should be forgotten. But given that silver is one of the few precious commodities for which there is some evidence in the sources, it is worth examining why.

There is no doubt that Arabia was silver-bearing in the past.[5] In the period of interest to us, silver was mined in Najd and the Yemen, and as mentioned already, the mines were under Persian control. Shamām, the mine in Najd that also yielded copper, was colonized by a thousand or several thousand Zoroastrians, and boasted two fire-temples, while Raḍrāḍ, the Yemeni mine in the territory of Hamdān, was run by the so-called "Persians of the Mine" who had started coming in the Jāhiliyya and who were still there in the ninth century, when the mine fell into ruin.[6] One account of the caravan which the Persian governor of the Yemen despatched to the Persian emperor duly states that it was loaded with silver ingots.[7] This was hardly the only occasion on which silver travelled to Iraq by land, for Raḍrāḍ was still provisioned by caravan from Iraq in Islamic times, and the caravans presumably carried something back.

None of this, however, does much to explain what role the Meccans may have played in the silver trade. They had no access to silver of their own. There is, at least, no mention of silver mines in the vicinity of Mecca, and they had, in any case, no wood with which to smelt it.[8] The

[4] Sprenger, *Leben*, III, 94 and the note thereto; Lammens, "République marchande," pp. 46 f. The only exception seems to be E. R. Wolf, "The Social Organization of Mecca and the Origins of Islam," p. 333. Wolf was a non-Islamicist who depended on Sprenger and Lammens for his information.

[5] Silver was part of the tribute paid by various Arab rulers to the Assyrians in the eighth century B.C. (Rosmarin, "Aribi und Arabien," pp. 8 f.), and Strabo lists it as one of the products native to Arabia which the Nabataeans did not have to import (*Geography*, XVI, 4:26). Both they and the Gerrheans seem to have been well provided with it. In 312 B.C., the Nabataeans were robbed of large quantities of silver, myrrh, and frankincense (Diodorus Siculus, *Bibliotheca*, XIX, 95:3), and in 205 B.C. the Gerrheans were forced to pay a huge tribute of silver, myrrh oil (*staktē*), and frankincense (Polybius, *History*, XIII, 9).

[6] Above, ch. 2, nn150, 160.

[7] Ṭabarī, *Ta'rīkh*, ser. I, p. 984; cf. also Lyall, *Mufaḍḍalīyāt*, I, 708 (*ad* CVI, 6), where the ingots are replaced by *āniya*, vessels.

[8] There were silver mines in unknown parts of Arabia, according to Hamdānī (*Jawharatayn*, p. 142 = 143; Dunlop, "Sources of Gold and Silver," p. 40), and some of the mines mentioned without specification of contents in connection with the Prophet's life could in

absence of silver from the trading agreement between Hāshim and the Byzantine emperor, from the tribute envisaged by the would-be king of Mecca for Byzantium, and from the gifts with which the Meccans hoped to coax the Negus into extraditing the Muslim refugees in Ethiopia certainly do not suggest that this was a commodity that they were in a position to export.[9] Why, then, is silver described as a major article of Qurashī commerce in connection with the raid at Qarada?

The answer is almost certainly because Qarada was located in Najd, an area that did yield silver, but yielded it to the Persians; or in other words, Quraysh would here seem to have been credited with commercial activities that were in fact performed by others. They could, of course, have purchased silver from the Persians or transported it as caravaneers in Persian service, but this is not what the Qarada story says. On the contrary, it makes it clear that it was by way of exception that the merchants of Mecca went to Najd. They only went to Qarada because they were threatened by Muḥammad, and they were sufficiently unfamiliar with the route to need a guide. The sources after Ibn Isḥāq make the guide in question, Furāt b. Ḥayyān al-ʿIjlī, an ally (*ḥalīf*) of Quraysh, implying that Quraysh made regular use of him;[10] but he is a straightforward foreigner in Ibn Isḥāq, and Wāqidī even has Ṣafwān b. Umayya exclaim in despair that he does not know the route to Iraq.[11] In short, the Qarada story has the Meccans go on an exceptional trip through unfamiliar territory which, as it happened, contained silver mines under Persian control; and it is only in connection with this trip that the Meccans are presented as silver exporters.[12] There can thus be

principle have been silver mines. But in practice, most of them seem to have been gold mines, and those that were unknown were presumably unknown because they were not exploited.

[9] For the references, see below, nn43-45.

[10] Thus as early as Ibn Hishām (*Leben*, p. 547).

[11] "They hired a man of Bakr b. Wā'il called Furāt b. Ḥayyān" (Ibn Isḥāq in Ibn Hishām, *Leben*, p. 547; similarly the other recensions). Wāqidī, *Maghāzī*, I, 197 f., where the guide is likewise a foreigner to those who make use of him.

[12] An exegetical story told *ad* 5:105 has a *mawlā* of Quraysh go to Syria or Ethiopia on trade carrying a silver cup (*jām*), sometimes said to have been inlaid with gold (several versions have been assembled by ʿAlī b. al-Ḥusayn Ibn ʿAsākir, *Ta'rīkh madīnat Dimashq*, x, 470 ff. The legal principles around which all the versions are structured are well brought out by Ismāʿīl b. ʿUmar Ibn Kathīr, *Tafsīr al-qur'ān al-ʿaẓīm*, II, 111 ff., where two ver-

little doubt that the Qurashī export of this commodity rests on a process of conflation.

This conclusion is reinforced by the story of the raid at ʿĪṣ in year 6, four years after that at Qarada. At ʿĪṣ, a Qurashī caravan was once more intercepted by Muḥammad's men. In Ibn Isḥāq's version it had carried money (rather than silver) to Syria under the care of Abū'l-ʿĀṣ b. al-Rabīʿ, being on its way back with unspecified things; but in other versions it is returning from Syria with silver belonging to Ṣafwān b. Umayya.[13] The tradition, in other words, asserts both that Quraysh exported silver to Syria and that they imported it from there, and this was the problem that worried Sprenger: they can hardly have done both in historical fact. Given that they are only presented as exporters of silver when they venture across to Najd, being importers of silver, or simply carriers of money, when they are back on their usual route, we may take it that it was not on the export of this commodity that they flourished.

For purposes of the present chapter, this conclusion suffices. It is worth noting, however, that the information on the Meccan silver trade illustrates a recurrent problem with the sources, that is, that apparently sober accounts of separate events turn out to be nothing but elaborations on a single theme. That the stories of the raids at Qarada and ʿĪṣ are doublets is obvious. In both stories a Qurashī caravan loaded with silver (coined or uncoined) is raided by Muḥammad's men. The silver is owned or guarded by Ṣafwān b. Umayya or Abū Sufyān in the Qarada story, by Ṣafwān b. Umayya or Abū'l-ʿĀṣ b. al-Rabīʿ in that about ʿĪṣ, and the Muslim commander is Zayd b. Ḥāritha in both.[14] It is hard to believe that the same commander twice intercepted a Meccan caravan loaded with the same commodity and manned by very much the same people. And when we are informed that a whole series of Meccan caravans was to fall into Muslim hands at ʿĪṣ about year 6, it is difficult not to conclude that this is the same episode in a third incarnation.[15] But the

sions are discussed). But this cup was meant as a gift for the king, and there is, of course, no question of claiming that Quraysh exported sophisticated silverware on a regular basis.

[13] Ibn Hishām, *Leben*, p. 469; Ibn Ishaq gives no place-name or date. Wāqidī, *Maghāzī*, II, 553 ff.; Ibn Saʿd, *Ṭabaqāt*, II, 87; cf. also Balādhurī, *Ansāb*, I, 377, 398 f. (without mention of the contents of the caravan).

[14] Wāqidī adds that Mughīra b. Muʿāwiya b. Abī'l-ʿĀṣ was also present on the second occasion (*Maghāzī*, II, 553).

[15] Ibn Hishām, *Leben*, p. 752; Wāqidī, *Maghāzī*, II, 627.

proliferations do not stop here. Some sources mention that Ḥuwayṭib b. ʿAbd al-ʿUzzā and ʿAbdallāh b. Abī Rabīʿa were present in the caravan at Qarada, together with Ṣafwān b. Umayya.[16] Elsewhere we are told that the Prophet borrowed 40,000 dirhams from Ḥuwayṭib b. ʿAbd al-ʿUzzā and ʿAbdallāh b. Abī Rabīʿa, and 50,000 from Ṣafwān b. Umayya, paying them back after the defeat of the Hawāzin.[17] And elsewhere still we learn that the booty taken by the Prophet from the Hawāzin was distributed among various people, including Ḥuwayṭib b. ʿAbd al-ʿUzzā, Ṣafwān b. Umayya, and Abū Sufyān; this booty included 4,000 ounces of silver.[18] We thus have a number of Qurashīs whose names are linked with silver, but in quite contradictory ways: the Prophet robs them of it as they are sending it to Syria, or bringing it back from there, or he borrows it from them and pays them back, or he gives it to them to win them over, having taken it from others. All the stories have in common is certain Qurashīs, the Prophet, silver. They thus testify to nothing but the existence of a theme, and the theme is the only evidence we ought to use, the rest being historically worthless elaboration. But shorn of the elaboration, the theme does not, of course, supply us with the information that we need.

This problem is not confined to cases where several versions of a particular story are known. Variant versions do not always survive, and even when they do, the Islamic tradition is so huge that one has not always read or recognized them: most of what passes for factual information about the rise of Islam is derived from stories read in isolation from their counterparts. The Islamic tradition on the rise of Islam, in fact, consists of little *but* stories, and the massive information that can be derived from these stories never represents straightforward fact. This is a point to which I shall return at greater length in the conclusion. In the

[16] Thus Wāqidī and Ibn Saʿd, but not Balādhurī, who merely mentions other *aʿyān*.

[17] Balādhurī, *Ansāb*, I, 363. There are several variations on this story, too: it was on the day of Ḥunayn (where the Hawāzin were defeated) that the Prophet asked Ṣafwān b. Umayya to lend him money (or coats of mail) (Aḥmad Ibn Ḥanbal, *al-Musnad*, VI, 465); it was in Mecca that he did so (Ṭabarī, *Taʾrīkh*, ser. 3, p. 2,357); it was when Ḥuwayṭib b. ʿAbd al-ʿUzzā converted that the Prophet asked him for a loan; Ḥuwayṭib later participated in the battle of Ḥunayn (Ṭabarī, *Taʾrīkh*, ser. 3, p. 2,329); and so on.

[18] Wāqidī, *Maghāzī*, III, 944 ff.; Ibn Saʿd, *Ṭabaqāt*, II, 152 f. The story is familiar from other sources, too, but without the silver (and silver was not included in all the booty distributed).

meantime, however, I shall suspend most of my source-critical doubts. The purpose of this part of the book is to examine what the Islamic tradition itself (as opposed to the secondary literature) says and implies about the nature of Meccan trade, and to see what sense we can make of this information on the assumption that it is basically correct. In accordance with the methodology adopted by the majority of Islamicists, I shall thus presume information to be authentic until the contrary can be proved. In other words, I shall accept all information on which there is widespread agreement in the tradition regardless of whether the story in connection with which it is offered is authentic or not (as long as it is not dictated by the moral of the story), but reject all claims contradicted by the tradition at large and/or by sources outside it (such as the claim that the Meccans exported silver). To give some concrete examples, I shall accept that Abū Sufyān traded in Syria, for all that some of the stories in which he does so are *dalā'il al-nubuwwa* stories, that is, miracle stories predicting or otherwise authenticating the prophethood of Muḥammad; but I shall reject the claim that he traded in the Yemen too because it is *only* in such stories that he does so, and the stories in question are inspired by Qur'ānic exegesis in their choice of locale. Similarly, I shall accept that Qurashīs might sell goods such as leather and perfume in Egypt, as does ʿAmr b. al-ʿĀṣ in a story predicting his conquest of this country; but I shall not commit myself as to whether ʿAmr b. al-ʿĀṣ used to do so, the choice of person being dictated by the point of the story, and I shall completely reject the claim that he (or other Qurashīs) would sell such goods in Alexandria, this claim being not only dictated by the point of the story, but also unconfirmed by the tradition at large and implausible on other grounds. In short, I shall accept everything that the Muslims at large remembered as their past, provided that their recollection is not obviously wrong or questionable. This methodology may be labelled minimal source criticism, and as will be seen, it is indefensible in the long run: one simply *cannot* make sense of the information given without assuming the recollection to be fundamentally wrong in one or more respects (or at least I cannot). But it is important to give the tradition the benefit of doubt and ourselves all the rope we could wish for: whether we will save or hang ourselves with it remains to be seen. What commodities other than silver, then, does the tradition associate with Meccan trade?

2. *Gold*

In Wāqidī's account of the raid at Qarada, the Qurashī caravan is loaded not only with silver but also with gold, and a story going back to Kalbī has it that ʿUmar once tried to smuggle gold into Syria.[19] One version of this story implies that Qurashī traders in Syria habitually carried gold with them.[20] Did the Meccans then owe their wealth to the export of gold to the Byzantine empire? Once again the answer is negative.

The presence of gold in the peninsula is well attested,[21] and there were gold mines in north Arabia no less than in the south.[22] There were even scholars who claimed one for Mecca, though this is clearly wrong.[23] Three gold mines in the vicinity of Mecca are mentioned in connection with the Prophet's life. The first is Buḥrān, which belonged to Ḥajjāj b. ʿIlāṭ al-Sulamī according to Ibn Isḥāq, and which was the

[19] Wāqidī, *Maghāzī*, I, 198. Zubayr b. Bakkār, *al-Akhbār al-muwaffaqiyyāt*, p. 625. It is cited from the *Muwaffaqiyyāt* by Ibn Ḥajar, *Iṣāba*, III, 12, no. 2,811, *s.v.* Zinbāʿ b. Sallāma, and summarized without mention of the gold in ʿAlī b. Muḥammad al-Māwardī, *Aʿlām al-nubuwwa*, p. 194, where the *isnād* goes back to Kalbī. A slightly different version is given in Abū'l-Baqāʾ Hibatallāh, *al-Manāqib al-mazyadiyya*, fols. 11a-b.

[20] "A caravan of Quraysh coming to Syria for trade without gold—impossible!" as Zinbāʿ, the customs officer, exclaims in Abū'l-Baqāʾ's account (*Manāqib*, fol. 11b).

[21] The classical sources usually locate the gold-bearing regions in south Arabia, cf. Agatharchides, §§ 95 ff.; Pliny, *Natural History*, VI, 161; von Wissmann, "Ōphīr und Ḥawīla." But Glaser conjectures that the gold exported from Ommana and Apologos (Ubulla) in the *Periplus*, § 36, came from the Yamāma (*Skizze*, II, 350, with reference to Hamdānī).

[22] Cf. Hamdānī, *Jawharatayn*, pp. 137 ff. = 136 ff.; Dunlop, "Sources of Gold and Silver," pp. 37 f.; Aḥmad b. Abī Yaʿqūb al-Yaʿqūbī, *Kitāb al-buldān*, pp. 316 f. = *Les pays*, pp. 154 f.; Wohaibi, *The Northern Hijaz*, pp. 160, 293. The gold that various Arab rulers paid to Assyrian kings presumably also came from the northern end of the peninsula (Rosmarin, "Aribi und Arabien," pp. 8 f.), as did perhaps also that of the Nabataeans (Strabo, *Geography*, XVI, 4:26).

[23] "Those who have information about Mecca say that at al-ʿAyr and al-ʿAyrah, two mountains overlooking Mecca, there is a mine [of gold]" (Hamdānī in Dunlop, "Sources of Gold and Silver," p. 37; *id.*, *Jawharatayn*, p. 137 = 136). But there does not appear to have been any mountains of these names in Mecca. It is in Medina that there is supposed to have been a mountain, or two, called ʿAyr (Yāqūt, *Buldān*, III, 751 f., *s.v.*; Abū ʿUbayd ʿAbdallāh b. ʿAbd al-ʿAzīz al-Bakrī, *Muʿjam mā istaʿjam*, pp. 688 f., *s.v.*). Even this contention, however, is problematic. ʿAyr and Thawr are mentioned in a tradition on the *taḥrīm* of Medina. But the Medinese themselves denied that there was a mountain by the name of Thawr in Medina, and Muṣʿab (al-Zubayrī?) also denied that there was one called ʿAyr (Bakrī, *Muʿjam*, pp. 222 f., *s.v.* Thawr).

object of one of the numerous raids organized by the Prophet in which no fighting took place.[24] The second is the so-called "Mine of B. Sulaym." According to Wāqidī, this was the mine that Ḥajjāj b. ʿIlāṭ owned, Buḥrān being simply the area in which it was located. We are told that, in fact, he owned several mines and that he would lend some of the gold that he derived from it to Meccan customers.[25] But the "Mine of B. Sulaym" was not located in or near Buḥrān; and according to Ibn Saʿd, it only began to be exploited in the caliphate of Abū Bakr.[26] If Ḥajjāj b. ʿIlāṭ lent gold to the Meccans, he must thus have had it from Buḥrān or elsewhere. Finally, we hear of the so-called Qabaliyya mines in the territory of Juhayna. The Prophet is said to have granted them or their income to a certain Muzanī, though Ibn Saʿd describes their revenues as going to the state in the caliphate of Abū Bakr.[27] There is no mention of them in connection with Meccan trade.

The sources thus do not suggest that Quraysh were involved in the mining of gold. They do assert that Quraysh would obtain gold from their neighbours, and that some of this gold would find its way to the north. But the reason why some of this gold would find its way to the north is clearly that it was a substitute for currency, not that it was an export commodity. Thus Wāqidī's elaborate account of the caravan threatened at Badr has it that various Meccans had contributed so many camels and so-and-so much gold to it, the value of the gold being identified now in terms of bullion and now in terms of currency. It is also as a substitute for currency that gold appears in the story of ʿUmar as a smuggler.[28] As has been seen, silver and dirhams are similarly inter-

[24] Ḥajjāj b. ʿIlāṭ: Ibn Isḥāq in the recension of Muḥammad b. Salama (Ḥamīdallāh, *Sīra*, no. 495) and that used by Yāqūt (*Buldān*, I, 498 f., *s.v.* Buḥrān), but not in that of Ibn Hishām (*Leben*, p. 544) or Ibn Ḥumayd (Ṭabarī, *Taʾrīkh*, ser. I, p. 1,368). The raids: Ibn Hishām, *Leben*, p. 544; Wāqidī, *Maghāzī*, I, 3, 196 f.

[25] Wāqidī, *Maghāzī*, II, 702 ff., (cf. I, 96); similarly Ibn Saʿd, *Ṭabaqāt*, IV, 269 f. (with lacuna); ʿAlī b. al-Ḥusayn Ibn ʿAsākir, *Tahdhīb taʾrīkh Dimashq al-kabīr*, IV, 48. A less elaborate version of this story was also known to Ibn Isḥāq (cf. Ibn Hishām, *Leben*, pp. 770 f., where he lends money of unspecified origin to the Meccans).

[26] Wohaibi, *The Northern Hijaz*, p. 133, cf. p. 71 (correcting Masʿūdī, whose confusion is caused by Wāqidī). Wāqidī presumably thought that a mine owned by a Sulamī must be Maʿdin B. Sulaym. Others thought that Sulamī mines produced silver (Ibn Ḥanbal, *Musnad*, V, 430; cf. Lammens, *Mecque*, p. 291). Ibn Saʿd, *Ṭabaqāt*, III, 213.

[27] Balādhurī, *Futūḥ*, pp. 13 f.; ʿAlī b. Aḥmad Ibn Ḥazm, *Jamharat ansāb al-ʿarab*, p. 201; Yāqūt, *Buldān*, IV, 33, *s.v.* al-Qabaliyya; Ibn Saʿd, *Ṭabaqāt*, III, 213.

[28] Wāqidī, *Maghāzī*, I, 27 f. (the gold being evaluated in terms of both *mithqāl*s and *dī-*

changeable in the stories of the raid at ʿĪṣ. What the sources describe is thus an import trade paid for in bullion, not an export trade of gold.[29] Gold is absent from Hāshim's trading agreement with the Byzantine emperor, the tribute envisaged by the would-be king of Mecca for the Byzantines, and the gifts with which the Meccans tried to bribe the Negus; and there is no record of imports of gold and silver on the Greco-Roman side.[30] Meccan trade thus cannot be identified as a trade in gold.

3. *Perfume*

As mentioned before, there is good evidence that the Meccans traded in perfume. The centre of the Arabian perfume industry was Aden. According to Marzūqī, it was so famous in pre-Islamic times that even Indian traders would have their perfume manufactured there, apparently supplying the raw materials themselves and, at all events, returning with *ṭīb maʿmūl*, the finished product. At the same time other traders would transport Yemeni perfume by land to Persia and the Byzantine empire.[31] On the Persian conquest of the Yemen the industry fell under Persian control, and one account of the tribute sent to the Persian king duly states that it included perfume.[32]

There is no evidence for Qurashī traders in Aden, or for Qurashī organization of caravans from there to Syria. But Quraysh do seem to have

---

nārs); Abū'l-Baqā', *Manāqib*, fols. 11a-b, where it is explained that the Ghassānids "used to take some of the gold which merchants had with them" (*kānū ya'khudhūna shay'an mimmā yakūnu maʿa'l-tujjār min al-dhahab*); in other words, it is assumed that merchants of any kind would carry some. In the Qurashī caravan everyone did: one merchant chose to bury his rather than to make a camel swallow it, as did ʿUmar and others. It is thus assumed that the quantities were small and distributed with individuals: gold was not what the caravan as such was carrying. The import of the exclamation cited above, n20, is clearly, "how could they engage in commercial transactions without money?" rather than "what are they bringing in to sell if they have no gold?"

[29] Elsewhere too it is taken for granted that the Meccans would pay for their purchases in bullion. Thus ʿAbbās is reputed to have taken twenty ounces of gold with him when he went to Badr, intending to spend it on food for his people; and Abū Bakr bought Bilāl for a *raṭl* of gold (ʿAlī b. Aḥmad al-Wāḥidī, *Asbāb al-nuzūl*, pp. 180, 337).

[30] Cf. below, nn43-45 and Miller, *Spice Trade*, p. 199.

[31] Marzūqī, *Azmina*, II, 164; compare the parallel, but shorter versions in Yaʿqūbī, *Ta'rīkh*, I, 314 (cited above, ch. 2 n59); Abū'l-ʿAbbās Aḥmad al-Qalqashandī, *Ṣubḥ al-aʿshā*, I, 411; and Abū Ḥayyān al-Tawḥīdī, *Kitāb al-imtāʿ wa'l-mu'ānasa*, I, 84.

[32] Lyall, *Mufaḍḍalīyāt*, I, 708 (*ad* CVI, 6). Aden was tithed by the Persian Abnā' (cf. the references to Marzūqī and Yaʿqūbī in the preceding note and Ibn Ḥabīb, *Muḥabbar*, p. 266).

participated in the distribution of Yemeni perfume in Arabia and beyond, starting, probably, in Najrān.[33] Thus ʿAbbās b. ʿAbd al-Muṭṭalib sold Yemeni perfume at Minā and elsewhere in the pilgrim season, whereas the mother of ʿAbdallāh b. Abī Rabīʿa sold it in Medina in the the caliphate of ʿUmar, her supplies being sent to her from the Yemen by her son; and Abū Ṭālib is also said to have traded in *ʿiṭr*, presumably Yemeni.[34] Of ʿAmr b. al-ʿĀṣ we are told that he used to sell leather goods and perfume in Egypt, an activity that once took him to Alexandria; Ḥakam b. Abīʾl-ʿĀṣ once went to Ḥīra for the sale of perfume; and after the conquests, *ṭīb* was among the gifts sent by ʿUmar's wife to the wife of Heraclius.[35] Perfume was thus a commodity for which the Meccans had a market not only in the Ḥijāz, but also outside Arabia.

It would nonetheless be hard to present Quraysh as large-scale suppliers of perfume to the Byzantine and Persian empires. The Byzantine empire had a perfume industry of its own, centred on Alexandria, and there is no record of imports of manufactured perfume on the Greco-Roman side.[36] On the contrary, the empire produced enough to export some of it to the Arabs themselves. Thus the Jews of Medina are said to have imported perfume from Syria to Medina in the time of the Prophet,[37] and it was also imported from there to Medina in Umayyad

[33] Cf. below, ch. 5, pp. 122 f.

[34] On ʿAbd al-Muṭṭalib, Ṭabarī, *Taʾrīkh*, ser. I, p. 1,162. On the mother of ʿAbdallāh b. Abī-Rabīʿa, *Aghānī*, I, 69 f.; Wāqidī, *Maghāzī*, I, 89; Balādhurī, *Ansāb*, I, 298 f.; Ibn Saʿd, *Ṭabaqāt*, VIII, 300. For other women who sold perfume in Medina at the time of the Prophet, see Ibn al-Athīr, *Usd*, V, 432, 548 f.; Ibn Ḥajar, *Iṣāba*, VIII, 56, 191, nos. 314, 1014, *s.vv.* al-Ḥawlāʾ and Mulayka wālida al-Sāʾib b. al-Aqraʿ. On Abū Ṭālib, Ibn Rusta, *Aʿlāq*, p. 215; Ibn Qutayba, *Maʿārif*, p. 249.

[35] On ʿAmr b. al-ʿĀṣ, Muḥammad b. Yūsuf al-Kindī, *The Governors and Judges of Egypt*, pp. 6 f. On Ḥakam b. Abīʾl-ʿĀṣ, *Aghānī*, XVII, p. 369. The parallel version in F. Schulthess, ed. and tr., *Der Dîwân des arabischen Dichters Ḥâtim Ṭej*, p. 29 = 48 f. (*ad* no. XLVIII), does not mention what he intended to sell at Ḥīra; but in both versions he is said to have had *ṭīb* with him with which he *ṭayyaba* his hosts after the meal he received on the way. This was presumably incense rather than perfume, but at all events a finished product once again. On ʿUmar's wife, Ṭabarī, *Taʾrīkh*, ser. I, p. 2,823.

[36] Miller, *Spice Trade*, pp. 199 f.

[37] Wāḥidī, *Asbāb*, p. 208 (*ad* 15:87); Muḥammad b. Aḥmad al-Qurṭubī, *al-Jāmiʿ li-aḥkām al-qurʾān*, X, 56 (both first adduced by Kister, "Some Reports," p. 77n). This is a crude piece of exegetical invention to which I shall come back in the last chapter, but the Jews are also presented as traders in perfume (of whatever origin) in Qays b. al-Khaṭīm, *Dīwān*, VII, 4 f.

times.[38] That the Arabs should have imported perfume while exporting their own is not implausible: they seem to have appreciated foreign aromatics even in antiquity.[39] But they can hardly have sold manufactured perfume in Alexandria, unless they bought it in Alexandria itself, and the story of ʿAmr's visit to this city is clearly apocryphal.[40] Where, then, in Byzantium did they sell it? Presumably at their customary markets in southern Syria: Gaza, Buṣrā, Adhriʿāt, and so forth;[41] or, in other words, they seem to have serviced the southernmost, and overwhelmingly Arab, communities of the Byzantine empire. This would agree with such evidence as we have for their activities in Iraq. The Persian empire presumably also had a perfume industry of its own, but Ḥakam b. Abī'l-ʿĀṣ had no intention of going further than Ḥīra, which had a market "in which the Arabs assembled every year."[42] He should thus be envisaged as a retailer selling his goods directly to private customers, not as a wholesaler catering to the Persian elite. The same is true of ʿAmr, who sold humble leather goods along with perfume. If the Qurashī perfume traders in Syria, Egypt, and Iraq were peddlers of an Arabian commodity in an Arab environment, it is less surprising that there should have been a market for them, and imports of this kind would naturally have gone unrecorded. But it is difficult to see how such activities could have sustained the growth of a city in the desert at a distance of one month's journey by caravan.

[38] Cf. *Aghānī*, XXII, 38, where a merchant sells *ʿitr* and *burr* in Medina, precisely the two commodities that Abū Ṭālib is said to have traded in (above, n34).

[39] Cf. above, ch. 3 n1. Moreover, there is no reference to Meccan imports of perfume from Syria unless one takes *laṭīma* to mean aromatics, in which case such imports would have been commonplace (cf. Fraenkel, *Fremdwörter*, p. 176). Wāqidī knew that *laṭīma* might mean *ʿiṭr* in particular, but he also knew that it might mean *tijāra* in general (*Maghāzī*, I, 32), and the sources frequently seem to use the word in this general sense.

[40] His presence is required there for predictive purposes, and the mode of prediction seems to be Persian (he is singled out as the future ruler of Egypt by a ball, compare Nöldeke, *Geschichte*, p. 29). Lammens also rejected it, though it was his sole evidence for the spice trade of the Meccans (cf. "République marchande," p. 47 and the note thereto).

[41] Cf. below, ch. 5, pp. 118 f.

[42] According to the *Aghānī*, XXIV, 62, the Persians even exported perfume to the Yemen: Kisrā sent a caravan loaded, among other things, with *ʿiṭr* to Bādhām, his governor of the Yemen. But this is simply one out of numerous versions of the same story, the Kisrā in question being now Anūshirwān and now Parwīz, and the caravan going now to the Yemen and now from it. For Ḥakam, see the references given above, n35.

4. Leather

Leather is the one commodity that is not only well attested, but also consistently associated with Qurashī exports. According to a well-known story that I shall henceforth refer to as Ibn al-Kalbī's *īlāf*-tradition, Hāshim founded the international trade of the Meccans by obtaining permission from the Byzantine emperor to sell leather goods and clothing in Syria.[43] It was hides, sacks of *qaraẓ* (a plant used in tanning), and skins filled with clarified butter that ʿUthmān b. al-Ḥuwayrith, the would-be king of Mecca, envisaged as a suitable tribute for the Byzantines some time after 570.[44] And it was leather that the Meccans presented to the Negus when they wanted him to extradite the Muslim refugees in Ethiopia, leather being the best Meccan product the Negus could think of.[45] ʿAmr b. al-ʿĀṣ similarly presented him with leather when, in a doublet of the above episode, he himself wanted to seek refuge in Ethiopia.[46] The Prophet used to trade in leather, as did his partner, and also ʿUmar, according to some, as well as Abū Sufyān, who once presented the Prophet with some.[47] ʿAmr b. al-ʿĀṣ sold not just perfume, but also leather in Egypt.[48] And when ʿAbd al-Raḥmān b. ʿAwf came to Medina, he displayed his business acumen, according to one version of the story, by buying skins, cottage cheese, and clarified butter on which he got rich, presumably by selling them in Syria, so that he soon had seven hundred camels carrying grain and flour from there.[49]

[43] Ibn Ḥabīb, *Munammaq*, p. 32; Ismāʿīl b. al-Qāsim al-Qālī, *Kitāb dhayl al-amālī wa'l-nawādir*, p. 199; Yaʿqūbī, *Ta'rīkh*, I, 280 f.; cf. Kister, "Mecca and Tamīm," p. 250. It is Ibn Ḥabīb who identifies the story as going back to Ibn al-Kalbī. It is reproduced, summarized and alluded to in many other sources, too, but usually without specification of the goods involved.

[44] Muḥammad b. Aḥmad al-Fāsī, *Shifā' al-gharām bi-akhbār al-balad al-ḥarām*, p. 143; Abū'l-Baqā', *Manāqib*, fol. 10b, where the *isnād* is traced back to ʿUrwa b. al-Zubayr. The date is fixed by the reference to the Persian conquest of the Yemen. That the goods in question were regarded as valuable is also suggested by Ibn Saʿd, *Ṭabaqāt*, VIII, 252, where Abū Bakr divorces Qutayla, giving her gifts of *qaraẓ*, clarified butter, and raisins.

[45] Ibn Hishām, *Leben*, p. 218; cf. Balādhurī, *Ansāb*, I, 232.

[46] Ibn Hishām, *Leben*, p. 716; Wāqidī, *Maghāzī*, II, 742.

[47] Muḥammad b. al-Ḥasan al-Shaybānī, *al-Kasb*, pp. 36, 41. Ibn Rusta, *Aʿlāq*, p. 215; Ibn Qutayba, *Maʿārif*, p. 250 (both on the professions of the *ashrāf*); A. Khan, "The Tanning Cottage Industry in Pre-Islamic Arabia," pp. 91 f.

[48] Kindī, *Governors*, p. 7.

[49] Ibn al-Athīr, *Usd*, III, 315. The version cited in ʿAbd al-Razzāq b. Hammām al-

We also hear something of the provenance of these goods. In Ibn al-Kalbī's story, the leather comes from the Ḥijāz, being picked up on the way to Syria by Meccan caravans, but some of it also seems to have come from Ṭā'if. Thus it was a caravan carrying leather, raisins, and (according to Wāqidī) wine from Ṭā'if that Muḥammad's men intercepted at Nakhla, between Ṭā'if and Mecca; and the leather industry of Ṭā'if is well known, though most of the evidence comes from later times.[50] If we go by the account of ʿUthmān b. al-Ḥuwayrith's ideas on tribute, leather was produced even in Mecca itself, though one story about the origins of Quṣayy's fortune implies that this had not always been so: Quṣayy, we are told, inherited it from a man who had come to Mecca for the sale of leather.[51] It was produced in Medina after the *hijra*, too, according to ḥadīth. The Prophet himself once fell asleep in the middle of tanning, apparently in Medina; Asmā' bint ʿUmays tanned forty skins the day her husband died; another widow was in the middle of tanning when the Prophet came to visit her: she wiped her hands of *qaraẓ* and presented him with a pillow stuffed with grass; and so forth.[52] It would, of course, be an idle task to defend the authenticity of these traditions, and the material relating to the sale of leather outside the Ḥijāz is not necessarily any better. It is clear, however, that those to whom we owe our sources took Meccan trade to have been a trade in leather above all. This is as far as we can go.

We thus have a problem on our hands. It is not likely that the inhabitants of a remote and barren valley should have founded a commercial empire of international dimensions on the basis of hides and skins. Sprenger, it is true, did his best to emphasize the commercial significance of the Arabian leather trade with reference to the high prices

Ṣanʿānī, *al-Muṣannaf*, VI, no. 10,411, however, omits the grain and flour and thus the evidence for foreign trade; and those in Ibn Saʿd, *Ṭabaqāt*, III, 125 f., have him sell unspecified things in the Medinese market and return with *samn* and *aqiṭ* that he has *earned* (similarly Muḥammad b. Ismāʿīl al-Bukhārī, *Le recueil des traditions mahométanes*, III, 50).

[50] Ibn Hishām, *Leben*, p. 424; Wāqidī, *Maghāzī*, I, 16; Ibn Saʿd, *Ṭabaqāt*, II, 11; Wāḥidī, *Asbāb*, p. 47. On the leather industry, cf. Lammens, *Ṭāif*, p. 226; Khan, "Cottage Industry," pp. 92 f. Both authors tend to treat information from the medieval geographers as information about pre-Islamic Arabia; but Ṭā'ifī leather appears as a highly esteemed product already in Ibn Ḥabīb, *Munammaq*, p. 73.

[51] Balādhurī, *Ansāb*, I, 49. Quṣayy inherited the money because the foreigner died without an heir; as retold by Lammens, he confiscated it (*Mecque*, p. 140).

[52] Khan, "Cottage Industry," pp. 91 f.

fetched by Arabian leather goods in medieval times.[53] But in the first place, the popularity of Arabian goods in the medieval Muslim world is likely to have owed more to the religious prestige of Arabia than to the intrinsic merits of its products. In the second place, the production of leather goods was in no way a Meccan monopoly in pre-Islamic or, for that matter, later times. The production would seem to have centred on south Arabia rather than the Ḥijāz. Leather was sold at Qabr Hūd in the Ḥaḍramawt,[54] and exported from Ṣanʿāʾ,[55] and Yemeni leather goods were among the things that Nuʿmān of Ḥīra would buy at ʿUkāẓ.[56] The Yemen also dominated the market in medieval times.[57] But wherever there was a pastoral economy there was a potential tanning industry, and leather would seem to have been produced all over the peninsula,[58] including, no doubt, the Syrian desert: skins had played an important role in the trade of Palmyra; and it was precisely with hides and skins that the rabbinic tradition associated Ishmaelite traders.[59] In the third place, the leather goods of the Meccans do not appear to have been very sophisticated. Leather was used for the most diverse articles in the Ḥijāz and elsewhere—tents, basins, buckets, saddles, oil skins, water skins, butter skins, belts, sandals, cushions, writing material, and, as has been seen, even boats.[60] But insofar as any of these articles qualified for clas-

[53] Sprenger, *Leben*, pp. 94 f. The anonymous author cited is Ibn al-Mujāwir.

[54] Marzūqī, *Azmina*, II, 163. It seems unnecessary to assume with Serjeant that *udum* might here mean "anything in which bread is dipped" and thus conceivably be a reference to spices (R. B. Serjeant, "Hūd and Other Pre-Islamic Prophets of Ḥaḍramawt," p. 125).

[55] Qalqashandī, *Ṣubḥ*, I, 411.

[56] Balādhurī, *Ansāb*, I, 101. The parallel account in *Aghānī*, XXII, 57, mentions much the same goods, but fails to specify that they were Yemeni, and Lammens accordingly took the leather to come from Ṭāʾif (cf. *Ṭāif*, p. 228).

[57] Khan, "Cottage Industry," pp. 93 ff. Cf. also Jāḥiẓ, *Tijāra*, pp. 34 f. = § 15.

[58] Cf. Ibn al-Mujāwir, *Descriptio*, I, 13; Dīnawarī, *Monograph Section*, nos. 413 ff., on tanning in Arabia; and note how the story in Balādhurī, *Ansāb*, I, 18, takes it for granted that people would gather *qaraẓ* there. Leather was tanned and/or sold at ʿUkāẓ (cf. Ṭirimmāḥ, IV, 25 in F. Krenkow, ed. and tr., *The Poems of Ṭufail Ibn ʿAuf al-Ghanawī and aṭ-Ṭirimmāḥ Ibn Ḥakīm aṭ-Ṭāʾyī*; Yāqūt, *Buldan*, III, 704 f., *s.v.* ʿUkāẓ). And the tribute paid by the Arabs to Nuʿmān of Ḥīra included leather, according to Fraenkel (*Fremdwörter*, p. 178; but the reference is wrong).

[59] J.-B. Chabot, *Choix d'inscriptions de Palmyre*, pp. 29 f. Above, ch. 2 n74; Great Britain, Foreign Office, *Arabia*, p. 68, where hides and skins are identified as the most important source of wealth in the area from Jabal Shammar northward.

[60] Lammens, *Ṭāif*, p. 227; Khan, "Cottage Industry," pp. 85 f.

sification as luxury products, they were made in the Yemen.[61] What the Meccans sold were crude products on a par with the cottage cheese, clarified butter, and *qaraẓ* with which they are associated, and this fits with Hāshim's assertion that they were cheap.[62] But if the Meccans dealt in cheap leather products destined for everyday use, why should the inhabitants of distant Syria have chosen to buy from them what was readily available at home? And if the Meccans transported their leatherware all the way to Syria, how *could* it have been cheap? Watt copes with the problem by dismissing the Qurashī leather trade as unimportant in comparison with that in frankincense and Indian luxury goods.[63] But given that there was no Qurashī trade in frankincense and Indian luxury goods, how did Mecca come to thrive? There is something here that does not fit at all.

5. *Clothing*

According to Ibn al-Kalbī's *īlāf*-tradition, Hāshim founded the international trade of the Meccans by obtaining permission to sell not just leather goods but also clothing in Syria.[64] Like the leather goods, the clothing is explicitly characterized as Ḥijāzī,[65] and it is implied that it was picked up, at least in part, from the Ḥijāzī tribes by Qurashī merchants on their way to Syria. They must thus have been woollens. They were no more sophisticated than the leather goods in which the Meccans traded: the "thick and coarse clothes of the Ḥijāz" are unfavourably contrasted with more refined varieties obtained elsewhere in a passage relating to the Umayyad period.[66] And again we are assured that they were cheap.

Clothing thus poses the same problem as leather. Leather goods can-

[61] This is presumably why Nuʿmān bought Yemeni rather than local leather goods at ʿUkāẓ (above, n56). Similarly, the Persian governor of the Yemen included leather goods such as ornamented belts in the tribute destined for the Persian king, whereas ʿUthmān b. al-Ḥuwayrith could think of nothing more sophisticated than *qaraẓ* and untanned hides for the Byzantines (*Aghānī*, XVII, 318; cf. Lyall, *Mufaḍḍalīyāt*, I, 708; above, n44).

[62] Above, n43.

[63] Watt, *Muhammad at Mecca*, p. 4.

[64] Above, n43.

[65] *Min udum al-Ḥijāz wa-thiyābihi*. Thus Ibn Ḥabīb, Qālī, and Yaʿqūbī, alike. It is presented as Yemeni by M. Ḥamīdallāh, "Al-īlāf, ou les rapports economico-diplomatiques de la Mecque pré-islamique," p. 299, and, following him, Baldry, *Textiles in Yemen*, p. 7.

[66] *Aghānī*, I, 310.

not have been rare in Syria, and cheap clothing there was certainly like coal in Newcastle. Syria had a textile industry of its own, as did Egypt, and in the late fourth century the Antiochene textile industry was capable of producing coarse cloth at prices so low that it could be sold as material suitable for the use of ascetics even in distant Rome. Moreover, plain weaving was practised throughout the countryside, and the majority of the population undoubtedly made do with clothing made by themselves or local craftsmen.[67] There was no lack of sheep in Syria, the Syrian desert being better sheep country than the Ḥijāz.[68] Yet the Meccans claimed that bulky woollens carried by caravan from the Ḥijāz to Syria at a distance of up to eight hundred miles would be cheaper for the Syrians than what they could buy at home. It makes no sense.

It makes even less sense if we consider that the Ḥijāzīs themselves imported clothing from Syria and Egypt. A Byzantine merchant is said to have sold an extremely expensive cloak in Mecca.[69] Ṣaffūriyya cloaks from Galilee were worn in Medina.[70] Ṭalḥa had Syrian cloth in the caravan with which he returned from Syria.[71] No fewer than seven caravans carrying clothes and other things are supposed to have come from Buṣrā and Adhriʿāt to the Jews of Medina in one day, and the Jews also appear as cloth merchants elsewhere.[72] Syrian and Coptic linen is mentioned in both poetry and prose, since Syria and Egypt were where the

[67] Jones, "Asian Trade," p. 6; *id.*, "Economic Life," p. 166. Note also that the treaty between the Prophet and the Jews of Maqnā required the latter to pay a quarter of what their women span (Balādhurī, *Futūḥ*, p. 60).

[68] Foreign Office, *Arabia*, p. 75.

[69] *Aghānī*, XVIII, 123. The beauty of *thiyāb al-Rūm* was proverbial in later times (Thaʿālibī, *Thimār*, p. 535).

[70] Ibn Ḥanbal, *Musnad*, IV, 75. Lammens had it that ʿUqba b. Abī Muʿayṭ had spent ten years in Ṣaffūriyya, but this is not correct. The story to which he refers has it that Umayya (not ʿUqba) spent ten years somewhere in Syria (in Jordan, according to Abū'l-Baqā', *Manāqib*, fol. 12a), where he adopted the child which his slave-girl had by a Jew from Ṣaffūriyya; this Jew was thus the real grandfather of ʿUqba (Lammens, *Mecque*, p. 119; Ibn Qutayba, *Maʿārif*, p. 139; Bakrī, *Muʿjam*, p. 609, *s.v.* Ṣaffūriyya, both from Ibn al-Kalbī; cf. also Ibn Ḥabīb, *Munammaq*, pp. 106 f.).

[71] Ibn Saʿd, *Ṭabaqāt*, III, 215.

[72] See the references given above, n37. I. Goldziher, ed., "Der Dîwân des Garwal b. Aus al-Ḥuṭeʾa," p. 185 (*ad* II, 3). Abū Bakr's Fadak cloak had presumably also been made or sold by Jews (Ibn Hishām, *Leben*, p. 985); and no fewer than 1,500 garments and 20 bales of Yemeni cloth were found at Khaybar on its conquest by Muḥammad (Wāqidī, *Maghāzī*, II, 664).

Meccans equipped themselves with cloth, as Lammens noted.[73] As has been seen, they also equipped themselves in the Yemen.[74] Clothing from Ṣuhār and Oman in general is likewise supposed to have been available in the Ḥijāz, and even trousers from Hajar are said to have been sold in the Ḥijāz.[75] One might, then, conclude that the Meccans are once more presented as having imported and exported the same commodity, but this is not quite correct. The clothing that they imported from the Mediterranean and elsewhere was made of linen, cotton, and other fine cloth, whereas that which they exported was woollen and coarse. In other words, the Meccans are presented as having risen to wealth by selling cheap clothes transported at a huge distance in exchange for expensive ones transported at a similar distance in return. If this is true, it is extraordinary. One can, of course, make a profit by selling large quantities of coarse clothing and buying small quantities of fine clothing that is subsequently sold at exorbitant prices in regions in which it is not normally available. But one cannot do so unless there are customers who find the coarse clothing sufficiently cheap to buy it. How could clothing originating in the Ḥijāz compete with that produced in southern Syria itself? There seems to be no simple answer to this question.

6. Animals

Most versions of Ibn al-Kalbī's *īlāf*-tradition mention only leather goods and clothing among the goods sold by the Meccans, but there are some exceptions. Qummī, as has been seen, enumerates leather, clothing, and overseas products such as pepper.[76] Jāḥiẓ and Thaʿālibī, on the other hand, omit both leather and clothing, but add that Quraysh would drive camels to Syria on behalf of the tribes through whose territory they passed.[77] There is nothing implausible about this claim, camels going well enough with leather and woollens, but it is probably mere elaboration, on a par with the pepper. Most accounts of Qurashī activities at

[73] Jacob, *Beduinenleben*, p. 149; Ṭirimmāḥ, IV, 28; Balādhurī, *Ansāb*, I, 100; *id.*, *Futūḥ*, p. 47. Lammens, *Mecque*, p. 300.

[74] Above, ch. 3 n177.

[75] Cf. Balādhurī, *Ansāb*, I, 507 f., on the Prophet's clothes; Ibn Saʿd, *Ṭabaqāt*, I, 327; Lammens, *Mecque*, p. 299n; *id.*, *Fāṭima et les filles de Mahomet*, p. 70. Ibn Ḥanbal, *Musnad*, IV, 352.

[76] Above, ch. 3, n159.

[77] ʿAmr b. Baḥr al-Jāḥiẓ, *Rasāʾil*, p. 70; Thaʿālibī, *Thimār*, p. 116.

markets in Syria certainly envisage them as selling inanimate goods (*baḍāʾiʿ*, *silaʿ*) rather than animals; and the only transaction in which we see a Byzantine merchant being paid in camels was conducted in Mecca rather than in Buṣrā.[78] A satirical poem does, however, taunt the Meccans with selling donkeys to the tribes of Daws and Murād.[79]

7. *Miscellaneous Foodstuffs*

As has been seen, ʿUthmān b. al-Ḥuwayrith thought of sending clarified butter to the Byzantines, whereas ʿAbd al-Raḥmān b. ʿAwf seems to have sold clarified butter and cottage cheese in Syria.[80] Yet the Syrian desert must have been better provided with such things than the barren environment of Mecca, and ʿAbdallāh b. Judʿān is reputed once to have sent two thousand camels to Syria for clarified butter, honey, and wheat with which he fed the Meccans and kept up his renown for generosity.[81] Once again we see the Meccans engaged in the peculiar activity of exporting coal to Newcastle while at the same time importing it from there. ʿUthmān is also said to have dealt in foodstuffs of unspecified kinds;[82] and one version of the list of the professions of the *ashrāf* has Abū Sufyān deal in oil along with leather. But oil (*zayt*) is presumably a mistake for raisins (*zabīb*, as in the parallel version), and the oil would, at all events, be an import from Syria;[83] whether ʿUthmān imported or exported his foodstuffs is not said.

8. *Raisins*

Lammens noted with surprise that the Meccans exported raisins from Ṭāʾif to Babylonia and even Syria, a land of vineyards.[84] It would indeed be surprising if they did, but the tradition does not claim as much. It is true that the caravan which Muḥammad's men intercepted at Nakhla was loaded with, among other things, raisins;[85] but this caravan was on its way from Ṭāʾif to Mecca, not to Syria. Abū Sufyān traded in

78 See the reference given above, n69.

79 Ibn Hishām, *Leben*, p. 707.

80 See the references given above, nn44, 49.

81 Ibn Kathīr, *Bidāya*, II, 218.

82 Shaybānī, *Kasb*, p. 41.

83 Ibn Qutayba, *Maʿārif*, p. 250; cf. Ibn Rusta, *Aʿlāq*, p. 215.

84 Lammens, *Mecque*, p. 289; *id.*, "République marchande," p. 46 (with reference to his *Ṭāif*); *id.*, *Ṭāif*, p. 148 (without references). The claim that raisins are often mentioned among the goods carried by Qurashī caravans is somewhat exaggerated.

85 See the reference given above, n50.

raisins, but we never see him send them any further afield than ʿUkāẓ.[86] Insofar as there was any exchange of raisins between Syria and the Ḥijāz, it was no doubt Syria that was the exporter.[87]

9. *Wine*

According to Wāqidī, the caravan that was intercepted at Nakhla was loaded with not only leather and raisins, but also wine, clearly from Ṭā'if; and ʿUqba b. Abī Muʿayṭ is supposed to have been a wine dealer.[88] Wāqidī's wine is an accretion on a par with the gold that he adds to the silver at Qarada and the silver that he adds to the booty at Ḥunayn, presumably inspired by the fact that leather, raisins, and wine were the three most famous products of Ṭā'if.[89] That Ṭā'ifī wine was drunk in Mecca is plausible enough, even if there was none in this caravan, and ʿUqba may also have traded in wine, for all we know. But Arabia did not export wine, and the Meccans do not seem to have played much of a role in the distribution of wine in the peninsula itself. Wine came primarily, though not exclusively, from Syria, as is clear from pre-Islamic poetry;[90] Syria was a "land of wine" in Arab eyes.[91] It was also from here that wine dealers tended to come, at least as far as northwest Arabia is concerned, many of them Jews, the rest presumably Christians.[92] It is Syrians, both Arab and non-Arab, who are credited with the sale of wine in Medina before the prohibition of alcohol.[93]

[86] Ibn Rusta, *Aʿlāq*, p. 215; cf. *Aghānī*, XIV, 223, where the fact that he married a daughter of a Thaqafī is explained with reference to his interest in raisins. Ibn Hishām, *Leben*, p. 590.

[87] Diḥya b. Khalīfa, for example, presented the Prophet with raisins, dates, and figs from Syria (Ibn Ḥabīb, *Munammaq*, p. 28). But elsewhere *zabīb* imported from Syria is a mistake for *zayt* (cf. for example Bukhārī, *Recueil*, II, 45 f.).

[88] Cf. above, n50. Ibn Rusta, *Aʿlāq*, p. 215; Ibn Qutayba, *Maʿārif*, pp. 249 f.

[89] Cf. Ibn Ḥabīb, *Munammaq*, p. 73, where Abraha is regaled with these three products on his arrival there.

[90] Cf. Jacob, *Beduinenleben*, pp. 96 ff.; Fraenkel, *Fremdwörter*, p. 157.

[91] Ibn Hishām, *Leben*, p. 136; Wāqidī, *Maghāzī*, II, 716. Compare also the oracular utterance cited in *Aghānī*, XXII, 110; Azraqī, *Makka*, pp. 54 f.

[92] Numerous attestations are given by Goldziher, "Ḥuṭej'a," p. 185 (*ad* II, 3); cf. also Lyall, *Mufaḍḍalīyāt*, LV, 10 and Lyall's note thereto (Jewish wine merchants from Golan). The wine merchants from Adhriʿāt and Wādī Jadar mentioned by Abū Dhu'ayb al-Hudhalī were Christian (J. Hell, ed. and tr., *Neue Huḏailiten-Diwane*, vol. I, IX, 11).

[93] Ibn al-Athīr, *Usd*, IV, 258; Ibn Ḥajar, *Iṣāba*, III, 67 f., no. 3,097, *s.v.* Sirāj al-Tamīmī; cf. also Ibn Ḥanbal, *Musnad*, II, 132, ult.

10. Slaves

ʿAbdallah b. Judʿān is said to have been a slave trader; he kept slave girls whom he would prostitute and whose offspring he would sell.[94] Though practices of this kind are attested elsewhere in Arabia, the information is of dubious value;[95] and at all events, the slave girls in question should probably be envisaged as Ethiopians and other foreigners rather than as Arab girls, taking us back to a question that has already been discussed.[96] But it is well known that the pre-Islamic Arabs were in the habit of enslaving each other in the course of intertribal raids and warfare, and one prisoner of war was sold by Hudhalīs in Mecca.[97] Even so, the possibility that the Meccans exported Arab slaves to Byzantium and elsewhere can be discounted. It is true that where tribesmen are in the habit of enslaving each other, slave traders are apt to arrive from outside; and if the Greeks and the Persians had gone to Arabia for their slaves, Quraysh might well have made a fortune on this trade. But, in fact, the slave traders of the ancient world left Arabia alone. The desert was too inhospitable and its inhabitants too mobile for organized slave raids on the part of the outsiders, and the Arabs themselves would seem to have had too strong a sense of ethnic unity to offer their captives for sale to outsiders after the fashion of Africans and Turks. There is considerable evidence in both the classical and the Islamic traditions for Greeks, Syrians, Persians, and others enslaved by the Arabs,[98] but scarcely any for Arab slaves abroad, and none whatsoever for Quarashī exports of this commodity.[99] In the absence of a foreign market, the

[94] Ibn Qutayba, *Maʿārif*, p. 250; Ibn Rusta, *Aʿlāq*, p. 215; Masʿūdī, *Murūj*, IV, 153 f.

[95] Prostitution of slave girls was practised at Dūmat al-Jandal (Ibn Ḥabīb, *Muḥabbar*, p. 264). It is also attested for Aden (Ibn al-Mujāwir, *Descriptio*, I, 7, according to whom it was the women of Mecca who had practised the same in the past). The practise was unknown to ʿAbdallāh's biographer in the *Aghānī*, VIII, 327 ff., as well as to Ibn Ḥabīb, *Munammaq*, pp. 171 ff., and Ibn Kathīr, *Bidāya*, II, 217 f.

[96] Cf. above, ch. 3, no. 22.

[97] J.G.L. Kosegarten, ed., *Carmina Hudsailitarum*, p. 116 (*ad* LVIII); cf. *Aghānī*, IV, 226.

[98] Cf. *Periplus*, § 20 (if you shipwreck, they enslave you); J. B. Segal, "Arabs in Syriac Literature before the Rise of Islam," pp. 102 f. (Malkā, a monk from Nisibis, enslaved); H. Lammens, *L'Arabie occidentale avant l'hégire*, p. 19 (Greek, Coptic, and other slaves of Byzantine origin); Ibn Hishām, *Leben*, pp. 139 f.; Ibn Saʿd, *Ṭabaqāt*, III, 85; Balādhurī, *Ansāb*, II, 47 (Persian slaves).

[99] An Arab slave was manumitted at Naupactos in the second century B.C. (R. Dareste,

trade in Arab slaves had no major centres. The creation and distribution of such slaves took place all over the peninsula, and there is no evidence that Mecca played a greater role in this process than any other market.[100]

11. Other

According to the list of the professions of the *ashrāf*, Saʿd b. Abī Waqqāṣ used to sharpen arrows.[101] So he may have done, but it is arrows from Yathrib, not from Mecca, that are proverbial in poetry.[102] Another Meccan is said to have manufactured and sold idols. Presumably he was not the only Meccan to have done so, given that every house in Mecca is supposed to have been equipped with one, and that even the bedouin would buy them.[103] But it is hard to imagine that the Meccans owed their wealth to the idol trade. There is not even any record of idols being sold to pilgrims.

We may now summarize. The Meccans exported one Yemeni commodity, perfume, and several Ḥijāzī ones: leather, clothing, possibly also camels and/or donkeys, and some clarified butter and cheese on occasion. None of the goods in question were rare in Syria, the Byzantine empire having a perfume industry, a textile industry, and a Syrian desert well provided with camels, sheep, and their various products; and the Meccans are frequently described as having returned with products identical with or similar to the ones they had sold. With the exception of Yemeni perfume, the goods in question do not seem to have been of superior quality. Most of them were bulky. Almost all were cheap. It is

---

B. Haussoullier, and T. Reinach, *Recueil des inscriptions juridiques greques*, II, 286). Ṣuhayb al-Rūmī, allegedly an Arab, was a slave in Byzantium on the eve of the rise of Islam (Ibn Saʿd, *Ṭabaqāt*, III, 226). The nearest we get to Qurashi export is the Prophet's sale of Jewish captives in Syria (below, ch. 7 n5).

[100] Had the Hudhalī prisoner of war not happened to have been captured near Mecca, he might have been sold at ʿUkāẓ (cf. below, ch. 7 n45). It was Kalbīs who sold Ṣuhayb al-Rūmī to a Meccan, not the other way round (Ibn Saʿd, *Ṭabaqāt*, III, 226). It was also Kalbīs who sold Salmān al-Fārisī to a Jew from Wādī'l-Qurā, who passed him on to a Jew from Yathrib (Ibn Hishām, *Leben*, pp. 139 f.).

[101] Ibn Rusta, *Aʿlaq*, p. 215; Ibn Qutayba, *Maʿārif*, p. 249. Other Qurashī *ashrāf* used to be butchers, smiths, and so forth, we are told, and all the information is clearly worthless.

[102] See for example Ṭirimmāḥ, XLVIII, 32; Ṭufayl, I, 57; ʿAmr b. Qamī'a, *Poems*, XIII, 27; A. A. Bevan, ed., *The Nakā'iḍ of Jarīr and al-Farazdak*, CV, 57.

[103] Wāqidī, II, 870 f.; partly reproduced in Azraqī, *Makka*, p. 78.

possible, indeed likely, that most of the information on which this conclusion is based is fictitious; but silver, gold, and pepper notwithstanding, the tradition is surprisingly agreed on the *kind* of goods that the Meccans traded. Naturally, even this fundamental point could be wrong. If so, there is nothing to be said on the subject of Meccan trade, and in the last resort this may well turn out to be the only sensible conclusion. But if the general picture drawn by the tradition is accepted, there is no doubt that the one to which we are accustomed should be drastically revised. In what follows I shall try to do precisely that.

5

WHERE WERE THE MECCANS ACTIVE?

We may start by considering the evidence for where the Meccans operated. The secondary literature generally informs us that they operated in Syria, the Yemen, Ethiopia, and Iraq, linking all four regions in a single commercial network. This claim rests on Ibn al-Kalbī's *īlāf*-tradition, which goes as follows.[1]

Meccan trade used to be purely local. Non-Arab traders would bring their goods to Mecca, and the Meccans would buy them for resale partly among themselves and partly among their neighbours.[2] This was how things remained until Hāshim, Muḥammad's great-grandfather, went to Syria, where he attracted the attention of the Byzantine emperor by cooking *tharīd*, a dish unknown to the non-Arabs. Having become friendly with the emperor, he persuaded the latter to grant Quraysh permission to sell Ḥijāzī leather and clothing in Syria on the ground that this would be cheaper for the Syrians. Next he returned to Mecca, concluding agreements with the tribes on the way. These agreements were known as *ilāf*s, and granted Quraysh safe passage through the territories of the tribes in question. In return, Quraysh undertook to act as commercial agents on behalf of these tribes, collecting their goods on the way to Syria and handing over what they had fetched on the way back.[3] Hāshim accompanied the first Meccan caravan to Syria, seeing to the fulfilment of the agreements and settling Quraysh in the towns and/or

[1] For the most important versions, see above. ch. 4, n43 (Yaʿqūbī's version being more of a loose paraphrase than the other two). There is another reasonably faithful version in Sulaymān b. Sālim al-Kalāʿī, *Kitāb al-iktifāʾ*, pp. 207 ff. (though it omits mention of the Meccan goods). The tradition is discussed by Ḥamīdallāh, "Rapports"; Simon, "Ḥums et īlāf"; and Kister, "Mecca and Tamīm."

[2] This point is also made in the paraphrase given by Thaʿālibī, *Thimār*, p. 115.

[3] Qālī's version has *taḥmila ilayhim* for *taḥmila lahum*. The tribesmen in question would receive both their *ra's mal* and their *ribḥ*, that is, what they had invested and what they had gained, the reward of Quraysh consisting exclusively in safe passage, it would seem. Versions such as Thaʿālibī's, however, make it clear that they took their cut of the *ribḥ*, too (*Thimār*, p. 116).

villages (*qurā*) of Syria; it was on this journey that he died in Gaza. His three brothers concluded similar treaties with the rulers of Persia, the Yemen, and Ethiopia, enabling Quraysh to trade in safety, and similar agreements with the tribes on the way, enabling them to travel to the countries in question without fear. All died in places implicitly presented as relevant to their trade. It was thanks to the activities of Hāshim and his brothers that the Meccans got rich.

This is an impressive account, and it is not surprising that modern scholars are inclined to accept it more or less at face value. But there is a snag. A number of traditionists, including Ibn al-Kalbī's own father, offer an account to precisely the opposite effect.

Meccan trade used to be international. The Meccans would go to Syria every summer and winter,[4] or to Syria in one season and to the Yemen in another.[5] (There is no reference to Meccan trade in Ethiopia or Iraq in this version.) They had to do so because other traders did not come to them.[6] But the effort was too much for them,[7] or it left them no time to pay attention to God.[8] So God told them to stay at home and worship Him, and they obeyed.[9] In order to make it possible for them to stay at home, God made Arabs from other parts of the peninsula bring foodstuffs to Mecca,[10] or alternatively it was Ethiopians whom He

[4] Jalāl al-dīn al-Suyūṭī, *Kitāb al-durr al-manthūr fī'l-tafsīr bi'l-ma'thūr*, VI, 397, citing ʿIkrima (Rūm and Shām, presumably meaning Syria in various guises rather than Anatolia and Syria).

[5] Ibn Ḥabīb, *Munammaq*, p. 262, citing Kalbī; Muqātil b. Sulaymān, *Tafsīr*, MS Saray, Ahmet III, 74/II, fol. 253a (I am indebted to Dr. U. Rubin for a copy of the relevant folio of the manuscript); Muḥammad b. Jarīr al-Ṭabarī, *Jāmiʿ al-bayān fī tafsīr al-qur'ān*, XXX, 199, citing ʿIkrima. The view that Quraysh traded in Syria in one season and the Yemen in another is not, of course, confined to these traditions.

[6] Muqātil, *Tafsīr*, fol. 253a.

[7] Kalbī in Ibn Ḥabīb, *Munammaq*, p. 262 (*ishtadda ʿalayhim al-jahd*); Muqātil, *Tafsīr*, fol. 253a; cited in Fakhr al-Dīn al-Rāzī, *Mafātīḥ al-ghayb*, VIII, 512 (*shaqqa ʿalayhim al-ikhtilāf lahum wa'l-iʿāda/al-dhahāb ilā'l-Yaman wa'l-Shām*).

[8] This rather than the sheer physical inconvenience is the point stressed in Ṭabarī, *Jāmiʿ*, XXX, 198 f.

[9] *Ibid.*, citing Ibn ʿAbbās (their journeys left them no *rāḥa*, so God prohibited them and told them to worship the lord of this house), ʿIkrima (God told them to stay in Mecca), and Ibn ʿAbbās again (God told them to cling to the worship of Him as they clung to the winter and summer journeys; He told them to stay in Mecca and worship Him instead of journeying to Ṭā'if); similarly Suyūṭī, *Durr*, VI, 397 f., citing ʿIkrima and Ibn ʿAbbās.

[10] Kalbī in Ibn Ḥabīb, *Munammaq*, p. 262, where the provisions come from Tabāla, Jur-

made do this.[11] At all events, the Meccans no longer left their sanctuary, or they only did so occasionally.[12] Meccan trade thus became purely local.

According to one exegete, it was on the rise of Islam that the international trade of the Meccans came to an end: when the Arabs began to come on pilgrimage to Mecca, and in delegations to the Prophet in Medina, the Meccans no longer needed to go to Syria for their provisions, we are told.[13] But the majority of exegetes implicitly describe this trade as having come to an end at some unidentified stage in the pre-Islamic past; and given that the sura in explanation of which we are told of this development is said to have been revealed in Mecca, this is the view that one will have to accept if one adopts the traditional approach to the sources. It follows that when Muḥammad began to receive revelations in Mecca, there no longer was such a thing as Meccan trade in the sense usually understood.

We thus have a situation analogous with that encountered in connection with silver: silver was what the Meccans exported, or maybe it was one of the things they imported; Meccan trade became international some time before the rise of Islam, or maybe it was then that it became local. The tradition asserts both A and not A, and it does so with such regularity that one could, were one so inclined, rewrite most of Montgomery Watt's biography of Muḥammad in the reverse.

How then do we resolve the problem at hand? Ultimately it is irresoluble. The rival stories are both of exegetical origin, both being told in explanation of *Sūrat Quraysh*, in which the enigmatic word *īlāf* occurs.[14] The common theme is Mecca's food supplies, but the theme is developed in diametrically opposed ways: Quraysh took over these supplies from others, or else they handed them over to others. It must have been well known whether Quraysh traded outside Mecca on the eve of Islam

ash, and coastal Yemen, being sent by sea to Jedda and by land to Muḥaṣṣab (between Mecca and Minā, cf. Yāqūt, *Buldān*, IV, 426, *s.v.*). None of the traditions cited by Ṭabarī have details of this kind.

[11] Muqātil, *Tafsīr*, fol. 253a, where the provisions likewise arrive at Jedda; Rāzī, *Mafātīḥ*, VIII, 512. One version of this tradition is also cited by Ḥamīdallāh, "Rapports," p. 302.

[12] According to Ibn ʿAbbās in Ṭabarī, *Jāmiʿ*, XXX, 198, ult., they would go on journeys or stay home as they pleased.

[13] Qummī, *Tafsīr*, II, 444.

[14] Cf. below, ch. 9.

or not; yet the exegetes were happy to assert both that they did and that they did not. As in the case of silver, the embellishments on the common theme would appear to have been made without concern for what was actually remembered.

Stories made up without concern for what was actually remembered cannot be used for a reconstruction of the past with which they purport to deal: those on the beginning and end of Meccan trade should both be rejected. Outright rejection of famous claims made in the Islamic tradition is, however, regarded as unacceptably radical by most Islamicists. Let us assume then that there is some historical recollection behind these stories after all, or rather behind one of them: inasmuch as it cannot be the case that the Meccans both did and did not trade outside Mecca on the eve of Islam, one of the two stories must be fundamentally wrong. Which one remembers right?

It is a basic principle of historical research that early information should be preferred to later claims. Kalbī and Muqātil are both earlier than Ibn al-Kalbī. If Kalbī remembered Meccan trade to have come to an end before the rise of Islam and his son remembered the opposite, the recollection of the father must be preferred to that of the son. This conclusion is reinforced by the fact that Ibn al-Kalbī's account is wrong in several respects. Most obviously, it is too schematic: four brothers initiate trading relations with four different regions, negotiating with four different rulers and making agreements with four different sets of tribes on the way. But it is also wrong in its assumption that the Byzantine emperor resided in Syria. Moreover, Quraysh are unlikely ever to have negotiated with emperors, as opposed to with Ghassānid and Lakhmid kings (who are, in fact, mentioned in some versions).[15] Further, the agreements concluded between Quraysh and other tribes cannot have been known as *īlāf*s.[16] And there cannot have been separate agreements with the tribes on the way to Ethiopia, be they known as *īlāf*s or otherwise: either the Meccans went to Ethiopia via the Yemen, in which case agreements existed already, or else they sailed there directly, in which case there were no tribes on the way. Clearly, Ibn al-Kalbī's story is not

[15] Thus Balādhurī, *Ansāb*, I, 59 (*mulūk al-Shām, mulūk al-ʿIrāq*); Ṭabarī, *Taʾrīkh*, ser. I, p. 1,089 (*mulūk al-Shām al-Rūm [sic] wa-Ghassān*, but Akāsira on the Iraqi side); *Nihāyat al-irab* cited by Kister, "Some Reports," pp. 61 f. (Jabala b. Ayham in Syria, but the Persian emperor in Iraq).

[16] Cf. below, ch. 9.

a factual account. It might be argued that at least it is more plausible than that supplied by his father: if the Meccans stopped trading in pre-Islamic times, how did they make a living? They must have found it hard to pay their bills by assiduous worship alone. But plausibility is no guarantee of truth, and Kalbī's story is, at any rate, quite plausible too: if the Meccans were guardians of a pre-Islamic temple, they could well have made a living by assiduous dispensation of religious services alone; how many other pre-Islamic guardians had to supplement their income by engaging in trade?

More seriously, the story offered by Kalbī and Muqātil is at odds with the tradition at large, and indeed with information elsewhere offered by Kalbī and Muqātil themselves.[17] But on the one hand, the idea that Quraysh were passive recipients of goods brought by others is quite common in the exegetical tradition. It is attested in both of the rival stories on Meccan trade: non-Arab traders used to bring goods to Mecca, as Ibn al-Kalbī says; non-Arab traders, or other Arabs, took over the task of provisioning Mecca, as Kalbī and Muqātil say. And it recurs in the comments on *Sūrat al-tawba*: unbelievers used to bring goods to Mecca; when God prohibited unbelievers from approaching the Holy Mosque, the task of provisioning Mecca was taken over by believing Arabs, or by unbelievers in the form of *jizya*.[18] The commentators here take it for granted that Mecca had always been provisioned by outsiders, continuing to be thus provisioned on the rise of Islam. On the other hand, the tradition at large could well be wrong. If eminent early authorities such as Kalbī, Muqātil, and indeed Ibn ʿAbbās hold that the Meccans stopped trading outside Mecca some time before the rise of Islam, should we not take it that their claim preserves a genuine recollection swamped by later accretions? The Qurashī trading caravans with which the tradition at large is so familiar could be dismissed as mere embellishment on an idea which, once it had entered the tradition, was bound to

[17] Thus Kalbī and Muqātil both know of a *mawlā* of Quraysh who traded in Syria or Ethiopia on the eve of Islam (cf. the references given below, n98), and of a Qurashī who traded in Persia at the same time (below, n126).

[18] By believers: Muqātil in Kister, "Some Reports," p. 79; ʿAbdallāh b. ʿUmar al-Bayḍāwī, *Anwār al-tanzīl wa-asrār al-taʾwīl*, I, 496 (*ad* 9:28). By unbelievers: Ṭabarī, *Jāmiʿ*, x, 66 f.; Suyūṭī, *Durr*, III, 227; Ibn Kathīr, *Tafsīr*, II, 346 f. (*ad* 9:28). Bayḍāwī had this solution, too: first God let the people of Tabāla and Jurash convert and bring provisions (cf. above, n10), and next He brought about the conquests.

generate elaborate stories: that such stories were made up is precisely what Ibn al-Kalbī's *īlāf*-tradition demonstrates. Ibn al-Kalbī's *īlāf*-tradition is late and wrong, and this is the crucial point: if we insist that there is historical recollection behind the stories on the beginning and end of Meccan trade, it is Kalbī's and Muqātil's account that we must accept. In short, a source-critical approach of the conventional kind leads us to the conclusion that the Meccans did not trade outside Mecca on the eve of Islam.

But this is obviously a source-critical charade. The stories on the beginning and end of Meccan trade are legends told in explanation of the Qur'ān, not of the past. The fact that Kalbī offered one story and his son another to the opposite effect does not mean that Kalbī offered recollection and his son invention, but on the contrary that neither was concerned with recollection at all: what they offered were simply stories that happened to be mirror-images of the same legendary theme. Whether the Meccans traded outside Mecca on the eve of Islam or not is a question that cannot be answered on the basis of these stories. Indeed, the very theme of trade could be legendary. This is the situation in which one turns to the early non-Muslim sources for help, but on this particular question they offer none: Pseudo-Sebeos and Jacob of Edessa do indeed tell us that Muḥammad was a trader, but not that Quraysh were traders too, or even that Muḥammad was one of them.[19] If one accepts that the Meccans traded outside Mecca on the eve of Islam, one does it on the basis of the Islamic tradition at large, and this is what I shall do, one of my concerns in this book being the extent to which the standard account of Meccan trade is defensible in terms of *any* evidence in this tradition. But in source-critical terms this is not a strong position, and the reader should take note of the methodological arbitrariness involved in this, as in any other, attempt to reconstruct the rise of Islam on the basis of the Islamic tradition: the very existence of the phenomenon to which this book is devoted could be questioned with reference to impeccable Muslim authorities.

Proceeding now on the assumption that the tradition at large is right, where do we find Quraysh in action? Since our present concern is the

[19] Sebeos, *Histoire*, p. 95; I. Guidi and others, eds. and trs., *Chronica Minora*, p. 326 = 250.

Qurashī export trade, I shall only deal with their presence in foreign countries (including the Yemen) in this chapter, reserving the question of where they traded in Arabia itself for Chapter 7.

SYRIA

There is complete agreement in the tradition that the Meccans traded (or used to trade) in Syria. This is, in fact, the only point on which agreement is total, and the commercial activities of Quraysh in Syria are far better attested than those elsewhere: it is typical that Ibn al-Kalbī's *īlāf*-tradition has concrete details only in connection with Syria, the parallel arrangements in the Yemen, Ethiopia, and Iraq being disposed of by duplication. All the exegetes who understand the two journeys mentioned in *Sūrat Quraysh* as trading journeys specify Syria as one of the destinations, and Syria is sometimes presented as the only land with which Quraysh had commercial relations.[20] Numerous individual Qurashīs are presented as having traded there. The list includes Umayyads such as Abū Sufyān,[21] Ṣafwān b. Umayya,[22] ʿUthmān,[23] Saʿīd b. al-ʿĀṣ,[24] and

[20] Thus, as mentioned already, Suyūṭī cites ʿIkrima for the view that Quraysh used to go to Rūm and Shām in winter and summer (*Durr*, VI, 397); and ʿIkrima is also invoked there for the view that they used to go to Syria in both winter and summer, travelling by different routes according to the season (*ibid.*, p. 398). Ibn Hishām takes it for granted that the two Qur'ānic journeys went to Syria, not Syria and somewhere else (*Leben*, p. 37). And Qummī, who identifies the two journeys as going to Syria and the Yemen, forgets the Yemen in his statement that Quraysh "no longer needed to travel to Syria" (*Tafsīr*, II, 444).

[21] See for example Ibn Hishām, *Leben*, p. 427; Wāqidī, *Maghāzī*, I, p. 28, where he is a member of the caravan that triggered the battle of Badr on its return from Syria; above, ch. 4, no. 1, where he tries to lead a caravan to Syria via Qarada; below, n52, where he visits Syria together with Umayya b. Abī'l-Ṣalt; and Ṭabarī, *Ta'rīkh*, ser. I, p. 1,561; *Aghānī*, VI, 345 (both citing Ibn Isḥāq), where he goes to Gaza during the armistice between Mecca and Medina.

[22] For his participation in the caravans raided at Qarada and ʿĪṣ, see above, ch. 4, no. 1. According to Wāqidī, *Maghāzī*, I, 197, Ṣafwān was of the view that Quraysh had only settled in Mecca in order to do trade with Syria and Ethiopia. But according to Fākihī, cited by Kister, "Some Reports," p. 77, Ṣafwān traded exclusively with Egypt.

[23] Thus Abū Nuʿaym Aḥmad b. ʿAbdallāh al-Iṣbahānī, *Dalā'il al-nubuwwa*, p. 70, citing Wāqidī, where he joins a caravan (*ʿīr*, misprinted as *ghayr*) to Syria and hears predictions of the Prophet.

[24] He was one of the Qurashī traders rounded up by ʿUthmān b. al-Ḥuwayrith in Syria (Ibn Ḥabīb, *Munammaq*, p. 180; Abu'l-Baqā', *Manāqib*, fol. 11a; Abū Dhi'b Hishām b. Shuʿba [Rabīʿa in Ibn Ḥabīb] al-ʿĀmirī is also said to have been taken).

the latter's sons, Abān,[25] Khālid, and ʿAmr;[26] Hashimites such as ʿAbd al-Muṭṭalib,[27] Ḥārith b. ʿAbd al-Muṭṭalib,[28] Abū Ṭālib[29] and the Prophet himself,[30] though Hāshimites other than the Prophet himself are more commonly associated with the Yemen;[31] famous members of other clans such as ʿAbdallāh b. Judʿan,[32] Abūl-ʿĀṣ b. al-Rabīʿ,[33] Talḥa,[34] Abū Bakr and his son,[35] ʿAmr b. al-ʿĀṣ,[36] as well as the sons of Abū Zamʿa and Abū Jahl (and/or Abū Lahab).[37] We also hear of non-

[25] Ibn Ḥajar, *Iṣāba*, I, 10, no. 2, *s.v.*; cf. *ibid.*, p. 181, no. 779, *s.v.* Bakkā'. This is yet another story of a trader hearing predictions of the Prophet in Syria.

[26] They were partners and would take turns going to Syria (Ibn Ḥabīb, *Munammaq*, p. 359).

[27] Cf. Ibn Saʿd, *Ṭabaqāt*, I, 120, where it is he or Abū Ṭālib who takes Muḥammad to Syria as a child.

[28] Ibn Ḥabīb, *Munammaq*, p. 441.

[29] Usually it is he who is said to have taken Muḥammad to Syria, cf. for example Ibn Saʿd, *Ṭabaqāt*, I, 153 ff. For further references, see below, ch. 9.

[30] Thus for example Ibn Saʿd, *Ṭabaqāt*, I, 129 f., 156. For a survey of the traditions on Muḥammad's visits to Syria, see below, ch. 9.

[31] Cf. below. If we discount the visits made by Hāshimites as guardians of Muḥammad, their association with Syria practically disappears.

[32] Ibn Ḥabīb, *Munammaq*, p. 171; cf. Ibn Kathīr, *Bidāya*, II, 217 f.

[33] He went to Syria carrying money partly owned by him and partly entrusted to him, being intercepted by the Muslims on the way back (cf. above, ch. 4 n13). He returned from Syria with a caravan carrying silver, being intercepted by the Muslims on the way at ʿĪṣ in year 6 (above, ch. 4, n13). He went to Syria with unspecified goods and was intercepted on his way back by Muslims operating on the coast during the armistice between Mecca and Medina, that is between years 6 and 8 (Mūsā b. ʿUqba in Ibn Ḥajar, *Iṣāba*, VIII, pp. 118 f., no. 684, *s.v.* Abū'l-ʿĀṣ b. al-Rabīʿ). According to Wāqidī, this episode was another battle at ʿĪṣ that had nothing to do with Abū'l-ʿĀṣ (above, ch. 4 n15). Wherever or whenever it happened, he was granted *jiwār* by Zaynab, his wife (and daughter of the Prophet), in illustration of the clause in the Constitution of Medina that *al-mu'minūn yad ʿalā man siwāhum, yujīru ʿalayhim adnāhum*.

[34] Ṭalḥa was in Syria at the time of the *hijra* (Ibn Hishām, *Leben*, p. 489; Balādhurī, *Ansāb*, I, 270), or he returned from there with a caravan at the time of the *hijra* of the Prophet (Ibn Saʿd, *Ṭabaqāt*, III, 215). A monk he met at Buṣrā knew that a prophet had appeared in Arabia (*ibid.*, Ibn Ḥajar, *Iṣāba*, III, 291, no. 4,259, *s.v.* Ṭalḥa b. ʿUbaydallāh).

[35] Abū Bakr was well know in Yathrib because he used to pass through it on his way to Syria (Ibn Saʿd, *Ṭabaqāt*, I, 233; cf. also Wāḥidī, *Asbāb*, p. 284). ʿAbd al-Raḥmān b. Abī Bakr also went to Syria *fī'l-tijāra* (*Aghānī*, XVII, 359; Ibn Ḥajar, *Iṣāba*, IV, 168, no. 5,143, *s.v.*).

[36] He was a member of the caravan that triggered the battle of Badr on its return from Syria (Ibn Hishām, *Leben*, p. 427; Wāqidī, *Maghāzī*, I, 28. Both mention Makhrama b. Nawfal as another participant).

[37] Zamʿa's *matjar* was Syria (Ibn Ḥabīb, *Munammaq*, p. 485). Abū Jahl's son was killed

Qurashīs going to Syria with Meccan caravans.[38] The Muhājirūn knew the way to Yathrib because their caravans used to pass it on their way to Syria.[39] The Prophet saw Meccan caravans between Mecca and Syria on his night journey to Jerusalem, and he himself continued to send merchandise there after the *hijra*.[40] Qurashī caravans going to and from Syria are well known from his attempts to intercept them. One such triggered the battle of Badr, and others were captured at Qarada and ʿĪṣ.[41] According to Wāqidī and the sources dependent on him, numerous other campaigns of the Prophet were also aimed at Qurashī caravans travelling between Mecca and Syria, with increasing success.[42] There was a Qurashī diaspora in Syria. Thus Hāshim is said to have settled Qurashīs in the *qurā* of Syria.[43] One Qurashī spent a whole year in Syria,[44] while another spent ten.[45] Yet another is said by way of insult

by a lion in the Ḥawrān, where he had gone for trade (Balādhurī, *Ansāb*, I, 131). Elsewhere it is a son of Abū Lahab (with or without Abū Lahab himself) who encounters a lion on a trading journey in Syria, though not always in the Ḥawrān (Abū Nuʿaym, *Dalā'il*, pp. 389 ff.; Māwardī, *Aʿlām*, p. 107; Ḥassān b. Thābit, *Dīwān*, I, 249 f.; II, 310, *ad* no. 249:1); but there were also some who made him trade at Ḥubāsha to the south of Mecca rather than in the Ḥawrān (*ibid.*, II, 310).

[38] Cf. Ibn Ḥabīb, *Munammaq*, pp. 173, 441, where a Tamīmī goes to Syria with Qurashīs, and Qurashīs who have gone to Syria with *ḥalīf*s become embroiled with Tamīmīs on the way.

[39] Balādhurī, *Ansāb*, I, 257.

[40] Ibn Hishām, *Leben*, pp. 267 and 975 f., where the merchandise is sent with Diḥya b. Khalīfa, who is plundered by Judhām, triggering Zayd b. Ḥāritha's expedition against the latter; cf. Wāqidī, *Maghāzī*, II, 564, where merchandise belonging to the Companions is sent with Zayd b. Ḥāritha, who is plundered by Fazāra, triggering the campaign against Umm Qirfa.

[41] Ibn Hishām, *Leben*, pp. 427 ff.; Wāqidī, *Maghāzī*, I, 19 ff. If we go by Wāqidī's account, there was not a single Meccan who did not have a trading interest in Syria, every Qurashī, indeed every Qurashī woman who owned anything at all, having contributed to this caravan (*ibid.*, p. 27). For Qarada and ʿĪṣ, see above, ch. 4, no. 1.

[42] Thus Ḥamza's expedition to the coast and the raids of Kharrār, Abwā', Buwāṭ, and ʿUshayra were all triggered by Qurashī caravans, according to Wāqidī, who here as so often knows more than Ibn Isḥāq (Wāqidī, *Maghāzī*, I, 9, 11 f.; cf. Ibn Hishām, *Leben*, pp. 419, 421 f.). No fighting took place and no caravans were captured in any of these raids, but later the Muslims captured practically every Qurashī caravan, as we are told in connection with another episode unknown to Ibn Isḥāq, the second raid at ʿĪṣ (Wāqidī, *Maghāzī*, II, 627). One such caravan coming from Syria was intercepted by nine recent ʿAbsī converts (Ibn Saʿd, *Ṭabaqāt*, I, 296, citing Wāqidī).

[43] See above, pp. 109 f.

[44] That is, Abān b. Saʿīd (Ibn Ḥajar, *Iṣāba*, I, 181, no. 779, *s.v.* Bakkā').

[45] That is Umayya, who is said to have left Mecca after losing a *munāfara* with Hāshim,

to have worked as a caravaneer in the Balqā'.[46] And there was no lack of Qurashīs for ʿUthmān b. al-Ḥuwayrith to round up in Syria at the time of his unsuccessful political ambitions.[47]

We are also given some information of how they went there[48] and where they went. One terminus was Gaza, visited by Hāshim and later by Abū Sufyān and other members of ʿAbd Manāf.[49] Another was Buṣrā (Bostra), the site of a famous fair at which Muḥammad himself is said to have traded once as Khadīja's agent.[50] The Meccans are also described as having visited Ayla and Adhriʿāt.[51] They do not seem to have frequented Jerusalem,[52] and the evidence for their presence in Damascus is somewhat feeble;[53] but they are sometimes said to have gone as far

thus starting the enmity between Umayyads and Hāshimites (Ibn Saʿd, *Ṭabaqāt*, I, 76; Ibn Ḥabīb, *Munammaq*, p. 106; Ibn Qutayba, *Maʿārif*, p. 139; Abū'l-Baqā', *Manāqib*, fol. 12a; cf. above, ch. 4, n70).

[46] Ḥassān b. Thabit, *Dīwān*, no. 206:2 (ed. Hirschfeld CCIX, 2).

[47] Ibn Ḥabīb, *Munammaq*, p. 180; Abū'l-Baqā', *Manāqib*, fol. 11a. The story in *Aghānī*, II, 243, would also testify to a Qurashī diaspora in Syria if "Sharāt" were not a mistake for "Sarāt" (cf. below, n92).

[48] Details about the routes followed are proffered by Wāqidī, *Maghāzī*, I, 28; II, 627; Bakrī, *Muʿjam*, pp. 416, 550, *s.vv.* Raḍwa, al-Maʿraqa; Suyūṭī, citing ʿIkrima via Ibn Abī Ḥātim (cf. above, n20); cf. also Lammens, *Mecque*, pp. 142 ff.

[49] Wāqidī, *Maghāzī*, I, 28, 200; cf. above, n21, for Abū Sufyān; above, p. 110, for Hāshim.

[50] On the fair, see Marzūqī, *Azmina*, II, 169 f.; on Muḥammad's visits, both as a child and as an agent of Khadīja, see the references given below, ch. 9. Ṭalḥa also visited Buṣrā, a traditional site for *dalā'il al-nubuwwa* stories (cf. above, n34). On the town itself, see *EI*[2], *s.v.* Boṣrā.

[51] They went by the coastal route via Ayla to Palestine in the winter and via Buṣrā and Adhriʿāt in the summer, according to ʿIkrima cited by Suyūṭī (above, n20); cf. also Wāqidī, *Maghazi*, I, 28.

[52] A late *dalā'il* story has it that Umayya b. Abī'l-Ṣalt al-Thaqafī went to "Gaza or Jerusalem," apparently accompanied by Abū Sufyān (Ibn Kathīr, *Bidāya*, II, 224). But Wāqidī would only admit Gaza (cf. below, n54), and the absence of Jerusalem from the traditions on Meccan trade is striking.

[53] In a variant version of the story referred to in the preceding note, Abū Sufyān and Umayya b. Abī'l-Ṣalt go on a trading journey to Syria, which takes them all the way to the Ghawṭa of Damascus, where they stay for two months (Ibn Kathīr, *Bidāya*, II, 220 ff., citing Ibn ʿAsākir; Ibn ʿAsākir, *Tahdhīb*, III, 115 ff.). It was in the Ḥawrān that a Qurashī trader encountered a lion according to some (above, n37), and it is implied that Abd al-Raḥmān b. Abī Bakr's trade took him to Damascus (*Aghānī*, XVII, 359 f.). Walīd b. al-Mughīra is said to have owed money to a bishop of Damascus by the name of Muqawqis (*sic*), but elsewhere he owes it to the bishop of Najrān (Ibn Ḥabīb, *Munammaq*, p. 226; Kis-

north as Jordan,[54] and Jacob of Edessa has Muḥammad trade in not only (Provincia) Arabia, Palestine, and Phoenicia, but also Tyre, a city that is not mentioned in Muslim accounts of Meccan trade at all.[55] On the whole, it is the desert towns and districts in the triangle formed by Gaza, Ayla, and Buṣrā that get the attention in the Islamic tradition, not the Hellenized cities of the coast and their hinterland.

Egypt

From Syria, Hāshim is supposed to have gone to Ankara on occasion;[56] but whatever lies behind this claim, it is not repeated in connection with the later Meccans.[57] There is, however, a fair amount of evidence linking them with Egypt. Thus ʿAmr b. al-ʿĀṣ is said to have sold perfume and leather there, as mentioned already.[58] Ṣafwān b. Umayya is supposed to have devoted himself exclusively to trade with this country.[59] Mughīra b. Shuʿba once went to Egypt for trade together with other Thaqafīs and Qurashīs.[60] One version of the Ḥudaybiyya treaty envisages the Meccans as passing through Medina on their way to Syria and

ter, "Some Reports," p. 73, citing Zubayr b. Bakkār); and elsewhere still it is a Thaqafī who owes money to him (Ibn Hishām, *Leben*, p. 273). A governor of Damascus is said once to have acted as judge in a dispute between two Arabs, but neither was a Qurashī (Balādhurī, *Ansāb*, I, 282). Watt's claim that the Meccans traded with Damascus and Gaza in the summer and the Yemen in the winter would seem to rest on his own exegesis of *Sūrat Quraysh* (cf. *EI²*, *s.v.* Ḳuraysh; compare also Watt, *Muhammad, Prophet and Statesman*, p. 1).

[54] They traded in Palestine and Jordan, according to Muqātil, *Tafsīr*, fol. 253a; and it was also in Jordan that Umayya spent his exile, according to Abū'l-Baqā' (above, ch. 4 n70). Wāqidī, on the other hand, is explicit that they, or at least the members of ʿAbd Manāf, did not go beyond Gaza (*Maghāzī*, I, 200).

[55] Guidi, *Chronica Minora*, p. 326 = 250.

[56] Ibn Saʿd, *Ṭabaqāt*, I, 75.

[57] They are sometimes said to have traded in Rūm (cf. the references given above, ch. 1 n10; above, n20; below, n72), and Lammens takes Rūm to mean Anatolia ("République marchande," p. 26, on the basis of the reference cited below, n72). But presumably it simply means the Byzantine empire in general. Conceivably, Hāshim's connections with Ankara arise from the fact that members of the Arab tribe of Iyād were believed to have settled there (*Aghānī*, XXII, 358).

[58] Kindī, *Governors*, pp. 6 f.

[59] Cf. above, n22.

[60] Aḥmad b. Yaḥyā al-Balādhurī, *Ansāb al-ashrāf*, fol. 1,211 l. 31 (I owe this reference to Dr. G. M. Hinds).

Egypt.[61] And Egypt replaces the Yemen in one version of the *īlāf*-tradition on Hāshim and his brothers.[62] Given that ʿAmr's visit to Alexandria is apocryphal, we have no information on where they went. One would expect them to have visited Sinai, a curiously familiar place in the Qurʾān,[63] as well as the eastern desert; but how much further they went is an open question.

The Yemen

The Yemen is generally described as the secondmost important *matjar*, place of trade, of the Meccans. Thus the two journeys mentioned in *Sūrat Quraysh* are commonly identified as journeys to Syria and the Yemen,[64] though the Yemen is sometimes omitted in favour of two journeys to Syria or one to Egypt or to Ethiopia.[65] Individual Qurashīs mentioned as having trading relations with the Yemen include Hāshimites such as ʿAbd al-Muṭṭalib (whose journeys are not, however, explicitly identified as trading journeys),[66] ʿAbbās b. ʿAbd al-Muṭṭalib[67] and Ibn ʿAbbās,[68] but above all Makhzūmīs: Abū Rabīʿa b. al-Mughīra,[69] Walīd

[61] Ṭabarī, *Jāmiʿ*, xxvi, 55 (*ad* 48:25).

[62] Suhaylī, *Rawḍ*, i, 48 (where the countries involved are Syria, Persia, Egypt, and Ethiopia); similarly Jāḥiẓ in Kister, "Mecca and Tamīm," p. 137 (Byzantium, Egypt, and Ethiopia).

[63] Cf. 23:20; 95:2 (the rest of the attestations refer to the Sinai of Moses).

[64] Cf. Muqātil, *Tafsīr*, fol. 253a; Ṭabarī, *Jāmiʿ*, xxx, 199; Qummī, *Tafsīr*, ii, p. 444; Ibn Ḥabīb, *Munammaq*, p. 262, citing Kalbī; ʿAbdallāh b. Muslim Ibn Qutayba, *Taʾwīl mushkil al-qurʾān*, p. 319; and numerous others.

[65] Cf. above, n20. For Egypt replacing the Yemen, see above, n62. For identification of the two *riḥlas* as journeys to Syria and Ethiopia, see Yaʿqūbī, *Taʾrīkh*, i, 280; ʿAbd al-Ḥamīd b. Abīʾl-Ḥusayn Ibn Abīʾl-Ḥadīd, *Sharḥ nahj al-balāgha*, iii, 457, citing Zubayr b. Bakkār; above, n22 (where Ṣafwān's view is of exegetical origin).

[66] Cf. Ibn Ḥabīb, *Munammaq*, pp. 123, 264 f., 538 f.; Azraqī, *Makka*, p. 99; *Aghānī*, xvi, 75; Ibn Qutayba, *Maʿārif*, p. 241, where he goes to the Yemen and stays with a king who tells him about hair-dye, or with some *ʿaẓīm* who predicts the Prophet, or goes to congratulate Sayf b. Dhī Yazan on the expulsion of the Ethiopians, receiving more predictions of the Prophet. That some of these journeys were envisaged as trading journeys is implied by Ibn Kathīr, *Bidāya*, ii, 251; Abū Nuʿaym, *Dalāʾil*, p. 89, where he goes to the Yemen *fī riḥlat al-shitāʾ*, this time to get predictions and advice from a rabbi.

[67] He would go to the Yemen for the purchase of perfume (Ṭabarī, *Taʾrīkh*, ser. i, p. 1,162). A lengthy *dalāʾil al-nubuwwa* story has him go to the Yemen together with Abū Sufyān (*Aghānī*, vi, 349).

[68] *Aghānī*, vi, 349.

[69] Azraqī, *Makka*, p. 175.

b. al-Mughīra,[70] Fākih b. al-Mughīra,[71] Hishām b. al-Mughīra and his sons,[72] as well as ʿAbdallāh b. Abīʾl-Rabīʿa[73] and ʿUmāra b. al-Walīd.[74] Makhzūmīs are also associated with the Yemen, as well as Ethiopia, in other ways.[75] *Dalāʾil al-nubuwwa* stories in which Abū Sufyān visits the Yemen can presumably be rejected,[76] but other Qurashīs are occasionally seen on trading journeys in the Yemen, too.[77] Explicit mention of caravans travelling between Mecca and the Yemen for purposes of trade is nonetheless rare.[78]

There is also little explicit information on where the traders went. Ibn

[70] He was one of the Qurashī traders who returned in a caravan from the Yemen (thus Ibn Ḥabīb, *Munammaq*, p. 163) or from Ethiopia via the Yemen (thus *ibid.*, p. 246; Ḥassān b. Thābit, *Dīwān*, p. 265); and the bishop of Najrān is said to have owed him money (above, n53).

[71] He, too, was a member of the caravan that returned from either the Yemen or Ethiopia (Ibn Ḥabīb, *Munammaq*, pp. 163, 246 f.).

[72] Hishām b. al-Mughīra met his wife, Asmāʾ bint Mukharriba, while staying at Najrān, presumably as a trader (Baladhūrī, *Ansāb*, I, 209; cf. Kister, "Some Reports," p. 64, where he appears among Meccan traders in Ṣanʿāʾ). Trading with *al-Rūm waʾl-uḥbūsh* is attested for his two sons in poetry (Goldziher, "Ḥuṭejʾa," p. 520, xxx, 6 f.; the scholiast adds Persia, though not the Yemen).

[73] He traded with the Yemen and sent perfume to his mother, Asmāʾ bint Mukharriba (who had married Abū Rabīʿa on the end of the marriage mentioned in the preceding note); she would sell it in Medina. He also had a large number of Ethiopian slaves (*Aghānī*, I, 64 f.).

[74] He is said to have gone to either Syria or the Yemen with ʿUmar as his hireling (Ibn Ḥabīb, *Munammaq*, p. 147); but he is more strongly associated with Ethiopia.

[75] Hubayra b. Abī Wahb fled to Najrān after the conquest, presumably because he had connections there (Balādhurī, *Ansāb*, I, 362; II, 41; Wāqidī, *Maghazī*, II, 847). ʿIkrima b. Abī Jahl also fled to the Yemen, according to some, with the intention of crossing from there to Ethiopia (below, n109). ʿUmāra b. al-Walīd traded in Ethiopia (below, n96), and there was a *dār al-ʿulūj* at which Ethiopians were to be found in the Makhzūmī quarter in Mecca (below, n104). The Makhzūmīs who are said to have returned from the Yemen in one version are said to have returned from Ethiopia in the other (above, nn70 f.); and though one Makhzūmī is associated with the Yemen, it is Ethiopian trade that is attested for his sons (above, n72). In a noncommercial vein, Makhzūmīs and others are said to have gone to the Yemen and to have run out of water in what appears to be a variant on the theme of the digging of the well (*Aghānī*, XV, 19; cf. below, ch. 9, p. 223).

[76] Cf. above, n67; cf. the even more elaborate story in Ibn ʿAsākir, *Tahdhīb*, III, 118 f.; Ibn Kathīr, *Bidāya*, II, 223, 224, where he alternates between Syria and the Yemen.

[77] Cf. Ibn Ḥabīb, *Munammaq*, pp. 140, 163, 246.

[78] Apart from the caravan returning from either the Yemen or Ethiopia and those in which Abū Sufyān are supposed to have gone, I have not come across any (cf. above, nn67, 70 f., 76).

al-Kalbī's *īlāf*-tradition merely has Muṭṭalib (who does in the Yemen what Hāshim does in Syria) die on his way to the Yemen in the nondescript place of Radmān[79] and contrary to what one might expect, they are not attested at Aden, the major Yemeni emporium and the ultimate source of Yemeni perfume at the time.[80] Ṣanʿāʾ is usually mentioned in political rather than commercial contexts.[81] A man from Ṣanʿāʾ is on record as having owed money to ʿAbd al-Muṭṭalib, and one version of the story of the desecration of Abraha's church places Qurashī merchants in this city.[82] But one of the rival versions places the events in Najrān,[83] and here we are on firmer ground. Thus it was in Najrān that Hishām b. al-Mughīra settled, and to Najrān that Hubayra b. Abī Wahb fled after the conquest of Mecca, just as it was to the bishop of Najrān that Walīd b. al-Mughīra owed money, according to some.[84] All three men were Makhzūmīs. ʿAbd al-Muṭṭalib is supposed to have been a friend of the bishop of Najrān,[85] and he also had a Jewish protégé (*jār*) from Najrān who used to trade in the markets of Tihāma.[86] It is Najrān

[79] Cf. Bakrī, *Muʿjam*, pp. 405, 695, *s.vv.* Radmān, Ghazza; Yāqūt, *Buldān*, II, 772 f., *s.vv.* Rudāʿ, Radmān; IV, p. 933, *s.v.* Waʿlān.

[80] Cf. above, ch. 4, no. 3.

[81] It is identified as the capital of Abraha and other Abyssinian rulers of the Yemen (Ibn Hishām, *Leben*, pp. 36, 43); and it was here, more precisely to Qaṣr Ghumdān, that Quraysh (led by ʿAbd al-Muṭṭalib) and others went to congratulate Sayf b. Dhī Yazan on the expulsion of the Abyssinians (Ibn Ḥabīb, *Munammaq*, pp. 538 ff.; *Aghānī*, XVII, 311 ff.; Azraqī, *Makka*, pp. 98 ff.; Abū Nuʿaym, *Dalāʾil*, pp. 56 ff.). But there is no account of Meccans visiting its fair, for all that it was one of some importance; cotton, saffron, dyestuffs, cloth, and iron were exchanged there, according to Marzūqī (*Azmina*, II, 164), cloaks, beads, and skins according to Qalqashandī (*Ṣubḥ*, I, 411), and Tawḥīdī (*Imtāʿ*, p. 85).

[82] Kister, "Some Reports," p. 75, and p. 64, citing *Nihāyat al-irab*. Alternatively, it was a group of Kinānīs who desecrated Abraha's church here (Ibn Ḥabīb, *Munammaq*, p. 68), the Kinānīs in question being intercalators enraged by Abraha's proposed diversion of the pilgrimage (Abū Nuʿaym, *Dalāʾil*, pp. 107 f., citing Ibn Isḥāq and others; Ibn Hishām, *Leben*, pp. 29 ff.).

[83] Kister, "Some Reports," p. 68; Abu Nuʿaym, *Dalāʾil*, p. 101. This story in its turn sounds like a variant of the one in which Ethiopians are robbed in Mecca (below, ch. 6, p. 143; and note that though the looting takes place in Najrān, the victim (Abraha's grandson, who had been on pilgrimage to Mecca in apparent ignorance of Abraha's proposed diversion of the pilgrimage) complains of what has happened to him in *Mecca*.

[84] Above, nn70, 72, 75.

[85] Kalāʿī, *Iktifāʾ*, p. 241 (yet another *dalāʾil* story).

[86] Ibn Ḥabīb, *Munammaq*, p. 94; similarly Balādhurī, *Ansāb*, I, 72 f., but without mention of the Najrānī origins of the Jew.

that is mentioned in the one passage suggestive of where the Meccans obtained their Yemeni perfume,[87] and they could certainly have bought their Yemeni clothing there, too.[88] It was to the tribe of Murād in the Najrān area that they were reputed to have sold donkeys.[89] They were also reputed to have sold them to Daws of the Sarāt, and it seems to have been from Daws and other tribes of the Sarāt that they obtained their Ethiopian slaves.[90] Abū Sufyān had an important Azdī ally (*ḥalīf*) from the Sarāt,[91] and Qurashī traders were apparently numerous there.[92] Qurashī traders also visited the annual fair at Ḥubāsha, six days' journey to the south of Mecca in the territory of Bāriq, an Azdī tribe; some of

[87] As mentioned already, Asmā' bint Mukharriba met Hishām b. al-Mughīra at Najrān (above, n72). What was she doing there? She was not a native of Najrān, her father being a Tamīmī and her mother a Bakriyya, and she was a widow when Hishām met her (Balādhurī, *Ansāb*, I, 209). Presumably, then, she was engaging in business (compare Khadīja, another widow who engaged in trade, and Hind bint ʿUtba, a divorcee who did the same, cf. below, ch. 6, p. 133). After she had settled in Medina, her business was in perfume that she received from the Yemen (above, n73). It is thus likely that she received it from Najrān.

[88] The Prophet imposed an annual tribute of two thousand cloaks on the Najrānīs (Balādhurī, *Futūḥ*, pp. 64 f.).

[89] Above, ch. 4, no. 6.

[90] Thus Bilāl is said to have been an Ethiopian *muwallad* (that is, non-Arab born in slavery in Arabia) from the Sarāt (Ibn Saʿd, *Ṭabaqāt*, III, 232; Balādhurī, *Ansāb*, I, 184). Anasa was likewise a *muwallad* from the Sarat, whereas Abū Kabsha was one from the land of Daws (Balādhurī, *Ansāb*, I, 478), and ʿĀmir b. Fuhayra was a *muwallad* of Azd (*ibid.*, p. 193). Nahdiyya was a *muwallada* of B. Nahd b. Zayd, presumably the Yemeni rather than the Syrian group of that tribe (*ibid.*, p. 196; cf. Caskel, *Ǧamhara*, II, s.v. Nahd b. Zaid). And it was at Ḥubāsha, a market located in Tihāma, that a black slave girl was sold (above, ch. 3, n170).

[91] That is Abū Uzayhir al-Dawsī, whose story is given in full in Ibn Ḥabīb, *Munammaq*, pp. 234 ff.; cf. also Ḥassan b. Thābit, *Dīwān*, II, 258 ff.; Ibn Hishām, *Leben*, pp. 273 ff. Abū Bakr also had a *ḥalīf* from the Sarāt (Ibn Saʿd, *Ṭabaqāt*, VIII, 276). And note that the *mawālī*, presumably freedmen, of ʿAbd al-Dār who claimed to be *ḥalīf*s of the latter presented themselves as Yemenis of Azd (*ibid.*, p. 246).

[92] Cf. *Aghānī*, II, 243. Here we are told that when Hishām b. al-Walīd killed Abū Uzayhir al-Dawsī, Abū Sufyān's above-mentioned *ḥalīf*, Quraysh sent someone to the Sharāt to warn *man bihā min tujjār Quraysh*, while at the same time an Azdī went to warn his own people. It makes no sense that Qurashī traders in Syria should have been warned, while those in the Sarāt would certainly have wanted to get out as soon as possible, so Sharāt must here be a mistake for Sarāt. Elsewhere we hear of a Qurashī in the Sarāt who was pursued by Dawsīs on the news of the murder of Abū Uzayhir and who was saved by a woman whose house he entered (Balādhurī, *Ansāb*, I, 136; Ibn Hishām, *Leben*, p. 276; Ḥassān b. Thābit, *Dīwān*, II, 263).

them bought cloth there.[93] Trading in "the Yemen" would thus seem to have meant trading in the area between Mecca and Najrān, on the fringes of the land occupied by Ethiopians and Persians, rather than in the Yemen itself.

Ethiopia

Ethiopia is a problematic case. It is identified as a Qurashī *matjar* of some importance in both Ibn al-Kalbī's account and elsewhere;[94] yet there is practically no concrete evidence on the trade in question. One story has Qurashī traders return from Ethiopia via the Yemen, but some hold the traders in question never to have gone further than the Yemen.[95] Another has ʿUmāra b. al-Walīd al-Makhzūmī sail to Ethiopia with ʿAmr b. al-ʿĀṣ for trade,[96] but the exegetical variants on this story make it reflect political rather than commercial relations.[97] Yet another exegetical

[93] Cf. below, ch. 7 n23. One Qurashī who bought cloth there was Ḥakīm b. Ḥizām (Bakrī, *Muʿjam*, p. 264).

[94] It was a *matjar* for Quraysh in which they found *rifāghan min al-rizq wa-amnan* (Ṭabarī, *Taʾrīkh*, ser. I, p. I, 181; similarly *id.*, *Jāmiʿ*, IX, 152, in connection with the Muslim migration there). A late version of the *īlāf*-tradition makes it the best land in which the Meccans traded (Kister, "Some Reports," p. 61, citing *Nihāyat al-irab*); and Ṣafwān b. Umayya is credited with the view that Quraysh only settled in Mecca for the sake of trade with Syria and Ethiopia (above, n22). "What is your business and why do you come to me if you are not traders?" as the Najāshī asks the emissaries of Quraysh who came for the extradition of the Muslims (Abū Nuʿaym, *Dalāʾil*, p. 197).

[95] Above, n70.

[96] *Aghānī*, IX, pp. 55 ff.; Ibn Isḥāq in the recension of Yūnus b. Bukayr in Ḥamīdallāh, *Sīra*, no. 211.

[97] The story in which ʿAmr and ʿUmāra go to Ethiopia on trade is about a Don Juan who overreaches himself and is denounced by ʿAmr to the Najāshī. It does not at first sight have much to do with the account in which ʿAmr goes to the Najāshī to secure the extradition of the Muslims or the doublet in which he thinks of seeking refuge in Ethiopia itself. In all three, though, ʿAmr is brought together with the Najāshī; and as Raven has demonstrated, the story about the Muslim refugees is an exegetical one spun around a Qurʾānic passage (3:198) with material borrowed from that about ʿUmāra and ʿAmr. This is confirmed by the fact that some sources let ʿUmāra and ʿAmr go together to Ethiopia to secure the extradition of the Muslims, letting ʿUmāra come to a sticky end on this rather than a separate occasion (thus Muṣʿab b. ʿAbdallāh al-Zubayrī, *Kitāb nasab Quraysh*, p. 322; Abū Nuʿaym, *Dalāʾil*, pp. 196 ff., citing ʿUrwa b. al-Zubayr; Ḥalabī, *Sīra*, pp. 322 ff.; cf. also the discussion in Balādhurī, *Ansāb*, I, 232 f.). Raven could well be right that the story in which ʿUmāra and ʿAmr go together for trade is the original one. It is certainly an excellent piece of storytelling. But all the stories involved could also be seen

story has a *mawlā* of B. Sahm, the clan of ʿAmr b. al- Āṣ, sail to Ethiopia for trade in the company of two Christian traders from Palestine, but a variant version has the *mawlā* go to Syria.[98] No doubt there will be other stories in the huge tradition; but the enthusiastic claim that "evidence for the brisk commercial intercourse between Mecca and Abyssinia is everywhere" can scarcely be said to be correct.[99]

There is no information on where the traders went in Ethiopia. The name of Adulis, the famous Ethiopian port, is unknown to the sources on pre-Islamic Arabia and the rise of Islam;[100] and though all the stories on Qurashīs in Ethiopia, be it as traders or as diplomats, involve the Negus, the tradition also fails to mention Axum. In fact, it would seem to be wholly ignorant of Ethiopian place names. Hāshim dies in Gaza and Muṭṭalib makes it to Radmān in Ibn al-Kalbī's *īlāf*-tradition, but their brother ʿAbd Shams is despatched in Mecca itself.

How then are we to envisage the trade between Mecca and Ethiopia? One suggestion is that is was the Ethiopians who came to Mecca (or at least Shuʿayba) rather than the other way round.[101] Of Ethiopians in

as different elaborations of common material; and if this is so, all the evidence we are left with is the common theme that ʿAmr b. al-ʿĀṣ had dealings with the Najāshī (cf. W. Raven, "Some Islamic Traditions on the Negus of Ethiopia").

[98] Cf. above, ch. 4 n12. It is in Kalbī's version that he goes to Syria (Ibn ʿAsākir, *Taʾrīkh*, x, 471), and in Muqātil's that he sails to Ethiopia (*ibid.*, pp. 471 f.). Since the silver cup that he carried was intended as a gift for the king in Kalbī's account, one would assume that the journey was originally to Ethiopia: the Byzantine king did not reside in Syria, whereas Quarashī traders are presented as having frequented the Najāshī. But then the non-Muslims who accompany him (and who are required for the legal point) are two Syrian Christians, Tāmīm al-Dārī and another, even in Muqātil's account, suggesting that both versions are conflations of earlier ones. The fact that the protagonist is a Sahmī (usually by *walāʾ*) should probably be taken to link the story to Ethiopia, though ʿAmr b. al-ʿĀṣ, as has been seen, traded in Syria, too. But then the protagonist is a *mawlā* of B. Hāshim in Kalbī's version, suggesting that there was once a story in which the journey went to the Yemen. The evidence is thus somewhat slippery.

[99] Shahid, "The Arabs in the Peace Treaty," p. 191.

[100] It is true that pre-Islamic and later poets mention ships known as *ʿadawlī*, and that these are generally taken to be from Adulis (thus Lammens, *Mecque*, p. 380, with numerous references; Jacob, *Beduinenleben*, p. 149; Hourani, *Seafaring*, p. 42). But Muslim scholars invariably identify them as coming from a port in Baḥrayn (Bakrī, *Muʿjam*, p. 648; Yāqūt, *Buldān*, III, p. 623, both *s.v.* ʿAdawlā), an identification that would seem to go back to Aṣmaʿī (thus the scholiast in Kuthayyir ʿAzza, *Dīwān*, II, 138). In view of the whereabouts of Ṭarafa, one of the earliest poets to mention these ships, this identification is likely to be right.

[101] Cf. Lammens, *L'Arabie occidentale*, p. 15; similarly Simon, "Ḥums et īlāf," pp. 223 f.

Mecca there is, in fact, some recollection. Thus one story about the origins of Quṣayy's fortune is that he killed and plundered an Ethiopian noble (*ʿaẓīm*) who had come to Mecca for trade.[102] One version of the story of how Meccan trade came to an end has it that Ethiopians would bring foodstuffs to Jedda (*sic*) so that the Meccans no longer had to make their tiresome journeys to Syria.[103] And the Makhzūmī quarter in Mecca is said to have had a *dār al-ʿulūj* at which Ethiopians were to be found.[104] Residues of Abraha's army are also supposed to have stayed behind in Mecca, working as craftsmen and shepherds.[105] Some, though not all, of these stories could be taken to reflect the presence in Mecca of Ethiopian freedmen rather than free traders; and the tradition is at all events adamant that the Meccans visited Ethiopia itself, where they had dealings with its ruler. The suggestion that Ethiopian traders would visit Mecca thus does not dispose of the problem.

Another possibility would be that Meccan trade with Ethiopia was not a trade with Ethiopia at all, but rather one with the Yemen under Ethiopian rule. It is the same clan, Makhzūm, which is associated with trade in both Ethiopia and the Yemen; and given the dearth of information on the Ethiopia trade, it is odd that some sources should present Meccan trade as one with Syria and Ethiopia, or Syria, Egypt, and Ethiopia, to the exclusion of the Yemen; if *ḥabasha* here meant Abyssinians who happened to be in the Yemen rather than Abyssinia itself, the claim would be less odd.[106] But though one source duly identifies the ruler from whom Quraysh obtained permission to trade in the Yemen as an Abyssinian,[107] the tradition does not go so far as to conflate this ruler, or other rulers of the Yemen, with the Negus himself. Moreover, it in-

[102] Ibn Ḥabīb, *Munammaq*, p. 18. The alternative story is that he inherited the fortune of a foreigner who had come to Mecca for the sale of leather (above, ch. 4 n51). Putting the two together, one might conclude that it was the Ethiopians who sold skins in Mecca rather than the Meccans who sold them in Ethiopia, a good example of the shapelessness of our evidence.

[103] Above, n11.

[104] Kister, "Some Reports," p. 73, citing Fākihī.

[105] Azraqī, *Makka*, p. 97.

[106] Cf. above, nn62, 65. The traditions identifying the journeys as going to Syria, Ethiopia, *and* the Yemen could be read in the same vein (Ibn Saʿd, *Ṭabaqāt*, 1, 75; cf. Thaʿālibī, *Thimār*, p. 115).

[107] Kister, "Some Reports," p. 61, citing *Nihāyat al-irab* (Abraha). In this version Hāshim himself concludes all four agreements.

sists that Qurashīs would cross the sea to get to Ethiopia. This solution is thus also unsatisfactory.

A third possibility is that Quraysh would trade with Ethiopia as residents in the Yemen rather than as citizens of Mecca. Insofar as they went to Ethiopia, they must have done so via the Yemen. The Muhājirūn are admittedly said to have sailed there directly from Shuʿayba; but they did so in ships, clearly foreign, that merely happened to put in there,[108] and it was to the Yemen that ʿIkrima b. Abī Jahl fled after the conquest of Mecca with the intention, according to Ṭabarī, of crossing to Ethiopia.[109] It was also via the Yemen that the above-mentioned traders in Ethiopia returned.[110] According to Wāqidī, ʿIkrima embarked somewhere on the coast of Tihāma (rather than at Aden),[111] and this agrees well enough with the information on where the Meccans traded in the Yemen. All this and the fact that the same Makhzūm are associated with Yemeni and Ethiopian trade could be taken to mean that Meccan residents in the Yemen participated in the local trade with Ethiopia, selling local rather than Meccan goods in Ethiopia and distributing Ethiopian goods locally rather than at the Meccan markets. The tradition does, of course, insist that it was Meccan rather than Yemeni leather goods that the Negus esteemed so highly, and generally thinks of the Ethiopia trade as conducted from Mecca itself; but this could be explained away, and we certainly never see Qurashīs distributing Ethiopian goods at markets such as ʿUkāẓ.[112] If Qurashī trade with Ethiopia was conducted by a diaspora in the Yemen, it would be less odd that the tradition remembers nothing about it except the fact that it existed.

Against this explanation must be set the fact that some accounts present the Ethiopia trade as an extension of Meccan links with Byzantine Syria rather than with the Yemen. Thus one version of the *īlāf*-tradition has it that it was the Byzantine emperor who obtained permission for

[108] Cf. above, ch. 1 n10.

[109] Ṭabarī, *Taʾrīkh*, ser. 1, p. 1,640, citing Ibn Isḥāq. Ibn Hishām, *Leben*, p. 819, merely says that he went to the Yemen. According to Wāqidī, *Maghāzī*, II, 851, he embarked somewhere on the coast of Tihāma; Wāqidī does not say that his destination was Ethiopia, but this can presumably be taken for granted.

[110] Cf. above, n70.

[111] Cf. above, n109.

[112] Syrian, Egyptian, and Iraqi goods were sold at one of the greatest fairs ever held at ʿUkāẓ, but apparently not Ethiopian ones (Marzūqī, *Azmina*, II, 168). Of the caravan returning from Ethiopia and/or the Yemen we are merely told that it carried the belongings of a Jadhīmī who had died in the Yemen (Ibn Ḥabīb, *Munammaq*, pp. 163, 246).

Quraysh to trade in Ethiopia.[113] An isolated tradition claims that ʿAbd Shams, the traditional founder of the Ethiopia trade, died in Gaza on a par with his brother Hāshim.[114] The *mawlā* who sails to Ethiopia with Christians from Palestine is presumably envisaged as setting out from Ayla.[115] And ʿAmr b. al-ʿĀṣ is supposed to have traded in Syria, Egypt, and Ethiopia alike. On the whole it seems reasonable to dismiss this evidence as triggered by, among other things, the well-known relations between Byzantium and Ethiopia and to stay with the explanation of the Ethiopia trade as one conducted by a diaspora in the Yemen.[116] But no solution seems to be exactly right.

What makes the problem so intractable is the fact that Ethiopia is extraordinarily prominent from a political and religious point of view in the traditions on the rise of Islam. Ethiopia is here a land beyond the sea in which both Muslims and non-Muslims will seek refuge, and the ruler of which is familiar to all, though especially to the Muslims: he receives them, refuses to hand them over, and in due course converts to Islam as the only foreign ruler to accept Muḥammad's invitation to adopt the new religion.[117] This fits well with the fact that there is a large number of Ethiopian loan words in Arabic relating, above all, to things religious

[113] Ibn Saʿd, *Ṭabaqāt*, I, p. 78.

[114] *Ibid.*, IV, p. 19, where the bishop of Gaza comes to Muḥammad at Tabūk and tells him that *halaka ʿindī Hāshim wa-ʿAbd Shams wa-humā tājirān wa-hādhihi amwāluhumā*. This is one out of several traditions in which Hāshim is presented as having been active shortly before the Prophet. Thus an account referred to already (above, nn 15, 107) presents him as having negotiated with Jabala b. Ayham in Syria, that is, the last Ghassānid king who died in exile after the Muslim conquest of Syria, though the ruler on the Persian side is Kavādh (d. 531)! The same account has Hāshim negotiate with Abraha, who also flourished too late (c. 540), especially if we consider that the Islamic tradition credits him with an expedition against Mecca in Muḥammad's year of birth (about 570). But Ibn Saʿd, *Ṭabaqāt*, I, 75, similarly cites Kalbī as saying that Hāshim negotiated the treaty between Quraysh and Heraclius (d. 641)! Chronologically, the tradition is completely at sea.

[115] Cf. above, n98.

[116] Some of the evidence could be dismissed on other grounds. Thus the fact that the *mawlā* sails to Ethiopia in the company of Syrian Christians could well be a result of conflation (cf. above, n98). ʿAmr's trade in Egypt (above, n58) is probably generated by the fact that he was the conqueror of Egypt; and his links with Ethiopia can also be queried, as will be seen: the ʿAmr with whom the tradition associates the Najāshī is not always identified as ʿAmr b. al-ʿĀṣ (cf. below, ch. 9, pp. 221 f.). He might thus have traded in Syria alone (above, n36).

[117] See for example, Ṭabarī, *Taʾrīkh*, ser. 1, pp. 1,568 ff.

(though many or most could in principle be south Arabian, too).[118] But it is not easy to say what sort of historical relations this evidence reflects. It is customary to explain it with reference to commercial links, a venerable approach inasmuch as early Muslim scholars did the same.[119] But hardly any of the loan words are commercial terms; the overwhelming majority entered Arabic via the Qur'ān, for all that Muḥammad neither traded in Ethiopia nor went there as a refugee; and practically nothing is known to the tradition about the trade that they are supposed to reflect. It would thus appear misguided to stretch such evidence as we have on trade in order to explain the mysterious Ethiopian link, this link being more likely to explain the evidence on trade when or if it is identified. Meanwhile, one can only say that however we are to envisage Qurashī trade with Ethiopia, it is unlikely to have played a major role in the Meccan economy.

Iraq

That leaves us with Iraq. Ibn al-Kalbī's *īlāf*-tradition asserts that the Meccans traded regularly there, and there is some concrete evidence in support of this claim. Thus one story has Abū Sufyān accompany a caravan of Qurashīs and Thaqafīs to Iraq,[120] while another displays him as a trader at Ḥīra.[121] It was also Abū Sufyān and/or Ṣafwān b. Umayya who accompanied the caravan intercepted by the Muslims at Qarada.[122] Ḥakam b. Abī'l-ʿĀṣ once went to Ḥīra for the sale of perfume.[123] And Musāfir b. Abī ʿAmr went there to earn money for a dower, engaging in trade, according to some, though others have it that he chose the eas-

[118] Nöldeke, *Neue Beiträge*, pp. 31 ff. The authority for the point that many of them could equally well be south Arabian is Professor A.F.L. Beeston (personal communication).

[119] Cf. Ṭabarī, *Ta'rīkh*, ser. 1, p. 1,181, citing Hishām b. ʿUrwa on the *hijra* to Ethiopia, explained with reference to the fact that Ethiopia was a *matjar* of Quraysh.

[120] *Aghānī*, XIII, 206, citing Haytham b. ʿAdī; cited from the *Aghānī* together with another version in Ibn Ḥajar, *Iṣāba*, V, 192 f., no. 6,918, *s.v.* Ghaylān b. Salama; an almost identical version is given by Muḥammad b. ʿAbdallāh al-Khaṭīb al-Iskāfī, *Luṭf al-tadbīr*, pp. 71 f. (I owe the last two references to Professor M. J. Kister.)

[121] *Aghānī*, IX, 52, citing Nawfalī.

[122] Above, ch. 4, no. 1.

[123] *Aghānī*, XVII, 369, citing Ibn al-Sikkīt and others.

ier method of asking Nuʿmān b. al-Mundhir for help.[124] And according to Ibn al-Kalbī himself, it was Qurashīs trading with Ḥīra who brought *zandaqa* to Mecca.[125] All the individuals mentioned are Umayyads, and the only destination seems to have been Ḥīra.[126] The *īlāf*-tradition adds no place names, despatching Nawfal, the founder of the Iraqi trade, at Salmān on the route to Iraq in Arabia itself. Some sources, however, add details on the relations that obtained between Quraysh and the tribes along the route in question.[127]

The trouble with these accounts is that they are so contradictory as to cancel one another out. Thus Ibn al-Kalbī claims that Nawfal obtained permission from the Persian emperor (or the king of Ḥīra) for Quraysh to trade in Iraq; but the story that has Abū Sufyān accompany a caravan of Thaqafīs and Qurashīs to Iraq makes Abū Sufyān exclaim that this is a dangerous undertaking because the Persian has *not* given them permission to trade in his land, which is no *matjar* to them.[128] Similarly, Ibn al-Kalbī claims that Nawfal concluded *īlāf*-agreements with the tribes on the way to Iraq, thereby obtaining safe passage for Quraysh; but other sources (themselves dependent on Ibn al-Kalbī) have it that Quraysh enjoyed automatic inviolability among most of the tribes along the Iraq route, either because Muḍar and their allies respected their direct and indirect ties of kinship with Quraysh or because they regarded Quraysh as holy men.[129] And both claims are contradicted in their turn by the story of Ḥakam b. Abī'l-ʿĀṣ, for Ḥakam sought *jiwar* from one of these

[124] *Aghānī*, IX, 50, 52 (he went to Ḥīra, he went to ask Nuʿmān's help, he went to Nuʿmān to acquire money for a dower); Muṣʿab, *Nasab Quraysh*, p. 136 (he went to Ḥīra for trade and died *ʿinda'l-Nuʿmān*).

[125] G. Monnot, "L'Histoire des religions," p. 29, citing Ibn al-Kalbī's *Mathālib al-ʿarab*.

[126] Traditions in which Qurashī traders go elsewhere in Iraq are not known to me, but there is one in which such a trader visits Persia proper. In explanation of Sūra 31:5 (*wa-min al-nās man yashtarī lahwa'l-ḥadīth*), Kalbī and Muqātil inform us that Naḍr b. al-Ḥārith, a member of ʿAbd al-Dār, used to go as a trader to Persia, where he bought Persian stories (however that is to be envisaged); he would tell these stories to Quraysh back in Mecca, saying that whereas Muḥammad told them of ʿĀd and Thamūd, he could tell them about Rustum, Isfandiyār, and the Persian emperors (Wāḥidī, *Asbāb*, p. 259). One would scarcely wish to postulate the existence of a Qurashī trade with Persia on the basis of this.

[127] Ibn Ḥabīb, *Muḥabbar*, pp. 264 f; Marzūqī, *Azmina*, II, 162, both from Ibn al-Kalbī.

[128] Above, n120. This contradiction was first noted by Simon, "Ḥums et īlāf", p. 228.

[129] Above, n127. It is Marzūqī who attributes inviolability to them on grounds of their connection with the sanctuary.

allies of Muḍar on his way to Iraq, or, in other words, he made *ad hoc* arrangements for his safety on the way in equal ignorance of Qurashī *īlāf*s and Qurashī inviolability among the tribes in question.[130] Further, we are told that when Quraysh took the route through the territory of Rabīʿa, they would be escorted by the sons of ʿAmr b. Marthad, the chief of Qays b. Thaʿlaba, from Bakr b. Wāʾil, thereby obtaining safe passage.[131] This is perhaps compatible with the existence of *īlāf*-agreements (though hardly with inviolability). But Abū Sufyān and Ṣafwān b. Umayya seem to have been ignorant of this arrangement, given that they were at a loss at what to do when Muḥammad forced them to take their caravan to Syria via the route to Iraq; and when a solution to their problem was proposed in the form of a guide from Bakr b. Wāʾil, who presumably served as their guarantor of safety as well, the guide in question was not a son of ʿAmr b. Marthad, but an unknown man by the name of Furāt b. Ḥayyān.[132]

The tradition thus asserts both that the Meccans had regular commercial relations with Ḥīra and that they did not. Presumably then they did not. For one thing, the tradition is more likely to have credited the Meccans with a fictitious *matjar* than to have denied them an historical one. For another, the assumption that they did not have regular commercial relations with this area seems to be the prevailing one. The Qarada story presupposes that Quraysh did not trade in Iraq; Abū Sufyān explicitly says as much as leader of the Qurashī-Thaqafī caravan; and Ḥakam b. Abīʾl-ʿĀṣʾ *jiwār* implies the same. Apart from Ibn al-Kalbī, no exegetes mention Iraq or Persia in explanation of the two (or two sets of) journeys mentioned in the Qurʾān. The descriptions of Qurashī relations with Muḍar and Rabīʿa along the Iraq route are given in connection with their visits to Dūmat al-Jandal (modern Jawf), and it is neither said nor implied that they used to continue to Ḥīra. The stories that depict Abū Sufyān and Musāfir as traders in Ḥīra have variants in which the trade is omitted,[133] and the same is true of Ibn al-Kalbī's account of

[130] Above, n123. The tribe from which he sought *jiwār* was Ṭayyiʾ, explicitly mentioned by Ibn Ḥabīb and Marzuqī as an ally of Muḍar that respected the inviolability of Quraysh.

[131] Above, n127.

[132] Cf. above, ch. 4 nn14 f.

[133] For Musāfir, see above, n124. It is in connection with Musāfir that we met Abū Su-

the spread of *zandaqa* in Mecca, a phenomenon of dubious historicity in itself.[134] Naturally, there is no reason to assert that Qurashī traders *never* ventured across to Ḥīra; but their visits must have been rare enough that it is meaningless to speak of a Qurashī trade with Iraq, a point that has in fact been made before.[135]

Meccan trade with foreign states was thus overwhelmingly a trade with Syria and its Egyptian neighbourhood, though commercial relations with the Yemen are also fairly well attested. By the Yemen, however, the sources seem to mean the area between Mecca and Najrān rather than the southernmost corner of the peninsula. From here, apparently, they would cross to Ethiopia, though precisely in what way they traded here is uncertain. They cannot be said to have had regular relations with Iraq.

---

fyān at Ḥīra, but it is only in one version that he is explicitly said to have gone there for trade (*Aghānī*, IX, pp. 50, 52).

[134] Cf. above, ch. 2 n170.

[135] Bulliet, *Camel and the Wheel*, pp. 295 f. (= n40); Donner, "Mecca's Food Supplies," p. 255, with reference to the Qarada story. Cf. also J.M.B. Jones, "*Al-Sīra al-nabawiyya* as a Source for the Economic History of Western Arabia at the Time of the Rise of Islam," 17 f. (where the absence of Persia and Iraq from the *īlāf*-tradition is noted together with the Qarada story).

6

WHAT MECCAN TRADE WAS NOT

We are now in a position to propose three negative points about the Meccan export trade. First, it was not a transit trade. Second, it was not a trade of the kind that attracted the attention of the inhabitants of Egypt and the Fertile Crescent. Third, it was not a trade that presupposed control of any trade routes in Arabia.

The first point is easily substantiated. The Meccans are usually envisaged as middlemen in a long-distance trading network. They are assumed to have collected goods, both native and foreign, in south Arabia and Ethiopia and to have transported them to Syria and Iraq for redistribution within the Byzantine and Persian empires. But the goods that they sold in the north were overwhelmingly of north Arabian origin, not south Arabian or Ethiopian, let alone Indian, Southeast Asian, or Chinese. They did purchase perfume in south Arabia for resale further north. But for one thing, most of it was sold in the Ḥijāz rather than the Byzantine and Persian empires. For another, there is nothing to suggest that any Meccan goods, be they perfume or other, were destined for redistribution withn these empires. There was a market for Ḥijāzī leatherware, clothing, and Yemeni perfume in the cities and villages of southern Syria, perhaps even in Ḥīra, but not in Antioch, Alexandria, Constantinople, or Ctesiphon. When Ibn al-Kalbī tells us that Hāshim settled Qurashīs in the towns and/or villages of Syria, he takes it for granted that the goods which they sold were intended for local consumption;[1] and this agrees with the way in which the Qurashī sellers of perfume are depicted.[2] And when we are told of Hind bint ʿUtba, the ex-wife of Abū Sufyān, that she borrowed 4,000 dinars from the treasury in the time of ʿUmar and set off to trade in the land of Kalb, the

[1] Cf. above, ch. 5, pp. 109 f. The same is implied by Hāshim's remark that it would be cheaper for the Syrians. Lammens nonetheless asserted that Quraysh did not sell manufactured articles, but only raw materials that the Byzantine industry could not do without (*Mecque*, p. 139).

[2] Above, ch. 4, no. 3.

Arab tribe in southern Syria,[3] we are hardly to take it that her commercial activities were radically different from those in which Khadīja or Abū Sufyān had engaged. The sources, in other words, assume the Meccans to have traded directly with private customers in southern Syria, not to have handed over their wares to wholesalers in Gaza or Damascus.[4] In short, Meccan trade is envisaged as an exchange of local goods. And this exchange is presented as having been conducted overwhelmingly within Byzantium and the Byzantine sphere of influence, not in the Sāsānid empire.

As regards the second point, it is obvious that if the Meccans had been middlemen in a long-distance trade of the kind described in the secondary literature, there ought to have been some mention of them in the writings of their customers. Greek and Latin authors had, after all, written extensively about the south Arabians who supplied them with aromatics in the past, offering information about their cities, tribes, political organization, and caravan trade; and in the sixth century they similarly wrote about Ethiopia and Adulis. The political and ecclesiastical importance of Arabia in the sixth century was such that considerable attention was paid to Arabian affairs, too; but of Quraysh and their trading centre there is no mention at all, be it in the Greek, Latin, Syriac, Aramaic, Coptic, or other literature composed outside Arabia before the conquests.

This silence is striking and significant. It is so striking that attempts have been made to remedy it. Thus we are told that Quraysh are indirectly attested in Pliny's *Dabanegoris regio*,[5] that Ptolemy mentions Mecca under the name of Macoraba,[6] a name supposed also to be reflected in Pliny's *portus Mochorbae*, identified as Jedda (*sic*),[7] and that Ammianus Marcellinus likewise mentions Mecca, this time under the name

[3] Ṭabarī, *Ta'rīkh*, ser. 1, pp. 2,766 f. Compare the similar story told *ibid.* about ʿUtba b. Abī Sufyān, who had engaged in trade as governor of the tribe of Kināna.

[4] Note also that the fact that Gaza was a port goes unmentioned in the traditions on Meccan trade.

[5] H. von Wissmann, "Makoraba," with reference to Pliny, *Natural History*, vi, 150.

[6] Cf. A. Grohmann, "Makoraba," with reference to Ptolemy, *Geography*, vi, 7: 32 and earlier literature. This identification has been accepted by *EI*[2], *s.v.* Kaʿba.

[7] Thus Grohmann, "Makoraba," citing Glaser with reference to Pliny, *Natural History*, vi, 150. Von Wissmann, on the other hand, locates *portus Mochorbae* opposite the island of Naʿmān in the northern end of the Red Sea and finds Jedda in Ptolemy's Arga Kōmē (H. von Wissmann, "Madiama," col. 539; *id.*, "Makoraba").

of Hierapolis.[8] All these suggestions should be dismissed out of hand. *Dabanegoris regio* cannot be construed as **Dhū Banī Quraysh*, "the (area) pertaining to Banī Quraysh," as von Wissmann would have it. For one thing, such a construction would be South Arabian rather than Arabic, the language one would have expected to be reflected here.[9] For another, the expression "Banū Quraysh" is impossible, Quraysh being no patronymic: as a descent group Quraysh were Banū Fihr. But above all, Pliny locates the region in question in southeast Arabia, more precisely somewhere between Ommana and the Ḥaḍramawt;[10] and the same is true of *portus Mochorbae*, mentioned in the same passage. That places explicitly identified as southeast Arabian should have been misconstrued as Qurashī domains says much about the intoxicating effect of Mecca on the source-critical faculties of otherwise sober scholars.[11] So does the identification of Ptolemy's Macoraba with Mecca, which has gained almost universal acceptance. It was first made on the ground that the names were vaguely similar and the location vaguely right, Macoraba being assumed to reproduce a name such as Makka-Rabba, "Great Mecca." But this is a most implausible construction,[12] which has since been replaced by *makrab* or *mikrāb*, meaning temple. But in the first place the root *krb* does not denote holiness in Arabic, as opposed to South Arabian, so that once again the language reflected would not be the one expected. In the second place, a name composed of the consonants *mkk* cannot be derived from the root *krb*.[13] It follows that Ptolemy would be referring to a sanc-

[8] Grohmann, "Makoraba," with reference to Ammianus Marcellinus, XXIII, 6: 47.

[9] In Arabic, of course, such a construction would mean "the owner of/the one endowed with B. Quraysh." It is not impossible that South Arabian (or for that matter Aramaic) was the *lingua franca* of the area at the time; but *lingua francas* do not normally affect place names.

[10] Pliny starts VI, 147, by saying that "we will now describe the coast from Charax onwards" and duly proceeds via Gerrha to Ommana and other ports on the Persian Gulf, which he reaches in VI, 149, arriving in south Arabia with its Chatramotitae and Sabaean frankincense in VI, 154. How then could VI, 150 refer to the coast near Mecca?

[11] Not that von Wissmann was noted for his sobriety, but Grohmann's identifications are no sounder, and there are examples of even wilder proposals by earlier scholars in his "Makoraba."

[12] It was justified with reference to names such as Rabbath-Moab or Rabbath-Ammon (cf. Grohmann, "Makoraba"). But the parallel is false inasmuch as these names are constructs, whereas Makka-Rabba is not. It would at all events have to be *Makka al-rabba*; but *rabb* is not used as an adjective in Arabic, nor is Mecca known as *Makka al-kubrā*.

[13] It is hard to share Rodinson's belief that the name of Mecca could be derived from the South Arabian form behind Macoraba, "perhaps by abbreviation" (*Mohammed*, pp. 38 f.).

tuary town which was *not* called Mecca. Why then identify the two? Rescue attempts such as *mikrāb Makka*, "the sanctuary of Mecca," are no better than Makka-Rabba, for all that we clearly need some sort of addition to account for the feminine form reflected in the Greek.[14] The plain truth is that the name of Macoraba has nothing to do with that of Mecca, and that the location indicated by Ptolemy for Macoraba in no way dictates identification of the two.[15] If Macoraba was located in an Arabic-speaking environment, its name is more likely to reflect an Arabic form such as **Muqarraba* than a derivation from South Arabian *krb*;[16] if it was located among speakers of South Arabian, it cannot have been the city of interest to us; and if Ptolemy mentions Mecca at all, he calls it Moka, a town in Arabia Petraea.[17] Naturally, there is no Mecca in Ammianus Marcellinus.[18]

[14] Cf. von Wissmann, "Makoraba." A name such as *mikrāb Makka* would presumably be rendered in Greek with a final *ka* rather than *ba*; it is unlikely that Macoraba should reproduce *mikrāb* with just a feminine ending taken from *Makka*. Buhl, who rightly notes that the name of Mecca cannot be derived from the Semitic word behind Macoraba, refers to Mecca's alternative name of Bakka, but this clearly does not help (F. Buhl, *Das Leben Muhammeds*, p. 103n).

[15] As von Wissmann asserts in his "Makoraba." Ptolemy locates Lathrippa at longitude 71, and this is accepted by von Wissmann as the longitude for Yathrib (cf. his Ptolemaic map of northern Arabia in "Madiama," col. 528). But Macoraba is located at longitude 73, or, in other words, two degrees further *east*, giving it a location somewhere in the middle of Arabia instead of near the coast (cf. the Ptolemaic map after Sprenger, Stevenson, and von Wissmann in Groom, *Frankincense*, p. 86, where this location is duly reproduced; and compare the actual relationship between Mecca and Medina at p. 192). Naturally, Pliny's longitudes and latitudes are inexact; but if they are inexact, one cannot identify places on the basis of them alone.

[16] Cf. Maqārīb, a place near Medina, in Yāqūt, *Buldān*, IV, 587, *s.v.*.

[17] Ptolemy, *Geography*, V, 17: 5 (this was drawn to my attention by M. A. Cook).

[18] Cf. Ammianus Marcellinus, *Rerum Gestarum Libri*, XXIII, 6: 47. Ammianus here lists seven *civitates eximiae* of Arabia Felix, that is, Geapolis, another five cities, plus Dioscuris (presumably Socotra). Grohmann noted that the five cities in question recur as *metropoleis* in Ptolemy, where they are listed in the same order and followed by *Dioskoridous polis*, too (*Geographia*, VI, 7: 35-45). This suggested to him that Ammianus and Ptolemy were using the same list and that Ammianus' Geapolis ought to be mentioned in Ptolemy, too. He proceeded to find it there in the form of Makoraba, arguing that a variant reading of Geapolis is Hierapolis, or, in other words, that Ammianus translated the name of the sanctuary town where Ptolemy merely transcribed it (Grohmann, "Makoraba"). This conjecture falls on the fact that Ptolemy mentions Geapolis under that very name (*Gaia polis*, VI, 7: 29). Hierapolis is thus a mistaken reading; and given that Makoraba is unlikely to have been Mecca, a reference to it would not have been a reference to Mecca, anyway.

That classical authors should have failed to mention Mecca and Quraysh is not a problem: why read them into Pliny and Ptolemy when it is authors such as Procopius, Nonnosus, and Syriac churchmen who ought to have referred to them? After all, we only make things worse by postulating familiarity on the part of Greco-Roman authors with both Mecca and Quraysh before they mattered, whereas neither was known after they had risen to commercial and political importance. It is the sixth-century silence that is significant, and this silence cannot be attributed to the fact that sources have been lost, though some clearly have.[19] The fact is that the sources written after the conquests display not the faintest sign of *recognition* in their accounts of the new rulers of the Middle East or the city from which they came. Nowhere is it stated that Quraysh, or the "Arab kings," were the people who used to supply such-and-such regions with such-and-such goods: it was only Muḥammad himself who was known to have been a trader.[20] And as for the city, it was long assumed to have been Yathrib. Of Mecca there is no mention for a long time; and the first sources to mention the sanctuary fail to give a name for it, whereas the first source to name it fails to locate it in Arabia.[21] Jacob of Edessa knew of the Kaʿba toward which the Muslims prayed, locating it in a place considerably closer to Ptolemy's Moka than to modern Mecca or, in other words, too far north for orthodox accounts of the rise of Islam; but of the commercial significance of this place he would appear to have been completely ignorant.[22] Whatever the implications of this evidence for the history of the Muslim sanctuary, it is plain that the Qurashī trading centre was not a place with which the subjects of the Muslims were familiar.

Assuming that there was such a thing as Qurashī trade, the silence of the sources must thus be explained with reference to the nature of the trade itself; and there is nothing in the Islamic tradition to suggest that

[19] Of Nonnosus' account, for example, only a short fragment survives in Photius. This account does mention a sanctuary of major importance; but the sanctuary is described as one active only in the holy months, on a par with ʿUkāẓ and other pilgrim fairs, so it is unlikely to have been a city, let alone a city called Mecca (cf. Nonnosus in Photius, *Bibliothèque*, I, 5 f.).

[20] Cf. above, ch. 5 n19.

[21] P. Crone and M. Cook, *Hagarism*, pp. 171 n8 (on the *Continuatio Arabica*, which gives Mecca an Abrahamic location between Ur and Ḥarrān), and 176 n48 (on the Khūzistānī chronicle and Bar Penkaye, who fail to give a name for it).

[22] *Ibid.*, p. 173 n30.

it *should* have attracted attention outside Arabia: the sale of leather goods, woollens, and perfume in places such as Buṣrā and Adhriʿāt was not likely to make headlines. If Quraysh were traders, their commercial activities were of a kind conducted in this area since time immemorial.

It follows that the traditional question of how and when the Meccans gained control of the routes between the Yemen, Syria, Ethiopia, and Iraq is meaningless; and the sources do not, in fact, assert that they were in control of any route or dominated the export trade of any particular locality, let alone that they monopolized the export trade of Arabia at large.

MECCA-SYRIA

The route between Mecca and Syria, traditionally identified as the northern end of the incense route, is assumed by modern scholars to have been controlled by the Ghassānids, who must have been ousted by Quraysh. Thus Simon has it that the fifth clause of the peace treaty between Byzantium and Persia in 561 furnishes decisive proof that the Ghassānids "actively pursued their commerce and without doubt controlled the Syrian part of the incense route."[23] But the clause in question orders the Arabs to bring their goods to Dara and Nisibis in *upper Mesopotamia*, forbidding them to smuggle their goods into the Byzantine and Persian empires by other routes.[24] What it regulates is thus an east-west trade between the Arabs of the Syrian desert and their settled neighbours, not a north-south trade between Syria, Iraq, and Arabia; indeed, why should a north-south trade have figured in a treaty between Byzantium and Persia at all? Whatever the Ghassānid involvement in the east-west trade, the treaty says nothing about their commercial policies in Arabia, and it neither proves nor implies that they were in control of any route. In fact we know nothing about the commercial policies of the Ghassānids, and they are not presented as commercial competitors of Quraysh in the sources.[25] Ibn al-Kalbī's *īlāf*-tradition has it that it was

[23] Simon, "*Ḥums* et *īlāf*," p. 226.

[24] Cf. Shahid, "The Arabs in the Peace Treaty," pp. 192 f.

[25] The story cited by Kister, "Mecca and Tamīm," p. 121, plays up Quraysh as true Arabs at the expense of the Ghassānids, but reflects no commercial rivalry.

non-Arab traders who were ousted by Quraysh, not Ghassānids; and what Quraysh took over was the task of supplying Mecca with necessities, not that of purveying luxury goods to the Byzantines. There simply is no evidence for a shift from Ghassānid to Meccan control of the northern route.

On the contrary, the tradition gives us to understand that numerous communities, both Arab and non-Arab, were commercially active in northwest Arabia side by side with Quraysh. Even Ibn al-Kalbī's claim that Quraysh ousted non-Arab traders from Mecca is contradicted by other material. Traders from Syria are supposed to have visited Mecca after Quṣayy's death,[26] and they were still there on the eve of Islam. Thus we are told that Byzantine traders were subject to tithes on entering Mecca.[27] One Byzantine merchant is on record as having sold an extremely expensive cloak there, and a certain Qimṭa al-Rūmī married his daughter to Nubayh b. al-Ḥajjāj, thereby making the latter's fortune.[28] Jewish traders settling in, or trading with, Mecca are also mentioned in connection with predictions of the Prophet.[29] As will be seen shortly, Yemeni traders were active in Mecca, too, as well as further north.

A similar picture is presented for Medina. Thus "Nabataeans" from Syria were still selling foodstuffs here toward the end of the Prophet's life: it was thanks to them that the Muslims were so well informed about Syrian affairs.[30] They carried grain and oil in their caravans,[31] and they

[26] Azraqī, *Makka*, p. 375, citing Mujāhid (they killed a gazelle in the *ḥaram*).

[27] *Ibid.*, p. 107.

[28] *Aghānī*, xviii, 123; Ibn Ḥabīb, *Munammaq*, p. 53.

[29] Thus, as mentioned already, ʿAbd al-Muṭṭalib had a Jewish *jār* from Najrān who used to trade in the *sūq*s of Tihāma (Ibn Ḥabīb, *Munammaq*, p. 94; this is the only Jew whose role is not predictive). A Jew settled in Mecca for trade at the time of the birth of Muḥammad, whose future prophethood was well known to him (Ibn Saʿd, *Ṭabaqāt*, i, 162; the version cited in Māwardī, *Aʿlām*, p. 153, omits the trade). A Jew from Taymāʾ who traded with Mecca or the Yemen predicted the Prophet to ʿAbd al-Muṭṭalib (Kalāʿī, *Iktifāʾ*, pp. 240 f.; Abū Nuʿaym, *Dalāʾil*, p. 122).

[30] Wāqidī, *Maghāzī*, iii, 989 f., 1,051; Ibn Hishām, *Leben*, p. 911.

[31] They are known now as *sāqiṭa* and now as *ḍāfiṭa*, and they carried *darmak* and oil to Medina, according to Wāqidī, *Maghāzī*, iii, pp. 989 f. Rifāʿa b. Zayd bought *darmak* from them (Balādhurī, *Ansāb*, i, 278; also cited in Ibn al-Athīr, *Usd*, iv, 263, and in ḥadīth collections). A Syrian who sold oil in Medina is mentioned in Ibn Ḥanbal, *Musnad*, v, 191. For *nabīṭ* or *anbāṭ ahl al-Shām* selling grain and oil in Medina at the time of the Prophet, see also Bukhārī, *Receuil*, ii, 45 f. (where the first tradition has *zabīb* for *zayt*); cf. *ibid.*, p. 7. For the *sūq al-nabṭ* in Medina, see Wāqidī, *Maghāzī*, i, 395.

would also visit Dūmat al-Jandal and the Yamāma, their imports from the Yamāma being dates.[32] Of a Christian trader from the Balqā' we are likewise told that he would sell grain in Medina in return for dates.[33] When Muḥammad's father went to Medina to buy dates, he was thus one of many traders there.[34] The sale of wine in Medina was dominated by Jews and Christians, as seen already, and the presence of Christian traders in Medina is taken for granted in other contexts, too.[35] As for the Jews of Medina, they are supposed to have engaged in caravan trade with Syria on a large scale, and one of them had business that took him to Wādī'l-Qura.[36] Even the Arabs of Medina would go to Syria for trade, if only in the context of predictions of the Prophet.[37]

In general, the Jews are said to have traded in commodities such as perfume, clothing, *kohl*, and wine.[38] Jewish Khaybar certainly played a major role in the distribution of Yemeni cloth in the north, and it was the site of an important fair.[39] Jews from Yathrib and the Yemen who had settled in the environs of Ṭā'if for purposes of trade were required to pay *jizya* on the rise of Islam.[40] The Arab inhabitants of Ṭā'if likewise engaged in trade, apparently often in collaboration rather than compe-

[32] Wāqidī, *Maghāzī*, I, 403. Muḥammad b. Yazīd al-Mubarrad, *al-Kāmil*, pp. 202 f.; the *sawāqiṭ* here include an Arab. Cf. also the definition of *sawāqiṭ* in Lane, *Lexicon*, *s.v.*.

[33] Ibn al-Athīr, *Usd*, II, 383; Ibn Ḥajar, *Iṣāba*, III, p. 157, no. 3,629, *s.v.* Saymūnā.

[34] ʿAbd al-Razzāq, *Muṣannaf*, V, 317.

[35] Above, ch. 4, no. 9. One of the stories told in explanation of Sūra 2:257 (*lā ikrāh fī'l-dīn*) is that an Anṣārī called Ḥuṣayn or Ḥuṣaynī or Abū'l-Ḥuṣayn had two sons who were converted to Christianity by Syrian traders in Medina; the Syrians were selling oil (*zayt*) or raisins (*zabīb*) or foodstuffs (*aṭʿām*) in general (Wāḥidī, *Asbāb*, pp. 58 f.; Ibn Kathīr, *Tafsīr*, I, 310 f.; Ibn Ḥajar, *Iṣāba*, II, 23, no. 1,753, *s.v.* Ḥuṣayn).

[36] For the seven caravans that are supposed to have come to the Jews of Medina from Buṣrā and Adhriʿāt in one day, see the references given above, ch. 4 n37. Note also Ibn Sunayna or Subayna, a Jewish merchant of Medina, according to Ibn Hishām, *Leben*, p. 553 (cf. Wāqidī, *Maghāzī*, I, 190 ff., where we are not, however, told that he was a merchant). Balādhurī, *Ansāb*, I, 486 (he bought Salmān al-Fārisī there).

[37] Ibn Saʿd, *Ṭabaqāt*, I, 165.

[38] Cf. above, ch. 4, nos. 3, 5, 9. For their trade in kohl, see Goldziher, "Ḥuṭej'a," p. 185.

[39] Cf. the large quantity of Yemeni cloth and garments found at Khaybar on its conquest by the Muslims (Wāqidī, *Maghāzī*, II, 664). On the fair, see Ibn Ḥabīb, *Muḥabbar*, p. 268; Marzūqī, *Azmina*, II, 161, 165. Note also the Ghassānid who fled to Ḥīra after having killed a fellow tribesman and posed there as a trader from Khaybar (Qālī, *Amālī*, p. 179).

[40] Balādhurī, *Futūḥ*, p. 56.

tition with the Meccans.[41] Even the occasional Najdī trader is met in the Ḥijāz.[42] Hudhalīs would go to Syria on trade, coming back, like so many, with predictions of the Prophet, and they visited Medina too, at least in the time of ʿUmar.[43]

Since much of this evidence relates to the period before the *hijra*, there is no question of explaining it with reference to the supposed "weakening of Mecca's monopoly" on the onset of hostilities between the Muslims and Quraysh; but its historical value can, of course, be queried on other grounds. Even so, the general point is clear, and there is some documentary evidence in its support: the Nessana papyri show us a group of Ishmaelites who were active at Nessana, some sixty kilometers from Gaza, and who traded in wool, camels, donkeys, grain, and the like, that is, in commodities similar to those handled by Quraysh at very much the same place and time.[44] For what it is worth, the evidence does not suggest that the Meccans dominated the exchange of goods between north Arabia and southern Syria, let alone that they enjoyed a monopoly of it. It could, however, be argued that they dominated the export of one particular commodity in north Arabia, that is, leather, though whether they actually did so is equally hard to prove or disprove.

The Yemen-Mecca

As far as the so-called southern end of the incense route is concerned, it is said that the Meccans took control of it in the wake of the Ethiopian conquest of the Yemen about 525. The occupation is assumed to have given rise to political disorders that affected economic life, though this, as has been noted, is "not crystal clear"; the Yemenis might thus have

[41] Cf. above, ch. 5, nn60 (Mughīra b. Shuʿba trading with Qurashīs in Egypt), 76 (Abū Sufyān trading together with Umayya b. Abī'l-Ṣalt), and 120 (Abū Sufyān leading a caravan of Qurashīs and Thaqafīs to Iraq). For a Ghāmidī who settled in Ṭā'if as a trader, see Ibn Ḥajar, *Iṣāba*, III, 240, no. 4,049, *s.v.* Ṣakhr b. Wadāʿa.

[42] Wāqidī, *Maghāzī*, I, 395, who here knows more than Ibn Isḥāq (cf. Ibn Hishām, *Leben*, p. 661).

[43] Hudhalīs in Syria: Ibn Saʿd, *Ṭabaqāt*, I, 161; Abū Nuʿaym, *Dalā'il*, p. 70; Hudhalīs in Medina: Ibn Ḥajar, *Iṣāba*, I, 275, no. 1,297, *s.v.* Jundab b. Salāma.

[44] C. J. Kraemer, Jr., ed. and tr., *Excavations at Nessana*, III, no. 89. The full list of commodities handled by them is wool, clothing, textiles, iron, camels, donkeys, horses, barley, wheat, oil, and other foodstuffs. In the Islamic tradition they would presumably have gone down as Nabataeans, *sawāqiṭ*, and the like.

lost their trade to the Meccans, in due course losing their political preeminence in Arabia to them, as well.[45] But there is no reason to believe that the Meccans inherited either power or commerce from the Yemen. As regards the former, it emerges from Justinian's negotiations with Esimphaios, that is Sumayfaʿ, the puppet king set up by the Ethiopians, that the Yemen was still politically influential in north Arabia in the early part of the reign of Justinian (527-565). The military and other exploits of Abraha, the Ethiopian usurper who followed Sumayfaʿ, also suggest that the Yemen under Ethiopian rule was a power of some consequence in Arabia. And the Persians who took over later certainly represented an even bigger one.[46] The fact that the Yemenis ceased to rule themselves does not mean that Arabia was henceforth afflicted with a political vacuum which it was the historical role of Mecca to fill.

As regards commerce, the reason why both Ethiopians and Persians displayed an interest in the Yemen is precisely that the Yemen mattered in the eastern trade, not that it had lost its importance to Mecca. The Yemen mattered because it was located on the way to the east, and it is a curious idea that while the giants were fighting for control of the coasts, a dwarf in the desert pinched the prize, causing Abraha to attack Mecca in dismay at a commercial success that did not, however, cause the Persians to leave the Yemen alone.[47] What sort of evidence, one wonders, can be adduced for all this?

One version of the *īlāf*-tradition places the inception of Qurashī trade with the Yemen in the reign of Abraha, that is after the Ethiopian conquest, though Abraha, who ruled about 540, cannot in fact have been a contemporary of Hāshim, Muḥammad's great-grandfather.[48] And some exegetes claim that the failure of Abraha's attack on the Kaʿba was crucial for the survival of Meccan trade, in the sense that the Meccans could not be traders without the sanctuary that Abraha was out to destroy.[49]

[45] Shahid, "The Arabs in the Peace Treaty," pp. 188 ff. In general, the introductory part of this article is one of the most intelligent presentations of the conventional view of Meccan trade. Cf. also J. Wellhausen, *Reste arabischen Heidentums*, p. 92: after the fall of the Himyarite kingdom Mecca seems to have become the largest and most powerful city in Arabia.

[46] Procopius, *Wars*, 1, 19, 14; 1, 20, 9; *EI*², *s.v.* Abraha (Beeston); cf. above, ch. 2, on the Persians.

[47] Cf. Watt, *Muhammad at Mecca*, p. 13; Hitti, *Capital Cities*, p. 9.

[48] Above, ch. 5 n107.

[49] Ibn Qutayba, *Mushkil al-Qur'ān*, p. 319.

Following these exegetes, Shahid links the sura assumed to refer to Abraha's defeat with that referring to Qurashī journeys, and reads the result as Qur'ānic evidence that the Meccans had established control of the incense route.[50] But whatever the merit of reading the two suras as a unit, the exegetes who link them merely say that the Meccans continued to trade after Abraha's defeat, and the Qur'ān itself says even less: the journeys are not identified as trading journeys in the book, nor were they always understood as such by the exegetes; their destination is not specified, and the exegetes do not always take them to have included journeys to the Yemen; and the incense route is unknown to Qur'ān and exegetes alike. The Meccans may well have started trading in the Yemen at the time of Abraha. A story set in the time of Abraha nonetheless has Yemeni traders, or Ethiopian traders from the Yemen, come to Mecca, where the Meccans, having suffered a bad period of drought and being apparently pastoralists, cannot resist the temptation to rob them. This is scarcely how their commercial takeover is usually envisaged.[51]

Simon accordingly postpones their takeover to the time of the *ḥilf al-fuḍūl*.[52] Since this alliance was formed when Muḥammad was in his twenties, or about 590, the crucial commercial expansion of the Meccans would thus have taken place so late that it cannot have affected Muḥammad's background much, though it could still be of importance for the conquests; but even this argument does not work. The *ḥilf al-fuḍūl* was an alliance sworn by a number of Meccans when a Yemeni trader sold goods in Mecca and failed to get his payment, the object of the alliance being to ensure that such incidents would not be repeated.[53] A story in which the Meccans vow to do justice to Yemeni traders in Mecca can hardly be said to suggest that they had ousted the traders in question, least of all when the sources show us the *ḥilf* in action by bringing a

[50] Shahid, "Two Qur'ānic Sūras," pp. 435 f.

[51] M. J. Kister, "The Campaign of Ḥulubān," pp. 429 f., reproducing the text of Balādhurī, *Ansāb*, fol. 811a. The text was first adduced in the above vein by Simon, "Ḥums et īlāf," pp. 221 f.

[52] Simon, "Ḥums et īlāf," pp. 222 f.

[53] Cf. Balādhurī, *Ansāb*, II, 12; *Aghānī*, XVII, 287 ff., 297 ff.; Ibn Ḥabīb, *Munammaq*, pp. 45 ff., 217 ff.; Ya'qūbī, *Ta'rīkh*, II, 16 f.; Jāḥiẓ, *Rasā'il*, pp. 71 ff.; Ibn Abī'l-Ḥadīd, *Sharḥ*, III, pp. 455 ff.; Kalā'ī, *Iktifā'*, p. 146. The trader is usually a Yemeni from B. Zubayd (Zayd in Kalā'ī) or Sa'd al-'Ashīra; but it is also suggested that he may have been a non-Arab (Ethiopian?), and in Ya'qūbī he is a northern Arab. The event is dated with reference to the Prophet's age at the time: he was twenty or in his twenties.

whole string of Yemeni traders to Mecca for unfair dealings that are duly put right.[54] The stories may well have blurred the true nature of the events they describe, as Simon argues; indeed, it would be more correct to say that they are legendary. But if stories in which the Meccans boast of having set up a board of complaints for Yemeni and other foreign traders in Mecca constitute "flagrant proof" ("preuve flagrante") that the Meccans "definitively eliminated the merchants of the Yemen from the commerce along the incense route and organized caravans to the Yemen themselves," then any evidence can be adduced as meaning anything we like. The stories are based on the assumption that Yemeni traders were active in Mecca on the eve of Islam; and though the non-Arab traders supplanted by Quraysh in Ibn al-Kalbī's story of Hāshim and his brothers could be understood as Ethiopians from the Yemen and other Yemenis, the tradition is in general innocent of the idea that the Meccans should have ousted them. The caravaneers who transported perfume from Aden to the Byzantine and Persian empires were presumably Yemenis; at least they are not identified as Qurashīs,[55] and Yemenis are said to have frequented the fair at Dūmat al-Jandal: far from trying to supplant them, Quraysh would provide them with escorts on the way.[56] The caravans to the Yemen that the Meccans are said to have organized for themselves are poorly attested in the tradition, and the maritime trade of the Yemenis was not, of course, affected by Mecca at all.[57] As usual, the information is not necessarily true; but true or false, it is the only information that we have, and there is no way in which it can be brought to support the notion of a shift from Yemeni to Meccan domination.

Ethiopia-Mecca

The Meccans may well have dominated the flow of goods from Ethiopia to Mecca, however we are to envisage the route in question. They can-

[54] Balādhurī, *Ansāb*, II, 13 f.; *Aghānī*, XVII, 297; Ibn Ḥabīb, *Munammaq*, pp. 47 ff., 341 ff.; Jāḥiẓ, *Rasā'il*, p. 73.

[55] Cf. Marzūqī, *Azmina*, II, 164.

[56] Ibn Ḥabīb, *Muḥabbar*, p. 264, with reference to the theme of Qurashī inviolability among Muḍarīs. The theme is developed differently in the parallel version given in Marzūqī, *Azmina*, II, 162.

[57] Cf. ch. 5 n78. For the Yemenis at Ayla, see ch. 2 n136.

not have had many competitors apart from the Ethiopians themselves, who took over from the Meccans or were ousted by them, depending on one's exegetical tastes.[58] But the trade between Ethiopia and Byzantium was maritime, as was that between Ethiopia and Persia insofar as it existed, and we never see Meccans handle Ethiopian goods in Arabia or further north. The idea that they enjoyed something like a monopoly on the trade between East Africa and the Mediterranean can accordingly be dismissed.[59]

Mecca-Iraq

In view of the fact that the Meccans hardly ever traded in Iraq, it is not a very plausible proposition that they should have come to dominate the route to this country, and the evidence traditionally adduced for the view that they did says nothing of the kind. Watt, Simon, and others identify the war or wars of Fijār, enacted about 590, as the occasion on which the Meccans took over from their Lakhmid rivals of Ḥīra.[60] As in the case of the Yemen, Iraq is thus added to the list of markets dominated by the Meccans at a stage so late that it cannot have mattered for the formation of Muḥammad, though it may still be of importance for the conquests. And again, the expedient goes against the tenor of the sources.

In the first place, the stories about the wars of Fijār are not about commerce at all. They are set at ʿUkāẓ because this is where people got together, not because trade was conducted there, and what they illustrate (very vividly, in fact) is life in a stateless society: one battle was triggered by amorous adolescents molesting a pretty girl,[61] another by a creditor who could not get his money back, and still others by Barrāḍ, an outlaw who had become an ally (*ḥalīf*) of Ḥarb b. Umayya and who killed the

[58] Cf. ch. 5, pp. 109-111.

[59] Cf. *EI*[2], *s.v.* Ḳuraysh (Watt).

[60] Watt, *Muhammad at Mecca*, pp. 14 f.; Simon, "Ḥums et īlāf," pp. 227 f.; Shahid, "The Arabs in the Peace Treaty," p. 191n; *EI*[2], *s.v.* Fidjār (Fück). The Prophet was fourteen, seventeen, twenty, or twenty-eight years old at the time, though some traditions imply that he was a minor (cf. E. Landau-Tasseron, "The 'Sinful Wars,' Religious, Social and Historical Aspects of *Ḥurūb al-Fijār*)."

[61] Elsewhere this story is set in Medina and told in explanation of the expulsion of B. Qaynuqāʿ (cf. Watt, *Prophet and Statesman*, p. 130).

escort of a caravan sent by Nuʿmān of Ḥīra to ʿUkāẓ, thus embroiling his ally and the latter's tribe in war with Qays, the tribal group to which the murdered man belonged.[62] In the first two episodes, Quraysh are presented as peacemakers, and it is the third that is adduced as leading to the Qurashī takeover: Barrāḍ, we are informed by Watt, acted in accordance with Qurashī desires, if not on Qurashī instructions, when he killed the leader of the Ḥīran caravan (which Watt misrepresents as being on its way to the Yemen rather than ʿUkāẓ).[63] But what we are actually told is that Barrāḍ was a good-for-nothing whom Ḥarb b. Umayya wanted to disown, though he was persuaded to let the alliance stand when Barrāḍ implored him to do so: Barrāḍ went to Ḥīra in order *not* to give trouble to his ally, though being what he was, he misbehaved again. In another version he kills a Khuzāʿī after having made the alliance with Ḥarb and flees to the Yemen, proceeding to Ḥīra from there without apparently even informing his ally of his whereabouts.[64] Either way, the events turn on the fact that he was a troublemaker;[65] and it was wounded pride, not a desire to further the policies of the Meccans, that caused him to murder the escort, the latter having mortally insulted him at Ḥīra.[66] According to the *Aghānī*, he made off with the caravan, taking it to Mecca, though he fled to Khaybar according to the other accounts. But the fact that the Meccans accept his presence in this version means

[62] For a vivid account of life at ʿUkāẓ, including the Fijār episodes, see Wellhausen, *Reste*, pp. 88 ff. The most important accounts of the wars are given by Ibn Ḥabīb, *Munammaq*, pp. 185 ff.; *Aghānī*, XXII, pp. 54 ff.; Balādhurī, *Ansāb*, I, 100 ff. But there are many others, all examined by Landau-Tasseron, "Sinful Wars."

[63] Watt, *Muhammad at Mecca*, p. 11 (where he "doubtless" knew that his action was in accordance with Meccan policy, though he was "presumably" pursuing his own ends); cf. p. 14 (where the fact that an ally of Quraysh made an unprovoked attack on a caravan from Ḥīra to the Yemen [*sic*] would mean that the Meccans were trying to close this route or ensure some control of it). We are explicitly told that Nuʿmān used to send a caravan to ʿUkāẓ every year and that this was one of them (*Aghānī*, XXII, 57; Balādhurī, *Ansāb*, I, 101; Ibn Ḥabīb, *Muḥabbar*, p. 195; *id.*, *Munammaq*, p. 191; Ibn Saʿd, *Ṭabaqāt*, I, 126 f. Compare also Yaʿqūbī, *Taʾrīkh*, II, 14; Ibn Ḥabīb, *Munammaq*, pp. 428 f.; Kister, "Ḥīra," p. 154, on Nuʿmān and this market.

[64] Thus Ibn Ḥabīb, *Munammaq*, p. 191; *id.*, *Muḥabbar*, p. 195.

[65] Cf. the heading *futtāk al-jāhiliyya* under which he is listed in Ibn Ḥabīb, *Muḥabbar*, pp. 192, 195 f.; compare Thaʿālibī, *Thimār*, p. 128. It is, of course, this problem that lies behind Watt's guarded formulation (above, n63).

[66] He had called him an "outlawed dog" to his face when he volunteered to escort the caravan.

no more than that they stood by the alliance, as well they might, since war was coming anyway. The story of Barrāḍ is the story of a misfit and the trouble he caused to everyone around him, and to read Qurashī machinations into it is to miss its point.

In the second place, Quraysh did not win the wars of Fijār; nobody did. What we are told is that Quraysh would mostly lose, but that in the end both parties got tired of fighting, whereupon they negotiated peace, counted their dead, and imposed blood money on the side that had inflicted more casualties than it had suffered. All this is typical of tribal war, not of struggles for commercial supremacy; and if commercial supremacy had been involved, Quraysh could scarcely be said to have achieved it. "Of the four battle days, Quraysh were victorious only in the third one, and were defeated in all the rest," as Landau-Tasseron notes.[67] In Watt's judicious formulation, however, we are informed that "as they were apparently successful, they presumably attained their object"; and in Simon's work the outcome has become a "crushing defeat" inflicted by Quraysh on their opponents, leading to the rise of Qurashī trade with Iraq.[68] Quraysh thus contrive to take control of the Iraq route by a combination of conjecture and misrepresentation.

The stories of the wars of Fijār are works of literature, not records of political or commercial history, as is true of most of our evidence on pre-Islamic Arabia. Whoever first told them was concerned to illustrate Jāhilī society as Jāhilī society had always been, using such episodes and personnel as were remembered; and it is for this that we should use them. The fact that one of these episodes happened to involve the capture of a caravan does not mean that we must attach deep economic or political significance to it:[69] when were caravans *not* being captured in Arabia? Nuʿmān himself had suffered numerous losses before.[70] No

[67] Landau-Tasseron, "Sinful Wars."

[68] Watt, *Muhammad at Mecca*, pp. 14 f.; Simon, "Ḥums et īlāf," p. 227.

[69] As does Simon, for example, not only in connection with the wars of Fijār but also in his discussion of the Persian caravan which was plundered by Tamīmīs ("Ḥums et īlāf," p. 227n).

[70] Cf. Kister, "Ḥīra," pp. 154ff.; Landau-Tasseron, "Sinful Wars," n60 (B. ʿĀmir); Ibn Ḥabīb, *Muḥabar*, pp. 195 f.; Yaʿqūbī, II, 14 f. (Balʿāʾ b. Qays, the Laythī chief who started raiding Nuʿmān's caravans after the latter had killed his brother); Segal, "Arabs in Syriac Literature", p. 108 (Thaʿlabīs from the Byzantine part of the Syrian desert who raid a caravan of Nuʿmān's).

doubt there were frequently tribal rivalries behind this kind of event, but we are making false economic history by elevating such rivalries into struggles for long-term commercial or political objectives.[71] The only commercial effect of Barrāḍ's action, apart from the loss to Nuʿmān, was the suspension of the fair at ʿUkāẓ that year. Quraysh did not oust the Lakhmids of Ḥīra from the route to Iraq in the 590s: the dynasty was abolished by the Persian emperor in 602, so that if the route was closed, as Watt surmises may have been the case, we must credit the fact to the Persians rather than Quraysh. Quraysh did not, at all events, begin to trade regularly in Iraq thereafter. It was Abū Sufyān, the son of Barrāḍ's Meccan ally, who described Iraq as a land in which Quraysh had no permission to trade; and it was still by way of exception that he and other Qurashīs ventured along the Iraq route to Qarada in 624.[72]

[71] Here I must disagree with Landau-Tasseron, who rejects Watt's interpretation of the Fijār wars but not the idea that Quraysh were trying to establish control of the Iraq route. The agents in this interpretation are B. ʿĀmir, who had previously raided one or several of Nuʿmān's caravans. It is postulated that B. ʿĀmir acted in accord with Quraysh and that the object of the aggression was to force Nuʿmān to grant B. ʿĀmir the privilege of escorting his caravans: it was only by having this privilege granted to a friendly tribe that Quraysh could achieve control of the route. But quite apart from being highly conjectural, this theory does not make much sense. B. ʿĀmir may well have intended to obtain the privilege of guarding Ḥīran caravans, but why should Quraysh have assisted them in this? Quraysh are supposed to have wanted control of the route in the sense that the goods that travelled along it went in Qurashī as opposed to Ḥīran or other caravans, or not at all; and it cannot have made much difference to them whether one tribe or the other had the privilege of guarding the caravans of their competitors. If B. ʿĀmir and Quraysh were in cahoots, Qurashī caravans could travel through ʿĀmirī territory regardless of whether B. ʿĀmir were escorts for the Ḥīrans or not; and if B. ʿĀmir wanted to be such escorts, they cannot have helped Quraysh in their supposed efforts to put an end to the Ḥīran caravans.

[72] Cf. ch. 4, pp. 87, 89.

7

WHAT MECCAN TRADE MAY HAVE BEEN

What can we say about the nature of Meccan trade in positive terms? Clearly, it was a local trade. Moreover, it was an Arab trade, that is to say, a trade conducted overwhelmingly with Arabs and generated by Arab rather than by foreign needs. But its precise nature is hard to pin down because of an overriding problem: how could a trade of this kind be combined with a trading centre in *Mecca*?

Meccan trade was a local trade in the sense that the commodities sold were of Arabian origin and destined for consumption in Arabia itself or immediately outside it. Some sources present the transactions of the Meccans as an export trade in return for which bullion was carried back, whereas others on the contrary describe it as an import trade for which bullion was carried to Syria.[1] But whatever the exact role of bullion in their transactions, most accounts envisage the Meccans as having sold commodities in Syria and elsewhere with a view to carrying others back. We do not know what they sold in Ethiopia, except perhaps skins,[2] nor do we know what they sold in the Yemen, except for donkeys. But Ethiopia can perhaps be discounted for purposes of Meccan (as opposed to Qurashī) trade; and though more information about Qurashī transactions in the Yemen would have been welcome, we do at least know that in Syria they sold hides, skins, leather goods of other kinds, clothing, perhaps also animals and clarified butter on occasion, as well as perfume. The commodities specified are in agreement with the modern observation that insofar as Arabia produces anything in excess of its domestic consumption, it is almost entirely due to the nomads and

[1] Cf. above, ch. 4, nos. 1-2.

[2] This is clearly implied by the Najāshī's fondness for Meccan skins (cf. above, ch. 4 nn45-46 f. As argued already, the skins and leather products may in fact have been Yemeni (cf. above, ch. 5, p. 127). Either way it should be noted that leather products are unlikely to have been any rarer in Ethiopia than they were in Syria; by the time of Ibn al-Mujāwir, at least, leather was tanned all over Arabia *and* Ethiopia (*Descriptio*, I, 13).

mountaineers.[3] And what the Meccans carried back was also goods of the kind one would expect. From Syria and Egypt, we are told, they imported fine cloth and clothing,[4] arms,[5] grain,[6] perhaps also oil,[7] fruit[8] and perfume on occasion.[9] From the Yemen they likewise obtained fine cloth and clothing,[10] as well as slaves, ultimately from Ethiopia,[11] "Indian swords,"[12] possibly foodstuffs,[13] and certainly the perfume that they would occasionally sell even abroad. What they bought in Ethiopia is unknown[14] and will again have to be discounted from the point of view of Meccan trade. But such information as we have leaves no doubt that their imports were the necessities and petty luxuries that the inhabitants of Arabia have always had to procure from the fringes of the Fertile Crescent and elsewhere, not the luxury goods with which Lammens

[3] Great Britain, Admiralty, *A Handbook of Arabia*, I, 24.

[4] Cf. above, ch. 4, no. 5.

[5] For Syrian swords from Buṣrā and elsewhere, see F. W. Schwarzlose, *Die Waffen der alten Araber*, p. 131. When the Prophet sold some of the captives of B. Qurayẓa in Syria, he bought weapons and horses in return (Wāqidī, *Maghāzī*, II, 523).

[6] The Meccans imported *ḥubūb*, *darmak* (fine flour), and clothes from Syria according to Qummī, *Tafsīr*, II, 444. ʿAbdallāh b. Judʿān once sent 2,000 camels to Syria for clarified butter, honey, and *burr* (Ibn Kathīr, *Bidāya*, II, 218). Bread is seen as coming from Syria in the account of how Hāshim fed the Meccans after a drought (cf. below, ch. 9, p. 207). The presence of bread and flour in Mecca is taken for granted in several traditions, without specification of origin (cf. Ibn Hishām, *Leben*, pp. 232, 531; Ibn Ḥabīb, *Munammaq*, p. 424; Rāzi, *Mafātīḥ*, VIII, 511). But few of the references given by Lammens for Meccan imports of Syrian grain actually refer to Mecca (cf. "République marchande," p. 47; *Mecque*, p. 307; *L'Arabie occidentale*, p. 22; most refer to Medina).

[7] This is a conjecture based on evidence referring to Medina and elsewhere (cf. Lammens, *Mecque*, p. 301; *id.*, "République marchande," p. 47; *id.*, *L'Arabie occidentale*, p. 22).

[8] Cf. Diḥyā b. Khalīfa's gift of dates, figs, and raisins from Syria to the Prophet (Ibn Ḥabīb, *Munammaq*, p. 28).

[9] This again is a conjecture based on evidence referring to Medina (cf. above, ch. 4, no. 3).

[10] Cf. above, ch. 4, no. 5.

[11] Cf. above, ch. 3 n169; ch. 5 n90.

[12] As conjectured by Jacob, *Beduinenleben*, p. 149; cf. also Schwarzlose, *Waffen*, pp. 127 f. Note that one version of the tribute dispatched by the Persian governor of the Yemen has it include swords (Lyall, *Mufaḍḍalīyāt*, I, 708).

[13] According to Lammens, *Mecque*, pp. 142, 302, the Meccans imported grain from the Sarāt; but he does not give any references. Masʿūdī has it that the month of Ṣafar owed its name to markets in the Yemen at which the Arabs would provision themselves; he does not, however, mention Quraysh in this context (*Murūj*, III, 417).

[14] Though it has been conjectured on lexicographical grounds that here, too, the return trade was in clothing (cf. Baldry, *Textiles in Yemen*, p. 8).

would have them equip themselves abroad.[15] The Meccans, in short, are presented as having exchanged pastoralist products for those of the settled agriculturalists within their reach, an activity also engaged in by the inhabitants of nineteenth-century Ḥā'il. The settlers of Ibn Rashīd's realm, according to Musil, would send at least four great caravans a year to Iraq. They would hire baggage camels from the Bedouin and load them with wool, goats' hair, camels' hair, clarified butter, camel fat, camel saddles, and so forth. They would often be accompanied by camel, sheep, and goat dealers, who would drive the animals they had purchased to Iraq and from there along the Euphrates to Syria, as well as by Bedouin who would sell their animals there and supply themselves with food and clothing.[16] What Musil describes for Ḥā'il in relation to Iraq is very much what the sources describe for Mecca in relation to Syria; and it is, of course, an activity that has been conducted in the peninsula ever since it was colonized by pastoralists.

Meccan trade was thus a trade generated by Arab needs, not by the commercial appetites of the surrounding empires, and it is as traders operating in Arabia rather than beyond its borders that the Meccans should be seen.[17] Arabia to them was not simply a route between the termini of a long-distance trade, but the very area on which their trade was focused. Thus they were active throughout western Arabia from Najrān to southern Syria and the Syrian desert, where they would visit Dūmat al-Jandal.[18] It was perhaps from Dūma that they would make their occasional visits to Ḥīra: this at least would explain both their ignorance of the route to Iraq from Mecca itself and the fact that it is Umayyads, otherwise associated with Syria, who are said to have made the visits in question. It was at all events in western Arabia itself that they had some of their most important markets, that is, the annual fairs held during the holy months at ʿUkāẓ,[19] Dhū'l-Majāz,[20] Majanna and Minā,[21] located in

[15] See for example Lammens, "République marchande," p. 47.

[16] A. Musil, *Northern Neǧd*, p. 241.

[17] Insofar as I have acquired any clarity of vision on this point, I owe it to the comments of Professor A.F.L. Beeston at a Byzantinist seminar in Oxford 1982, at which I presented a preliminary version of this book.

[18] Ibn Ḥabīb, *Muḥabbar*, p. 264 (where they are only said to have provided escorts for others going there); Marzūqī, *Azmina*, II, 162 (where they go in their own right). I know of no concrete illustration of Qurashīs at Dūma.

[19] Ibn Ḥabīb, *Muḥabbar*, pp. 266 f.; Marzūqī, *Azmina*, II, 165; Yaʿqūbī, *Taʾrīkh*, I, 314. The wars of Fijār, discussed in the previous chapter, are all set at ʿUkāẓ.

[20] It was at ʿUkāẓ and Dhū'l-Majāz that the Meccans traded before their trade went in-

the vicinity of Ṭā'if and Mecca. And they are also said to have visited other annual fairs in the region, such as Badr to the north of Mecca[22] and Ḥubāsha to the south.[23] Indeed, they are even said to have visited a fair as distant as Rābiya in the Ḥaḍramawt.[24] In central and eastern Arabia, however, they do not seem to have had much business,[25] though the occasional Qurashī is met in the Yamāma.[26] One tradition claims that the Meccans obtained regular food supplies from the Yamāma, but this is unlikely to be correct.[27] Central and eastern Arabia must have

---

ternational (Thaʿālibī, *Thimār*, p. 115). They are often portrayed as trading there after it had done so (cf. Ibn Ḥabīb, *Munammaq*, p. 236; Ibn Hishām, *Leben*, p. 274; Jāḥiẓ, *Rasā'il*, p. 76; Ibn Saʿd, *Ṭabaqāt*, I, 152).

[21] The presence of Qurashī traders at Majanna is attested only in Wāqidī, *Maghāzī*, I, 388 (where it sounds like mere embroidery). For a Qurashī trader at Minā, see Ṭabarī, *Ta'rīkh*, ser. I, p. 1,162. But all the pilgrim fairs are envisaged as fairs for the Meccans in the sources (see for example Bakrī, *Muʿjam*, p. 660, *s.v.* ʿUkāẓ).

[22] Thus Wāqidī, *Maghāzī*, I, 384, 387; cf. Ibn Saʿd, *Ṭabaqāt*, II, 13. This sounds like more embroidery.

[23] Thus it was at Ḥubāsha rather than at Buṣrā that Muḥammad traded as Khadīja's agent, according to some (ʿAbd al-Razzāq, *Muṣannaf*, V, 320; Ḥassān b. Thābit, *Dīwān*, II, 310; Yāqūt, *Buldān*, II, 192 f., *s.v.*, with an alternative location of the fair at Medina). It was located in Azdī territory six days journey to the south of Mecca, according to Azraqī (*Makka*, p. 131), and was the greatest *sūq* of Tihāma, according to Bakrī (*Muʿjam*, pp. 262, 264; Bakrī also knew that the Prophet had attended this fair).

[24] Ibn Ḥabīb, *Muḥabbar*, p. 267; Marzūqī, *Azmina*, II, p. 165. Again, I know of no concrete illustration of Qurashīs there; the traders who visit the Ḥaḍramawt in Ibn Ḥabīb, *Munammaq*, p. 321, are Kinānīs.

[25] Nobody seems to claim that they visited fairs such as Dabā or Ṣuḥār in Oman. Ibn Ḥabīb does claim that they would act as escorts to caravans visiting Mushaqqar in Baḥrayn (*Muḥabbar*, p. 265); but this claim rests on the belief that Quraysh were inviolable in all Muḍarī territory thanks to Muḍarī respect for kinship ties, a most implausible idea (Muḍar was far too large a group for relations between its members to have been comparable to that between fellow-tribesmen), and Marzūqī merely says that Mushaqqar was visited by all Arab tribes, presumably meaning that it was a fair of major importance, not necessarily that it was visited by Quraysh, as well (Azmina, II, 162 f.).

[26] Thus Bujayr b. al-ʿAwwām is said to have gone to the Yamāma as a trader and to have been killed there by an Azdī in revenge for Abū Uzayhir (Ibn Ḥabīb, *Munammaq*, p. 250). Some versions omit the trade (Balādhurī, *Ansāb*, I, 136; Caskel, *Ǧamhara*, II, s.v. Buǧair b. al-ʿAuwām).

[27] Thus we are told that Thumāma b. Uthāl cut off the supply of grain from the Yamāma to Mecca on his conversion (Ibn Hishām, *Leben*, p. 997; Kister, "Mecca and Tamīm," p. 135). This is a story of exegetical origin. In explanation of Sūra 23:78 (*wa-laqad akhadhnāhum bi'l-ʿadhāb*) we are told that the Prophet prayed for the Meccans to be afflicted with seven years of famine "like the years of Joseph" and that Abū Sufyān com-

been commercially linked with Iraq in those days no less than they were in later times—and all the more so in those days thanks to the Persian presence.

The sources thus describe the Meccans as having been active in an area extending from Syria to the fringes of the Yemen, with somewhat obscure extensions into the Ḥaḍramawt in the east and Ethiopia in the west. This was the area that they united in a single commercial network, not Syria, the Yemen, Ethiopia, and Iraq, or, in other words, not the countries surrounding western Arabia, but western Arabia itself. The fact that parts of this area had been incorporated in the Byzantine and Persian empires should be dismissed as irrelevant. Quraysh did not trade with Byzantine Syria, let alone Sāsānid Iraq. They traded with Syria, or more precisely *in* Syria, occasionally also in Iraq, because southern Syria and Ḥīra formed part of Arabia in all respects except one.

If we think of this area as a single one, Meccan trade takes on the appearance not so much of an export-import trade as of a distribution of diverse goods within Arabia itself. Southern Syria and its Egyptian fringes were no doubt the most important settled economy within this area; but it should still be seen as belonging to Arabia, and agriculturalist products handled by the Meccans came from the Yemen and Ṭā'if, too.[28] Similarly, it was not just in Syria and Egypt that the Meccans sold pastoralist products, such goods being exchanged within the peninsula, as well.[29] If the Meccans were *tujjār al-ʿarab*, as Ibn al-Kalbī insists,[30]

plained to him, saying that Muḥammad had killed fathers with the sword and sons with hunger; in response, this verse was revealed. Alternatively, the famine arose because Thumāma had cut off the food supplies from the Yamāma, and this was why Abū Sufyān went to complain (Ṭabarī, *Jāmiʿ*, XVIII, 30 f.; Suyūṭī, *Durr*, v, 13; Ibn Kathīr, *Tafsīr*, III, 252; Ṭūsī, *Tibyān*, VII, 384 f.; Qurṭubī, *Tafsīr*, XII, 143). But some took the Qur'ānic *ʿadhāb* to be a reference to Badr (Suyūṭī, *Durr*, v, 14) or the conquest of Mecca (Qurṭubī, *loc. cit.*) rather than a famine. As in the case of all exegetical stories, the event itself is of doubtful historicity, and the sources do not in general envisage Mecca and the Yamāma as closely linked until after the conquests: by the mid-Umayyad period both Mecca and Medina received food supplies from the Yamāma and Baḥrayn (Aḥmad b. Yaḥya al-Balādhurī, *Ansāb al-ashrāf*, XI, 139 f.; note that it is Ibn ʿAbbās, an exegete, who invokes the story of Ibn Uthāl here).

[28] As regards the Yemen, this has been shown already; as regards Ṭā'if, note Abū Sufyān's sale of raisins from there at ʿUkāẓ (above, ch. 4, no. 8).

[29] Quraysh selling donkeys in the Sarāt and buying camels and sheep, presumably for their own use, in Mecca (cf. below, ch. 8 n56).

[30] Ibn al-Kalbī in his *īlāf*-tradition (cf. the references given above, ch. 4 n43), where

they were traders of the Arabs in the sense of suppliers to them; and this is, in fact, also how both Ibn al-Kalbī's *īlāf*-tradition and its mirror image on the end of Meccan trade present them. Non-Arabs used to bring goods to Mecca, we are told, until Quraysh took over this task, or else it was Quraysh who used to do it until non-Arabs took over. Either way, trade is seen as an activity engaged in for the sake of a purely Arab problem—the provisioning of Mecca—and Syria, the Yemen, Ethiopia, and Iraq are simply so many places from which provisions were obtained, not links in an overall commercial network. Naturally, these and other accounts are both chauvinistic and qur'anically inspired,[31] but the tradition at large agrees with them. The sources have no sense whatever of imperial needs that could be exploited by Quraysh, only of Arab, primarily Meccan, needs that had to be fulfilled. If there is any truth to the sources, the Meccans thus fulfilled a role similar to that of the inhabitants of Ḥā'il or the ʿUqayl. The ʿUqayl (or, strictly speaking, the wholesale dealers employing agents known as ʿUqayl) exported camels to Syria and Egypt, to a lesser extent also Iraq, and imported goods such as coffee, rice, spices, and arms in return, distributing them among the Arabs from their centres in the Qaṣīm.[32] Like the merchants of Ḥā'il, they were *tujjār al-ʿarab*. What they exported was nothing very rare or precious, and what they imported certainly were not opulent luxuries. Nonetheless, their activities made them very rich. It is traders of this kind, not Minaeans or Sabaeans, still less Italian merchant republics, that one should have in mind when thinking about Quraysh.[33]

This conclusion raises two further questions. First, it reinstates the problem of Meccan commercial dominance. As has been seen, we cannot credit the Meccans with control of any routes in Arabia, but should we envisage them as dominating the exchange of goods in the peninsula itself? Naturally, they cannot have done so in the whole of Arabia. No

---

Hāshim describes Quraysh as such to the Byzantine emperor, for all that we have just been told that Quraysh did not trade outside Mecca at the time.

[31] Cf. the overtones of Abraham's prayer for sustenance and safety (2:120) in Ṭabarī's account of the Ethiopian *matjar* (cited above, ch. 5 n94).

[32] A. Musil, *The Manners and Customs of the Rwala Bedouins*, pp. 278 f.; cf. also Foreign Office, *Arabia*, p. 73.

[33] Cf. Lammens, "République marchande," p. 29; Hitti, *Capital Cities*, p. 9.

trading people ever did;[34] and Quraysh, as noted already, are not commonly seen in action in central or eastern Arabia. Equally, the fact that they had to coexist with Byzantine, Yemeni, Jewish, and various other traders in western Arabia itself means that it is difficult to credit them with a dominance such as that enjoyed by Ḥā'il, that is, a dominant position in the general exchange of pastoralist and agriculturalist products within a specific region. And it is also hard to award them a dominance such as that enjoyed by the ʿUqayl, who controlled the export trade in a specific commodity (camels) throughout all or most of the peninsula: inasmuch as the Meccans do not seem to have handled Yemeni leather goods,[35] such control as they had of this trade must have been limited to northwest Arabia. The question thus reduces to whether they dominated the exchange of goods at the pilgrim fairs of this region.[36] Here the evidence is somewhat inconclusive.

It is customary to present the Meccans as having controlled these fairs. Indeed, the fairs in question are often described in a fashion which the innocent reader might take to suggest that the Meccans owned them. But this, at least, they did not. The fairs were cooperative ventures. The sites were located in the territories of various tribes (all non-Qurashī), but subject to no authority, being devoid of permanent inhabitants.[37] In the holy months, when the use of arms was forbidden, large numbers of tribesmen would come together here as pilgrims and as traders: ʿUkāẓ, for example, attracted visitors from Quraysh, Hawāzin, Khuzāʿa, Gha-

[34] Even the Minaeans, who probably came closer to it than any other trading people, had to coexist with Sabaeans, Gerrheans, Gebbanites, and no doubt others, too.

[35] The only suggestion of a Qurashī interest in Yemeni leather goods is the *adīm Khawlānī* that was used as writing material by the Prophet in Medina (Wāqidī, *Maghāzī*, I, 13). Presumably it came from Khawlān in the Yemen rather than the Syrian village of that name (cf. Yāqūt, *Buldān*, II, 499, *s.v.*; leather is mentioned as writing material elsewhere in the literature, too, but without indication of its provenance). But this scarcely suffices to establish a Qurashī trade in such goods.

[36] There were clearly pilgrim fairs elsewhere in the peninsula, too. Thus the *sawāqiṭ* who imported dates from the Yamāma visited the Yamāma, not the Ḥijāz, in the holy months (Mubarrad, *Kāmil*, p. 202).

[37] Azraqī, *Makka*, p. 131 (ʿUkāẓ was in the territory of Naṣr of Qays ʿAylān, Majanna in that of Kināna, and Dhū'l-Majāz, apparently, in that of Hudhayl). Simon goes to the other extreme when he presents these tribes as having dominated the fairs ("Ḥums et īlāf," p. 215). Wellhausen correctly observes that "niemand war hier Herr im Hause" (*Reste*, p. 92).

ṭafān, Aslam, and others.[38] We are told that arms would be deposited with a Qurashī at ʿUkāẓ, and this certainly shows that Quraysh were respected there.[39] But so were Tamīm, for it was Tamīmīs who had the function of hereditary judges;[40] and the view that they had it by gracious permission of Quraysh rather than by common consent is unpersuasive.[41] This point apart, the view that Quraysh enjoyed particular importance at the pilgrim fairs arises largely from the fact that the pilgrim fairs were of particular importance to them, which is not quite the same thing. Naturally, we hear more about Quraysh at these fairs than about other participants: it was, after all, they who produced the Prophet. But it was at ʿUkāẓ that agents of Nuʿmān of Ḥīra sold Iraqi goods, buying Yemeni ones in return;[42] and though it may have been Qurashīs who carried the Yemeni goods there, we are not told that this was so. Others, moreover, offered goods such as camels and cattle,[43] swords,[44] slaves,[45] precious metals,[46] and clarified butter.[47] And we are hardly to take it that the sale of leather and raisins at ʿUkāẓ was in the hands of Quraysh alone.[48] In short, one does not get the impression that the pilgrim fairs

[38] Ibn Ḥabīb, *Muḥabbar*, p. 267; Marzūqī, *Azmina*, II, 165. Yaʿqūbī merely says that the participants were Quraysh and other Arabs, mostly of Muḍar (*Taʾrīkh*, I, 314).

[39] *Aghānī*, XXII, 59.

[40] The numerous attestations of this point are lined up by Kister, "Mecca and Tamīm," pp. 145 ff.

[41] With all due respect to Kister, who sees Quraysh as having entrusted this and other functions to Tamīm (cf. the preceding note).

[42] For his annual caravans to ʿUkāẓ, see above, ch. 6 n63; for his purchase of Yemeni goods there, see ch. 4 n56.

[43] Marzūqī, *Azmina*, II, 168.

[44] Cf. *Aghānī*, XI, 119, where a killer disposes of his victim's sword at ʿUkāẓ, implying that this was the place where one sold whatever one might wish to get rid of.

[45] Khadīja's nephew bought Zayd from Qaynīs at ʿUkāẓ (Ibn Saʿd, *Ṭabaqāt*, III, 40); it was also here that Fākih b. al-Mughīra bought the woman who was to become the mother of ʿAmr b. al-ʿĀṣ; like Zayd she was the victim of a raid (Ibn al-Athīr, *Usd*, IV, 116).

[46] Marzūqī, *Azmina*, II, 168 (*naqd*). Presumably it was here that the Meccans obtained some of their bullion.

[47] *Aghānī*, I, 209.

[48] For Abū Sufyān's sale of raisins at ʿUkāẓ, see Ibn Hishām, *Leben*, p. 590. For the leather trade there, see ch. 4, nn56, 58. There is also a reference to the sale of leather at Dhū'l-Majāz in Nābigha al-Dhubyānī, *Dīwān*, no. VI, 14 f., where it is sold by a Ḥirmiyya. Was she a Meccan? Lammens proposed to emend her into a Jarmiyya (*Mecque*, pp. 154n, 264 f.).

would have lost importance if the Meccans had withdrawn; they certainly survived the conquests, falling into desuetude only in the late Umayyad period and thereafter.[49] None of this, of course, rules out the possibility that Quraysh dominated the distribution of Syrian and Egyptian goods at these fairs and other markets in Arabia.[50] But like the possibility that they dominated the leather trade in the north, this hypothesis can be neither proved nor disproved.

The second question is a more important one: how was it possible for Quraysh to engage in a trade of the kind described from Mecca? Exchanges of pastoralist products for those of settled agriculturalists usually take place between communities located within reasonable distance of each other, such as Ḥā'il and Iraq, or between settled communities and Bedouin who, though sometimes very far away, regularly visit the communities in the course of their migratory cycle. But Mecca is separated from southern Syria by a distance of some eight hundred miles; the Meccans were not Bedouin; and the goods that they sold, moreover, were readily available in Syria itself. The Meccans, in short, are described as having gone on regular journeys of an arduous nature and one month's duration in order to sell coal in Newcastle, being of the opinion that what they sold would be cheaper than the local varieties, and frequently returning with local varieties of the very goods that they had sold. It makes no sense.

It is true that the inhabitants of pre-oil Arabia are known to have covered huge distances for small rewards,[51] and there is an example of a trading people doing precisely that in the above-mentioned ʿUqayl, who collected their camels all over the peninsula for sale in Damascus

[49] ʿUkāẓ was abandoned in the wake of Abū Ḥamza's conquest of Mecca in 129 A.H., Dhū'l-Majāz and Majanna sometime thereafter (Azraqī, *Makka*, p. 131. Lammens wrongly postulates that they were suppressed in the course of Muḥammad's blockade of Mecca, or at least after the *fatḥ*, when the merchants of Mecca transferred to Medina, cf. *Mecque*, p. 112).

[50] For the sale of Syrian, Egyptian, and Iraqi goods at ʿUkāẓ, see Marzūqī, *Azmina*, II, 168, where it is not said, however, that they were sold by Quraysh. The Iraqi goods referred to are presumably those dispatched by the king of Ḥīra (cf. above, ch. 6 n63).

[51] "The light-bodied Arabian will journey upon his thelûl, at foot-pace, hundreds of leagues for no great purpose" (Doughty, *Travels*, II, 534).

and elsewhere.[52] The ʿUqayl thus specialized in a commodity that was also available in Syria itself, and the fact that they could do so shows that transport costs must have been low. If the ʿUqayl could do it with camels, why should Quraysh have been unable to do it with hides and skins?

The answer is because camels can walk, whereas their disembodied hides and skins cannot. The ʿUqayl operated as itinerant traders, dispersing among the tribes every year and returning with as many camels as a man can manage, or more if they hired herders to accompany them part or all of the way, as they frequently seem to have done.[53] Bedouin and itinerant traders have in common the fact that travelling is simply another form of living to them: the activity involves few or no extra expenses. But hides and skins, not to mention woollens, have to be carried, and the quantities that an individual can carry are limited. Quraysh are accordingly presented as having organized caravans; and though some of their goods were picked up on the way, according to Ibn al-Kalbī's *īlāf*-tradition, Mecca must have been the primary centre of collection inasmuch as it was from here that the caravans set out. But caravan trade means transport costs: goods simply cannot be transported by caravan without expenses over and above what it would cost for the people involved to subsist on the way. Animals have to be hired, containers to be provided, drivers to be paid, and arrangements for fodder, food, and water on the way have to be made.[54] The loss of an occasional caravan, moreover, is a far more expensive matter than the loss of an occasional ʿUqaylī.

There are examples of caravaneers carrying humble goods for a long way in Arabia, too. Thus natives of nineteenth-century ʿUnayza, a city in the Qaṣīm, found it worth their while to transport clarified butter collected from the local Bedouin all the way from ʿUnayza to Mecca, covering some 450 miles and spending twenty days or more on the way.[55] We are told that they would recoup by charging twice as much for their

[52] Cf. the references given above, n32.

[53] Musil, *Rwala*, p. 280.

[54] Later evidence shows the transport costs of caravan trade to have been surprisingly low (cf. Steensgaard, *Carracks, Caravans and Companies*, pp. 31 ff.). As soon as a desert had to be negotiated, though, transport costs rose steeply (*ibid.*, p. 39); and the calculations apply only to caravan trade in valuable goods: "of course, for cheaper goods it was an altogether different matter" (*ibid.*, p. 39, with an example at p. 40).

[55] Doughty, *Travels*, II, pp. 481 ff., cf. p. 345.

goods as they were worth locally, and Wāqidī likewise has the Meccans making a gross profit of 100% in Syria.[56] Where, then, is the difference? The journey to Syria was much longer, but even so the Meccan enterprise can hardly be said to have been of a different order.

The parallel breaks down in two ways, however. First, the ʿUnayzīs were servicing tourists in a city that produced nothing in itself, and that also lacked a fertile hinterland; clarified butter *was* a rare commodity in Mecca, and prices were scarcely an objection. But southern Syria in the sixth and seventh centuries was neither a tourist land nor a land so deprived of resources as Mecca and environs. The customers of Quraysh were tribesmen, villagers, and townsmen who produced most of what they needed themselves and who could have obtained most of what they needed in addition from local caravaneers such as the Christian Ishmaelites who operated at Nessana. They were under no constraint to buy their hides, clarified butter, or coarse clothing from traders coming from almost twice as far away as the ʿUnayzīs. In short, it is hard to believe that there was a market in southern Syria for humble goods transported from so far afield.

Second, the ʿUnayzīs had their base in the Qaṣīm, the fertile part of central Arabia in which the ʿUqayl organization also had its centre, whereas Quraysh had theirs in the Ḥijāz, or more precisely in the lowlands thereof known as Tihāma. Not only Mecca but the entire Ḥijāz is described in the modern literature as patchy in terms of agriculture, poor in terms of pasture land, and generally quite unproductive.[57] The exegetes inform us that Quraysh engaged in trade precisely because there was no other way in which they could make a living in Mecca.[58] But the idea that trade in other people's commodities is something one can pull out of one's sleeve for purposes of occupying places unsuitable for human, or at least settled, occupation is somewhat naive. How, for example, did a city bereft of pasture land provide fodder for the 1,000 or even 2,500 camels of which their caravans are sometimes said to have been composed?[59] The figures are, of course, quite unrealistic,[60] but

[56] Doughty, *Travels*, II, 487; Wāqidī, *Maghāzī*, I, p. 200, cf. p. 387. Wāqidī's details, unknown to Ibn Isḥāq, are common in the literature after him.

[57] Foreign Office, *Arabia*, pp. 9, 11, 89; Admiralty, *Handbook of Arabia*, I, 98 ff.

[58] Thus for example Ibn Qutayba, *Mushkil al-Qurʾān*, p. 319.

[59] Cf. Wāqidī, *Maghāzī*, I, 12, 27, on the caravans that the Prophet tried to intercept at

they serve to highlight the problem. The Meccans had to import all their foodstuffs, and presumably fodder too, not to mention the *qaraẓ* which they used in tanning.[61] Some of their provisions, notably fruit, came from neighbouring Ṭā'if, a city that God is supposed to have moved from Syria to Arabia for the express purpose of ensuring that the Meccans had something to eat.[62] But man does not live on fruit alone, still less do beasts, and other foodstuffs had to be imported from further afield.[63] But foodstuffs imported from far away must have been expensive, and grain carried by caravan from Syria at a distance of some eight hundred miles must have been incredibly costly: that which Medina, some two hundred miles to the north of Mecca, imported from southern Syria is explicitly said to have been a luxury that only the rich could afford.[64] How, then, could the Meccans at large afford it? How, in other words, could they trade in Syria from a place that was not only far away, but also devoid of food and other amenities that human beings and other animals generally require to engage in activities of any kind?

The standard answer to this question is that Mecca was a sanctuary that attracted pilgrims. Quraysh, we are told, began by trading with the pilgrims and in due course extended their sphere of activities, no doubt spending some of their pilgrim money in Syria. I shall come back to this hypothesis in the next chapter. All I wish to say here is that even if it were true, it would not solve the problem. How could the Meccans cope with thousands of pilgrims, their mounts, and other animals on top of the local human and animal population? It was possible after the con-

Buwāṭ and Badr. As usual, the information is unknown to Ibn Isḥāq, but commonly reproduced in the literature after Wāqidī.

[60] Though they are generally taken at face value (thus even by Groom, *Frankincense*, p. 162, despite his firsthand knowledge of Arabia). The number of camels is far too high and the ratio of men to camels far too low: 30 men manage 1,000 camels and 100 men 2,500 camels in Wāqidī; but 70 men (30 of them drivers) manage 170 camels in Doughty (*Travels*, II, p. 488). The only reason why we find the size of Wāqidī's caravans plausible is that we know of huge pilgrim carvans going to Mecca in Islamic times. Wāqidī was, of course, familiar with these caravans, too.

[61] Cf. Ibn al-Mujāwir, *Descriptio*, I, 32, where Mecca imports *qaraẓ* from ʿAqīq.

[62] Azraqī, *Makka*, p. 41; cf. also Ibn al-Mujāwir, *Descriptio*, I, 22, where we are told under a different *isnād* that Ṭā'if used to be *min arḍ Filasṭīn*.

[63] Cf. above, p. 150.

[64] Cf. the *ḥadīth* of Rifāʿa b. Zayd (Balādhurī, *Ansāb*, I, 278; Ibn al-Athīr, *Usd*, IV, 263; and elsewhere).

quests, but only thanks to regular imports of grain from Egypt (by sea, of course), lavish digging of wells, and other forms of attention from the rulers of the Middle East, who had infinitely more resources at their disposal than the pre-Islamic Meccans. As far as pre-Islamic Mecca is concerned, the more people we choose to place in it, the more imports of expensive food by caravan we need to postulate. Naturally pilgrim money ought to have helped, if pilgrim money was indeed available. But even if we accept that Mecca was an object of pilgrimage in pre-Islamic times, we have to confront the problem that the Meccans are almost invariably said *not* to have traded with the pilgrims.[65] And even if we are willing to impugn the veracity of the sources on this point, we are still left with the problem that the Meccans invested their money in commodities of the kind that could not be transported from Mecca to Syria by land without becoming more expensive than Syrian varieties of similar or higher quality. Why would the Syrians buy these commodities? How could Quraysh afford to import necessities at such a price and on such a scale? Why, in short, was Qurashī trade a viable enterprise?

There are at least four ways in which this problem could be solved. All four, however, require rejection of at least one proposition on which there is total agreement in the sources; in other words, all four require the adoption of a more sceptical attitude to these sources than has prevailed so far in this work. So far I have analyzed discrepancies between the secondary literature and the sources, and between statements made in the sources themselves, without querying the fundamental reliability of the tradition; on the contrary, I have presupposed it: this is how I have isolated the body of evidence with which we must now try to reconstruct the nature of Meccan trade. But now it seems that the overall reliability of the tradition *must* be queried: the sources are agreed on what can scarcely be called other than mutually contradictory propositions. Some readers may be inclined to accept these propositions *bilā kayf*, arguing that Meccan trade was as described, however little sense it may appear to make; but this seems an unsatisfactory solution. If Meccan trade existed, it must have been trade of an intelligible kind; and if the sources fail to describe it as such, then we must consider the possibility that the sources are at fault.

If we chose to do so, the first and most obvious hypothesis to try out

[65] I shall take up this point in the following chapter.

is that the trading centre of Quraysh was located much closer to Syria than modern Mecca, that is to say, somewhere in the northern Ḥijāz within easy reach of Buṣrā, Adhriʿāt, and Gaza. If Quraysh were based in this area, they would no longer be engaged in the peculiar task of selling imported coal in Newcastle, but rather in that of distributing coal of local origin in Newcastle and environs; and the fact that they frequently bought identical or similar goods for themselves would cease to be odd. In favour of this idea, it could be said that the relationship between Mecca and Syria comes across as unusually close in the sources. Just as the Meccans would visit Syria, so Syrian and other Byzantine traders would visit Mecca;[66] and Mecca was also linked with Byzantine Syria in political terms. Thus Quṣayy is said to have received Byzantine assistance for his conquest of Mecca,[67] while ʿUthmān b. al-Ḥuwayrith thought that the Byzantines might like to have a client king there.[68] It was from the Syrian desert that Quṣayy arrived for his conquest of the city, more precisely from the land of ʿUdhra, a Quḍāʿī tribe; and his Quḍāʿī relatives participated in the conquest, too.[69] Indeed, the Qurashī link with Byzantium was such that it was a Qurashī in Syria, according to Theophanes, who gave warning to the Byzantines when the Muslim invasion of Syria began.[70] Topographically, Syria was also far better known to Quraysh than any other *matjar* of theirs. Names such as Buṣrā, Adhriʿāt, Zarqā', Maʿān, Balqā', Sharāt, and Gaza are mentioned with some frequency, and the sights of southern Syria are treated as landmarks familiar to the Meccans at large.[71] Thus when Āmina was

[66] Cf. above, ch. 6 nn26-28.

[67] Ibn Qutayba, *Maʿārif*, p. 279.

[68] Cf. Fāsī, *Shifā'*, pp. 143 f.; Abū'l-Baqā', *Manāqib*, fols. 10b-11a (these are the sources referred to previously in connection with ʿUthmān's envisaged tribute); Ibn Ḥabīb, *Munammaq*, pp. 178 ff.; Muṣʿab al-Zubayrī, *Nasab Quraysh*, pp. 209 f.; Aḥmad b. Yaḥyā al-Balādhurī, *Ansāb al-ashrāf*, iv b, 126 f.; Kalāʿī, *Iktifā'*, pp. 316 f.; cf. also Kister, "Mecca and Tamīm," p. 140n.

[69] On the death of Quṣayy's father, his mother married an ʿUdhrī and went to live in Syria, taking Quṣayy with her; on learning his true origins, Quṣayy returned to Mecca and conquered it from Khuzāʿa with the help of his half-brother Rizāh, who came *fī jamʿ min al-Shām wa-afnā' Quḍāʿa* (Ibn Ḥabīb, *Munammaq*, pp. 16 f., 82 ff.; Yaʿqūbī, *Ta'rīkh*, i, 273 ff.; Ibn Hishām, *Leben*, pp. 75 f.; Balādhurī, *Ansāb*, i, 48 ff. The story is told in other sources, too).

[70] Theophanes, *Chronographia*, i, 335, A.M. 6123 (a *Korasenos* called Koutaba; cf. *ibid.*, p. 355, A.M. 6169, where Muʿāwiya has a council of *amīr*s and *Korasenōn*, Qurashīs).

[71] The Meccan familiarity with Syrian towns such as Buṣrā also impressed Lammens (*Mecque*, p. 142).

pregnant and a great light shone forth from her, it was the castles of Buṣrā, not those of Yathrib or the Yemen, that she could see by it;[72] and God himself was of the opinion that the Meccans would pass by the petrified remains of Lot's people in southern Palestine "in the morning and in the evening."[73] One would not have guessed from this remark that the Meccans had to travel some eight hundred miles to see the remains in question.

Quraysh, of course, also traded at the pilgrim fairs, and these are said to have been located near modern Ṭā'if and Mecca.[74] But the pilgrim fairs were held during annual festivals, not once a week or every day, and contrary to what is often asserted, no advantage was to be derived from a location close to them: throughout most of the year they were deserted.[75] Once a year they attracted visitors from far afield, and Quraysh may well have been among those who were willing to cover large distances in order to participate. But for purposes of everyday life, trading had to be conducted somewhere else; and this somewhere else, it could be argued, was the northern Ḥijāz and southern Syria.

If we adopt this position, we have another problem on our hands: how do we account for the evidence linking Mecca with the Yemen and Ethiopia? Direct trading relations between Mecca and Ethiopia could be denied and those between Mecca and the Yemen could be belittled: it is not implausible that a successful trading community in the north should have despatched occasional caravans to the Yemen. But this is to evade the problem rather than to solve it. Meccan trade in the Yemen is described as more than incidental; there is a fair amount of material on Meccan relations with tribes to the south of modern Mecca, notably Daws of Azd Sarāt;[76] and both the Yemen and Ethiopia are politically prominent in the sources on the rise of Islam.

[72] Ibn Hishām, *Leben*, p. 102; Ibn Sa'd, *Ṭabaqāt*, I, 102, 149 (*quṣūr* and *aswāq* of Buṣrā); 'Abd al-Razzāq, *Muṣannaf*, v, 318 (*quṣūr* of Syria).

[73] Qur'ān, 37:138. The exegetes naturally take the observation to refer to Qurashīs on trading journeys, Sudūm being on their way to Syria (see for example Ṭabarī, *Jāmi'*, XXIII, 56; Bayḍāwī, *Anwār*, II, 333).

[74] 'Ukāẓ was located one *barīd* from Ṭā'if on the Ṣan'ā' road, Majanna one *barīd* from Mecca, and Dhū'l-Majāz one *farsakh* from 'Arafa (in its turn located about thirteen miles east of Mecca on the road to Ṭā'if), cf. Azraqī, *Makka*, p. 131. On the fairs in general, see Wellhausen, *Reste*, pp. 87 ff. For further references, see below, ch. 8 n11.

[75] "Sonst war es ein toter Flecken," as Wellhausen observes with reference to 'Ukāẓ (*Reste*, p. 92).

[76] Cf. Ibn Ḥabīb, *Munammaq*, pp. 234 ff., 280 ff.

Given that there is no way of eliminating the overriding importance of Syria, it might thus be argued that Quraysh had two trading centres rather than one, possibly to be envisaged as an original settlement and a later offshoot. Whichever might be the original settlement, there would be a centre in the north, associated above all with Umayyads, and another somewhere in the south, associated primarily with Hāshimites and Makhzūmīs, the two being linked by common origin, commercial relations, and marriage ties. Such a hypothesis would wreak much more havoc in the traditional account of Muḥammad's life than a mere relocation of Mecca. Yet, as will be seen, Muslim accounts of the Meccan sanctuary also suggest that more than one place is being described.

A third possibility is that we should make a sharp distinction between Mecca and Qurashī trade, or in other words, envisage Quraysh as a trading people operating more or less independently of the place in which they were recruited. Such trading peoples are well known from pre-oil Arabia. Thus Pliny's Gebbanitae as reconstructed by Beeston originated, perhaps, in the Niṣāb area, but operated all over southwest Arabia, handling frankincense, cinnamon, and other aromatics wherever they went, and setting themselves up in a number of towns outside their homeland, which does not appear to have functioned as the centre of either collection or distribution.[77] Similarly, the ʿUqayl were active wherever there were camels. The families who organized the trade were settled in the Qaṣīm, where the agents likewise tended to be recruited. But though the Qaṣīm to some extent served as the centre of collection and distribution, much of the trade was conducted outside it.[78] There is an even more striking example in the Kubaysīs, all or most of whom came from Kubaysa in Iraq, but who operated as itinerant traders in Arabia, trading practically everywhere, it seems, except in Kubaysa itself.[79] All three peoples specialized in certain commodities as types of trade rather than a certain region, and in the case of the Kubaysīs and ʿUqaylīs this was clearly a result of the dispersed nature of both goods and customers. Since Quraysh likewise handled goods produced everywhere in the peninsula, it makes sense that they should have been widely dispersed, operating as far away as Syria and the Ḥaḍramawt, and even Ethiopia, without much overall connection between their ac-

[77] Cf. Beeston, "Pliny's Gebbanitae"; *id.*, "Some Observations," pp. 7 f.

[78] Cf. the references given above, n32.

[79] Musil, *Rwala*, p. 269.

tivities in north and south. Mecca would simply be the place of recruitment, to some extent perhaps of organization, but not the centre of collection. There would not be any one centre of collection, but rather numerous minor ones; and insofar as there was any centre of distribution, this was clearly the pilgrim fairs, notably ʿUkāẓ and Dhū'l-Majāz, not Mecca—a point to which I shall come back. This model would have the additional advantage of making Quraysh extremely well connected, especially in the western half of the peninsula, without crediting them with a political predominance or "Meccan commonwealth" supposedly built up on the Ethiopian conquest of the Yemen.

The sources, of course, insist that Mecca was the centre of Qurashī trade, being the city for which all imports were destined and from which all caravans set out; and though Ibn al-Kalbī has Qurashī caravaneers pick up goods from local tribes on the way to Syria in his *īlāf*-tradition, neither he nor any other source known to me envisages them as trading on the way. What is more, if we distinguish between Mecca and Qurashī trade, we run into problems with the traditional account of how Muḥammad forced Mecca to surrender. But, on the one hand, the ʿUqaylī model could perhaps be modified to avoid this problem. Thus it might be argued that Mecca was a transfer point for most goods handled by Quraysh even though most buying and selling took place outside it: *pace* Ibn al-Kalbī and others, they *did* trade on the way. On the other hand, it could be argued that the traditional account of how Muḥammad forced Mecca to surrender should be rejected. For one thing, the number of caravans threatened or intercepted by Muḥammad is considerably larger in Wāqidī than in Ibn Isḥāq: the three caravans that are plundered by the Muslims over a period of five or six years in the latter's work scarcely suffice to explain why a trading city of major importance, let alone one backed by a "Meccan Commonwealth" should have surrendered to a nest of robbers. And if the number of caravans involved increased at the same exponential rate of growth before Ibn Isḥāq as it did between Ibn Isḥāq and Wāqidī, we soon arrive at a stage at which not a single one remains. For another thing, it is by no means obvious that Mecca did surrender peacefully. "We trampled upon Mecca by force with our swords," as ʿAbbās b. Mirdās remembered it.[80] "The Muslims advanced their swords against them, beating so that one could hear

[80] Ibn Hishām, *Leben*, p. 860; republished with notes and further references in ʿAbbās b. Mirdās, *Dīwān*, XXIV, 8.

nothing except the cries of men in battle," as another poet put it.[81] "Our swords have left you a slave, and ʿAbd al-Dār, their leaders, are slave girls," as Ḥassān b. Thābit boasted.[82] And early lawyers were also of the opinion that Mecca had been conquered by force.[83] There is thus no reason to reject the ʿUqaylī model simply because it is at odds with the received version of Muḥammad's life.

Yet whichever model we adopt, the fact remains that two areas in particular are reflected in the traditions on the Prophet's life, that is, southern Syria and the northern Ḥijāz on the one hand, the Sarāt and other places to the south of modern Mecca on the other. Why should this be so? Where was Muḥammad active before the *hijra*, and which was the city that he forced to surrender or conquered by force? Where was the sanctuary? There appears to be no way of making sense of Qurashī trade without undermining the tradition at large.

Finally, it could be argued that the entire attempt to reconstruct the nature of Meccan trade is futile. If the sources assert that the Meccans stopped trading outside Mecca or started doing so, exported commodities in return for which they were paid in bullion or exported bullion in return for which they bought commodities, or exported commodities in return for others, then one has every right to suspect that what the sources preserve is not recollections of what Meccan trade was like, but rather versions of what early storytellers thought it could have been like, each version being perfectly plausible in itself because it is based on knowledge of the kinds of trade that were conducted in Arabia. If this is so, it is not surprising that the traditions fail to add up to a coherent picture, nor should we attempt to make them do so. It would not be the case that certain details are wrong and others right, but that all should be dismissed as embroidery on general themes such as trade, wealth, raids, and the like.

[81] J. Wellhausen, ed. and tr., "Letzter Teil der Lieder der Hudhailiten," p. 31 = 137 (no. 183), where it is attributed to Abū Raʿʿās al-Sāhilī. The poem is also cited in Ibn Hishām, *Leben*, p. 818, with much the same story about the author, here Ḥimās b. Qays (similarly Wāqidī, *Maghāzī*, II, 823, without the poem). But we are now assured that the poem does not refer to the conquest of Mecca as such, only to an isolated pocket of resistance led by the three men whose names are mentioned in the poem.

[82] Ḥassān b. Thābit in Ibn Hishām, *Leben*, p. 829 (= *Dīwān*, ed. Hirschfeld, no. I, lines 22 f.). ʿArafat rejected this line (*Dīwān*, I, 19 f.).

[83] Kister, "Some Reports," p. 87.

There is nothing in the present state of research to indicate which of these hypotheses would be most profitable to pursue. All presuppose that the sources are wrong on certain fundamental points; and since this proposition has not, so far, been widely accepted, we lack a sense of where and in what respects their version of the events leading to the rise of Islam is at its weakest: the fact that Meccan trade itself should have been treated as unproblematic in the secondary literature is a case in point. It should be clear from these hypotheses, though, that Mecca itself is no less of a problem than Meccan trade. Exactly where it was is far from clear. In what follows I shall show that *what* it was is equally uncertain.

8

THE SANCTUARY AND MECCAN TRADE

The genesis of Meccan trade is conventionally explained with reference to the fact that Mecca was a *ḥaram* or sanctuary area. On the one hand, it was the object of an annual pilgrimage. It thus became a pilgrim fair, "a typical . . . combination of pilgrim center and marketplace," as Donner puts it.[1] On the other hand it was inviolable, no bloodshed being permitted within it. It was thus apt to attract settlers and visitors all the year round, and according to Watt it became a commercial center because it was a place "to which men could come without fear of molestation."[2] It is not always clear in the secondary literature whether it was the annual pilgrimage or the permanent inviolability, or both, that stimulated the growth of trade; nor is it always clear when the sanctuary began to have its stimulating effect: according to some, Mecca was a cultic and commercial center even in antiquity, though it is more commonly said only to have developed into one on its occupation by Quraysh.[3] There is not, however, any disagreement on the basic point: one way or the other, Meccan *ḥaram* and Meccan trade were intimately linked, as practically every author on the subject states.[4] But why has this proposition gained axiomatic status?

As regards antiquity, the proposition is gratuitous in that we do not know anything about trade in Mecca before its occupation by Quraysh. The belief arises from the identification of Mecca with Ptolemy's Macoraba. But this identification is untenable, as has already been shown;

[1] F. M. Donner, *The Early Islamic Conquests*, p. 51.

[2] Watt, *Muhammad at Mecca*, p. 3.

[3] Mecca is conjectured to have been a major cultic and commercial centre even in antiquity in Grohmann, "Makoraba"; similarly Hitti, *Capital Cities*, pp. 4 f.; and Donner believes it to have functioned as a pilgrim fair for centuries before the rise of Islam (*Conquests*, p. 51). For other views, see the discussion in Simon, "Ḥums et īlāf," p. 206n.

[4] See for example Lammens, "République marchande," pp. 33 f.; Margoliouth, *Mohammed*, pp. 13 f.; Rodinson, *Mohammed*, p. 39; Shaban, *Islamic History*, 1, 3; Hitti, *Capital Cities*, p. 5; Kister, "Some Reports," p. 76.

and even if it were not, it would not enable us to say anything about the city, inasmuch as Ptolemy offers no information about it apart from the longitude and latitude at which it was located.[5] The Islamic tradition has it that the Amalekite and Jurhumite rulers of Mecca used to collect tithes from traders there, but is otherwise silent on the subject.[6]

It could, moreover, be argued that Quraysh were traders even before they occupied Mecca. An ʿUqla inscription dating from about 270-278 A.D. enumerates *Qršhtn* as guests of a Ḥaḍramī king along with representatives of Tadmar, Kašd, and Hind.[7] The *Qršhtn* are assumed to be Qurashī women; and if the other guests were Palmyrenes, Chaldaeans, and Indians, the meeting presumably had something to do with trade.[8] If so, Quraysh would appear to have been traders of some importance as early as the third century A.D.; and since they only settled in Mecca two centuries later or so,[9] their trade could evidently not owe anything to the sacred status of this city. One would not, however, wish to attach too much importance to this inscription. Khadīja, Asmāʾ, Hind, and other female traders notwithstanding, it is odd that Quraysh should have been represented by fourteen women and not a single male, fourteen also being too many in view of the fact that the hypothetical Palmyrenes, Chaldaeans, and Indians only sent two representatives. Whatever the women were doing in the Ḥaḍramawt, they had hardly been sent there to discuss trade.[10] If their identification as Qurashī women is correct, Quraysh must have enjoyed an importance in the third century of which the Islamic tradition preserves no recollection at all, and this is a startling thought. But the importance was not necessarily commercial, and the identification could be wrong. There may have been trade in Mecca be-

[5] Cf. above, ch. 6, pp. 134-36.

[6] *ʿAghānī*, xv, 12 f.; Masʿūdī, *Murūj*, III, 99.

[7] A. Jamme, ed. and tr., *The Al-ʿUqlah Texts (Documentation Sud-Arabe, III)*, pp. 38, 44 (Ja 919, 931). Both parts of the inscription have been published before, but the crucial words had not yet been deciphered (cf. *Repertoire d'Épigraphie Sémitique*, VII, nos. 4,859, 4,862).

[8] Jamme takes the identification of the women as Qurashī for granted and considers the possibility that the Hindites were Indians, but makes no suggestions regarding the identity of Tadmar and Kašd (*Al-ʿUqlah Texts*, pp. 17, 25, 38 f., 45). It is to Professor A.F.L. Beeston that I owe the suggestion that we may here be seeing Indians, Chaldeaeans, Palmyrenes, and Quraysh together (personal communication).

[9] Cf. *EI*[2], *s.v.* Ḳuṣayy.

[10] Jamme offers no speculations on what they might be doing, though he too thinks that there must have been more than trade to the meeting (*Al-ʿUqlah Texts*, p. 25).

fore its occupation by Quraysh, and Quraysh may have been traders before they occupied the city; but the fact of the matter is that we know nothing about either question.

What, then, do we know about the relationship between the Meccan *ḥaram* and Qurashī trade after the Qurashī occupation of the city? On this question the tradition offers a fair amount of information. We may start by considering whether Mecca was a pilgrim fair.

The tradition is almost unanimous that it was *not* a pilgrim fair. A famous list of pre-Islamic fairs enumerates some sixteen fairs as having been of major importance in Arabia before Islam. Not one of the several versions of this list mentions Mecca.[11] What is more, there is no question of Mecca having been somehow forgotten. We are told that three of the fairs in question, that is, ʿUkāẓ, Dhū'l-Majāz, and Majanna, were held in the holy months. Having traded there, people would perform their ritual duties at ʿArafa (located in the vicinity of these fairs just outside Mecca) and then go home.[12] Thus one version. More commonly we are told that they would prepare for the pilgrimage to Mecca. This they would do on the day of *tarwiya* (8 Dhu'l-ḥijja) by calling a halt to trade and transferring from ʿUkāẓ or Dhū'l-Majāz to ʿArafa.[13] On this day, too, they would be joined by all those who had not attended the fairs in question, having nothing to buy or sell.[14] No trade was conducted at ʿArafa or Minā.[15] *A fortiori*, no trade was conducted in Mecca itself.

[11] The fullest version is given in Marzūqī, *Azmina*, II, 161 ff.; shorter ones are found in Ibn Ḥabīb, *Muḥabbar*, pp. 263 ff.; Abū Ḥayyān, *Imtāʿ*, I, 83 ff.; Yaʿqūbī, *Ta'rīkh*, I, 313 f.; Qalqashandī, *Ṣubḥ*, I, 410 f. The section relating to the pilgrim fairs is also reproduced in a somewhat different form in Azraqī, *Makka*, pp. 129 ff.; Ibn Ḥabīb, *Munammaq*, pp. 274 f. Some additional material is cited in Bakrī, *Muʿjam*, pp. 660 f.; Yāqūt, *Buldān*, III, 704 f., both *s.v.* ʿUkāẓ. In general, see also S. al-Afghānī, *Aswāq al-ʿarab fi'l-jāhiliyya wa'l-Islām*.

[12] Thus Abū Ḥayyān, *Imtāʿ*, p. 85 (*thumma yaqifūna bi-ʿArafa wa-yaqḍūna mā ʿalayhim min manāsikihim thumma yatawajjahūna ilā awṭānihim*).

[13] Yaʿqūbī, *Ta'rīkh*, I, 314; Ibn Ḥabīb, *Munammaq*, p. 275; *id.*, *Muḥabbar*, p. 267; Marzūqī, *Azmina*, II, p. 166; Azraqī, *Makka*, p. 129. Compare also *Aghānī*, XXII, p. 57, where the fair of ʿUkāẓ is envisaged as continuing right up to the beginning of the pilgrimage.

[14] Azraqī, *Makka*, p. 129; Marzūqī, *Azmina*, II, 166.

[15] Azraqī, *Makka*, p. 130, cf. p. 129: *kāna yawm al-tarwiya ākhira aswāqihim*. Ibn Ḥabīb, *Munammaq*, p. 275.

The list of pre-Islamic fairs goes back to Ibn al-Kalbī, but the section on the pilgrim fairs is derived from his father's *Tafsīr*, presumably *ad* 2:194.[16] By way of background to this verse, other exegetes also inform us that the pre-Islamic Arabs used not to trade during the pilgrimage, that is in a state of *iḥrām*;[17] accordingly, we are told, no trading was conducted at either ʿArafa or Minā.[18] That none was conducted in Mecca itself is once more left implicit. Alternatively, we are informed that the pre-Islamic Arabs did trade during the pilgrimage, or that some of them did:[19] it was the early Muslims rather than the pagans who felt the combination of trade and pilgrimage to be wrong.[20] But the places at which the pagans are said to have traded during the pilgrimage are once more specified as ʿUkāẓ, Dhū'l-Majāz, and Majanna, not as Mecca, Minā, or ʿArafa, so Mecca still is not envisaged as a pilgrim fair. Either way, God himself put an end to the qualms in question when he revealed 2:194: "it is no fault in you that you should seek bounty from your lord." It was then that people began to trade at ʿArafa, Minā, and, once more implicitly, Mecca itself during the pilgrimage.[21] Indeed, given that ʿUkāẓ,

[16] Ibn al-Kalbī is identified as the authority for the full list in Marzūqī, whereas Kalbī is given as the authority for the section relating to the pilgrim fairs and related matters in Azraqī (*Makka*, p. 122). The *isnād* in Azraqī is Kalbī from Abū Ṣāliḥ from Ibn ʿAbbās, indicating that the information comes from Kalbī's lost *Tafsīr* (cf. F. Sezgin, *Geschichte des arabischen Schrifttums*, I, 34 f. Sezgin's belief that the work is extant remains to be proved, cf. below, ch. 9 n59).

[17] Ṭabarī, *Jāmiʿ*, II, 158 ff., citing Mujāhid and ʿAmr b. Dīnār, both from Ibn ʿAbbās; similarly M. J. Kister, "Labbayka, Allāhumma, Labbayka . . . . On a Monotheistic Aspect of a Jāhiliyya Practice," pp. 37 f., citing Muqātil and others; cf. also *id.*, "Some Reports," p. 76 and the note thereto (where the evidence is interpreted differently).

[18] Ṭabarī, *Jāmiʿ*, II, 159, citing Mujāhid on ʿArafa and Saʿīd b. Jubayr on Minā.

[19] Cf. Yaʿqūbī, *Taʾrīkh*, I, 298, where the Ḥums and the Ḥilla are presented as having differed on this point.

[20] Ṭabarī, *Jāmiʿ*, II, 159 f.; Muḥammad b. al-Ḥasan al-Ṭūsī, *al-Tibyān fī tafsīr al-Qurʾān*, II, 166; Ibn Kathīr, *Tafsīr*, I, 239 f.; Wāḥidī, *Asbāb*, pp. 41 f. (The view that it was the pre-Islamic Arabs who felt trade during the pilgrimage to be wrong is also mentioned in the latter two works.)

[21] Cf. Azraqī, *Makka*, pp. 130 f. ("they used not to buy and sell on the day at ʿArafa or during the days at Minā, but when God brought Islam he allowed them to do so; for God, exalted is he, revealed in his book, "it is no fault in you that you should seek bounty from your lord" [and when ʿUkāẓ, Dhū'l-Majāz, and Majanna were abandoned] they made do with the fairs of Mecca, Minā, and ʿArafa"). Note also the reflections of the same idea in the comments *ad* 22:28 f., where the *manāfiʿ* are frequently understood as a reference to

Dhū'l-Majāz, and Majanna were not incorporated in the Muslim pilgrimage, Mecca, Minā, and ʿArafa were strictly speaking now the only pilgrim fairs, though the old fairs continued to be held until the end of the Umayyad period.[22]

In connection with 2:194 the exegetes are thus agreed that Mecca only became a pilgrim fair on the rise of Islam. In connection with 9:28, however, they say the opposite. By way of background to this verse, we are told that the pagan Arabs used to bring merchandise, almost invariably identified as foodstuffs, to Mecca during the pilgrimage. When God prohibited idolators from approaching the Holy Mosque, the Meccans thus feared for their livelihood, and this is why God reassured them, saying that "if you fear poverty, God shall surely enrich you." He enriched them by making the people of Jedda, Ḥunayn, and Ṣanʿāʾ, or Tabāla and Jurash, convert so that the Meccans no longer had to trade with infidels in order to obtain their food,[23] or else by making the infidels pay *kharāj* and *jizya* so that the Meccans did not have to trade at all.[24]

This story is a variation on the theme of Mecca's food supplies and the end of Meccan trade that we have come across already.[25] Being one variation among others, it is not weighty evidence; and, moreover, it depicts the Meccans as passive recipients of supplies brought by others rather than as active exploiters of a pilgrim trade. It is nonetheless the only evidence known to me for the proposition that Mecca was a pilgrim fair. Here, as in the case of the Meccan spice trade, the axiomatic truths of the secondary literature have only a tangential relationship with the evidence presented in the sources.

The axiomatic status of the proposition that Mecca was a pilgrim fair is all the more surprising in that as early as 1887 Wellhausen argued with

---

trade: *rakhaṣa lahum fī'l-rukūb wa'l-matjar*, as Mujāhid explains (Ṭabarī, *Jāmiʿ*, xvii, 98; also cited *ibid.*, ii, 159, *ad* 2:194).

[22] Azraqī, *Makka*, p. 131.

[23] Muqātil in Kister, "Some Reports," p. 79; Bayḍāwī, *Anwār*, i, 496.

[24] Ṭabarī, *Jāmiʿ*, x, 66 f.; Suyūṭī, *Durr*, iii, p. 227; Ibn Kathīr, *Tafsīr*, ii, 346 f.; Bayḍāwī, *Anwār*, i, 496; cf. also Ṭūsī, *Tibyān*, v, 201.

[25] Above, ch. 5, pp. 110 f. Note that it is the people of Tabāla and Jurash who figure in Kalbī's account of how the Meccans obtained their provisions after the two journeys had become too much for them, as also in Bayḍāwī's account of how they obtained their provisions after the unbelievers were forbidden to approach the Holy Mosque.

some cogency that Mecca was not an object of pilgrimage at all in pre-Islamic times.[26] As I shall show, Wellhausen's hypothesis makes effortless sense of the evidence. The pre-Islamic Arabs *did* trade during the pilgrimage. But they did not trade in *Mecca* during the pilgrimage, because the pilgrimage did not go to Mecca before the rise of Islam.

That the pre-Islamic Arabs traded during the pilgrimage is easily shown. ʿUkāẓ, Dhū'l-Majāz, and Majanna were *ḥaram*s which one would visit in the holy months,[27] that is to say, as pilgrims. They were also *ḥaram*s at which people would trade. The pre-Islamic Arabs thus traded during the pilgrimage, and naturally they did so in a state of *iḥrām*, the consecrated state of pilgrims: how could they be pilgrims if they were not in this state? Ibn Ḥabīb informs us that Quraysh would never go to Dhū'l-Majāz except in a state of *iḥrām*.[28] Quraysh were also in a state of *iḥrām* at ʿUkāẓ when the war of Fijār provoked by Barrāḍ broke out.[29] And according to Azraqī, nobody would go to either ʿUkāẓ, Dhū'l-Majāz, or Majanna except in a state of *iḥrām* (*illā muḥrimīn bi'l-ḥajj*).[30] Our sources no doubt take it that people would go in this state because trading at the fairs in question was followed by the pilgrimage to ʿArafa, Minā, and Mecca, but this is evidently wrong. If people went in a consecrated state to holy places in the holy months, they were going as pilgrims to the places in question. Visiting ʿUkāẓ, Dhū'l-Majāz, and Majanna was part of the pilgrimage, not a prolegomenon to it. In short, it was as pilgrims that visitors to ʿUkāẓ, Dhū'l-Majāz, and Majanna would engage in trade.

From ʿUkāẓ, Dhū'l-Majāz, and Majanna the pilgrims would proceed to ʿArafa and Minā. But would they proceed to Mecca, too? Wellhausen denied it on the ground that the Muslim pilgrimage is still conducted largely outside Mecca, a point hard to dispute. Though it begins in Mecca, its formal start is at ʿArafa; and though it ends in Mecca, too, its real termination is at Minā, this being where sacrifices are made and

[26] Wellhausen, *Reste*, pp. 79 ff.

[27] "He brought it to the market of ʿUkāẓ in the *ḥaram*," as we are told of someone trying to sell a sword at ʿUkāẓ, where he was killed in the *ḥaram* (*Aghānī*, XI, 119). For the dates of the fairs, see the references listed above, n11.

[28] Ibn Ḥabīb, *Munammaq*, p. 275.

[29] Ibn Ḥabīb, *Munammaq*, p. 196 (*qadima sūq ʿUkāẓ fa-wajada'l-nās bi-ʿUkāẓ qad ḥaḍarū'l-sūq wa'l-nās muḥrimūn li'l-ḥajj*).

[30] Azraqī, *Makka*, p. 132.

heads are shaved, whereupon the state of *iḥrām* is abandoned.[31] This suggests that the visits to Mecca have been added to an originally independent ritual, and there are two further points in support of this view. First, as Wellhausen himself noted, the religious offices connected with the pilgrimage to ʿArafa were in the hands of Tamīmīs and others, not of Qurashīs: Quraysh are presented as responsible only for the pilgrims in Mecca itself.[32] Second, Mecca is an odd place in which to end the *ḥajj*. Minā and ʿArafa were uninhabited places devoid of guardians and permanent inhabitants, being active only in the holy months. So also were ʿUkāẓ, Dhū'l-Majāz, and Majanna, the *ḥarams* with which the pilgrimage started: the five sanctuaries outside Mecca form a natural group. But Mecca was a city with a permanent population and a shrine endowed with guardians. It was thus a shrine on a par with that of Allāt at Ṭā'if or al-ʿUzzā at Nakhla, not a desert sanctuary. The pilgrimage was a ritual performed at times and places in which everybody downed arms and nobody was in control: a sanctuary owned by a specific tribe does not belong in this complex.

It could, of course, be argued that the pilgrimage had been extended to Mecca even in pre-Islamic times, and this is how Lammens saw it: the originally independent sanctuaries of ʿArafa and Minā, according to him, had been reduced to mere stations on the way to Mecca even before the rise of Islam by the enterprising Quraysh in the course of their commercial expansion.[33] But this is unlikely to be correct. In the first place, the tradition is too eager to dissociate ʿArafa and Minā from the other desert sanctuaries, attaching them to Mecca instead. When the exegetes tell us that the pagan Arabs used to abstain from trading during the pilgrimage (meaning the Muslim pilgrimage to ʿArafa, Minā, and Mecca), or that they did trade during the pilgrimage (but only during the pagan pilgrimage to ʿUkāẓ, Dhū'l-Majāz, and Majanna), they are concerned to present Minā and ʿArafa as places of particular holiness. But people did

[31] Wellhausen, *Reste*, pp. 79 ff.

[32] Wellhausen, *Reste*, p. 83 n; cf. *ibid.*, p. 81; below, p. 188; Kister, "Mecca and Tamīm," pp. 141 f., 155. Kister argues against Wellhausen on the ground that it was Quraysh who had invested Tamīm (the holders of the most important offices) with their functions: Tamīm were thus integrated in the Meccan system. But since the sources make it clear that no Qurashīs had ever held the offices in question, it is hard to see how they could have been in a position to delegate them.

[33] Lammens, "République marchande," p. 35.

not stop trading at Minā and conceivably not even at ʿArafa.[34] If ʿArafa and Minā had been stations on the way to Mecca even in pre-Islamic times, the tradition would scarcely have needed artificial linkage mechanisms of this kind. Second, it is striking that the exegetical discussions of trade or no trade during the pilgrimage are focused on ʿArafa and Minā to the exclusion of Mecca: people would abstain from trade during the pilgrimage, that is, at ʿArafa and Minā; they would trade during the pilgrimage, but not at ʿArafa and Minā; when God allowed them to trade during the pilgrimage, they began to trade at ʿArafa and Minā. There is no reference to Mecca in these discussions, Mecca being added by way of afterthought only in Azraqī's account.[35] Indeed, Azraqī explicitly points out that the permission to trade referred to "the pilgrim stations (*mawāsim al-ḥajj*), that is Minā, ʿArafa, ʿUkāẓ, Majanna, and Dhū'l-Majāz; for these were the pilgrim stations (*fa-hādhihi mawāsim al-ḥajj*)."[36] That Mecca itself is supposed to have been a pilgrim station is here totally forgotten. Third, the tradition implicitly concedes that the pilgrimage stopped short of Mecca even in Muḥammad's time. When Muḥammad was looking for tribes to give him shelter, he toured the pilgrim fairs in the vicinity of Mecca for seven or ten years instead of awaiting the arrival of the pilgrims in Mecca itself.[37] It was at such a pilgrim station (*mawsim*) that he first met the future Anṣār, according to some.[38] Of negotiations with pilgrims in Mecca itself there is no recollection whatsoever.[39] And, as just seen, one version of the list of pre-Islamic

[34] Minā is explicitly counted as a pre-Islamic fair in Marzūqī, *Azmina*, II, 161. For the pilgrim trader (*dājj*) at Minā, see also Ṭabarī, *Jāmiʿ*, II, 159 (*ad* 2:194), where it is asserted that he would abstain from trading there; Azraqī, *Makka*, p. 399, where it is implied that he would not. For ʿAbbās b. ʿAbd al-Muṭṭalib selling Yemeni perfume at Minā in the pilgrim season, see above, ch. 4, n34. There is no comparable evidence for ʿArafa.

[35] Cf. above, n21.

[36] Azraqī, *Makka*, p. 130.

[37] Cf. Ibn Hishām, *Leben*, pp. 281 f., where only Minā is explicitly mentioned; Ibn Saʿd, *Ṭabaqāt*, I, pp. 216 f. (the Prophet would follow the pilgrims every year in their *manāzil* at the *mawāsim*, the places mentioned being ʿUkāẓ, Majanna, Dhū'l-Majaz, and Minā); similarly Abū Nuʿaym, *Dalāʾil*, p. 247, citing Wāqidī; Bakrī, *Muʿjam*, p. 661 (*s.v.* ʿUkāẓ), citing Abū'l-Zubayr from Jābir. But note how Ibn Saʿd equates touring these fairs with staying in Mecca.

[38] Ibn Hishām, *Leben*, p. 286; Ibn Saʿd, *Ṭabaqāt*, I, p. 217 (where the Yathribīs are shaving their heads; cf. p. 221; Abū Nuʿaym, *Dalāʾil*, pp. 253, 261, citing Ibn Isḥāq and ʿUrwa b. al-Zubayr.

[39] There are several rivals to the conventional story of how Muḥammad met the Anṣār

fairs explicitly says that visitors to the pilgrim fairs would go home on their completion of the ritual at ʿArafa.

It is thus reasonable to conclude with Wellhausen that Mecca was not an object of pilgimage in pre-Islamic times. It follows that it was no pilgrim fair, either;[40] and with the exception of the story told *ad* 9:28, there is in fact no evidence in the tradition of a trade with the pilgrims who are supposed to have arrived there in the Jāhiliyya. All or most pilgrims are said to have been supplied with food and drink free of charge, the Meccans having agreed to let themselves be taxed for this purpose.[41] Such clothes as the pilgrims might need were typically given or lent to them

at ʿAqaba, and some locate the first meeting at Mecca; but the Anṣār who go to Mecca do not go as pilgrims. Thus one account has two Khazrajīs go to Mecca to submit a *munāfara* (boasting competition) to ʿUtba b. Rabīʿa; the Prophet preached Islam to them and they converted, returning to Medina with the new religion (Ibn Ḥajar, *Iṣāba*, I, 32, no. 111; II, 172, no. 2,432, *s.vv.* Asʿad b. Zurāra and Dhakwān b. ʿAbd Qays. Both men figure in the conventional account, too). Alternatively, a group of Aws went to Mecca to invoke Qurashī help against Khazraj. They stayed with ʿUtba b. Rabīʿa. Quraysh refused to help, but Muḥammad offered Islam and one converted (Iyās b. Muʿādh), though he died soon thereafter. The Awsīs had pretended to go to Mecca for the *ʿumra*, but their meeting with Muḥammad nonetheless took place at Dhū'l-Majāz (Ibn Saʿd, *Ṭabaqāt*, III, 437 f.; Ibn Hishām, *Leben*, pp. 285 f. [with fewer details]; cf. the brief version in Balādhurī, *Ansāb*, I, 238). Yet another first convert was Abū'l-Haytham, apparently envisaged as having come to Mecca on the occasion just mentioned (Ibn Saʿd, *ibid.*, p. 448). Alternatively, the first convert was Suwayd b. al-Ṣāmit, who came to Mecca on *ʿumra* or pilgrimage and who also died soon after his conversion (Ibn Hishām, *Leben*, pp. 284 f.; also cited in Ṭabarī, *Taʾrīkh*, ser. I, pp. 1,207 f.; cf. Balādhurī, *loc. cit.*). Here, at first sight, we have a pilgrim meeting Muḥammad in Mecca. But since Muḥammad is described as touring the pilgrim fairs at the time, Mecca here means the *mawāsim* in its vicinity, presumably Dhū'l-Majāz (as in the second story). Yet another story has Anṣārīs come to Mecca *fī umūr lahum*; Qays b. al-Khaṭīm was favourably impressed by the Prophet, but died before the year was over (Balādhurī, Ansāb, I, 238).

[40] Wellhausen himself curiously chose to dodge this conclusion: "to some extent Mecca can also be counted as one of the markets of the pilgrimage," he claimed (*Reste*, p. 91). But of pilgrim trade in Mecca he adduced no evidence; and the fact that the tradition localizes a certain event that took place in a *mawsim* now at ʿUkāẓ or Dhū'l-Majāz and now at Mecca is surely attributable to the very development that he himself identified, the substitution of Mecca for ʿUkāẓ and Dhū'l-Majāz in the Muslim pilgrimage.

[41] Cf. Ibn Hishām, *Leben*, p. 87, where Hāshim institutes the *rifāda* with a fine speech to the effect that the pilgrims are God's guests. At p. 83 it is Quṣayy who institutes it with the same speech, though this time the *rifāda* is intended only for pilgrims who cannot pay for themselves.

along with other necessities, the only reward of their Meccan hosts, according to some, being a share in the pilgrims' sacrifices.[42] And it was to neighbouring tribes, not to pilgrims, that the Meccans were reputed to have sold idols.[43] For the flourishing trade with pilgrims in Mecca described, for example, by Margoliouth, there is no support in the tradition, while that presented by Lapidus in fact refers to ʿUkāẓ.[44]

This is not to deny that Quraysh owed much of their wealth to the pilgrimage. "How did they make a living if *not* from the pilgrimage?" as ʿUmar asks in response to the question on the legitimacy of combining pilgrimage and trade.[45] But the pilgrimage on which they flourished was the pagan one to sanctuaries outside Mecca, above all ʿUkāẓ and Dhū'l-Majāz. These were the pilgrim fairs at which "people made a living in the Jāhiliyya," the *mawāsim al-ḥajj* that constituted their *matjar*, their place of trade.[46] When we are told that Quraysh used to trade only with those who came to Mecca, Mecca is more or less automatically glossed as meaning Dhū'l-Majāz and ʿUkāẓ:[47] here as elsewhere "Mecca" is an

[42] Cf. Kister, "Mecca and Tamīm," pp. 136 and the note thereto, 137, 139.

[43] Cf. above, ch. 4, no. 11.

[44] Cf. Margoliouth, *Mohammed*, p. 13. It is true that Hubal's guardians charged a fee for oracular advice; but it is Quraysh themselves, not foreign pilgrims, who are presented as the customers (a point to which I shall return shortly). A visitor's tax is attested for Byzantine traders, but again not for pilgrims (cf. Azraqī, *Makka*, p. 107). Lammens takes the *ḥarīm* mentioned by Ibn Durayd to be a tax on pilgrims (cf. *Mecque*, p. 140; Muḥammad b. al-Ḥasan Ibn Durayd, *Kitāb al-ishtiqāq*, p. 282). In fact, however, the *ḥarīm* was a share in the pilgrims' sacrifices that Qurashī hosts would receive in return for looking after them and providing for their needs (cf. Kister, "Mecca and Tamīm," p. 136n. And even this interpretation could be disputed; cf. the alternative story about Ẓuwaylim, the *mānīʿ al-ḥarīm*, cited *ibid.* from Balādhurī). Lapidus, "The Arab Conquests," p. 59; compare Wellhausen, *Reste*, pp. 89 f.

[45] Ṭabarī, *Jāmiʿ*, II, 160; Ibn Kathīr, *Tafsīr*, I, 240 *(wa-hal kānat maʿāyishuhum illā fī'l-ḥajj?)*.

[46] *Kāna ʿUkāẓ wa-Dhū'l-Majāz aswāqahum fī'l-jāhiliyya yuqīmūnahā mawāsim al-ḥajj wa-kānat maʿāyishuhum minhā* (Bayḍāwī, *Anwār*, I, 145). *Kāna matjar al-nās fī'l-jāhiliyya ʿUkāẓ wa-Dhū'l-Majāz* (Tabarī, *Jāmiʿ*, II, 159, citing ʿAmr b. Dīnār from Ibn ʿAbbās). *Kānat ʿUkāẓ wa-Majanna wa-Dhū'l-Majāz aswāqan fī'l-jāhiliyya* (Ibn Kathīr, *Tafsīr*, I, 239, citing the same). All statements are made in explanation of 2:194, which was revealed *fī mawāsim al-ḥajj*.

[47] *Kānat Quraysh lā tutājiru illā maʿa man warada ʿalayhā Makkata fī'l-mawāsim wa-bi-Dhī'l-Majāz wa-sūq ʿUkāẓ wa-fī'l-ashhur al-ḥurum* (Thaʿālibī, *Thimār*, p. 115). This passage clearly does not describe three alternative places or dates of arrival: *fī'l-mawāsim* is synon-

abbreviation (or tendentious substitution) for the pilgrim fairs at which the Meccans traded.[48] The pilgrim fairs were "the markets of Mecca":[49] Mecca itself was not a fair. ʿUkāẓ, Dhū'l-Majāz, and Majanna, "these were the markets of Quraysh and the Arabs, and none was greater than ʿUkāẓ."[50] The sources thus make it clear that sanctuaries did contribute to Qurashī wealth; but it was sanctuaries other than that of Mecca which made the contribution.

It might still be argued that Mecca, though not an object of pilgrimage, nonetheless attracted visitors in Rajab, when the *ʿumra* was made, and that these visitors stimulated trade.[51] But for one thing, it could be argued that the *ḥajj* and the *ʿumra* were destined for the same sanctuary: if the *ḥajj* stopped short of Mecca, the *ʿumra* did, as well.[52] For another thing, there is only the feeblest suggestion that the *ʿumra* generated trade.[53] And though Hubal, the deity accommodated in the Kaʿba, may

ymous with *fīʾl-ashhur al-ḥurum*, and it was only in the *ashhur al-ḥurum* that people came to Dhū'l-Majāz and ʿUkāẓ. The first and the last *wa* thus do not mean "and," but rather "that is," and the passage might be translated as follows: "Quraysh used only to trade with those who came to them at Mecca in the pilgrim season, that is at Dhū'l-Majāz and the market of ʿUkāẓ in the holy months."

[48] Events located at Mecca in one source will be located at Dhū'l-Majāz or ʿUkāẓ in another (cf. above, n40; and compare the equivalence of Mecca and Dhū'l-Majāz in n39). When Ibn Saʿd says that the Prophet "stayed in Mecca for as long as he stayed, calling the tribes to God and offering himself to them every year at Majanna, ʿUkāẓ and Minā," he is implicitly turning the pilgrim fairs into parts of Mecca without saying anything incorrect (*Ṭabaqāt*, I, 217; similarly p. 216). When the sources speak of the pilgrim fairs as "the markets of Mecca" (cf. the following note), they again tend to envisage them as extensions of Mecca rather than as markets outside it at which the Meccans traded; and naturally the modern reader follows suit.

[49] Bakrī, *Muʿjam*, p. 660, *s.v.* ʿUkāẓ: ʿUkāẓ, Majanna, and Dhū'l-Majāz were *aswāq li-Makka*; cf. Ibn Saʿd, *Ṭabaqāt*, VIII, 323: Dhū'l-Majāz was a *sūq min aswāq Makka*.

[50] Yāqūt, *Buldān*, III, 705, *s.v.* ʿUkāẓ, citing Wāqidī; cf. Ibn Ḥabīb, *Muḥabbar*, p. 267 (*kānat ʿUkāẓ min aʿẓami aswāq al-ʿarab*).

[51] Cf. Wellhausen, *Reste*, pp. 84, 97 ff.

[52] This was not Wellhausen's view, but compare Nonnosus' description of an Arabian sanctuary of the same type as the complex of pilgrim fairs known from the Islamic tradition, possibly even identical with it: it was visited in all three holy months, including Rajab (below, nn127-28). And note that the *ʿumra* seems to go to Dhū'l-Majāz in one of the accounts of the conversion of Medina cited above, n39.

[53] One version of the *ḥilf al-fuḍūl* story has it that the Yemeni who was wronged in Mecca has come to make the *ʿumra* and engage in trade (*qadima Makka muʿtamiran bi-biḍāʿa*, thus

for all we know have attracted visitors all the year round,[54] there is little to indicate that Mecca was a market of major importance at all. It had a *sūq*,[55] and there is occasional mention of Hudhalīs, Kinānīs, and others selling camels, sheep,[56] slaves,[57] and other commodities there.[58] Ṣafwān b. Umayya is said to have sold Egyptian imports in the lower part of the city,[59] and a Tamīmī is said to have had his *matjar* in Mecca (but the parallel version omits the *matjar*, and a variant version also fails to mention trade).[60] Byzantine traders are said to have visited Mecca, and Jews are also supposed to have been active there, as we have seen already.[61] But the sources give us to understand that Qurashī trade was conducted

---

Ibn Abi'l-Ḥadīd, *Sharḥ*, III, 464; Kalāʿī, *Iktifāʾ*, p. 146, both citing Zubayr b. Bakkār). But in the prediction story cited in Kalāʿī, *Kitāb al-iktifāʾ*, pp. 240 f.; Abū Nuʿaym, *Dalāʾil*, p. 122, the Yathribīs who make the *ʿumra* are merely accompanied by a trader, a Jew who evidently was not making the *ʿumra* himself. I know of no other stories in which *ʿumra* and trade are mentioned together.

54 There is no indication of seasonal patterns in accounts of visits to Hubal. For the votive offerings that he received, see Azraqī, *Makka*, pp. 31, 49. Compare the votive offerings received by Allāt (above, ch. 3 n4). Votive offerings are not, of course, evidence of trade.

55 Thus Nubayh b. al-Ḥajjāj found it hard to maintain his two wives on what he earned during the day in the *sūq* of Mecca (Ibn Ḥabīb, *Munammaq*, p. 52). Abū Jahl was sitting *fī nāḥiyat min al-sūq* when a Zubaydī came to complain to the Prophet about an injustice (Balādhurī, *Ansāb*, I, 130—a variation on the *ḥilf al-fuḍūl* story).

56 Thus an Irāshī sold camels to Abū Jahl, who refused to pay, whereupon Muḥammad redressed the injustice (Ibn Hishām, *Leben*, p. 257; Balādhurī, *Ansāb*, I, 128; Abū Nuʿaym, *Dalāʾil*, pp. 166 f.). A Sulamī sold camels to a Meccan who likewise refused to pay (Ibn Ḥabīb, *Munammaq*, p. 164). A Hudhalī selling sheep in Mecca caught sight of Abū Jahl (Balādhurī, *Ansāb*, I, 128. All these are more variations on the *ḥilf al-fuḍūl* theme).

57 A Hudhalī sold a prisoner of war in Mecca (above, ch. 4, n97). Since Dhū'l-Majāz was located in Hudhalī territory it is, however, possible that Mecca here stands for Dhu'l-Majāz.

58 A Kinānī sold an unspecified commodity in Mecca (Ibn Ḥabīb, *Munammaq*, pp. 275 f.). Two ʿAbdīs are supposed to have sold trousers from Hajar there (above, ch. 4 n75). And *idhkhir* was exchanged there for *ḥamḍ* (above, ch. 3 n49).

59 Kister, "Some Reports," p. 77, citing Fākihī.

60 Ibn Abī'l-Ḥadīd, *Sharḥ*, III, pp. 465 f.; Ibn ʿAsākir, *Tahdhīb*, VII, 329; cf. Kister, "Mecca and Tamīm," pp. 130 f. Both tell a story about a Tamīmī protégé of Zubayr b. ʿAbd al-Muṭṭalib who got slapped by Ḥarb b. Umayya in Mecca. Ibn ʿAsākir does not, however, mention that the Tamīmī had come to Mecca for trade; and trade is also absent from the story in which it is a protégé of Khalaf b. Asʿad who gets slapped by Ḥarb b. Umayya (*Rasāʾil*, p. 76; cited by Ibn Abī'l-Ḥadīd, *Sharḥ*, III, 457).

61 Cf. above, ch. 5, p. 139.

overwhelmingly *outside* Mecca, in Syria, the Yemen, and elsewhere, and above all at the pilgrim fairs.

One is thus inclined to be suspicious of the claim that Qurashī trade developed because men could come to Mecca without fear of molestation. Actually, here, as so often, Mecca has been conflated with the pilgrim fairs around it. The only time at which people could *come* to Mecca without fear of molestation was in the holy months; but the holy months did not, of course, owe their existence to the Meccan sanctuary, and it was to ʿUkāẓ, Dhū'l-Majāz, and other pilgrim fairs that Meccans and others alike would go during the months in question. The advantage that Mecca is believed to have derived from its sacred status (apart from the pilgrimage that has already been discussed) is a permanent inviolability which meant that people could *live* there without fear of molestation, be it by neighbouring tribes or private enemies elsewhere. The exegetes make much of the claim that Mecca was exempt from raids and other violence, God having granted it immunity from perils of this kind in response to Abraham's prayer for safety and sustenance;[62] and it is often stated in the secondary literature that Mecca attracted outlaws, fugitives, and others in need of refuge. Be this as it may, the exegetes develop the theme of inviolability in a fashion precisely opposite to Watt when it comes to trade. It is not that others could come to Mecca without fear of molestation, but on the contrary that the Meccans themselves could *go away* from Mecca without such fear. Whereas other Arabs, we are told, were unable to leave their territories without risking being raided, Quraysh were safe wherever they went, their connection with the sanctuary conferring inviolability on them.[63] If they were raided by mistake, their property would be restored to them on discovery of their identity because, as it was said, a Qurashī is inviolable everywhere.[64]

This idea is not confined to the exegetes. Thus one version of the list

[62] Ṭabarī, *Jāmiʿ*, xxx, p. 172; Suyūṭī, *Durr*, vi, 397; Rāzī, *Mafātīḥ*, viii, 513; Ṭūsī, *Tibyān*, p. 414 (the latter without reference to Abraham); cf. Qur'ān, 14:40. All are commenting on Sūra 106.

[63] Ṭabarī, *Jāmiʿ*, xxx, 172, citing Qatāda and Ibn Zayd; Suyūṭī, *Durr*, vi, 398, citing Qatāda; Ibn Qutayba, *Mushkil al-Qur'ān*, p. 319; Rāzī, *Mafātīḥ*, viii, 513.

[64] Kalāʿī, *Iktifā'*, p. 78, citing Abū ʿUbayda (*al-Qurashī bi-kulli baladin ḥarām*); similarly Qatāda in Ṭabarī, *Jāmiʿ*, xxx, 172.

of pre-Islamic fairs has it that all Muḍar and their allies (though not all Arabs, as implied by the exegetes) regarded Quraysh as inviolable because of their association with the *bayt*.[65] And Jāḥiẓ contrives to find a reference to this inviolability in a pre-Islamic poem, though this time in a contemptuous vein: being mere traders, we are told, Quraysh would seek refuge in their *bayt* and, on leaving it, decorate themselves with *muql* and the bark of trees in order to make themselves recognizable to potential attackers. In short, there is evidence that Quraysh were regarded as holy men, not holy dispensers of justice as Serjeant would have it, but rather holy traders.[66]

The claim is not altogether implausible. Traders have often been regarded as inviolable in Arabia, though they have not often had a sanctuary to make their inviolability respectable.[67] And guardians of holy places have similarly tended to enjoy inviolability, though they have not often used it to be traders. That Quraysh were regarded as inviolable is nonetheless hard to accept.

First, who acknowledged the inviolability of Quraysh? Not all Arabs, for not all Arabs recognized the sanctity of Mecca, as the tradition itself admits.[68] It could be the case that all Muḍar and their allies did, as Marzūqī claims. But according to Ibn Ḥabīb's version of the same passage, it was on grounds of kinship rather than holiness that these tribal groups would refrain from raising Quraysh: no Muḍarī or ally of a Muḍarī would molest Muḍarī merchants, he says, meaning that Qaysī or Tamīmī merchants enjoyed the same protection as the supposedly holy men of Quraysh.[69] In fact, however, Quraysh can scarcely have enjoyed automatic protection on either ground, for the story of Hāshim's *īlāf*-agreements takes it for granted that they had to make special agreements for their safety on the way wherever they went. And the story of Ḥakam b. Abī'l-ʿĀṣ's *jiwār* similarly presupposed lack of automatic protection,

[65] Marzūqī, *Azmina*, II, 162.

[66] Jāḥiẓ, *Tria Opuscula*, p. 63. Cf. R. B. Serjeant, "Ḥaram and Ḥawṭah, the Sacred Enclave in Arabia."

[67] And despite the sanctuary, they clearly are not respectable in Jāḥiẓ's discussion. The poem on which he is commenting explicitly says that trade is despised (*wa'l-tijāra tuḥqaru*), and Jāḥiẓ explains that this is because traders could not defend themselves. Quraysh are thus pariahs here rather than holy men.

[68] Cf. Kister, "Mecca and Tamīm," pp. 142 ff.

[69] Ibn Ḥabīb, *Muḥabbar*, p. 264.

though it presupposes lack of special agreements as well, at least on the route to Iraq.[70] To restate the point in concrete terms, we are told by Marzūqī and Ibn Ḥabīb that Ṭayyi' would refrain from raiding Quraysh because they were allies of Muḍar, who respected the sanctity of Mecca or maybe just Muḍarī kinship ties. But others tell us that, on the contrary, Ṭayyi' were among the tribes who did not respect the sanctity of Mecca and who would even raid pilgrims in the holy months. Indeed, it was because Ṭayyi' and others did not respect the sanctity of Mecca that Hāshim had to negotiate *īlāf*-agreements.[71] Nonetheless, it was also from Ṭayyi' that Ḥakam was obliged to seek *jiwār*. One is thus disinclined to believe that either Muḍar or their allies regarded Quraysh as exempt from acts of aggression.

Second, how could Quraysh claim inviolability? To be inviolable in tribal Arabia was to be excluded from the tribal commonwealth in which prestige was determined largely by military strength. One could be excluded because one was too holy to compete, as in the case of the saint, or because one was to weak to do so, as in the case of the pariah; but either way one had to renounce the use of force: one evidently cannot claim to be *both* inviolable *and* a competitor in military terms. But Quraysh were a warlike people. It is true that there are suggestions to the contrary. Thus they are often said to have abstained from raiding;[72] the Jews of Medina attributed their defeat at Badr to their lack of military experience;[73] and Jāḥiẓ explains that traders in pre-Islamic Arabia, including Quraysh, were despised for their inability to defend themselves, an explanation that conjures up pariahs.[74] But the tradition at large is innocent of the idea that they were either unwilling or unable to fight. There are stories in which they engage in Bedouin-style raids, or set out to avenge their dead, and long accounts of their wars with the Azd and other tribes, not to mention the wars of Fijār or their campaigns against Muḥammad.[75] Even members of trading caravans would gallantly engage in military skirmishes with other tribes on behalf of

[70] Cf. above, ch. 5 n123.

[71] Kister, "Mecca and Tamīm," pp. 118 f., 142, citing Thaʿālibī, Jāḥiẓ, and others.

[72] *Ibid.*, pp. 136 f., 138, citing Jāḥiẓ and Ḥalabī.

[73] Ibn Hishām, *Leben*, p. 383.

[74] Cf. above, nn66, 67.

[75] Cf. Ibn Ḥabīb, *Munammaq*, pp. 150 f., where they leave Mecca to raid and plunder tribes as far away as Lakhm and Balī. See also pp. 124 ff., 146 f., 164, 235 ff.

weaker groups; and ʿAbd al-Dār, the actual guardians of the Kaʿba, had no more renounced the use of arms than had the rest of Quraysh.[76] Naturally, saints are not always so much above the use of force as they are supposed to be; but if they fight, they do so to the accompaniment of protests, and of such there are none in the tradition.[77] Who, moreover, supplied practically all the leaders of the conquests? It is hard to believe that generals such as Khālid b. al-Walīd or ʿAmr b. al-ʿĀṣ started as men too holy (or too weak) for direct participation in the use of force.

Third, it is clear that the sources confuse temporary inviolability during the holy months with permanent inviolability arising from association with a sanctuary, the second institution being the only one to have survived the rise of Islam. When Jāḥiẓ says that Quraysh would decorate themselves with *muql* and bark on leaving their sanctuary, he takes it that the inviolability which the outfit advertised arose from the sanctuary and was exclusive to its Qurashī inhabitants. But according to Abū ʿUbayda, the inhabitants of Yathrib would similarly decorate their turrets with ropes and stalks of palm leaves when they wished to make the *ʿumra* or the pilgrimage: everyone would know that they had gone into a state of *iḥrām*, and they would thus be granted free passage.[78] Or again, Ibn al-Kalbī informs us that pilgrims and traders in the holy months would decorate themselves with garlands of hair and tufts of wool to notify that they were exempt from the normal rules of tribal relations; pilgrims and traders coming from Mecca, though, would use bark, precisely as Jāḥiẓ says.[79] And Azraqī has it that garlands of bark were also donned by those who had used violence in the *ḥaram* as a means of averting retaliation.[80] In all three cases, the visual display ad-

[76] Ibn Ḥabīb, *Munammaq*, pp. 170, 441; Balādhurī, *Ansāb*, I, 102.

[77] Cf. R. B. Serjeant, *The Saiyids of Ḥaḍramawt*, pp. 15, 17, 19.

[78] Ibn Ḥabīb, *Munammaq*, p. 327. The transmitter's name is given as Ibn Abī ʿUbayda.

[79] Marzūqī, *Azmina*, II, 166 f. The details are given in connection with the *dājj*, the trader in the holy months, but the introductory paragraph makes it clear that they apply to the *ḥājj* as well.

[80] Azraqī, *Makka*, p. 132. If someone killed, slapped, or beat another in the *ḥaram* (of the pre-Islamic sanctuary fairs), he would make a garland of bark and say *anā ṣarūra* (not *ḍarūra*, as in Wüstenfeld's edition) and thus avoid retaliation. (The expression is explained as a claim of ignorance of the sanctity of the area, cf. Lane, *Lexicon*, *s.v.*) For the comparable use of crowns by pilgrims in antiquity, see Gaudefroy-Demombynes, *Pèlerinage*, p. 285. (The conjecture that *idhkhir* was used for *qilāda*s by the Meccans is not, however, supported by the sources.)

vertises a temporary state of inviolability, not a permanent exclusion from the tribal commonwealth in which aggressive relations obtain. What Jāḥiẓ is describing, as emerges above all from Ibn al-Kalbī's information, is Quraysh leaving Mecca in a state of *iḥrām*. They have donned their garlands of bark and *muql* because they are on their way to sanctuaries such as ʿUkāẓ and Dhū'l-Majāz, which they were in the habit of visiting as pilgrims and traders in the holy months, and this is why they are inviolable: their inviolability arises from the fact that they are on their way to sanctuaries, not from their residence in one, and they would share this inviolability with everybody else who visited the sanctuaries in question. Quraysh have become a special group in Jāḥiẓ' account by the same method of expropriation of information that we have already encountered in connection with the pilgrimage: features common to sanctuaries outside Mecca have become characteristics unique to Mecca. It is presumably the same process that lies behind the claims of inviolability for Quraysh in the exegetical literature, though Qur'ānic inspiration on the one hand and the replacement of holy months by holy men in Islamic Arabia on the other must both have contributed to the misconception.[81]

[81] In fact, holy men of the type envisaged by the exegetes are not attested at all for pre-Islamic Arabia outside the exegetical literature. They are well known from modern Ḥaḍramawt, and it was on the basis of modern observations (rather than the exegetical literature) that Serjeant proposed to cast Quraysh as such. Serjeant's argument that the Ḥaḍramī *manṣab*s perpetuate a pre-Islamic institution is persuasive enough; but if the institution existed in pre-Islamic Arabia, it presumably existed in those areas in which it is found today. It is practically unknown to modern north Arabia (a fact worthy of a better discussion than that offered by M. E. Meeker, *Literature and Violence in North Arabia*). There are plenty of modern *kāhin*s without sacred enclaves, and plenty of sacred enclaves (here, as in the south, usually tombs of saints) without guardians. But the guardians who occupy these enclaves in the Ḥaḍramawt, protecting the *ḍuʿafā'* who settle there and resolving disputes for the tribes around it (by way of reward for their recognition of its inviolability), have no counterpart in the north: even the *sharīf*s of Mecca fail to conform to the specifications. It is thus unlikely that the institution was found in north Arabia in pre-Islamic times; and given that Quraysh were warlike and engaged in trade instead of the settlement of disputes (a point to which I shall come back), the exegetical claims to the contrary are not persuasive. Serjeant reads every *sayyid* and *sharīf* in pre-Islamic Arabia as a holy man, for all that the terms in question simply meant "noble" at that time (cf. *Sayids of Ḥaḍramawt*, pp. 4 ff.); and Donner obliges by presenting every pre-Islamic guardian as a Ḥaḍramī *manṣab*, for all that pre-Islamic guardians had altogether different functions (cf. *Early Islamic Conquests*, pp. 34 ff.). Both thus misrepresent the pre-Islamic evidence while, at the same time, ignoring the modern evidence for north Arabia.

In what way, then, can the Meccan sanctuary be said to have assisted the growth of Meccan trade? It was not an object of pilgrimage, and the pilgrims whom the tradition insists on bringing there did not engage in trade. It may well have attracted visitors on a par with other Arabian shrines such as that of al-ʿUzza at Nakhla, but we are hard put to demonstrate that this assisted Meccan trade in any way (and did it stimulate trade at Nakhla?). The tradition regards this trade as having flourished because Quraysh were willing to go away, not because others were willing to come to them. But the *ḥaram* did not facilitate Qurashī operations outside it. All our stereotyped notions about the relationship between the Meccan sanctuary and Meccan trade, in fact, apply to the pilgrim fairs. ʿUkāẓ, Dhū'l-Majāz, Majanna, and so forth were sacred enclaves to which people could come without fear of molestation (that is, in the holy months) and in which no bloodshed was permitted (be it during the holy months or all the year round); it was these *ḥarams* that were objects of a pre-Islamic pilgrimage, generating trade, and it was here that disputes were settled and debts repaid. Whatever the precise relationship between these sanctuaries, it was they which mattered for Qurashī trade: in commercial terms the *ḥaram* of Mecca was redundant.

We thus find ourselves in the same situation as in the previous chapter: an analysis of discrepancies between the secondary literature and the sources, and of conflicting information within these sources, leads to evidence suggesting that a more radical hypothesis should be pursued. If the Meccan *ḥaram* attracted no pilgrims, conferred no inviolability on its inhabitants and in no way affected economic activities, in what sense did it exist at all? To enquire whether Mecca was a *ḥaram* in pre-Islamic times or not is, of course, to call for a reexamination of the tradition going beyond the scope of a book on trade; but it is worth pointing out here that the sources corroborate the impression that the sacred status of Mecca may be of Islamic rather than pre-Islamic origin in three major ways.

First, there is a problem with the proposition that guardians of a sacred enclave should have made a living as traders. This point is highlighted by the Ḥaḍramī model proposed by Serjeant for Mecca. In Serjeant's Ḥaḍramawt a holy lineage (nowadays composed of descendants of the Prophet) presides over a holy territory (nowadays the tomb of a saint), in which others settle to engage in trade, crafts, and other occupations regarded by the tribesmen as despicable. Those who engage in these occupations are *ḍuʿafāʾ*, weaklings who cannot protect themselves and who owe their freedom from tribal molestation to the prestige of the presiding saint. But if Quraysh were a holy lineage, who were their *ḍuʿafāʾ*? Quraysh did not preside over a pariah population of traders, tanners, sweepers, and servants, but on the contrary worked as tanners and traders themselves, whence the odd suggestion of both holy men and outcasts in Jāḥiẓ's discussion of them.[82] How could they be both? No doubt guardians of sacred places, be they pre-Islamic or Islamic, have seen fit to engage in trade at various times; and trade has not been uniformly despised in Arabia, nor are Quraysh usually presented as having lost status by engaging in it. But with the exception of Quraysh, guardians with commercial interests have not actually identified themselves as traders, still less have they chosen to trade in person. The fact is that trading can never have been a proper activity for those in charge of holy places. However praiseworthy the activity may have been when performed by others, guardians cannot be *caravaneers*: what sort of guardian spends his time shifting raisins, hides, and perfume between the Yemen, Ṭāʾif, and Syria and haggling at the markets of Buṣrā and ʿUkāẓ? Quite apart from the undignified nature of the idea, guardians are supposed to stay by their shrines and receive a constant stream of visitors desirous of such services as they may be reputed to perform. Yet Quraysh were always on the move, engaged in tasks below their dignity. Even ʿAbd al-Dār, the actual guardians of the Kaʿba, would seem to have been traders, and the Hāshimites, supposedly in charge of functions linked with the pilgrimage, certainly were.[83] No wonder that God told Quraysh to stay at home and worship him: the exegetes apparently also felt that guardianship and trade were incompatible.

Second, Quraysh do not seem to have performed any of the services expected of pre-Islamic guardians. Practically all guardians of pre-Islamic shrines were diviners, that is to say, they would foretell the outcome of events, advise on the suitability or otherwise of intended action,

[82] Cf. above, p. 181. For Serjeant, see "Haram and Hawtah"; cf. *id.*, *Sayids of Ḥaḍramawt*.

[83] It was an ʿAbdarī who was said to have worked as a caravaneer in the Balqāʾ; but this was admittedly said by way of insult (above, ch. 5 n46). It was also an ʿAbdarī who was reputed to have traded in Persia (ch. 5, n126).

and generally know that which is unknown, always in a practical context.[84] Yet neither ʿAbd al-Dār nor Quraysh at large were *kuhhān*. We see them practise divination as laymen equipped with their own do-it-yourself divination kits,[85] but not as professionals dispensing their art on behalf of visitors to Mecca. On the contrary, they themselves were customers of professional diviners. Sometimes they would seek out *kāhins* and *kāhinas* far away from Mecca or in Mecca itself, and sometimes they would consult the oracular arrows of Hubal, the deity which the Kaʿba is said to have accommodated.[86] It makes sense that Hubal's guardian should have practised divination, but it is odd that he was not apparently a Qurashī. Admittedly, some sources listing the real and imagined offices of pre-Islamic Mecca place the *azlām*, the divinatory arrows, with Quraysh;[87] but they fail to do so in connection with Hubal. Usually the administrator of his arrows is completely anonymous. Hubal had a guardian (*ḥājib*), we are told. His divinatory arrows were administered by "the one who administered the arrows" (*ṣāḥib al-qidāḥ*).[88] It was "the guardians of the sanctuary" (*sadanat al-bayt*) who would handle the arrows on behalf of Qurashīs in search of oracular advice.[89] What guardi-

[84] Cf. T. Fahd, *La divination arabe*, p. 110; Wellhausen, *Reste*, pp. 131 ff. Note that pre-Qurashī guardians of the Kaʿba are also said to have practised *kihāna* (Ibn Ḥabīb, *Munammaq*, pp. 346, 405).

[85] Surāqa b. Mālik consulted his arrows on the question of whether he should try to catch the Prophet on the latter's escape from Mecca: the arrows were on God's side (Ibn Hishām, *Leben*, p. 331). Abū Sufyān is reputed to have had his arrows with him at Ḥunayn (*ibid.*, p. 845; Wāqidī, *Maghāzī*, III, 895). For other examples (both Qurashī and non-Qurashī), see Fahd, *Divination*, pp. 181n, 186 f.

[86] Cf. Ibn Ḥabīb, *Munammaq*, pp. 20 f. 105 f., 107 f. (Khuzāʿī *kāhin* in ʿUsfān, a *kāhin* in ʿUsfān), 109 f. (a *kāhin*), 112 ff. (Saṭīḥ *al-kāhin* in the Yemen; this story is also told in *Aghānī*, IX, 53 f.). For other examples, see below, ch. 9, p. 219. On Hubal's divinatory arrows see Ibn Hishām, *Leben*, pp. 97 f.; Azraqī, *Makka*, pp. 31, 58, 73 f. (citing Ibn Isḥāq); Hishām b. Muḥammad Ibn al-Kalbī, *Kitāb al-aṣnām*, p. 28; cf. also *EI*² *s.v.* Hubal. We see them in use mainly in connection with ʿAbd al-Muṭṭalib, who consulted them over the digging of the Zamzam and the proposed sacrifice of his son (Ibn Hishām, *Leben*, pp. 94, 97 ff.). Azraqī also displays them in use on an earlier occasion (*Makka*, p. 107), but the parallel passage in Ibn Saʿd omits both Hubal and the arrows (*Ṭabaqāt*, I, 146). According to Wāqidī, Quraysh consulted them on whether or not to fight the battle of Badr (*Maghāzī*, I, 33).

[87] Cf. Lammens, *Mecque*, p. 163; *id.*, "République marchande," pp. 30 f.

[88] Azraqī, *Makka*, p. 74 (citing Ibn Isḥāq); Ibn Hishām, *Leben*, pp. 94, 97.

[89] Fahd, *Divination*, p. 181n, citing Azharī.

ans? Who are these people officiating in the Kaʿba in the name of the one deity said to have had its place inside the Kaʿba itself,[90] exercising the one function known to have been characteristic of pagan priests? The answer would seem to be members of Ghāḍira b. Ḥubshiyya, a Khuzāʿī lineage of the same ancestry as Ḥulayl b. Ḥubshiyya, the lineage in which the guardianship of the Meccan sanctuary is said to have been vested before the Qurashī occupation of Mecca. Both are usually presented as persons rather than groups: Ḥulayl was the last Khuzāʿī guardian;[91] Ghāḍira, his brother, was in charge of Hubal's divinatory arrow at some stage, apparently in Qurashī Mecca, and would dispense his services in return for a dirham and a sacrificial animal.[92]

Now we are told that when Quṣayy conquered Mecca, he graciously decided to leave the *ijāza* of the pilgrimage at ʿArafa in the hands of Tamīmīs, that at Muzdalifa in the hands of ʿAdwānīs, intercalation in the hands of Kinānīs, and some unspecified function in the hands of Murra b. ʿAwf of Dhubyān.[93] As has been seen, he also "allowed" Tamīmīs to continue as hereditary judges at ʿUkāẓ.[94] And it would now appear that he likewise allowed Khuzāʿīs to remain in charge of Hubal in the Kaʿba. If so, what religious functions can Quraysh be said to have taken over on their conquest of the *ḥaram*? They did not divine, they did not cure, they did not adjudicate: they simply kept the Kaʿba in repair and supplied food and drink for the pilgrims.[95] Quraysh were thus

[90] Thus Ibn Hishām, *Leben*, p. 97; Azraqī, *Makka*, p. 58 and elsewhere. Wāqidī, however, moves him outside (*Maghāzī*, II, 832).

[91] Ibn Ishām, *Leben*, p. 75; cf. Caskel, *Ǧamhara*, II, *s.v.* Ḥulail b. Ḥabašīya.

[92] Azraqī, *Makka*, p. 133; cf. Ibn Hishām, *Leben*, p. 97, where we are told that Quraysh would pay a hundred dirhams and a *jazūr* to the *ṣāḥib al-qidāḥ*; Caskel, *Ǧamhara*, II, *s.v.* Ġāḍira b. Ḥabašīya.

[93] Ibn Hishām, *Leben*, p. 80; cf. pp. 30, 76 ff.

[94] Cf. above, ch. 7, p. 156.

[95] The list of famous judges given in Ibn Ḥabīb, *Muḥabbar*, pp. 132 ff.; Yaʿqūbī, *Taʾrīkh*, I, 299 f., does include Qurashīs, and a fuller version of this list is given by Ibn Ḥabīb, *Munammaq*, pp. 459 f.; Fāsī, *Shifāʾ*, pp. 142 f. But it is clear from Fāsī's remarks that the Qurashī judges are envisaged as having adjudicated among Quraysh only (he points out that they owed their office to the common consent of Quraysh, not to a position of power). There are no examples of Qurashīs being sought out as judges in intertribal disputes (it is clearly as an interested party that Saʿīd b. al-ʿĀṣ acts as *ḥakam* in the dispute between Quraysh and Layth reported in Ibn Ḥabīb, *Munammaq*, pp. 137 f.; it is as laymen that they intervene in the first Fijār disputes, the *ḥakams* at ʿUkāẓ being Tamīmīs); and it

priests whose only function was to get together in order to dig, build, and assemble food. They would go on arduous journeys to gather provisions, collecting hides and woollens for sale in Syria, selling raisins at 'Ukāẓ, donkeys in the Sarāt, and returning with all sorts of goods from Syria and the Yemen; and they would make assiduous use of spades and trowels on their return. But they did not perform a single service of the kind that men enjoying a special relationship with the holy were expected to render in pre-Islamic Arabia. What sort of guardians are these?

Third, what deity did Quraysh represent? The Meccan shrine accommodated Hubal, and there are supposed to have been several minor divinities in its vicinity, their number becoming prodigious in some sources.[96] But as has just been seen, Quraysh do not appear to have been guardians of Hubal, and it evidently was not idols such as Isāf and Nā'ila that provided their *raison d'être*. Who, then? The Qur'ān inveighs against Allāt, al-'Uzzā, and Manāt (53:19 f.); and these goddesses seem to have played a much more important role in Qurashī religion than Hubal, who is not mentioned in the Qur'ān and who is not prominent in the tradition, either.[97] But Quraysh were not guardians of these

---

certainly was not for the settlement of disputes that pilgrims were supposed to have come to Mecca.

[96] There is said to have been no fewer than 360, all of which collapsed when the Prophet recited Sūra 17:82 on the conquest of Mecca (Azraqī, *Makka*, pp. 75 f., citing Ibn Isḥāq; Wāqidī, *Maghāzī*, II, 823; cf. Ibn Hishām, *Leben*, pp. 824 f.; Ibn al-Kalbī, *Aṣnām*, p. 31). There is something to be said for Lüling's view that the number represents that of days in a year (G. Lüling, *Die Wiederentdeckung des Propheten Muhammad*, p. 168).

[97] Cf. Wellhausen, *Reste*, p. 75. It is by Allāt and al-'Uzzā that Quraysh swear (Ibn Hishām, *Leben*, p. 116, cf. p. 566; Wāqidī, *Maghāzī*, II, p. 492). And it is Allāt and al-'Uzzā that converts denounce (Ibn Hishām, *Leben*, pp. 205 f.; Balādhurī, *Ansāb*, I, 185 f.). In general, Allāt and al-'Uzzā come across as the major deities of Quraysh (cf. Balādhurī, *Ansāb*, I, 230; Wāqidī, *Maghāzī*, I, 35). Zayd b. 'Amr, the pre-Islamic *ḥanīf*, did renounce Hubal, too (for some obscure reason replaced by Ghanm in the manuscripts, cf. Ibn Hishām, *Leben*, p. 145; A. Guillaume, tr., *The Life of Muhammad*, p. 100n; Wellhausen, *Reste*, p. 75); and some converts are made to renounce all the major idols attested for Quraysh (Balādhurī, *Ansāb*, I, 185, citing Wāqidī; cf. Wāqidī, *Maghāzī*, II, 493). Abū Sufyān invoked Hubal at Uḥud (Wāqidī, *Maghāzī*, I, 296 f.; also cited elsewhere); and Hubal is sometimes said to have been the greatest idol of Quraysh (Wāqidī, *Maghāzī*, II, 832; Azraqī, *Makka*, p. 73; Ibn al-Kalbī, *Aṣnām*, p. 27). But Abū Sufyān also invoked al-'Uzzā at Uḥud (Wāqidī, *Maghāzī*, I, 297; Balādhurī, *Ansāb*, I, 327; compare Ibn Hishām, *Leben*, p. 811, on Allāt's cavalry); and al-'Uzzā is also said to have been the greatest idol of Quraysh (cf. the follow-

goddesses, or any one of them: it was outside Mecca at shrines guarded by other people that they would worship them, al-ʿUzzā at Nakhla being their greatest idol, according to Ibn al-Kalbī.[98]

The tradition clearly envisages them as guardians on behalf of Allāh, the God of Abraham and the future God of Islam. "We are the sons of Abraham, the people of the holy territory (*ḥurma*), the guardians of the shrine (*wulāt al-bayt*), and the residents of Mecca," as Quraysh would say.[99] The Kaʿba was "the holy house of Allāh" (*bayt allāh al-ḥarām*), and "the holy house of Allāh and his friend Abraham."[100] Like other Arabs, Quraysh had corrupted their Abrahamic monotheism by the adoption of polytheist gods.[101] But it was they who maintained the crucial features of Abrahamic monotheism that survived: belief in Allāh and the conduct of pilgrimage to his house.[102] And it was because of this role that they enjoyed a position of superiority in Arabia.[103]

How much truth is there to this account? The belief that Abraham had bequeathed a monotheist religion to his Arab descendants is attested for northwest Arabia as early as the fifth century in a Greek source.[104] It

---

ing note). She is well attested in the theophoric names of Quraysh, whereas Hubal is not. In fact, no theophoric name seems to be attested for him at all; and though Hubal figures as a personal name, it does not do so among Quraysh (cf. Caskel, *Ǧamhara*, II, *s.v.*; Lüling's view that Hubal should be identified as Abel seems unacceptable, cf. *Wiederentdeckung*, pp. 169 ff.).

[98] Ibn al-Kalbī, *Aṣnām*, pp. 14 ff., 27; cf. Wellhausen, *Reste*, pp. 24 ff.

[99] Ibn Hishām, *Leben*, p. 126, where they invent the Ḥums on this ground.

[100] Ibn Hishām, *Leben*, pp. 31, 33; cf. p. 15, where Jewish rabbis confirm that this was so.

[101] Cf. Ibn Hishām, *Leben*, pp. 15, 51.

[102] The pilgrimage is identified as Abrahamic in, for example, Masʿūdī, *Murūj*, III, 99 (with reference to Qur'ān, 2:121); Ibn Hishām, *Leben*, p. 126; and the pilgrims are guests of Allāh and visitors to his *bayt*, *ibid.*, pp. 83, 87.

[103] Ibn Hishām, *Leben*, p. 126; cf. Ibn Ḥabīb, *Muḥabbar*, p. 264; Marzūqī, *Azmina*, II, 162.

[104] Cf. Sozomen, *Kirchengeschichte*, VI, 38, 10ff. = *The Ecclesiastical History of Sozomen*, pp. 309 f. Sozomen, a fifth-century native of Gaza whose mother tongue could well have been Arabic (his name was Salamanes), informs us that the Arabs descend from Ishmael and Hagar, that such being their descent they abstain from pork and observe other Jewish practices, and that insofar as they deviate from the practices of the Jews, this must be ascribed to the lapse of time and contact with other nations: Moses only legislated for the Jews whom he led out of Egypt, and the inhabitants of the neighbouring region (*sc.* Arabia)

is thus not impossible that Quraysh should have adopted Abrahamic descent and beliefs even before Islam, though it is hard to believe that the whole of Arabia could have done the same. But if Quraysh saw themselves as guardians on behalf of Abraham's God, all while acknowledging the existence of other deities, their reaction to Muḥammad becomes exceedingly hard to understand. When Muḥammad attacked polytheism, Quraysh reacted with a vigorous defence of Allāt, Manāt, al-ʿUzzā, and to some extent even Hubal, invoking them in battle against Muḥammad and demanding belief in them from the converts whom they tried to make recant.[105] In other words, they reacted by mobilizing all the deities in whom they had no vested interest against the very God they were supposed to represent. If they owed their superior position in Arabia to their association with Abraham's God, why was it the pagan deities they chose to defend? And if Abraham's God was the God of their fathers, why was it the pagan gods they chose to describe as ancestral?[106] The tradition clearly has a problem on its hands in that it wishes to describe Quraysh as monotheists and polytheists alike: on the one hand they were repositories of the aboriginal monotheism that Muḥammad was to revive; and on the other hand they were polytheist zealots against whom Muḥammad had to fight.[107] They cannot have been both

---

probably soon forgot the laws imposed on them by their forefather Ishmael. All this could, of course, be Christian inference from the Bible. But Sozomen goes on to say that since then Arab tribes have heard of their true origin from the Jews and returned to the observance of Jewish laws and customs: even at the present day, he says, there are Arabs who regulate their lives according to Jewish precepts. What Sozomen's information adds up to is that by the fifth century the Arabs themselves had become familiar with the idea that they were Abrahamic monotheists by origin, at least in the Gaza area (a Qurashī *matjar*), and that some of them reacted by becoming what the Islamic tradition describes as *ḥanīf*s (on whom see now U. Rubin, "Ḥanīfiyya and Kaʿba. An Inquiry into the Arabian Pre-Islamic Background of Dīn Ibrāhīm"). It is worth noting that they owed the idea to contact with Jews, not with Christians.

105 Cf. above, n97.

106 Ibn Hishām, *Leben*, pp. 167 ff., on the Qurashī reaction to Muḥammad's public preaching: *yā Abā Ṭālib inna ibn akhīka qad sabba ālihatanā wa-ʿāba dīnanā wa-saffaha aḥlāmanā wa-ḍallala ābāʾanā . . . lā naṣbiru ʿalā hādha min shatm ābāʾinā wa-tasfīh aḥlāminā wa-ʿayb ālihatinā . . . qad khālafa dīnaka wa-dīn ābāʾika.*

107 The pre-Islamic Arabs at large are similarly displayed now as future monotheists and now as disbelievers. (When they abstain from buying and selling during the pilgrimage, they are proto-Muslims; but when they trade during the pilgrimage and are forbidden to

in historical fact. If we accept that they resisted Muḥammad more or less as described, the claim that they represented the God of Abraham must be dismissed.

This does not, of course, rule out the possibility that they represented an indigenous deity known as Allāh, and it is as guardians of such a deity that they are generally envisaged in the secondary literature. But this hypothesis is also problematic.

Admittedly, up to a point it makes good sense. Allāh is associated with a black stone, and some traditions hold that originally this stone was sacrificial.[108] This suggests that it was the stone rather than the building around it which was *bayt allāh*, the house of god, and this gives us a perfect parallel with the Old Testament *bethel*. The cult of the Arab god Dusares (Dhū Sharā) also seems to have centred on a black sacrificial stone.[109] According to Epiphanius, he was worshipped together with his mother, the virginal Kaabou, or in other words *kāʿib* or *kaʿʿāb*, a girl with swelling breasts.[110] A similar arrangement is met in a Nabataean inscription from Petra that speaks of sacrificial stones (*nṣyb*ʾ = *anṣāb*) belonging to "the lord of this house" (*mr*ʾ *byt*ʾ) and al-ʿUzzā, another *kāʿib* lady.[111] If we assume that *bayt* and *kaʿba* alike originally referred to the Meccan stone rather than the building around it, then the lord of the Meccan house was a pagan Allāh worshipped in conjunction with a female consort such as al-ʿUzzā and/or other "daughters of God."[112] This would give us a genuinely pagan deity for Quraysh and at the same time explain their devotion to goddesses.[113]

But if Quraysh represented Allāh, what was Hubal doing in their

---

approach the Holy Mosque, they are proto-*dhimmīs*.) But it is, understandably, in connection with the Prophet's own tribe that this dual perspective is most marked. Compare below, ch. 10, p. 233.

[108] It owed its colour to the pagan practice of pouring blood and intestines over it (cf. U. Rubin, "Places of Worship in Mecca"). But as might be expected, there are also other explanations of its colour.

[109] J. H. Mordtmann, "Dusares bei Epiphanius," p. 104, citing Suidas.

[110] *Ibid.*, pp. 101 f.

[111] T. Nöldeke, "Der Gott *Mr*ʾ *Byt*ʾ und die Kaʿba," p. 184.

[112] Cf. Wellhausen, *Reste*, p. 24. Note that al-ʿUzzā appears as the mother of Allāt and Manāt in the poem cited by Ibn Hishām, *Leben*, p. 145.

[113] But it would, of course, also require rejection of the contention that they worshipped al-ʿUzzā (and/or other "daughters of God") at sanctuaries other than the Kaʿba.

shrine? Indeed, what was the building doing? No sacrifices can be made over a stone immured in a wall, and a building accommodating Hubal makes no sense around a stone representing Allāh. Naturally Quraysh were polytheists, but the deities of polytheist Arabia preferred to be housed separately. No pre-Islamic sanctuary, be it stone or building, is known to have accommodated more than one male god, as opposed to one male god and female consort. The Allāh who is attested in an inscription of the late second century A.D. certainly was not forced to share his house with other deities.[114] And the shrines of Islamic Arabia are similarly formed around the tomb of a single saint. If Allāh was a pagan god like any other, Quraysh would not have allowed Hubal to share the sanctuary with him—not because they were proto-monotheists, but precisely because they were pagans.

One would thus have to fall back on the view that Allah was not a god like any other. On the one hand, Allāh might simply be another name for Hubal, as Wellhausen suggested: just as the Israelites knew Yahwe as Elohim, so the Arabs knew Hubal as Allāh, meaning simply "God."[115] It would follow that the guardians of Hubal and Allāh were identical; and since Quraysh were not guardians of Hubal, they would not be guardians of Allāh, either. But as Wellhausen himself noted, Allāh had long ceased to be a label that could be applied to any deity. Allāh was the personal name of a specific deity, on a par with Allāt, not merely a noun meaning "god"; and in the second century this deity had guardians of his own.[116] When ʿAbd al-Muṭṭalib is described as having prayed to Allāh while consulting Hubal's arrows, it is simply that the sources baulk at depicting the Prophet's grandfather as a genuine pagan, not that Allāh and Hubal were alternative names for the same god.[117] If Hubal

[114] J. T. Milik, "Inscriptions grecques et nabatéennes de Rawwāfah," p. 58 (I am indebted to Dr. G. M. Hinds for drawing my attention to this inscription). A certain Šaʿdat here identifies himself as priest (*'fkl*) of *'lh'* and builder of his temple (*byt'*).

[115] Wellhausen, *Reste*, pp. 75 f.; cf. p. 218.

[116] Cf. above, n114.

[117] Ibn Hishām, *Leben*, pp. 94, 98 (the first passage is defective in the Wüstenfeld edition, "Allāh" having fallen out, but cf. Ibn Hishām, *al-Sīra al-nabawiyya*, ed. M. al-Saqqā and others, 147; the second passage was adduced by Wellhausen from Ṭabarī, *Ta'rīkh*, ser. 1, p. 1,076, cf. p. 1,077). Similarly (on another occasion) Ibn Isḥāq in the recension of Yūnus b. Bukayr (Ḥamīdallah, *Sīra*, no. 28); compare Ibn Isḥāq in the recension of Ibn Hishām, where Hubal is omitted (*Leben*, pp. 106 f.).

and Allāh had been one and the same deity, Hubal ought to have survived as an epithet of Allāh, which he did not. And moreover, there would not have been traditions in which people are asked to renounce the one for the other.[118]

On the other hand, Allāh might have been a high God over and above all other deities. This is, in fact, how Wellhausen saw him, and he has been similarly represented by Watt.[119] It is not how he appears in the inscriptional material, in which he is very much the god of a particular people;[120] and the fact that he was known as Allāh, "the god," is no indication of supremacy: Allāt, "the goddess," was not a deity over and above al-ʿUzzā or Manāt. But he could, of course, have developed into such a god, as the Qur'ānic evidence adduced by Wellhausen and Watt suggests. If we accept this view, however, we are up against the problem that he is unlikely to have had guardians of his own in this capacity. Viewed as a high god, Allāh was too universal, too neutral, and too impartial to be the object of a particularist cult, as Wellhausen noted; no sanctuary was devoted to him *except* insofar as he had come to be identified with ordinary deities.[121] A high god in Arabia was apparently one who neither needed nor benefitted from cultic links with a specific group of devotees. (Wellhausen may of course be wrong: maybe a high god in Arabia *did* benefit from such links. But if so, we are back at the problem of why Allāh was made to share these links with Hubal.)

If Quraysh were guardians on behalf of an Allāh above all other deities, they must thus have started as guardians of someone else. But as has been seen, they do not appear to have been guardians of Hubal, and Hubal was not identified with Allāh, nor did his cult assist that of Allāh in any way.[122] And if we postulate that they started as guardians of an or-

[118] Cf. above, n97.

[119] He was the highest god (Wellhausen, *Reste*, p. 76), different from the *Götzen* (*ibid.*, pp. 218 f.), and above tribal and cultic divisions (*ibid.*, pp. 219, 221 ff.). Cf. W. M. Watt, "The 'High God' in Pre-Islamic Mecca"; *id.*, "The Qur'ān and Belief in a 'High God.' "

[120] He was the god of Rubat, the tribe to which the guardian belonged, cf. Milik, "Inscriptions," p. 58, adducing an inscription in which Ilāhā is asked to regard the tribe of Rubat with benevolence.

[121] Wellhausen, *Reste*, pp. 219, 221.

[122] *Pace* Fahd in *EI*², *s.v.* Hubal, where we are told that "in the field of popular piety at least, it eclipsed the other deities in the Meccan pantheon, to such an extent that there has been some speculation whether the unanimity regarding this cult did not help prepare the

dinary Allah who subsequently developed into a supreme deity, we reinstate the problem of Hubal's presence in his shrine. The fact is that the Hubal-Allāh sanctuary of Mecca is an oddity; can such a shrine have existed in historical fact? There would seem to be at least two sanctuaries behind the one depicted in the tradition, and Quraysh do not come across as guardians of either.

Their supposed guardianship notwithstanding, Quraysh appear as laymen in the sources. It is as laymen that they seek out *kāhin*s and *kāhina*s when in trouble and consult Hubal's arrows for expert advice. It is likewise as laymen that they are free to be devotees of as many gods as they like, joining the crowds of Kinānīs and other Muḍarīs around al-ʿUzzā at Nakhla,[123] visiting Allāt at Ṭā'if and Manāt at Qudayd, making annual pilgrimages to an idol at Buwāna,[124] and joining the annual *ḥajj* to sanctuaries outside Mecca. There is nothing in this behaviour to suggest special identification with or interest in a particular god, and at no point do we see Quraysh in the role of professional dispensers of religious services to others. The tradition credits them with a guardianship by presenting Mecca as the *ḥaram* in which the Abrahamic pilgrimage culminated: when we see Quraysh leave their city in a state of *iḥrām* we are not to take it, the sources insist, that Quraysh are going as pilgrims to other places, but on the contrary that they are leaving so as to return as pilgrims to the very city from which they had come. There was nothing to the guardianship apart from the pilgrimage. Quraysh were thus guardians in the sense that they looked after the Muslim pilgrimage to the sanctuary of the Muslim God: all genuinely pagan functions were in the hands of others. Take away the Muslim elements and the guardianship dissolves, leaving Quraysh as ordinary traders.

---

way for Allāh." But what the evidence shows is precisely that the cult of Allāt and al-ʿUzzā eclipsed that of Hubal (cf. above, n97); and Fahd has misunderstood Wellhausen, to whom he refers as an authority for his view. Wellhausen was out to explain why one hears so *little* about Hubal, not why he was so popular; and his solution was that Hubal *was* Allah, not that he prepared the way for him: the two names referred to one and the same deity.

[123] This shrine was venerated by Quraysh, Kināna, and all Muḍar, according to Ibn Hishām, *Leben*, p. 839; cf. also Ibn al-Kalbī, *Aṣnām*, pp. 18, 27.

[124] For Buwāna, see Ibn Saʿd, *Ṭabaqāt*, I, 158, 161; III, 380; Kalāʿī, *Iktifā'*, p. 257. It is one of the idols renounced in Balādhurī, *Ansāb*, I, 185.

The relationship between Mecca and Qurashī trade may now be summarized as follows. Qurashī trade is said to have developed because Mecca was a halt on the incense route, because it was located at the crossroads of all major trade routes in Arabia, and especially because it was a sanctuary that attracted pilgrims once a year and afforded constant protection to those who wished to settle there. All these claims would appear to be wrong. Mecca was not located on the incense route, still less at the crossroads of all the major routes in Arabia. It was not an object of pilgrimage. It was not a sanctuary, or if it was, Quraysh were not apparently its guardians. And it did not, in fact, afford protection to those who settled there: settlers in Mecca owed their safety to alliances with members of Quraysh, not to the supposed sanctity of the Meccan territory.[125] The site was barren, devoid of a fertile hinterland except for Ṭā'if, ill-equipped for maritime trade, and much too far away for a caravan trade with Syria of the kind that the sources describe.

Did Quraysh really have their trading center in this place? If we accept that they did, we will have to grant that Quraysh became traders despite the nature of the place in which they settled, not because of it; and we will also need to reinterpret the nature of their trade, conceding that it must have been conducted largely independently of Mecca, in some variation or other of the ʿUqaylī model. If we reject the identification of their center with modern Mecca, we can relocate them somewhere in northwest Arabia and thus accept the picture presented on their trade; but in return we are left with a southern connection of an enigmatic kind. Either way, the sources on the rise of Islam are wrong in one or more fundamental respects.

From the point of view of the rise of Islam, the problem may be restated as follows. We seem to have all the ingredients for Muḥammad's career in northwest Arabia. Qurashī trade sounds perfectly viable, indeed more intelligible, without its south Arabian and Ethiopian extensions, and there is a case for a Qurashī trading center, or at least dias-

[125] All foreigners in Mecca were either *ḥalīf*s or *mawālī* of Qurashīs; yet an asylum is supposed to afford protection to those who cannot find *people* to help them. Barrāḍ was an outlaw who sought refuge in Mecca, but he owed his safety there to his alliance with Ḥarb b. Umayya: had Ḥarb chosen to disown him, he would have been no safer in Mecca than anywhere else (cf. above, ch. 6, p. 146).

pora, in the north. One might locate it in Ptolemy's Moka.[126] Somewhere in the north, too, there was a desert sanctuary of pan-Arabian importance, according to Nonnosus.[127] Mecca originated as a desert sanctuary, according to Kalbī;[128] it still sounds like one in the accounts of Muʿāwiya's building activities there;[129] and the sanctuary that

[126] Cf. above, ch. 6 n17.

[127] "Most of the Saracens, those of the Phoinikōn and those beyond it and beyond the Taurenian mountains, consider as sacred a place dedicated to I do not know what god, and assemble there twice a year. Of these gatherings, the first lasts a whole month and goes on until the middle of spring . . . the other lasts two months. . . . While these gatherings last, they live, says Nonnosus, in complete peace not only with each other, but also with all the people who live in their country. They claim that even the wild beasts live in peace with men and, what is more, among themselves" (Nonnosus cited by Photius, *Bibliothèque*, I, 5 f.; cf. Wellhausen, *Reste*, p. 101). The Phoinikōn are presumably the Palm Groves of Procopius (*Wars*, I, 19, 7 ff.; II, 3, 41) on the northern Red Sea Coast. The Taurenian mountains ought to be Jabal Ṭayyi'. If so, the sanctuary was presumably located somewhere in the north. As noted before, Epiphanius' month of *Aggathalbaeith* (*Ḥijjat al-bayt*) also suggests the existence of a pilgrim centre in the north (*EI*², *s.v.* ḥadjdj).

[128] Bakrī, *Muʿjam*, p. 58: Hishām said that Kalbī said, "people would go on pilgrimage and then disperse, so that Mecca would remain empty, nobody being there." Noted by Wellhausen, *Reste*, p. 92. Given the transfer of information from the pilgrim fairs, this clearly suggests that the first Muslim sanctuary simply *was* one or more of these fairs. Such a hypothesis would, however, require relocation of one or more of the fairs in question in the north. Lammens was not averse to relocation (cf. *Mecque*, pp. 131n, 153 f.), and it would be neat to conflate the pilgrim fairs with Nonnosus' *ḥaram*, identifying both with the first sanctuary of Islam. (Nonnosus' sanctuary was visited first for a month and next for two, whereas the pilgrim fairs were only visited during the two months of Dhū'l-Qaʿda and Dhū'l-Ḥijja. But if the *ʿumra* of Rajab also went to the pilgrim fairs rather than to Mecca [as it seems to do above, n39], this problem disappears.) It would, of course, also be simplistic in the sense that there must have been several pilgrim centres in pre-Islamic Arabia. But if we choose not to identify Nonnosus' *ḥaram* with the pilgrim fairs, we must acknowledge that a sanctuary of major importance in Arabia disappeared without leaving any trace whatever in the tradition. And if we similarly choose not to identify it with the first sanctuary of Islam, this silence becomes particularly odd: a rival *ḥaram* of such importance ought to have been an object of invectives.

[129] When Muʿāwiya began his building activities in Mecca, there was a storm of protest, not only because he had no right to plant orchards in a place that God himself had described as devoid of cultivation but also because it was felt that Mecca ought to be a place "with wide unbuilt spaces . . . accessible to everyone" (Kister, "Some Reports," pp. 86 ff.). People used to pitch their tents anywhere in the sanctuary area, and this was how things ought to remain (*ibid.*, pp. 86 f.). Compare the conscious (and successful) effort to keep Minā unpopulated (*ibid.*, p. 88; Azraqī, *Makka*, p. 400; cf. Yāqūt, *Buldān*, IV, 643, *s.v.*).

Muʿāwiya turned into "towns and palaces"[130] must have been located somewhere in the north.[131] Jewish communities are well attested for northwest Arabia. Even Abrahamic monotheism is documented there,[132] and the prophet who was to make a new religion of this belief was himself a trader in northwest Arabia. Yet everything is supposed to have happened much further south, in a place described as a sanctuary town inhabited since time immemorial,[133] located, according to some, in an unusually fertile environment,[134] associated with southern tribes

[130] Cf. Kister, "Some Reports," p. 88, where ʿĀʾisha reproves Muʿāwiya for having turned Mecca into *madāʾin wa-quṣūr*, whereas God had made it free for all (Fākihī).

[131] Cf. the *qibla* of the pre-Umayyad mosque of Kufa (Balādhurī, *Futūḥ*, p. 276) and those of the Umayyad mosques of Wāsiṭ and Ishaf Beni Junayd (Crone and Cook, *Hagarism*, p. 23, adducing archaeological evidence and Jāḥiẓ, *Rasāʾil*, p. 296). For Jacob of Edessa's observations on the *qibla*, see *ibid.*, p. 173 n30. There is, of course, no question of explaining away this evidence with reference to the assumption that Christian authors were so prejudiced against Islam that they could not tell east or west from south (Jacob of Edessa), or that the conquerors themselves had so little sense of direction that they could not tell west from south (Balādhurī, the archaeological evidence). It could be argued that the Umayyad had officially adopted a *qibla* facing *jihat* (as opposed to *ʿayn*) *al-Kaʿba*, which would allow them an orientation from due west to due south in Iraq, due east to due south in Egypt (cf. D. A. King, "The Practical Interpretation of Qurʾān 2.144: Some Remarks on the Sacred Direction in Islam." I owe my knowledge of this paper to Dr. G. M. Hinds). It is, however, somewhat unlikely that recent conquerors with a strong sense of where they came from should have adopted a simplistic *qibla* notion popular with *ʿulamāʾ* in medieval Central Asia and Spain. The fact that the two Umayyad mosques of Iraq are both orientated too far north by about 30 degrees (in fact 30 and 33) suggests that the Umayyads were aiming at precision. So does the tradition that the mosque of ʿAmr b. al-ʿĀṣ in Egypt pointed too far north and had to be corrected in the governorship of Qurra b. Sharīk (Crone and Cook, *Hagarism*, p. 24). And Jāḥiẓ certainly did not explain the deviant *qibla* of Wāsiṭ as an instance of orientation towards *jihat al-Kaʿba*: as far as he was concerned, it was plain wrong. The evidence for an Islamic sanctuary in northwest Arabia thus remains impressive.

[132] Cf. above, n104.

[133] Or more precisely since Abraham (cf. Ibn Hishām, *Leben*, p. 51). Note that it was a real city, not just a scatter of encampments: already in the days of the Amalekites and Jurhummites it was ruled by proper kings, one in the lower part and one in the upper part of the city, who could collect tithes (cf. above, n6). When Quṣayy settled Quraysh in Mecca, he continued the collection of tithes (Ibn Saʿd, *Tabaqat*, I, 70).

[134] Thus the story of the migration of Ketura and Jurhum has these two tribes settle in Mecca on grounds of its lush vegetation (Ibn Hishām, *Leben*, pp. 71 f.; *Aghānī*, XV, 12; Azraqī, *Makka*, pp. 45, 47). The Amalekites also benefitted from its fertility (Azraqī, *Makka*, p. 50; Ṭabarī, *Taʾrīkh*, ser. I, p. 278). It was still *kathīr al-shajar waʾl-ʿiḍāh waʾl-*

such as Jurhum and Khuzāʿa, linked with Ethiopia and the Yemen, and endowed with a building accommodating Hubal and his priests.[135] Why? What is the historical relationship between these places? Whatever the solution, we are unlikely to find it with the methodology that currently prevails in the field.

---

salam when Quṣayy occupied it (Ibn Saʿd, *Ṭabaqat*, I, 71). It is characterized as *muʿtalij al-baṭḥāʾ*, "a plain with luxuriant herbage" in Ibn Hishām, *Leben*, p. 65 (cf. Lane, *Lexicon*, *s.v. iʿtalaja*). Ibn al-Zubayr was the son of *muʿtalij al-biṭāḥ* (ʿUbaydallāh Ibn Qays al-Ruqayyāt, *Dīwān*, XLVII, 1; translated "dichtest bewachsenenen der Thalgründe [von Mecca]"); and a later ʿAlid boasted of being the same (D. S. Margoliouth, ed. and tr., *The Table-Talk of a Mesopotamian Judge*, p. 51 = 56; translated "the meeting-place of the low grounds"). It could, of course, be argued that these statements merely reflect other people's ideas about qualities required in a sanctuary (cf. Crone and Cook, *Hagarism*, p. 22 and n16 thereto; A. J. Wensinck, *The Ideas of the Western Semites Concerning the Navel of the Earth*, pp. 34 f.). On the other hand, if there is any reality to the sanctuary town in question, it makes sense that it should have been located in a fertile environment.

[135] Hubal clearly belongs in a town, not in an open-air sanctuary. He had Khuzāʿī guardians. He was introduced by a Khuzāʿī, too (ʿAmr b. Luḥayy/Rabīʿa, the ancestor of Khuzāʿa, who was guardian of the Meccan shrine). It is true that epigraphically he seems to be a northern rather than a southern divinity (cf. EI^2, *s.v.*), that Ibn al-Kalbī credits his introduction to Khuzayma, the ancestor of Kināna, rather than to ʿAmr b. Luḥayy (*Aṣnām*, p. 28; repeated by Ibn Saʿd, *Ṭabaqāt*, I, 69; Balādhurī, *Ansāb*, I, 37), and that ʿAmr b. Luḥayy himself is supposed to have imported him from the north: he brought him from the Balqāʾ (Ibn Ḥabīb, *Munammaq*, pp. 353 f.), or from Hīt in the Jazīra (Azraqī, *Makka*, pp. 31, 58, 73, 133). But the one Qurashī who is associated with Hubal is ʿAbd al-Muṭṭalib (cf. above, n117), and ʿAbd al-Muṭṭalib is consistently associated with the south: he journeys to the Yemen (above, ch. 5 n66), negotiates with Abraha in the story of the elephant (Ibn Hishām, *Leben*, pp. 33 ff.), and goes to Ṣanʿāʾ to congratulate the Yemenis on the expulsion of the Ethiopians (above, ch. 5 n81). Note that ʿAlī is also associated with the south: he was sent on campaign to the Yemen by the Prophet on two occasions (Ibn Hishām, *Leben*, p. 999); and the author of the "Secrets of Simon b. Yoḥai" apparently believed him to be a Yoktanid from the Ḥaḍramawt (cf. Crone and Cook, *Hagarism*, p. 178 n68). As noted several times before, there was also a strong Yemeni contingent with ʿAlī at Ṣiffīn and in the following of Mukhtār (according to W. M. Watt, *Islam and the Integration of Society*, pp. 105 f., the entire development of Shīʿism can be credited to Yemeni influence). Yet Muḥammad himself is consistently associated with Syria, except for the tradition in which he trades at Ḥubāsha.

PART III

CONCLUSION

9

THE SOURCES

This is a book in which little has been learnt and much unlearnt. Part of what has been unlearnt is a cluster of ideas without support in the sources, but a good deal more consists of contentions made by the sources themselves. That the sources on the rise of Islam are of questionable historical value has long been recognized. The trend until recently, however, has been toward general acceptance of their veracity, and the secondary literature frequently treats them as straightforward historical reports. This they are not, as should be clear already, and most of our conventional knowledge about the rise of Islam will have to be unlearnt when this is recognized. What kind of sources are they, then?

Leaving aside sources outside the Islamic tradition, the bulk of our information on the rise of Islam is derived from the Qur'ān and the amorphous mass of material subsumed under the label of ḥadīth, that is, the countless traditions on the sayings and doings of the Prophet, the Companions, and other early figures that are preserved in exegetical, historical, legal, and other works, as well as in special ḥadīth collections. There is, of course, material on pre-Islamic Arabia of a quite different kind: tribal tradition, poetry, information derived from Sāsānid annals, and so forth. Such material is of decisive importance for our reconstruction of the context in which the new religion arose, and some use has been made of it in the present work. It poses problems of its own that must be left aside here. As soon as we start asking questions about the actual rise of the new religion, however, we find ourselves heavily dependent on Qur'ān and ḥadīth, and it is to these two sources that the present chapter is devoted.

The Qur'ān is generally, though not invariably, regarded as a contemporary source, or in other words as the preaching of Muḥammad himself. Whether or not this is correct, the Qur'ān does not offer much historical information, and what it does offer is formulated in a style so allusive that it is largely unintelligible on its own. Without the help of the exegetical literature one would not be able to identify the historical events referred to in verses such as "it is He who restrained their hands from you, and your hands from them, in the hollow of Mecca, after He had made you victorious over them" (48:24); "God has already helped you on many fields, and on the day of Ḥunayn, when your multitude was pleasing to you, but it availed you naught, and the land for all its breadth was strait for you, and you turned about, retreating" (9:25); "O believers, remember God's blessings upon you when the hosts came against you . . . there it was that the believers were tried . . . and when the hypocrites . . . said, 'God and His messenger promised us only delusion.' And when a part of them said, 'O people of Yathrib, there is no abiding here for you, therefore return.' And a part of them were asking leave of the Prophet, saying 'our houses are exposed,' yet they were not exposed; they desired only to flee" (33:9 ff.); "and God most surely helped you at Badr, when you were utterly abject" (3:119). This last verse seems intelligible because the story of the battle of Badr is very familiar. It is not, however, familiar from the Qur'ān. If the Qur'ān were our only source on the rise of Islam, we would know that the rise of the new religion had something to do with a man called Muḥammad, who claimed to be an apostle of God and who operated somewhere in northwest Arabia, apparently in the vicinity of Lot's remains in the Balqā'; but we would not be able to say anything about the historical events that led to the acceptance of his message.[1]

For practical purposes, our sources are thus exegetical ḥadith plus ḥadīth of other kinds. It is not generally appreciated how much of our information on the rise of Islam, including that on Meccan trade, is derived from exegesis of the Qur'ān, nor is it generally admitted that such information is of dubious historical value. I should like to illustrate the nature of this information with reference to *Sūrat Quraysh*, a sura that we have already encountered on several occasions.[2]

[1] Cf. M. Cook, *Muhammad*, pp. 69 f. Cf. also J. Wansbrough, *Quranic Studies*, p. 56: "the role of the Qur'ān in the delineation of an Arabian prophet was peripheral: evidence of a divine communication but not a report of its circumstances. . . . The very notion of biographical data in the Qur'ān depends on exegetical principles derived from material external to the canon."

[2] Cf. above, chs 4 and 5, on what and where the Meccans traded.

Sūrat Quraysh consists of four lines that may be rendered as follows:

1. For the *īlāf* of Quraysh,
2. their *īlāf* of the journey in winter and summer.
3. So worship the lord of this house, who fed them against a hunger
4. and gave them security from a fear.

Īlāf has been left untranslated because its meaning is uncertain; also, some exegetes read the initial *li* as an expression of surprise rather than as a preposition meaning "for."[3] But otherwise the translation is straightforward. What then does the sura say?

It mentions a journey in summer and winter. The context gives no indication of what journeys are intended, but the exegetes are ready to assist. The journeys, we are told, were the greater and lesser pilgrimages to Mecca: the *ḥajj* in Dhū'l-ḥijja and the *ʿumra* in Rajab.[4] Alternatively, they were the migrations of Quraysh to Ṭā'if in the summer and their return to Mecca in the winter.[5] Or else they were Qurashī trading journeys. Most exegetes hold them to have been trading journeys, but where did they go? They went to Syria, we are told: Quraysh would travel by the hot coastal route to Ayla in the winter and by the cool inland route to Buṣrā and Adhri'āt in the summer.[6] Or else they went to Syria and somewhere else, such as Syria and Rūm, however that is to be understood,[7] or Syria and the Yemen, as is more commonly said: Quraysh would go to Syria in the summer and to the Yemen in the winter, when Syria was too cold,[8] or else to Syria in the winter and the Yemen in the summer, when the route to Syria was too hot.[9] Alternatively, they went

[3] Cf. Ṭabarī, *Jāmiʿ*, xxx, 198.

[4] Rāzī, *Mafātīḥ*, viii, 512.

[5] Ibn ʿAbbās in Ṭabarī, *Jāmiʿ*, xxx, 171. Also reproduced elsewhere.

[6] Suyūṭī, *Durr*, vi, 398, citing ʿIkrima. Muqātil similarly has them travel by the coastal route in the winter; but instead of having them travel by the inland route in the summer, he has them go to the Yemen (*Tafsīr*, fol. 253a).

[7] Suyūṭī, *Durr*, vi, 397, once more citing ʿIkrima; similarly Ḥusayn b. Aḥmad Ibn Khālawayh, *Mukhtaṣar fī shawādhdh al-qur'ān*, p. 180.

[8] Ṭabarī, *Jāmiʿ*, xxx, 171, citing Ḍaḥḥāk, Kalbī, Ibn Zayd, and ʿIkrima (the latter specifying Buṣrā and the Yemen), also cited by Suyūṭī; Ibn Qutayba, *Mushkil al-qur'ān*, p. 319; Bayḍāwī *Anwār*, ii, 620; Qummī, *Tafsīr*, ii, 444; Ibn Ḥabīb, *Munammaq*, p. 262, citing Kalbī.

[9] Muqātil, *Tafsīr*, fol. 253a.

to Syria and Ethiopia: to Syria in the summer and Ethiopia in the winter, or maybe the other way round.[10] Or they went to Syria, the Yemen, *and* Ethiopia[11]; or to Syria and Rūm on the one hand and the Yemen and Ethiopia on the other;[12] or to Syria, the Yemen, Ethiopia, and Iraq: to Syria in the summer and to the rest in the winter, according to those who specify.[13] Several of these views are offered outside the exegetical literature proper, though clearly in explanation of the Qur'ān. It is clearly also in explanation of the Qur'ān that we are told of Hāshim's institution of the two journeys,[14] or of one of them,[15] or of all four, [16] though the classical exegetical literature omits this point.

What does the sura say about these journeys? Verse 3 proceeds, "so worship the lord of this house," implying that there was a logical relationship between worship and journeys, and all the exegetes agree that this is so. But in what way? According to some, Quraysh are here being told to worship God because He enabled them to go on these journeys, thereby securing provisions for Mecca,[17] or because He enabled them to continue to do so despite the Ethiopian threat to Mecca.[18] According to others, they are being told to worship God as much as they travel,[19] or to worship Him instead of traveling, the journeys leaving them no time to do so.[20] And according to still others, they are being told to worship

[10] Wāqidī, *Maghāzī*, I, 197 (to Syria in the summer and Ethiopia in the winter); Ya'qūbī, *Ta'rīkh*, I, 280 (the other way round); Ibn Abī'l-Ḥadīd, *Sharḥ*, III, 457 (where no seasons are specified).

[11] Ibn Sa'd, *Ṭabaqāt*, I, 75, citing Kalbī.

[12] Tha'ālibī, *Thimār*, p. 115; cf. Jāḥiẓ, *Rasā'il*, p. 70.

[13] Cf. above, ch. 5 n1. The seasons are supplied by Balādhurī, *Ansāb*, I, 59.

[14] Cf. Balādhurī, *Ansāb*, I, 58; Ibn Sa'd, *Ṭabaqāt*, I, 75; Ṭabarī, *Ta'rīkh*, ser. 7, p. 1,089.

[15] Namely, the journey to Syria. Only Ya'qūbī seems to have noticed that the story of Hāshim and his three brothers conflicts with the claim that Hāshim *sanna al-riḥlatayn*: according to him, Hāshim instituted the two journeys to Syria and Ethiopia, whereupon his brothers went into action, one of them *renewing* the treaty with Ethiopia (*Ta'rīkh*, I, 280, 282).

[16] Cf. Kister, "Some Reports," pp. 61 f.

[17] Bayḍāwī, *Anwār*, II, 620; this is also the exegesis implicit in Ibn al-Kalbī's story of Hashim and his brothers.

[18] Ibn Qutayba, *Mushkil al-qur'ān*, pp. 319 f.

[19] Ṭabarī, *Jāmi'*, XXX, 199.

[20] *Ibid.*, p. 198, citing Ibn 'Abbās (*nahāhum 'an al-riḥla . . . fa-lam yakun lahum rāḥa*); similarly Ibn 'Abbās in the tradition identifying the two journeys as going to Ṭā'if and back, and 'Ikrima, *ibid.*, p. 199 (*fa-amarahum an yuqīmū bi-Makka*); Ibn Khālawayh,

Him because He put an end to these journeys, Ethiopians and/or others having taken over the provisioning of Mecca.[21]

So far, then, God has told Quraysh to worship Him as much as/because of/instead of two journeys of uncertain character and destination, which is very much what one can infer from the sura itself. But He also mentions that He has freed them from a certain hunger. What is He referring to?

According to some, He is referring to the fact that He enabled Quraysh to provision Mecca. This He did by letting Hāshim institute the two journeys,[22] or by defeating the Ethiopians so that they could continue to go on these journeys,[23] at any rate by means of these journeys,[24], or alternatively by putting an end to these journeys, letting others bring provisions to Mecca.[25] But according to others, the verse refers to a specific famine in Mecca. Either it was the pre-Islamic famine to which Hāshim reacted by importing bread from Syria: he made it into *tharīd* and fed it to his starving fellow-tribesmen, an activity to which he owed his name.[26] Or else it was the later famine with which Quraysh were afflicted by God in response to Muḥammad's prayer: when they converted, it came to an end.[27] Still others, though, propose that the verse refers to the hunger with which Qurashī families were afflicted in pre-Islamic times when impoverished families would withdraw to the desert until they died: Hāshim put an end to this practice by instituting the two

Mukhtaṣar, p. 180. Kalbī (cited by Ibn Ḥabīb, *Munammaq*, p. 262) and Muqātil (*Tafsīr*, fol. 253a), on the other hand, stress that the journeys were tiresome.

[21] Muqātil, *Tafsīr*, fol. 253a; Qummī, *Tafsīr*, II, 444.

[22] This is the implicit exegesis of the claim that Hāshim *sanna al-riḥlatayn*, as well as of Ibn al-Kalbī's story of Hāshim and his brothers.

[23] Ibn Qutayba, *Mushkil al-qur'ān*, p. 319.

[24] Bayḍāwī, *Anwār*, II, 620; Ṭūsī, *Tibyān*, x, 413 f.

[25] Ṭabarī, *Jāmi'*, xxx, 198; Qummī, *Tafsīr*, II, 444; Muqātil, *Tafsir*, fol. 253a; cf. also Kalbī in Ibn Ḥabīb, *Munammaq*, pp. 262 f.

[26] Ibn Ḥabīb, *Munammaq*, p. 263; Ibn Sa'd, *Ṭabaqāt*, I, 75 f.; Balādhurī, *Ansāb*, I, 58; Ṭabarī, *Ta'rīkh*, ser. I, p. 1,089. That this story is of exegetical origin is clear from the *isnād* given in Ibn Sa'd and Balādhurī (Kalbī from Abū Ṣāliḥ from Ibn 'Abbās); it is told in connection with *ḥadīth al-īlāf* in Ibn Ḥabīb (once more from Kalbī).

[27] Rāzī, *Mafātīḥ* VIII, 512, citing Kalbī. Kalbī thus had three explanations of the hunger, though this is the only one which is explicitly cited as such; cf. the previous note, where it is the hunger to which Hāshim reacted, and Ibn Ḥabīb, *Munammaq*, p. 263, where it is also implied to be the general hunger from which Quraysh were freed when others brought foodstuffs to Mecca, and where the wording is reminiscent of that cited by Rāzī.

trading journeys, attaching every poor man to someone rich, and letting rich and poor share in the proceeds until all were equally rich.[28] In short, the import of God's words on hunger are uncertain.

In what sense, then, did God free them from fear, as stated in verse 4? According to many, He freed them from fear of the road. This He did by letting Hāshim conclude *īlāf*-agreements with the tribes on the way to Syria and elsewhere,[29] or by conferring inviolability on them wherever they went,[30] or by putting an end to their journeys so that they could stay at home,[31] or by making Mecca itself inviolable.[32] According to others, however, the fear in question was fear of the Ethiopians, the verse being a reference to the defeat of the *aṣḥāb al-fīl*.[33] Alternatively, it was fear of leprosy,[34] or fear that the future caliphate might pass from Quraysh,[35] or fear in every sense of the word.[36] In short, the fear was either general or specific, and if specific of disputed nature.

We are thus left with the enigmatic word *īlāf* of lines 1-2. The exegetes disagreed over its reading: was it to be read *īlāf*, *ilāf* or *ilf*?[37] And they were even more divided over its meaning. Some took it to mean "habit" (of going on journeys),[38] others proposed "clinging to" (these journeys

[28] Rāzī, *Mafātīh*, VIII, 511, citing ʿAṭāʾ from Ibn ʿAbbās; similarly Suyūṭī, *Durr*, VI; 397, citing Zubayr b. Bakkār's *Muwaffaqiyyāt* (it is not found in the published part of this work); cf. Kister, "Mecca and Tamīm," pp. 122 f.

[29] Thus, implicitly, Ibn al-Kalbī's *īlāf*-tradition. The exegetical origin of this story is confirmed by Jāḥiẓ, *Rasāʾil*, p. 71 (where this and other accounts are explicitly characterized as *tafsīr āmanahum min khawf*), and Thaʿālibī, *Thimār*, p. 115 (where the story is told with the comment that Hāshim was the first to make the *īlāf* mentioned by God).

[30] Ṭabarī, *Jāmiʿ*, XXX, 200, citing Qatāda (twice); also reproduced by Suyūṭī; Ibn Qutayba, *Mushkil al-qurʾān*, p. 319.

[31] Qummī, *Tafsīr* II, 444.

[32] Ṭabarī, *Jāmiʿ*, XXX, pp. 199 f., citing Ibn ʿAbbās (on God's response to Abraham's prayer) and others; similarly Suyūṭī, *Durr*, VI, 397; Ṭūsī, *Tibyān*, X, 414. This also seems to be Muqātil's interpretation (*Tafsīr*, fol. 253a).

[33] Thus Aʿmash and Zubayr b. Bakkār in Suyūṭī, *Durr*, VI, 398; similarly Bayḍāwī, *Anwār*, II, 620.

[34] Thus several traditions in Ṭabarī, *Jāmiʿ*, XXX, 200; Ibn Ḥabīb, *Munammaq* p. 263, citing Kalbī (according to whom no Qurashī was ever afflicted with this disease); Ṭūsī, *Tibyān*, X, 414 (fear of the enemy or of leprosy); Bayḍāwī, *Auwār*, II, 620.

[35] Rāzī, *Mafātīḥ*, VIII, 513, with reference to other interpretations, too.

[36] Thus Ṭabarī himself (*Jāmiʿ*, XXX, 200).

[37] See for example Ibn Khālawayh, *Mukhtaṣar*, p. 180; Ṭabarī, *Jāmiʿ*, XXX, 197.

[38] Ibn al-Kalbī in Ibn Ḥabīb, *Munammaq*, p. 263; Ibn Saʿd, *Ṭabaqāt*, I, 75 (*daʾb*).

and/or the worship of God),[39] still others proposed "mutual love" or "harmony" (obtaining on these journeys and elsewhere);[40] some took it to mean "blessing" (conferred by these journeys),[41] and still others took it to mean "pacts" or "protection" (negotiated by Quraysh for their safety on these journeys, or for the collection of taxes devoted to Mecca's defence).[42]

In short, the sura refers to the fact that Quraysh used to trade in Syria, or in Syria and the Yemen, or in Syria and Ethiopia, or in all three, and maybe also in Iraq, or else to their habit of spending the summer in Ṭā'if, or else to ritual visits to Mecca. It celebrates the fact that they began to trade, or that they continued to do so, or that they stopped; or else it does not refer to trade at all. It alludes to a Meccan need for imported foodstuffs, or to a Meccan famine, or to a Meccan habit of committing suicide by starvation; it refers to Qurashī agreements with other tribes, or to Qurashī inviolability, or to the inviolability of Mecca or its need for defence, or to its safety after the Ethiopian defeat, or to Qurashī exemption from leprosy, or the Qurashī monopoly on the caliphate; and it does all this using a word that means habit, or clinging to, or mutual love, or divine blessing, or pact and protection.

What the exegetical tradition has to say on *Sūrat Quraysh* may thus be reduced to the following: in this sura God tells Quraysh to worship Him, referring to two journeys of uncertain nature and destination, reminding them of an exemption from hunger and fear that could be interpreted in a variety of ways, and using a word to which any meaning derivable from the root *'lf* could be imputed.[43] Taken in its entirety, the

[39] Ṭabarī, *Jāmiʿ*, xxx, 198 (*luzūm*); similarly Ibn Khālawayh, *Mukhtaṣar* p. 180; Ibn Qutayba, *Mushkil al-qur'ān*, pp. 319 f.

[40] Ṭabarī, *Jāmiʿ*, xxx, 198 (*ulfa*); similarly Zubayr b. Bakkār in Suyūṭī, *Durr*, x, 397 (with reference to Hāshim's mixing of rich and poor); Ṭūsī, *Tibyān*, x, 413; cf. also Rāzī, hafāfih, VIII, 510 f.

[41] Ṭabarī, *Jāmi'*, xxx, 198 (*niʿma*).

[42] Cf. Ibn al-Kalbī's *īlāf*-tradition. *Īlāf* is glossed as *ʿuhūd* in Ibn Ḥabib, *Muḥabbar*, p. 162, as *amn* in Masʿūdī, *Murūj*, III, 121. The idea that the agreements were about taxes for the defence of Mecca is mentioned as an alternative interpretation of the verse on *khawf* in Jāḥiẓ, *Rasā'il*, p. 70.

[43] With the exception of *niʿma*, all the meanings proposed for Qur'ānic *īlāf* are ramifications of the root meaning of *'lf*, as pointed out by A. Brockett, "Illustrations of Orientalist Misuse of Qur'ānic Variant Readings."

tradition says nothing that cannot be inferred from the text of the sura itself.

It is thus clear that the exegetes had no better knowledge of what this sura meant than we have today. What they are offering is not their recollection or what Muḥammad had in mind when he recited these verses, but, on the contrary, so many guesses based on the verses themselves. The original meaning of these verses was unknown to them. Either it had never been known to them or else there had been a gradual drift away from it.[44] In any case, it was lost to the tradition, on a par with the original significance of the mysterious letters of the Qur'ān, or the meaning of Qur'ānic *kalāla*.[45]

It follows that we cannot use this tradition for a reconstitution of the meaning of *Sūrat Quraysh*: like the exegetes, we have only the Qur'ānic text itself to go by. Conversely, we evidently cannot adduce *Sūrat Quraysh* as Qur'ānic confirmation of facts volunteered within this tradition. It may well be that Quraysh spent their summers in Ṭā'if, traded with Syria, and had particularly harmonious relations among themselves, as well as agreements with other tribes going back to Hāshim. But inasmuch as we do not know the nature of the Qur'ānic journeys or the meaning of Qur'ānic *īlāf*, the Qur'ān cannot be taken to confirm any of these propositions, let alone all of them. Given the allusive style of the Qur'ān, the validity of this point is not limited to *Sūrat Quraysh*: whenever the Qur'ān is said to confirm points made in the tradition, it turns out to be the tradition that confirms itself.

But did Quraysh spend their summers at Ṭā'if, and did they have agreements known as *īlāfs* going back to Hāshim? What, in other words, is the historical value of information offered in explanation of Qur'ānic passages such as *Sūrat Quraysh*? In principle, such information could be

[44] As might be inferred from Brockett, "Illustrations," though Brockett's thesis is that the Muslims had *not* forgotten the original meaning and sound of Qur'ānic utterances, let alone been unaware of them from the start. Brockett concedes that the preservation of the meaning of the text was never as strict as that of the wording, or, in other words, that the meaning might be forgotten; and he believes the scholars to have regarded it as their duty to extract as many meanings as possible from the text, or, in other words, to invent. Loss of original meaning on the one hand and invention of new ones on the other add up to a gradual drift away from the original import of the revelation.

[45] Cf. Cook, *Muhammad*, p. 72; and D. S. Powers, "The Islamic Law of Inheritance Reconsidered: a New Reading of Q. 4:12B," especially pp. 74 ff.

perfectly correct: whatever the meaning of Qur'ānic *īlāf*, the exegetes clearly knew the root on the basis of which they tried to explain it; and whatever the meaning of *Sūrat Quraysh*, they must similarly have known the history in the light of which they tried to interpret it. Yet in practice it is clear that much or most of the information thus offered is false.

Thus the exegetes *ad Sūrat Quraysh* inform us that Quraysh went on trading journeys to Syria, and if there is any truth to the Islamic tradition at all, this must be accepted as correct. Yet even this simple fact has been twisted by exegetical use. Because the Qur'ān mentions a journey in both summer and winter, the exegetes had to adapt their knowledge of Qurashī trade to accomodate this indication of a seasonal pattern. Hence Quraysh are said to have gone to Syria by different routes in summer and winter, or, more commonly, to have gone to Syria in the summer and somewhere else in the winter (or the other way round), though there is no indication in the tradition at large that this was so: some Qurashīs would seem to have traded in Syria, but not in the Yemen or Ethiopia, while others traded in the Yemen and/or Ethiopia, but not in Syria; and the Qurashīs in question presumably visited their *matjar* more than once a year.[46] Modern Islamicists generally take the two annual trading journeys literally, accepting that Quraysh would visit Syria in the summer.[47] But at the same time they also accept the traditional date for the battle of Badr, for all that the caravan involved in this battle must have departed for Syria in the winter, being on its return from there in March.[48] There is evidently no reason to accept the historicity of the information triggered by the Qur'ānic mention of two journeys.

Similarly, the claim that Quraysh would migrate to Ṭā'if in the summer sounds plausible enough, and it has been accepted by modern scholars such as Lammens and Watt.[49] But inasmuch as it is badly attested outside the exegetical tradition, the chances are that it was invented.[50]

[46] Cf. above, ch. 5. But note how the late *dalā'il al-nubuwwa* story referred to in ch. 5 n 76 has Abū Sufyān alternate between Syria and the Yemen.

[47] See for example *EI*², *s.v.* Ḳuraysh (Watt).

[48] *Ibid.*, *s.v.* Badr (Watt).

[49] Lammens, *Ṭāif*, pp. 160 ff.; Watt, *Muhammad at Mecca*, p. 138.

[50] Possibly under the influence of later conditions. After the conquests, the desirability of spending the summer at Ṭā'if and the winter and/or spring at Jedda and/or Mecca became something of a *topos* (cf. Yāqūt, *Buldān*, III, 500, *s.v.* Ṭā'if; *Aghānī*, VI, 205). A satir-

There is certainly no indication of a seasonal retreat to Ṭāʾif in the accounts of Muḥammad's life, and Mecca was full of Quraysh during the summer in which Muḥammad and his Companions are said to have made their *hijra* to Medina.[51]

The proposition that Quraysh had agreements known as *īlāf* can also be rejected. If *īlāf* had been a technical term for an institution of central importance for the Meccans, as also for the tribes with which they were in contact, it would have been a very familiar word. Yet later scholars, many of them Meccans, were puzzled by it. They disagreed over its pronunciation and also over its meaning, and where some took it to be a singular, others understood it as a plural.[52] All this shows clearly enough that this was a word that they had never encountered before.[53] In fact, Hāshim's supposed *īlāf*-agreements owe their existence to the Qur'ān mention of freedom from fear: Quraysh were freed from fear by agreements known as *īlāf* guaranteeing them safety on the way, or by inviolability arising from their residence in the *ḥaram*, or by inviolability in the *ḥaram* alone, or by agreements, similarly known as *īlāf*, guaranteeing them a contribution toward the defence of this *ḥaram*. Taken in isolation, each suggestion sounds convincing. But that merely goes to show that they were made by men familiar with the manners and customs of Arabia: their utterly contradictory nature demonstrates that they were made without concern for the manners and customs of historical Mecca. There is accordingly no reason to accept any one of them as true,[54] and

ical poet applied this *topos* to the pre-Islamic Quraysh in a contemptuous vein (Jāḥiẓ, *Tria Opuscula*, pp. 62 f.), and it was to be applied even to a pre-Islamic deity (Azraqī, *Makka*, p. 79). It may thus have been the same *topos* that the exegetes read into the Qur'ān.

[51] Muḥammad is supposed to have arrived in Medina in September (EI^2, *s.v.* hidjra [Watt]); and according to one passage in Ibn Isḥāq, he only left Mecca after all his Companions had safely arrived (Ibn Hishām, *Leben*, p. 323; but cf. *ibid.*, p. 339, where Muḥammad leaves first, all his Companions following later).

[52] It is normally understood as a singular (on a par with *da'b, luzūm, amn*); but Ibn Ḥabīb's *wa'l-īlāf al-ʿuhūd* shows that he took it to be a plural (*Muḥabbar*, p. 162).

[53] Cf. Cook, *Muhammad*, p. 72; cf. also Shahid, "Two Qur'ānic Sūras," p. 432, for a similar, if less radical, conclusion.

[54] As a historian, one is inclined to be impressed by the detail that Quraysh would act as commercial agents for the tribes on the way. In fact, however, this is simply a development of the theme *kafāhum al-mu'na*, shared by Ibn al-Kalbī's *īlāf*-tradition and the rival story, alike. In Ibn al-Kalbī's story the crucial idea behind the commercial agency is that Quraysh saved their associates the trouble of travelling to the markets of Syria or elsewhere themselves: *fa-kafāhum mu'nat al-asfār* (Jāḥiẓ *Rasā'il*, p. 70), *li-yakfiyahum mu'nat*

the modern tendency to accept all of them as such is certainly quite illegitimate.[55] The information is here engendered by the wording of the Qur'ān *regardless* of such historical information as may have been available on Quraysh in pre-Islamic times.

The fact of the matter is that the Qur'ān generated masses of spurious information. The story about Hāshim's *īlāf*-agreements is not an originally independent account now wrongly told in explanation of Sūra 106, still less is it an account confirmed by this sura. On the contrary, it is engendered by it: without this sura it would not exist. It does not represent a vague recollection of how Meccan trade began, nor does the rival story offer recollections of how it came to an end: Meccan trade obviously neither began nor ended in this way.

Of such exegetical stories there are countless examples. It is precisely because the exegetical literature offers a *story* in explanation of practically every verse that the exegetical literature is so popular a hunting ground for historians. When, for example, God tells the believers that He has given them "seven *mathānī* and the glorious Qur'ān" (15:87), we are told by way of background that seven caravans belonging to the Jews of Medina arrived from Buṣrā and Adhriʿāt in one day carrying rich goods, or alternatively that Muḥammad and his men saw these caravans at Adhriʿāt, and that either way Muḥammad's men wanted to plunder them, but that God restrained them, saying that He had given them

al-asfār (Thaʿālabī, *Thimār*, p. 116), *fa-yakfūnahum ḥumlānahā* (Qālī, *Amālī*, p. 199; Ibn Ḥabīb, *Munammaq*, p. 33). But in the rival story the crucial idea is that God saved Quraysh the trouble of travelling to these markets: *wa-kafāhum Allāh al-riḥlatayn* (Ibn Ḥabīb, *Munammaq*, p. 262), *kafāhum Allāh ʿazza wa-jalla mu'nat al-shitā' wa'l-ṣayf* (Muqātil, *Tafsīr*, fol. 253a), *kafāhum al-mu'na* (Ṭabarī, *Jāmiʿ*, xxx 171). There is no recollection of arrangements specific to Mecca behind these assertions.

[55] See for example Shaban, *Islamic History*, 1, 6 f.: "Makkan merchants would . . . take such goods with them to Syria and, on their return, would pay back their would-be partners their capital and all their profits. In return these tribesmen would guarantee the safety of the Makkan caravans in their territories. This was probably the original form of *īlāf*, pact of security, which was the most widely applied. Other forms of *īlāf* involved a payment of tax by the tribesmen wishing to take part in trade, but unable to guarantee the safety of Makkan caravans in their territories. Hāshim collected these taxes to enable him to organize the defence of those caravans." Jāḥiẓ makes it quite clear that the arrangements supposedly referred to in the Qur'ān were of *either* the one type *or* the other (*Rasā'il*, pp. 70 f.). But Shaban wants both to be historical and duly supplies a different context for the two, discretely changing the purpose of the taxes in question from defence of Mecca to a commercially more interesting defence of Meccan caravans.

something better than that, namely the seven *mathānī* and the Qur'ān.[56] Not all exegetical stories are quite so crude, but a great many well-known facts about the rise of Islam are likely to be exegetical inventions of this kind. Do the Qur'ānic references to orphans reflect the historical fact that Muḥammad was an orphan, or did Muḥammad become an orphan by way of amplification on the Qur'ān? When the Qur'ān speaks of hearts being "brought together," is it referring to a historical group of people whose "hearts were brought together" after the conquest of Mecca (*al-mu'allafa qulūbuhum*), or did this people come into existence because the Qur'ānic allusions had to be explained and fleshed out? If the second point of view is adopted, the conventional account of the rise of Islam collapses.

The exegetical literature testifies to what the exegetes chose to believe rather than to what they remembered: their information on Mecca shows what sounded plausible to them, not what Mecca was like in historical fact. What sounded plausible to the majority of exegetes has been accepted in this book as the nearest one can get to historical fact, but it must be admitted that the nearest is not very near. If the exegetes found it equally plausible that the Meccans should have traded and that they should have stopped doing so, that they should have traded during the pilgrimage and abstained from doing so, that they should have been holy men and not holy men, plausibility in their eyes was clearly determined by exegetical rather than historical concerns. Moreover, the exegetes were evidently familiar with Arabia in general, and some of their contradictory accounts about Mecca must have been based on such general knowledge rather than knowledge of Mecca. When they credit the Meccans with a leather trade, did they actually remember the Meccans to have traded in leather, or was leather simply a plausible commodity with which to credit them? If the second point of view is adopted, all the positive claims advanced in this book collapse, along with the conventional account.

How reliable, then, is the nonexegetical tradition? From what has been said, it should be plain that much of the apparently historical tradition

[56] Qurṭubī, *Jāmi'*, x, 56; Wāḥidī, *Asbāb*, p. 208 (where the caravans arrive in Medina); Bayḍāwī, *Anwār*, I, 655 (where they are seen at Adhri'āt). Ṭabarī similarly interprets 15:88 as an injunction not to covet the property of others, but without recourse to the story about the caravans (*Jāmi'*, xiv, 38).

is in fact of exegetical origin. Thus the story of Hāshim and his journeys owes its existence to *Sūrat Quraysh*, for all that it is in historical rather than exegetical works that it survives. Similarly, the numerous historical events said to have triggered a revelation (the raid at Nakhla, the battle of Badr, the oath of allegiance at Ḥudaybiyya, Muḥammad's encounters with *munāfiqūn*, and so forth) are likely to owe at least some of their features, occasionally their very existence, to the Qur'ān. As for what remains, some is legal and doctrinal ḥadīth in historical guise; that such material reflects the religious preoccupations of later generations rather than their historical recollection is now generally accepted.[57] But there is also a good deal of historical narrative that seems to be largely or wholly devoid of exegetical, doctrinal, or legal inspiration, and the nature of this material is of crucial importance. How could it *not* represent a more or less faithful recollection of historical events? In fact, its historical value is slight. Like much exegetical ḥadīth, it is the work of storytellers.

That storytellers played a major role in the formation of the exegetical tradition is no secret, and the stories of the beginning and end of Meccan trade are characteristic examples of their contribution. Being almost perfect mirror images of each other, they are contrary developments of the theme, and there are also different developments of minor themes within them.[58] This is characteristic of oral storytelling, and both the

[57] Cf. J. Schacht, "A Revaluation of Islamic Traditions"; *id.*, "On Mūsā b. 'Uqba's Kitāb al-Maghāzī."

[58] Cf. the contrary developments of *kafāhum al-mu'na*, above, n 54. Compare the different developments of the theme of *akhṣaba*: when the Meccans found the effort of travelling back and forth between Syria and the Yemen too much, *akhṣaba Tabāla wa-Jurash wa-ahl sāḥil al-baḥr*, and these people took over the task of carrying provisions to Mecca (Kalbī in Ibn Ḥabīb, *Munammaq*, p. 262); when the Meccans disbelieved in Muḥammad, Muḥammad asked for them to be afflicted with years like the years of Joseph, whereupon they suffered drought and hardship; but when they converted, *fa-akhṣabat al-bilād wa-akhṣaba ahl Makka* (Kalbī in Rāzī, *Mafātīḥ*, VIII, 512). When Hāshim made *īlāf*-agreements with the tribes of Arabia, *fa-akhṣabat Quraysh* (Tha'ālibī, *Thimār*, p. 116; Jāḥiẓ, *Rasā'il*, p. 71). When Hāshim imported bread from Syria and fed the Meccans, *fa-kāna dhālika awwalla khiṣbihim* (Ibn Ḥabīb, *Munammaq*, p. 103). Note also the role of Hāshim's *tharīd*: he cooks it in Mecca during a year of famine, thus freeing the Meccans from hunger (above, n 27), or he cooks it in Syria where it attracts the attention of the Byzantine emperor, with much the same result (above, chapter 5, p. 109). This theme is used in other hostility between Hāshimites and Umayyads (Ibn Ḥabīb, *Munammaq*, pp. 103 ff.; Ibn Sa'd, *Ṭabaqāt*, I, 75 f.). Or he cooks it at Minā, 'Arafa, and Mecca in illustration of the Meccan solicitude for pilgrims

stories in general and particular themes such as Hāshim and his *tharīd* show the genre to have been a popular one. Now, as mentioned already, it is a characteristic feature of Muslim exegesis that it consists in the first instance of a story. We hear of people, caravans, wars, disputes over land or booty, marriages and divorces, love and emotional entanglements of other kinds: it is almost invariably concrete human relationships of this kind that cause God to intervene, sending down a verse. This is an approach typical of popular, not scholarly, thinking, and it is predominant in the works of early exegetes such as Kalbī and Muqātil[59] Classical exegetes such as Ṭabarī may omit the story, having developed hermeneutical interests of a more sophisticated kind; but even when they do so, the story underlies the interpretation advanced.[60] It is clear, then, that much of the classical Muslim understanding of the Qur'ān rests on the work of popular storytellers, such storytellers being the first to propose particular historical contexts for particular verses.[61] It should also be clear that this is the major reason why the exegetical tradition is so unreliable a guide to the original meaning of the Qur'ān and history alike: as might be expected of storytellers, they made up their stories in complete disregard or ignorance of both.

It is, similarly, thanks to the contribution of storytellers that the historical tradition is so short of authentic information. Their role in the formation of the sources on the rise of Islam is manifest in three major ways.

(Ya'qūbī, *Ta'rīkh*, I, 280; Ibn Sa'd, *Ṭabaqāt*, I, 78). The activity always explains his name.

[59] Cf. Wansbrough, *Quranic Studies*, pp. 122 ff., where it is typical of Muqātil, but not of Kalbī. As Wansbrough himself says, however (*ibid.*, p. 144), the work that he cites as Kalbī's *Tafsīr* cannot be the work of Kalbī himself. When Kalbī's *Tafsīr* is cited in the tradition, be it exegetical, historical, or legal, it invariably offers a story, such as that about the end of Meccan trade preserved by Ibn Ḥabīb (*Munammaq*, pp. 262 f.), the drought with which the Prophet punished the Meccans cited by Rāzī (*Mafātīḥ*, VIII, 513), the drought to which Hāshim responded by cooking *tharīd* (above, n 27), the *mawlā* who traded in Syria with a silver cup (above, ch. 5, n 98), or the *qatīl Isrā'īl* who occasioned the institution of the *qasāma* (P. Crone, "Jāhilī and Jewish Law: the *Qasāma*," p. 175). It follows that the ascription to him of the utterly different *Tafsīr* extant in a number of manuscripts must be rejected (*ibid.*, n 111).

[60] Thus Ṭabarī and other exegetes omit mention of Hāshim in connection with Sūrat Quraysh, but still identify the journeys as trading journeys. Ṭabarī omits the story of the caravans told *ad* 15:88, but interprets the passage no differently.

[61] Cf. Wansbrough, *Quranic Studies*, pp. 122 ff.

First, here as in the exegetical tradition, we are given utterly contradictory information. Several examples have been given already in connection with trade. I should now like to add some of more fundamental importance.

It is well known that Medina on the eve of Islam (= Yathrib) was torn by feuds. Ibn Isḥāq does not tell the full story of these feuds, but he refers to them on several occasions,[62] and they play a crucial role in his account of how Muḥammad came to be accepted there: the Yathribīs who decide to throw in their lot with him explain that their people is divided by hatred and rancour to an unusual degree, and they express the hope that "perhaps God will unite them through you."[63] Yet Ibn Isḥāq also informs us that when Muḥammad came to Yathrib, he found that the Yathribīs had a leader called Ibn Ubayy whom they were just about to crown their king. "None of his people contested his authority, and the Aws and Khazraj never rallied to one man before or after him, until the coming of Islam, as they did to him."[64] This exceptional state of unison was possible because Ibn Ubayy, though a Khazrajī, collaborated closely with a man of Aws. The diadem for his coronation had already been made, but on the arrival of the Prophet his followers abandoned him, and this is why he became a *munāfiq*.[65] Ibn Isḥāq, in other words, first tells us that Muḥammad stepped into a political vacuum in Yathrib and next that he snatched away authority from a well-established ruler in Yathrib. Never had Yathrib been so disunited, or else it had never been so united. The contradiction is beyond harmonization.[66]

Now Ibn Isḥāq cites both stories on the authority of ʿĀṣim b. ʿUmar b. Qatāda, an Anṣārī who, according to Ibn Ḥajar, "had knowledge of the *maghāzī*, and *siyar*, and who was invited to sit in the mosque of Damascus and tell about the *maghāzī* and the virtues of the Companions,

[62] Cf. Ibn Hishām, *Leben*, pp. 285 f., 385.

[63] *Qad taraknā qawmanā wa-lā qawma baynahum min al-ʿadāwa waʾl-sharr mā baynahum* (Ibn Hishām, *Leben*, p. 287). The passage is mistranslated in Guillaume, *Life of Muhammad* p. 198 ("we have left our people, for no tribe is so divided by hatred and rancour as they," as opposed to "when we left our people, they were in a worse state of hatred and rancour than any other people").

[64] Ibn Hishām, *Leben*, p. 411.

[65] *Ibid.*; cf. *EI*², s.v. ʿAbd Allāh b. Ubayy (Watt).

[66] It is all the more irresoluble in that the Aws were supposed to have won the battle of Buʿāth, fought shortly before the arrival of the Prophet (Ibn Hishām, *Leben*, pp. 385 f., cf. 285 f.). Yet when he arrived, Yathrib allegedly had a Khazrajī ruler.

which he did."[67] ʿĀṣim, in other words, was a storyteller, and what Ibn Isḥāq reproduces here is some of the stories with which he entertained the Damascenes. Evidently, his assignment was not to give boring lectures on history, but rather to evoke an emotional response to the great deeds of the Prophet and his Companions so as to commit people to Islam. And this he did, in the first story by stressing the pitiful state of the Medinese before God in His mercy sent them a prophet, and in the second story, by building up the immense opposition that Muḥammad had to overcome in Medina, using the opportunity to flesh out Qur'ānic references to *munāfiqūn*. The fact that the two stories are utterly contradictory no doubt went unnoticed both by himself and his audience, just as it has gone unnoticed by later historians, because they are told for different purposes in different context, each one of them making emotional sense on its own.

There is a similar contradiction in Ibn Isḥāq's presentation of the Jews in Medina on the eve of Islam. On the one hand, we are told that they used to side with their Arab allies in the feuds conducted by the latter, fighting against each other with a lamentable lack of monotheist solidarity: was not the Torah in their hands by which they knew what was forbidden and what allowed?[68] This is meant to evoke the response "what *has* Judaism come to? A good thing that we now have Islam." But on the other hand we are also told that the Jews were molested as a people by their pagan neighbours, with the result that they were united in the hope for a prophet who would kill their Arab oppressors.[69] Here the Jews display no lack of monotheist solidarity, because here we are meant to see them as representatives of the monotheist tradition that was oppressed by paganism and that Muḥammad was to indicate (though as it happened, he killed the Jews rather than their Arab oppressors, the Arabs having hastened to convert). Once again, the stories are told with complete disregard for what the situation in Medina may or may not have been like in historical fact.

In historical fact it is more likely that there were feuds than kings in Medina: on this question we have a tradition used by the storytellers but not invented by them.[70] But if there were feuds in Medina, the storytellers must have invented the power of Ibn Ubayy. They must also

[67] Aḥmad b. ʿAlī Ibn Ḥajar al-ʿAsqalānī, *Tahdhīb al-tahdhīb*, v, 53 f., *s.v.*

[68] Ibn Hishām, *Leben*, p. 372.

[69] *Ibid.*, p. 286; cf. pp. 373 f., 378.

[70] Cf. J. Wellhausen, "Medina vor dem Islam," based largely on the *Aghānī*.

have invented something, possibly everything, about the position of the Jews.

The second way in which the contribution of the storytellers is manifest is in the tendency for apparently independent accounts to collapse into variations on a common theme. I have already commented on this phenomenon, but I should now like to examine its significance in greater detail.

The sources are familiar with a large number of stories, all of which are variations on the theme of "Muḥammad's encounter with representatives of non-Islamic religions who recognize his as a future prophet."[71] According to one set of traditions, this encounter took place when Muḥammad was a small child still (in practically all versions) in the care of his foster mother. He was seen by Ethiopian Christians who wanted to kill him, or by *kāhin*s at ʿUkāz or an *ʿarrāf* there, or by a *kāhin* or *ʿarrāf* at Dhū'l-Majāz, or by a *kāhin* in Mecca, all of whom similarly wanted to have him killed, or by a seer at Mecca who wanted to take him away.[72] According to another set of traditions, the encounter took place when Muḥammad was aged nine or twelve. He was taken to Syria by Abū Ṭālib (or ʿAbd al-Muṭṭalib)[73] and was seen by Jews of Taymā', or by a nameless monk in a nameless place, or by Baḥīrā, a Christian monk at Buṣrā, or by Baḥīrā in an unnamed place,[74] or by Baḥīra, a Jewish rabbi.[75] In these versions, too, the Jews (or the Greeks) are after him, with the result that he is quickly taken away.[76] Yet another set of traditions hold the encounter to have taken place when he was twenty-five.

[71] This example was suggested to me by M. A. Cook.

[72] Ethiopian Christians: Ibn Hishām, *Leben*, p. 107; Jews: Ibn Saʿd, *Ṭabaqāt*, I, 113; at ʿUkāẓ: ʿAbd al-Razzāq, *Muṣannaf*, v, 317; Ibn Saʿd, *Ṭabaqāt*, I, 151; cf. Abū Nuʿaym, *Dalā'il*, p. 117; at Dhū'l-Majāz: Abū Nuʿaym, *Dalā'il*, pp. 95, 116 f.; Kalāʿī, *Iktifā'*, pp. 237 f., citing Wāqidī; a *kāhin* in Mecca: Ibn Saʿd, *Ṭabaqāt*, I, 166; a seer: Ibn Hishām, *Leben*, pp. 114 f.

[73] Cf. Ibn Saʿd, *Ṭabaqāt*, I, 120.

[74] Jews of Taymā': ʿAbd al-Razzāq, *Muṣannaf*, v, 318; monk: Ibn Saʿd, *Ṭabaqāt*, I, 120, 153; Baḥīrā at Buṣra: Ibn Hishām, *Leben*, pp. 115 ff.; Ibn Saʿd, *Ṭabaqāt*, I, 153 f.; Abū Nuʿaym, *Dalā'il*, pp. 125 ff.; Baḥīrā elsewhere: Ibn Saʿd, *Ṭabaqāt*, I, 121; Balādhurī, *Ansāb*, I, 96 f. His journey to Syria at the age of nine is also mentioned in Ibn Ḥabīb, *Muḥabbar*, p. 9; Yaʿqūbī, *Ta'rīkh*, II, 13, but without reference to the encounter with *ahl al-kitāb*.

[75] Ibn Kathīr, *Bidāya*, II, 286, citing Suhaylī from Zuhrī's *Siyar*.

[76] Compare also Abū Nuʿaym, *Dalā'il*, pp. 119 f., where Muḥammad is recognized as a future prophet by a Jew in Medina at the age of six; the Jew informed Muḥammad's maternal relatives there, whereupon Āmina became afraid and took him away.

Abū Ṭālib told him to go to Syria to make some money, so he joined Khadīja's caravan and was seen by a nameless monk in a nameless place, or by Nasṭūrā/Nasṭūr al-Rāhib at the market of Buṣrā.[77] Only one version refers to Jews being after him here.[78] In all stories, however, he is recognized as a future prophet because of his orphanage, the redness of his eye, the fact that he sits under a certain tree, or because of a combination of these.[79]

That these accounts represent some fifteen different versions of the same event is unlikely to be disputed by anyone. Which one of them is true, then? Evidently none. The story itself is of the kind which, as Watt puts it, is "not true in the realistic sense of the secular historian."[80] What the sources offer are fifteen equally fictitious versions of an event that never took place.

To Watt this is not a major problem because the event in question is miraculous and thus to be rejected anyway. As he sees it, one handles miracle stories by simply discounting the miraculous elements and accepting the information that remains as historically sound. Thus he accepts as historically correct the claim that Muḥammad traded in Syria as Khadīja's agent, even though the only story in which we are told as much is fictitious.[81] It is similarly, to him, a historical fact that ʿAbd al-Muṭṭalib dug the well of Zamzam in Mecca, though this information is likewise derived from a miracle story.[82] And all the information that the tradition offers on Muḥammad's mother he likewise accepts at face

[77] Mont: Ibn Hishām, *Leben*, pp. 119 f.; cf. Balādhurī, *Ansāb*, I, 97 f., without mention of the encounter with *ahl al-kitāb*; Nasṭūrā: Ibn Saʿd, *Ṭabaqāt*, I, 129 ff., 156 f.; Kalāʿī, *Iktifāʾ*, pp. 258 ff., citing Wāqidī; Abū Nuʿaym, *Dalāʾil*, pp. 131 ff., citing the same.

[78] Namely, Abū Nuʿaym's.

[79] Cf. H. Hirschfeld, *New Researches into the Composition and Exegesis of the Qoran*, p. 22; cf. also *EI*² *s.v.* Baḥīrā.

[80] Watt, *Muhammad at Mecca*, p. 33.

[81] *Ibid.*, p. 38. It is true that Watt tells the story as "the traditional account," thus avoiding the question of its historicity. But Muḥammad's *continuing* service as Khadīja's agent or partner is presented as a straightforward fact, for all that it is an inference from the same "traditional account." The tradition that Muḥammad traded in partnership with Sāʾib b. Abīʾl-Sāʾib in the Jāhiliyya seems to be unaware of his partnership with or agency on behalf of Khadīja (cf. Azraqī, *Makka*, p. 471; Shaybānī, *Kasb*, p. 36); and as Watt notes, there are not further records of his having travelled to Syria again, be it on behalf of Khadīja or others.

[82] Watt, *Muhammad at Mecca*, p. 31; cf. Ibn Hishām, *Leben*, pp. 91 ff; Kalāʿī, *Iktifāʾ*, pp. 216 f. (likewise from Ibn Isḥāq).

value, except for incidents of a supernatural nature.[83] Source criticism to Watt thus consists largely in adopting a secular stance. *Mutatis mutandis*, the wall of Jericho did not collapse at the sound of Joshua's trumpets, but otherwise the Biblical account is reliable; Jesus did not feed thousands with a couple of fishes and loaves, but the Sermon on the Mount was enacted precisely as the Gospels describe.

Storytellers do not however distinguish between true and false in the realistic sense of the secular historian, and what they did to supernatural incidents surrounding Muḥammad's life they did to natural incidents as well. They did not put their imagination only into supernatural events, reverting to the role of faithful transmitters as soon as straightforward history was involved. If they could produce fifteen equally fictitious versions of a miraculous episode, they could also produce fifteen equally fictitious accounts of an apparently historical event. The fact that so many stories in the tradition are variations on a common theme testifies to this very fact.

For example, ʿAmr b. al-ʿĀṣ is supposed to have gone to Ethiopia on three (or two) occasions. First he went there in order to trade together with ʿUmāra b. al-Walīd, whom he denounced to the Najāshī. Next (or, according to some, on the same occasion) he went to the Najāshī armed with leather in order to secure the extradition of the Muslim refugees in Ethiopia; he denounced them to the Najāshī, though the latter refused to comply with his wishes. Finally, he went, once more armed with leather, to seek refuge at the Najāshī's court himself.[84] On this occasion he met another ʿAmr there, that is ʿAmr b. Umayya al-Ḍamrī: he denounced him to the Najāshī, though again without success.[85] ʿAmr b. Umayya had been sent by the Prophet in connection with the Muslim refugees in Ethiopia, or the marriage of Umm Ḥabība, or as a scout, or for unspecified reasons, or to summon the Najāshī to Islam.[86] The Najāshī converted, and when ʿAmr b. al-ʿĀṣ denounced ʿAmr b. Umayya to him, he refused to extradite him, whereupon ʿAmr b. al-ʿĀṣ converted at his hands.[87]

[83] Cf. *EI*[2], *s.v.* Āmina (Watt).

[84] Cf. the references given above, ch. 4 nn 45-56; ch. 5 nn 96-97.

[85] Ṭabarī, *Taʾrīkh*, ser. 1, pp. 1,601 ff., citing Ibn Isḥāq; Ibn Hishām, *Leben*, pp. 716 ff.; ʿAbd al-Raḥmān b. ʿAbdallāh Ibn ʿAbd al-Ḥakam, *Futūḥ Miṣr*, pp. 252. f.; cf. Raven, "Some Islamic Traditions."

[86] Raven, "Some Islamic Traditions."

[87] Cf. above, n 85.

These stories are no different from those on Muḥammad's encounter with Jews and others. Being non-miraculous, they do not violate any laws of nature, of course, and in that sense they could be true. In fact, they are clearly not. All are elaborations on a common theme, "ʿAmr and the Najāshī." The ʿAmr in question is either good or bad, the bad one being armed with leather, and all the stories are combinations and recombinations of the same motifs: refuge, extradition, denunciation, and conversion. Watt selects as historically true the tradition that ʿAmr b. Umayya was sent to Ethiopia in connection with the Muslim refugees in Ethiopia, or Umm Ḥabība's marriage, rather than to summon the Najāshī to Islam.[88] Here as elsewhere, his source criticism thus consists in adopting a secular stance: the nature of the source material remains unnoticed.

Given the proliferation of variant versions in the tradition, we clearly cannot adopt a literal-minded approach to any one alleged event: which version of the event in question are we to be literal about? If the tradition offers two, five, or fifteen versions of a certain event, we evidently ought to reconstitute this event on the basis of them all. Yet this is precisely what we cannot do. What is the original event behind the theme of ʿAmr and the Najāshī or of certain Qurashīs and silver? We cannot even tell whether there *was* an original event: in the case of Muḥammad's encounter with Jews and others there was not. Either a fictitious theme has acquired reality thanks to the activities of storytellers or else a historical event has been swamped by these activities. The result is that we are left with little but spurious information: the fact that the stories consist of themes and subthemes in different combinations means that we cannot get *behind* the storytellers.

What the tradition offers is thus a mass of detailed information, none of which represents straightforward *facts*. Naturally, much of this information could be correct in the sense that the storytellers presumably drew on their historical knowledge for the circumstantial details with which they embellished their accounts. But this merely amounts to saying that the tradition offers us information of the kind that sounded plausible to storytellers, which does not take us very far. One storyteller

[88] W. M. Watt, *Muhammad at Medina*, pp. 345 f., with reference to the fact that "Muḥammad was a wise and far-seeing statesman" who would not have sent envoys to foreign rulers inviting them to convert: "to appeal to these princes at this period to accept Islam would have done more harm than good."

found it plausible that Muḥammad should have traded in Syria as Khadīja's agent; another preferred to let him act as such at Ḥubāsha, to the south rather than to the north of Mecca.[89] One storyteller had ʿAbd al-Muṭṭalib dig his well in Mecca; another let him dig it at Ṭā'if, with precisely the same events attached.[90] It evidently is not a *fact* that ʿAbd al-Muṭṭalib dug the well of Zamzam, still less does it show him to have been "a man of energy and initiative" who caused the position of his clan to improve.[91] The only facts we have are facts about the tradition, not about the past that it purports to narrate. It is an interesting fact about the tradition that it should have attached holy figures such as ʿAbd al-Muṭṭalib and Muḥammad now to one place and now to another, and it is facts of this kind, not the supposedly historical events narrated, that constitute our genuine evidence on the rise of Islam.

The third way in which the contribution of the storytellers to the tradition on the rise of Islam is manifest is the steady growth of the information. It is obvious that if one storyteller should happen to mention a raid, the next storyteller would know the date of this raid, while the third would know everything that an audience might wish to hear about it. This process is graphically illustrated in the sheer contrast of size between the works of Ibn Isḥāq (d. 767) and Wāqidī (d. 823), that of Wāqidī being much larger for all that it covers only Muḥammad's period in Medina. But practically any incident narrated by both illustrates the same point. The raid of Kharrār, for example, is told as follows by the two.[92]

Ibn Isḥāq: "Meanwhile the Messenger of God had sent Saʿd b. Abī Waqqāṣ on compaign with eight men from among the Muhājirūn. He went as far as Kharrār in the Ḥijāz, then he returned without having had a clash with the enemy (*wa-lam yalqā kaydan*)."

[89] Cf. above, ch. 7 n23.

[90] Cf. Ibn Ḥabīb *Munammaq*, pp. 98 ff. and the references given there. Given that all versions of this story have *mā'*, the editorial emendation of this word into *māl* should be rejected. According to Yaʿqūbī, *Ta'rīkh*, I, 284 ff. 288 ff., ʿAbd al-Muṭṭalib dug *both* the Zamzam and, about the same time, a well in Ṭā'if, with much the same effects on both occasions.

[91] Watt, *Muhammad at Mecca*, p. 31.

[92] Ibn Hishām, *Leben*, pp. 422 f.; Wāqidī, *Maghāzī*, I, 11.

Wāqidī: "Then the Messenger of God (may God bless him and give him peace) appointed Saʿd b. Abī Waqqāṣ to the command against Kharrār—Kharrār being part of Juḥfa near Khumm—in Dhū'l-Qaʿda, eighteen months after the *hijra* of the Messenger (may God bless him and give him peace). Abū Bakr b. Ismāʿīl b. Muḥammad said on the authority of his father on the authority of ʿĀmir b. Saʿd on the authority of his father [*sc.* Saʿd b. Abī Waqqāṣ]: the Messenger of God (may God bless him and give him peace) said, 'O Saʿd, go to Kharrār, for a caravan belonging to Quraysh will pass through it.' So I went out with twenty or twenty-one men, on foot. We would hide during the day and travel at night until we arrived there on the morning of the fifth day. We found that the caravan had passed through the day before. The Messenger had enjoined upon us not to go beyond Kharrār. Had he not done so, I would have tried to catch up with it."

Unlike Ibn Isḥāq, Wāqidī knows the exact date of the expedition, and also the whereabouts of Kharrār (which is more than was known to anyone else);[93] he knows that the purpose of the expedition was to intercept a caravan, that the men went on foot, but travelled only at night, that it took them five days, and that the reason why no fighting took place is that the caravan had come and gone; he even knows that the number of participants in the raid was larger than hitherto assumed—and naturally he knows all this on the impeccable authority of the leader of the expedition himself. This is typical of Wāqidī. He will always give precise dates, locations, names, where Ibn Isḥāq has none, accounts of what triggered the expedition, miscellaneous information to lend colour to the event, as well as reasons why, as was usually the case, no fighting took place. No wonder that scholars are fond of Wāqidī: where else does one find such wonderfully precise information about everything one wishes to know? But given that this information was all unknown to Ibn Isḥāq, its value is doubtful in the extreme. And if spurious information accumulated at this rate in the two generations between Ibn Isḥāq and Wāqidī, it is hard to avoid the conclusion that even more must have accumulated in the three generations between the Prophet and Ibn Isḥāq.

[93] Cf. Yāqūt, *Buldān*, II, 408, *s.v.*: it is a place in the Ḥijāz (= Ibn Isḥāq), or a place near Juḥfa (= Wāqidī), or a valley of Medina, or a watering place in Medina, or a place in Khaybar.

Now it has long been recognized that *some* of our evidence on the rise of Islam goes back to storytellers; but it is usually assumed that the storytellers simply added some legends and fables to a basically sound tradition that existed already, possibly distorting this tradition to some extent, but on the whole doing no damage that we cannot simply deduct.[94] This is a gross underestimation of their contribution. In the case of *Sūrat Quraysh*, Ibn Ubayy, the Jews of Medina, ʿAmr and the Najāshī, ʿAbd al-Muṭṭalib's well, Muḥammad and Khadīja, it was the storytellers who created the tradition: the sound historical tradition to which they are supposed to have added their fables simply did not exist.[95] It is because the storytellers played such a crucial role in the formation of the tradition that there is so little historicity to it. As storyteller followed upon storyteller, the recollection of the past was reduced to a common stock of stories, themes, and motifs that could be combined and recombined in a profusion of apparently factual accounts. Each combination and recombination would generate new details, and as spurious information accumulated, genuine information would be lost.[96] In the absence of an alternative tradition, early scholars were forced to rely on the tales of storytellers, as did Ibn Isḥāq, Wāqidī, and other historians. It is because they relied on the same repertoire of tales that they all said such similar things, as Jones has pointed out. Wāqidī did not plagiarize Ibn Isḥāq, but he did not offer an independent version of the Prophet's life, either: what he, Ibn Isḥāq, and others put together were simply so many selections from a common pool of *qāṣṣ* material.[97] And it is for the same reason that they came to agree on the historicity of events that never took place, such as ʿAmr's adventures at the Najāshī's court. Nobody can have remembered these adventures, but nobody remembered anything to the contrary, either. The sources are agreed on the historicity of these adventures because there were well-known stories about them: the consensus is based on scholarly examination of secondary material, not on con-

[94] Cf. W. M. Watt, "The Materials Used by Ibn Isḥāq," pp. 25 f.; cf. also *EI*², *s.v.* ḳāṣṣ and the literature cited there.

[95] The nearest we get to one is the tradition on the feuds of Medina, which contradicts the information on Ibn Ubayy: there is none on Ibn Ubayy himself.

[96] This is a point that I have tried to demonstrate before with reference to the fate of the Constitution of Medina in Ḥadīth (cf. P. Crone, *Slaves on Horses*, p. 7). But I overlooked the role of the storytellers in this loss.

[97] Cf. J.M.B. Jones, "Ibn Isḥāq and al-Wāqidī," pp. 46 f., 51.

tinuous transmission of a historical tradition. There *was* no continuous transmission. Ibn Isḥāq, Wāqidī, and others were cut off from the past: like the modern scholar, they could not get *behind* their sources.

That there was no continuous transmission is a fundamental point which I should like to corroborate with references to the date of the battle of Badr. The history of this date illustrates the role played by the Qur'ān in the formation of the tradition at the expense of recollection. The agents may or may not have been storytellers in this particular case, but either way the moral is the same: as new information was created, earlier information was lost.

What is the date of the battle of Badr? There is complete agreement in the tradition that it is Ramaḍān, year 2.[98] What we are concerned with here is the month. On the face of it the month is confirmed by the Qur'ān: here Ramaḍān is given as the month of the *furqān* (2:181); and the "day of *furqān* on which the two parties met" (8:42) is identified by the exegetical tradition as the battle of Badr. The combination of scholarly unanimity and what appears to be scriptural confirmation would thus make the month in which the battle of Badr took place one of the few unshakable facts of early Islamic history. Naturally, it is not of great importance in itself, but a correctly preserved date for so early an event would do something to vindicate the general reliability of the historical tradition. There is, of course, a weak link in the argument in that the Qur'ān itself does not identify the "day of *furqān*" as the battle of Badr; and the *furqān* that was "sent down" in Ramaḍān scarcely sounds like a reference to a battle. Sceptics might thus argue that the Qur'ān, far from confirming the date given in the tradition, actually generated it. But until recently such sceptics had the unanimity of the tradition against them.

In 1956, however, Grohmann published an eighth-century papyrus from Khirbat al-Mird in Palestine. The papyrus is fragmentary and Grohmann's reading is undoubtedly wrong in places; but unless he has totally misread it, the papyrus gives us a deviant date for the battle of Badr.[99]

[98] Cf. J.M.B. Jones, "The Chronology of the *Maghāzī* Textual Survey," p. 247.

[99] A Grohmann, ed. and tr., *Arabic Papyri from Ḫirbet el-Mird*, no. 71. The possibility that Grohmann misread the papyrus is real: one fragment (no. 28), which he took to be an official letter probably referring to taxation, has since turned out to be a fragment of the Qur'ān (cf. M. J. Kister, "On an Early Fragment of the Qur'ān"; the photograph of the

The papyrus begins by listing some names, of which only Wāqid b. ʿAbdallāh, B. ʿAdī b. Kaʿb, Mughīra, and Ḥakam are legible or easily reconstructed. In line six it mentions the date of "fourteen months from Muḥarram" and states that "they went out to Badr." In line seven we are told that "they met at Badr," the date being now given as "eighteen months from Muḥarram." The last line mentions Muḥammad, Mecca, Quraysh, and a certain Majīd.

The battle of Badr is not supposed to have taken place fourteen or eighteen months from Muḥarram, but rather twenty-one months from it (the Muḥarram involved being the first month of the first Muslim year). If we count fourteen and eighteen months from Muḥarram, we arrive either at Ṣafar and Jumāda II or at Rabīʿ I and Rajab, depending on whether or not we include Muḥarram itself in the count. We do not arrive at Ramaḍān.

Abbott did not like this fact, and together with Grohmann she set out to spirit it away. This she did by proposing, first, that the author of the fragment was not counting from Muḥarram, but rather from Rabīʿ I, the month in which the *hijra* actually took place (as does Wāqidī, for example); and second that the first of the two dates given by the fragment should be taken to refer to an earlier event known as the first battle of Badr.[100] (There are no fewer than three "battles" of Badr. The first is a minor episode in which no fighting took place; the second is *Badr al-qitāl* or the classical battle; the third does not concern us here.)

Let us assume then that Abbott is right: the author counted from the month of the *hijra*, that is Rabīʿ I. Counting fourteen months from Rabīʿ I does not get us to the right month for the first battle of Badr, still less for the second[101] But counting eighteen months from Rabīʿ I does get us to Ramaḍān, the proper month for the second or classical battle of

papyrus at p. 166 makes Grohmann's failure to recognize the passage quite understandable). In this particular case, however, his reading of the papyrus fits so well with other evidence (as will be seen) that the possibility is remote.

[100] Grohmann citing Abbott in Grohmann, *Arabic Papyri*, p. 105.

[101] The first battle of Badr took place in Jumāda II, year 2, according to Ibn Isḥāq (this date is implicit in Ibn Hishām, *Leben*, p. 423, and explicit in Khalīfa b. Khayyāṭ, *Taʾrīkh*, I, 16). And this is the date that Abbott and Grohmann equate with the first date given in the papyrus. But Jumādā II, year 2, is fifteen or sixteen months from Rabīʿ I, year 1 (depending on whether Rabīʿ I is included in the count or not), not fourteen. The second battle was eighteen or nineteen months from Rabīʿ I.

Badr, provided that we omit Rabīʿ I itself from the count. Wāqidī does not, his date being nineteen months from the *hijra*.[102] But this is scarcely an objection. Whatever the first date may refer to, we would thus seem to have saved the traditional date for the battle of Badr.

There is, or course, a problem. The fragment is eight lines long; within those eight lines the author informs us twice that he is counting from Muḥarram: one might thus be inclined to believe that he is counting from Muḥarram. If so, we have an author of the mid-eighth century who was under the impression that a battle or battles known by the name of Badr had been fought fourteen and/or eighteen months from Muḥarram, in other words not in Ramaḍān.

What, then, are the events described? *Pace* Grohmann and Abbott, the fragment does not refer to the first battle of Badr. This "battle," alias the raid of Safawān, is one out of two episodes involving Kurz b. Jābir and pasturing camels at Medina.[103] No Wāqid, ʿAdī b. Kaʿb, Mughīra, or Ḥakam are mentioned in connection with this episode in any classical source.[104] It is, however, well known that the second or real battle of Badr was preceded by a raid at Nakhla in which Muḥammad's men captured a Meccan caravan on its way from Ṭāʾif. The participants in this raid included *Wāqid* b. ʿAbdallāh and ʿĀmir b. Rabīʿa of *B. ʿAdī b. Kaʿb* on Muḥammad's side, and ʿUthmān b. ʿAbdallāh b. *al-Mughīra* together with *Ḥakam* b. Kaysān on the Meccan side.[105] There can thus be no doubt that the papyrus describes the raid of Nakhla followed by the battle of Badr. The two dates given are either the dates of Nakhla and Badr, respectively, or alternative dates for the battle of Badr alone.

[102] Wāqidī, *Maghāzī*, I, 2.

[103] Cf. Ibn Hishām, *Leben*, p. 423; Wāqidī, *Maghāzī*, I, 12 (Kurz raided the camels of Medina and the Prophet went in pursuit of him; Wāqidī adds that the camels were stationed in the Jammāʾ area). For the second occasion, see Ibn Hishām, *Leben*, pp. 998 f. (Kurz went in pursuit of some tribesmen who had raided pasturing camels in the Jammāʾ area); Wāqidī, *Maghāzī*, II, 568 ff. (somewhat different).

[104] The sources checked are Ibn Hishām, *Leben*, p. 423; Khalīfa, *Taʾrīkh*, I, 16; Wāqidī, *Maghāzī*, I, 12; Ibn Saʿd, *Ṭabaqāt*, II, 9; Ibn Ḥabīb, *Muḥabbar*, p. 111; Ṭabarīkh, ser. I, p. 1,271.

[105] Ibn Hishām, *Leben*, pp. 423 ff.; Ṭabarī *Taʾrīkh*, ser. I, pp. 1,274 ff.; Wāqidī, *Maghāzī*, I, 13 ff. Ibn Isḥāq explicitly characterizes ʿĀmir b. Rabīʿa as a member of B. ʿAdī b. Kaʿb (though Ṭabarī omits him altogether). Grohmann read the first letter of Ḥakam's patronymic as *ṣād* rather than *kāf*, but given the state of the papyrus, this is not an objection.

If the former, we have here a deviant date for the raid at Nakhla and another for the battle of Badr.[106] If the latter, we have two deviant dates for Badr.

In the tradition as we have it these dates have disappeared. Why? Presumably because scriptural passages came to be identified as references to the events in question. If Nakhla is referred to in 2:214, the raid took place in a holy month, not in Ṣafar or Rabīʿ I. If Badr is referred to in 2:181, the battle took place in Ramaḍān, not in Jumāda II or Rajab. The Qur'ānic allusions would thus seem to have generated the classical dates, causing earlier ones to be lost.

They were not lost without a trace, however: they were dumped on the raid of Safawān. Why is this episode known as the first battle of Badr? We are told that the Prophet went in pursuit of Kurz b. Jābir and returned on reaching Safawān: this is why the incident is known as the raid of Safawān. But in the course of so doing he came near to Badr: this is why it is also known as the battle of Badr. One is not entirely convinced by this explanation. The incident is dated to fourteen or eighteen months from Muḥarram, or more precisely fifteen/fourteen and eighteen/seventeen months from Muḥarram, depending on whether Muḥarram itself is included in the count.[107] The raid of Safawān thus carries not only the name of the battle of Badr, but also its preclassical dates (or those of Badr and Nakhla). Safawān, in short, is where the non-Qur'ānic dates for Badr (or Badr and Nakhla) were unloaded.

Yet if it had not been for this papyrus, we would never have known. The tradition as we have it displays not the slightest hesitation over the date of the battle of Badr, and the complete unanimity clearly suggests that Badr had always been remembered as a battle fought in Ramaḍān. In fact, it was not remembered as such at all. The month was supplied by the Qur'ān at the *cost* of recollection, and alternative dates (be they

[106] Nakhla is unanimously dated to Rajab, year 2 (cf. Jones, "Chronology," p. 247). This is eighteen or nineteen months from Muḥarram, the date given in the papyrus for the battle of Badr. Either the two events are envisaged as having taken place in the same month, though there are two months between them in the tradition as we have it, or else Nakhla is envisaged as having taken place some time before its classical date. Given that the papyrus offers the date of fourteen months from Muḥarram for an event that could be Nakhla, the latter is presumably the case.

[107] Fourteen months according to Ibn Isḥāq, eighteen according to Wāqidī (cf. above, nn 101, 104).

right or wrong) were still current in the mid-eighth century. Unanimity in this case does not testify to continuous transmission, but on the contrary to the accumulated loss of information. As in the case of ʿAmr's adventures in Ethiopia, the consensus was based on secondary material that has obliterated the past, not on genuine remains with which it can be reconstituted.

"Once the modern student is aware of the tendencies of the early historians and their sources . . . it ought to be possible for him to some extent to make allowance for the distortion and to present the data in an unbiased form; and the admission of 'tendential shaping' should have as its corollary the acceptance of the general soundness of the material."[108] This is Watt's methodology, and it represents a common attitude to the sources on the rise of Islam. It must be said to rest on a misjudgement of these sources. The problem is the very mode of origin of the tradition, not some minor distortions subsequently introduced. Allowing for distortions arising from various allegiances within Islam such as those to a particular area, tribe, sect, or school does nothing to correct the tendentiousness arising from allegiance to Islam itself. The entire tradition is tendentious, its aim being the elaboration of an Arabian *Heilsgeschichte*, and this tendentiousness has shaped the facts as we have them, not merely added some partisan statements that we can deduct.[109] Without correctives from outside the Islamic tradition, such as papyri, archaeological evidence, and non-Muslim sources, we have little hope of reconstituting the original shapes of this early period.[110] Spurious information can be rejected, but lost information cannot be regained.

108 Watt, *Muhammad at Mecca*, p. xiii.
109 Cf. Wansbrough, *Quranic Studies*, pp. 57 f.
110 Cf. Crone and Cook, *Hagarism*, part 1.

10

THE RISE OF ISLAM

Having unlearnt most of what we knew about Meccan trade, do we find ourselves deprived of our capacity to explain the rise of Islam? If we take it that trade is the crucial factor behind the appearance of a prophet in Arabia, the spread of his message there, and the Arab conquest of the Middle East, then the answer is evidently yes. But, in fact, Meccan trade cannot be said ever to have provided a convincing explanation for any of these events.

The view that Meccan trade is the ultimate cause of the rise of Islam is Watt's. The reader may begin to feel that there has been enough polemic against Watt in this book, and this is a view which its author shares. But to disagree with the conventional account is of necessity to disagree with the *fons* and *origo* of this account: throughout the present work the reader can treat the name of Watt as a shorthand for "early Islamic historians in general" and take polemical attention as a backhanded compliment to him. It is thanks to the enormous influence exercised by his work that a general appraisal of the theories that dominate the field takes us back to Watt for a final round.

According to Watt, the Qurashī transition to a mercantile economy undermined the traditional order in Mecca, generating a social and moral malaise to which Muḥammad's preaching was the response.[1] This hypothesis is clearly weakened by the discovery that the Meccan traded in humble products rather than luxury goods, but it is not necessarily invalidated thereby. Even so, however, there are other reasons why it should be discarded.

In the first place, it is unlikely that so brief a period of commercial wealth should have sufficed to wreak much havoc in Meccan society. In

[1] This thesis is presented in Watt, *Muhammad at Mecca* and *Muhammad at Medina*; also *Muhammad, Prophet and Statesman*, *Islam and the Integration of Society*, *The Cambridge History of Islam*.

the nineteenth century, for example, the town of Ḥā'il enjoyed a meteoric rise to commercial importance, comparable to that described for Mecca, without there being any indication of a correspondingly swift breakdown of traditional norms.[2] Why should there have been? It takes considerably more than a century of commercial success to undermine the tribal order of a population that has been neither uprooted nor forced to adopt a different organization in connection with its economic activities. Caravan trade is not capitalist in any real sense of that word, and Watt's vision of the Meccans as financiers dedicated to a ruthless pursuit of profit occasionaly suggests that he envisages them as having made a transition to the twentieth century.[3]

In the second place, the evidence for a general malaise in Mecca is inadequate. According to Watt, the Qur'ān testifies to an increasing awareness of the difference between rich and poor and a diminishing concern on the part of the rich for the poor and weak even among their own kin, orphans in particular being ill-treated; further, the Qur'ānic stress on acts of generosity implies that the old ideal of generosity had broken down to the point that the conduct of the rich would have been looked upon as shameful in the desert, while at the same time the Qur'ānic emphasis on man's dependence on God suggests that the Meccans had come to worship a new ideal, "the supereminence of wealth."[4] But the Qur'ān does not testify to an increasing awareness of social differentiation or distress: in the absence of pre-Qur'ānic evidence on the subject, the book cannot be adduced as evidence of change. And charges of excessive attachment to wealth and neglect of others, especially the poor and the weak, are standard items in the repertoire of monotheist preachers, as is the theme of man's dependence on God: how different would Muḥammad's preaching have been, one wonders, if he had begun his career in Medina, or for that matter elsewhere?[5] It is not very likely that there should be a one-to-one correspondence between the objective factors that led to the appearance of a prophet in Arabia and Muḥammad's subjective perception of his mission: prophets are heirs to a prophetical tradition, not to a sociological habit of viewing their society from outside.

[2] Cf. Musil, *Northern Neǧd*, p. 241.

[3] Cf. Watt, *Muhammad at Mecca*, pp. 19, 72 ff.

[4] *Ibid.*, pp. 72f., 75, 78.

[5] Cf. Wansbrough, *Quranic Studies*, p. 126, on "the orphan's lot."

Leaving aside the Qur'ān, then, to what extent does the tradition corroborate Watt's diagnosis? Viewed as pagan enemies of Islam, the Meccans are accused of neglect of kinship ties and other protective relationships, as well as a tendency for the strong to "eat" the weak.[6] But viewed as proto-Muslims, they are praised for their harmonious relations.[7] The conduct of trade in particular is supposed to have been characterized by cooperation between rich and poor; indeed, by the time of the rise of Islam there no longer were any poor.[8] Both claims, of course, merely illustrate the point that what the tradition offers is religious interpretation rather than historical fact. If we go by the overall picture suggested by this tradition, there is, however, no doubt that Watt's diagnosis is wrong. In social terms, the protection that Muḥammad is said to have enjoyed from his own kin, first as an orphan and next as a prophet, would indicate the tribal system to have been intact, as Watt himself concedes, adding that the confederate status of foreigners in Mecca would indicate the same.[9] It was, as Abū Sufyān said, *Muḥammad* who disrupted traditional kinship ties with his preaching.[10] From the point of view of morality, traditional tribal virtues such as generosity were both esteemed and practised: wealthy Meccans such as ʿAbdallāh b. Judʿān would have been astonished to learn that their conduct would have been looked upon as dishonourable in the desert.[11]

In religious terms, the Meccans are depicted as zealots on behalf of their pagan shrine as well as devotees of a string of other deities by whom they swore, after whom they named their children, and whom they took with them in battle against the Muslims. Watt interprets the

[6] Cf. Ibn Hishām, *Leben*, p. 219 (from Jaʿfar b. Abī Ṭālib's interview with the Najāshī, cf. Wansbrough, *Quranic Studies*, pp. 38 ff.).

[7] Cf. the interpretation of *īlāf* in *Sūrat Quraysh* as *ulfa* (above, ch. 9 n 40).

[8] Cf. the references given above, ch. 9 n28.

[9] Watt, *Muhammad at Mecca*, p. 18.

[10] Abu Sufyān said so in connection with the complaint mentioned above, ch.7 n. 27, where the references are given. Compare Kistes, "Mecca and Tamīm," p. 124. Watt's observation that reactions to Muḥammad did not always follow tribal ties accordingly has no bearing on the state of tribal ties before Muḥammad's appearance (*Muḥammad at Mecca*, p. 19).

[11] Ibn Judʿān was famed for the grandiose scale on which he fed the Meccans (cf. *Aghānī*, VIII, 327 ff.; Ibn Kathīr, *Biddāya*. II, 218). Other Meccans were similarly noted for their generosity toward the poor and needy of their clans (Kister, "Mecca and Tamīm," pp. 123 ff.; in general, this work is a good antidote to Watt's).

violations of the *ḥaram* during the wars of Fijār as "probably a sign of declining belief."[12] But obviously holy places and months were violated from time to time: Muḥammad himself is supposed to have violated a holy month without having lost belief in it;[13] and if the Meccans had come to regard such violations as unobjectionable, they would hardly have referred to the wars in question as *ḥurūb al-fijār*, "the sinful wars."[14] The fact that the Meccans carried their pagan deities with them into battle does not mean that "the remnants of pagan belief in Arabia were now at the the level of magic"[15]: we are hardly to take it that the remnants of Islam were similarly at the level of magic by the time of the battle of Ṣiffīn, in which the soldiers are said to have carried Qur'āns with them, or that Christians who wear crosses are mere fetishists. Watt concedes that "in view of the opposition to Muḥammad at Mecca it is conceivable that some small groups there—perhaps those specially concerned with certain religious ceremonies—had a slightly higher degree of belief."[16] But a slightly higher degree of belief among small groups with possibly special functions scarcely provides an adequate explanation for the magnitude of this opposition.

The fact is that the tradition knows of no malaise in Mecca, be it religious, social, political, or moral. On the contrary, the Meccans are described as eminently successful; and Watt's impression that their success led to cynicism arises from his otherwise commendable attempt to see Islamic history through Muslim eyes. The reason why the Meccans come across as morally bankrupt in the sources is not that their traditional way of life had broken down, but that it functioned too well: the Meccans preferred their traditional way of life to Islam. It is for this that they are penalized in the sources; and the more committed a man was to this way of life, the more cynical, amoral, or hypocritical he will sound

[12] Watt, *Muhammad at Mecca*, pp. 23 f.

[13] Cf. Watt, *Muhammad at Medina*, pp. 5 ff., on the raid of Nakhla, supposedly conducted in the holy month of Rajab. Compare *Aghānī*, XIII, 3: "Qaysaba b. Kulthūm al-Sakūnī . . . went on pilgrimage. When the Arabs went on pilgrimage in the Jāhiliyya, they used not to molest one another. When he passed B. ʿĀmir b. ʿUqayl, they attacked him, took him prisoner and took all his property and whatever he had with him." The norm is explained so as to elucidate the nature of the violation, not so as to suggest that it had ceased to be observed.

[14] Landau-Tasseron also rejects Watt's interpretation ("Sinful Wars").

[15] Watt, *Muhammad at Mecca*, p. 24.

[16] *Ibid.*, p. 23.

to us: Abū Sufyān cannot swear by a pagan deity without the reader feeling an instinctive aversion to him, because the reader knows with his sources that somebody who swears by a false deity is somebody who believes in nothing at all.

In the third place, the Watt thesis fails to account for the fact that it was in Medina rather than in Mecca that Muḥammad's message was accepted.[17] In Mecca, Muḥammad was only a would-be prophet, and if he had stayed in Mecca, that is what he would have remained. This makes sense, given the general absence of evidence for a crisis in Mecca: if Muḥammad himself had conceived his monotheism as a blueprint for social and moral reform in Mecca, he must soon have changed it into something else. It was outside Mecca, first in Medina and then elsewhere in Arabia, that there was a market for his monotheism: the Meccans had to be conquered before they converted. It follows that the problems to which Muḥammad's message offered a solution must have been problems shared by the Medinese and other Arabs to the exclusion of the Meccans. In short, they were problems that had nothing to do with Meccan trade.

Is this surprising? Ultimately, the Watt thesis boils down to the proposition that a city in a remote corner of Arabia had some social problems to which a preacher responded by founding a world religion. It sounds like an overreaction. Why should a blueprint for social reform in Mecca have caused the entire peninsula to explode? Clearly, we must concentrate on such factors as were common to Arabia, not on those that were peculiar to Mecca; the more unusual we consider Mecca to have been, the more irrelevant we make it to the explanation of the rise of Islam.

Watt is not, of course, unaware of the need to explain the success of Muḥammad's message outside Mecca. But having linked its genesis with Meccan trade, he is forced to identify a second set of problems to account for its success in Medina; and having opted for problems arising from a transition to a settled life in Medina, he needs a third set of problems to account for its spread in Arabia at large, this time opting for a general spiritual crisis: "there was a growing awareness of the existence of the individual in separateness from the tribe, with the consequent

[17] This point is stressed by Aswad, "Social and Ecological Aspects," pp. 420, 429, and taken for granted by Serjeant, "Haram and Hawtah."

problem of the cessation of his individual existence at death. What was the ultimate destiny of man? Was death the end?"[18]

The changes and transitions in question would, however, seem to be largely of Watt's own making. As regards the feuds with which the Medinese had to cope, they did not arise from a transition to settled life, but simply from settled life in general. It is a mistake to regard tribal organization as peculiar to nomads and sedentarization as necessarily leading to alternative forms of organizations, norms, and beliefs.[19] The settled people of pre-oil Arabia were tribally organized, like the Bedouin, and they subscribed to much the same norms and beliefs; both settled and nomadic life was typically life under conditions of statelessness. Watt is right that sedentarization created a greater need for authority,[20] but the material resources required for the creation and maintenance of stable state structures simply were not available. Accordingly, Arabian settlements were usually plagued by feuds; those characteristic of Medina in the sixth century would appear to have been no different from those characteristic of most Arabian settlements, including Medina, in the nineteenth.[21] The feuds to which Muḥammad offered a solution were a constant of Arabian history, not a result of change. It was only the solution that was new. The novelty of the solution lay in the idea of divinely validated state structures; and it was Muḥammad's state, not his supposed blueprint for social reform, which had such powerful effect on the rest of Arabia.

As for the spiritual crisis, there does not appear to have been any such thing in sixth-century Arabia, in the sense normally understood[22] There is no feeling in Muḥammad's biography of burning questions and long-

[18] Watt, *Muhammad at Mecca*,p. 19; also pp. 142 f.

[19] Cf. *Ibid.*, p. 16, where tribal solidarity is presented as essential for survival in desert conditions; *ibid.*, pp. 19, 74 ff., where it is nomadic rather than merely tribal ways that the Meccans are losing; and *ibid.*, p. 142, where nomadic standards and customs are incompatible with a settled way of life.

[20] Watt, *Muhammad at Mecca*, p. 143.

[21] Cf. Doughty, *Travels*, I, 328 f., 527 (Taymā' and in general); C. Huber, *Voyage dans l'Arabie centrale*, p. 16 (Jawf); W. G. Palgrave, *Narrative of a Year's Journey through Central and Eastern Arabia (1862-3)*, I, 62, 119 (Jawf, the Najd); J. L. Burckhardt, *Travels in Arabia*, p. 373 (Medina); C. Snouck Hurgronje, *Mekka in the Latter Part of the 19th Century*, pp. 8 f. (Mecca); cf. Philby, *Heart of Arabia*, II, 165 (Sulayyil).

[22] Compare G.-H. Bousquet, "Observations sociologiques sur les origines de l'Islam," pp. 73, 81.

debated issues finally resolved. Instead, there is a strong sense of ethnogenesis. The message of this biography is that the Arabs had been in the peninsula for a long time, in fact since Abraham, and that they had finally been united in a state. Muḥammad was neither a social reformer nor a resolver of spiritual doubts: he was the creator of a people.

The impulse behind Watt's attempt to identify social changes and spiritual crises in Arabia comes from his conception of religion as a set of ultimate truths concerning the nature and meaning of life: what is the destiny of man? Is death the end? When religion is thus conceived, it usually takes a fundamental change in people's way of life and outlook to make them abandon their beliefs, and the process tends to be accompanied by pangs of conscience and spiritual pain. If we assume that the pre-Islamic Arabs shared this conception of religion, it follows from the rapid spread of Islam in the peninsula that there *must* have been a fundamental change—which to most of us conjures up an image of socioeconomic change—with accompanying spiritual crisis. All we need to do then is to identify the nature of this crisis. The immense appeal of Watt's work on the rise of Islam rests on the fact that he thought along these very intelligible lines and came up with a socioeconomic change of the requisite kind: the Meccans were making a transition to a capitalist economy and losing their faith in the process. How very familiar; the Meccans were just like us. But an explanation that credits our own experience to a simple society is unlikely to be right. What sort of socioeconomic change and spiritual crisis preceded the Israelite adoption of Yahweh? How much thought about the ultimate destiny of man went into the Icelandic adoption of Christianity by vote of parliament? None, apparently. Similarly in the case of Islam. Islam originated in a tribal society, and any attempt to explain its appearance must take this fact as its starting point.

What, then, was the nature of religion in tribal Arabia? The basic point to note here is that tribal gods were ultimate sources of phenomena observable in this world, not ultimate truths regarding the nature and meaning of life. More precisely, they were ultimate sources of all those phenomena that are of great importance in human society, but beyond direct human control: rain, fertility, disease, the knowledge of soothsayers, the nature of social groups, and so forth. They were worshipped for the practical services they could render in respect of these phenomena. As Wellhausen noted, they differed from more spirits only in that they had names and cults devoted to them; without a name a deity could not be invoked and manipulated, and the very object of the cult was to make the deity exercise its power on behalf of its devotees.[23] "Ilāhā, regard the tribe of Rubat (with benevolence)," as a third-century inscription says.[24]

This being so, tribal gods neither required nor received emotional commitment, love, or loyalty from their devotees. Thus a famous story informs us that "in the days of paganism Banū Ḥanīfa had a deity made of dates mixed with clarified butter. They worshipped it for a long time. Then they were hit by a famine, so they ate it."[25] In much the same pragmatic spirit a modern Bedouin vowed half of whatever he might shoot to God. Having shot some game, he ate half, left the other half for God and departed; but feeling hungry still, he crept back and successfully stole God's part, and ate it, boasting that "God was unable to keep his share, I have eaten his half as well as mine."[26] Now if hunger could make a tribesman eat or cheat his god without remorse, then it is obvious that practical needs could likewise make him renounce or exchange this god for another without compunction. "We came to Saʿd so that he might get us together, but Saʿd dispersed us; so we have nothing to do with Saʿd," as a pre-Islamic tribesman is supposed to have said in disgust when his idol scared his camels away.[27] In much the same fashion a whole tribe abandoned its native gods for Christianity when its chief was cured of childlessness by a Christian monk.[28] And the numerous other Arabs who found the medical facilities of the Christian God sufficiently impressive to adopt Him as their own are unlikely to have found the act of conversion any more difficult.[29] A god was, after all, no

[23] Wellhausen, *Reste*, pp. 213 f.

[24] Cf. the reference given above, ch. 8 n117.

[25] Ibn Qutayba, *Maʿārif*, p. 266.

[26] A. Jaussen, *Coutumes des arabes au pays de Moab*, pp. 288 f.

[27] Ibn al-Kalbī, *Aṣnām*, p. 37; also cited in Ibn Hishām, *Leben*, p. 53.

[28] Sozomen, *Kirchengeschichte*, vi, 38: 14 ff. *Ecclesiastical History*, p. 310.

[29] The holy man who converted Najrān to Christianity was a healer, according to Ibn Hishām, *Leben*, p. 21. Ephraim the Stylite also worked cures among his Arab devotees (T. Nöldeke, *Sketches from Eastern History*, p. 221, cf. p. 219). The Christian sources are in general quite remorseless about the role of medical miracles in the spread of their creed, be it in Arabia or elsewhere, and Christian saints continued to cure Arabs even after the conquests, though they could no longer demand conversion (as opposed to fiscal and other

more than a powerful being, and the point of serving him was that he could be expected to respond by using his power in favour of his servants. A modern Tiyāha tribesman who was being swept away by a flood screamed in great rage at God, "I am a Tihi! I am a Tihi! God, if you don't believe it, look at the brand on my camels."[30] Obviously, if a deity was so inefficient as to unleash floods against his own followers, or so weak as to be unable to protect them from famine, or to keep his own share of some game, or to work miraculous cures, then there was reason to eat, cheat, abuse, denounce, or abandon him. "What were two little words?" as Doughty was asked on one of the numerous occasions on which attempts were made to convert him, "pronounce them with us and it shall do thee no hurt." The idea that a believer might be personally committed to a deity, having vested the ultimate meaning of his life in it, did not occur to any of these men. Those who tried to convert Doughty were evidently thoroughly committed to Islam, but not to Islam as a saving truth of deep significance to them as individuals. Convert, settle, and we will give you palm trees, as they told Doughty; in other words, be one of ours. Allāh was a source communal identity to them, not an answer to questions about the hereafter.[31] And the numerous people who tried to convert him or to penalize him for his Christianity on other occasions were likewise people who neither knew nor cared much about Islam as a saving truth, but who were outraged by his open denial of the God who validated their society.[32]

---

privileges) by way of payment for successful treatment (cf. Brock, "John of Dailam," *passim*).

[30] G. W. Murray, *Sons of Ishmael*, p. 44.

[31] Doughty, *Travels*, I, 556. On the occasion cited, the saving qualities of Islam were invoked as a last resort, Doughty being an obstinate man who refused to care for the things of this world: "what were two little words? Pronounce them with us and it shall do thee no hurt. Khalīl [= Doughty], believe in the saving religion, and howbeit thou care not for the things of this life, yet that it may go well with thee at last" (Doughty, *Travels*, I, 556). The speakers were villagers. Elsewhere Doughty noted that it was only with difficulty that the Bedouin could imagine a future life (*ibid.*, p. 282; similarly A. Blunt, *Bedouin Tribes of the Euphrates*, II, 216 ff.).

[32] Doughty himself characterized Bedouin fanaticism as "a kind of national envy or Semitic patriotism" (*Travels*, I, 569); and the reason why he found their obsession with religion hypocritical is clearly that they were not religious in his sense of the word, that is, they did not care very much about abstract truth or ritual observance (cf. *ibid.*, II, 53). Having understood that religion in Bedouin (or indeed Arabian) society was a kind of patriotism, he ought also to have understood that he placed himself in the position of an out-

Now, just as tribal gods did not articulate great spiritual truths, so also they were not deeply entrenched in everyday life.[33] Pre-Islamic (or for that matter pre-modern) Arabia was strikingly poor in mythology, ceremonial, ritual, and festivals. Religious life was reduced to periodic visits to holy places, stones, and trees, to sacrifice and consultation of diviners; most Bedouin managed with even less than that;[34] and these practices were not closely associated with belief in specific gods. The great annual pilgrimage was apparently not conducted in the name of any one deity, and the remaining practices could effortlessly be switched from one deity to another; all survived into modern times, among Muslim and Christian tribesmen alike. Renouncing one god for another thus did not require any change in either outlook or behaviour, unless the new deity carried with him a behavioural programme antithetical to tribal norms. In principle, the Christian deity did carry with him such a programme, though in practice the holy men active in Arabia were in no position to ensure that conversion amounted to more than two little words. But the Muslim deity did not. On the contrary, he endorsed and ennobled such fundamental tribal characteristics as militance and ethnic pride. Despite the Qur'ānic suspicion of Bedouin, it

law by his open denial of the God who sanctioned this society (cf. *ibid.*, II, 254, where his *rafīq* threatens to kill him on the ground that "with a Nasrāny who need keep any law? Is not this an enemy of Ullah?"). But he was too bent on seeing himself as a martyr to concede this point.

[33] And note that the validity of this point is not limited to the Bedouin. The Ḥanīfa who ate their idol were settled villagers, not Bedouin. The man who offered Doughty palm trees in return for conversion was no Bedouin, either. And in general, Doughty's account of reactions to his Christianity in Arabia reveals no difference of outlook between settled and Bedouin, except that the fanaticism of the former tended to be more intense (cf. *Travels*, I, 95).

[34] The Bedouin of the inner desert have no holy places, sacred objects, or mediators between man and God (Musil, *Northern Neǧd*, p. 257). They pay no attention to the saintly graves they come across near villages, dismissing the saints in question as belonging to villagers and herders of goats and sheep, not Bedouin (*id.*, *Rwala*, pp. 417 f.). Bedouin attitudes to the superstitions of the settled are well caught in the statements recorded by Murray in Sinai: "there is a grave . . . [in Egypt, on which] those women who desire offspring go and break bottles, and they think it does them good. Also those who wish to be married go before an old man and pay him a good round sum for writing their names in a book. And they think *that* does them good!" (Murray, *Sons of Ishmael*, p. 150). "The *jinn* abound in our mountains, but nobody but a *fellah* would fear them. Now, wolves are really dangerous!" (*ibid.*, p. 156).

was only on the development of classical Islam in the Fertile Crescent that the celebrated antithesis between *muruwwa* and *dīn*, manliness and religiosity, emerged.

It is thus clear that the mass conversion of Arabia to Islam does not testify to any spiritual crisis, religious decadence, or decline of pagan belief.[35] Indeed, in behavioural terms, the better part of Arabia was still pagan in the nineteenth century. What the mass conversions show is that Muḥammad's God had something very attractive to offer here and now. When Saʿd, the pre-Islamic deity, scared away the camels of his devotees, the latter concluded that "Saʿd is just a rock": the power that he was supposed to have exercised had proved unreal. But when Muḥammad established himself, they concluded that "Allāh is great." The Arabs converted to Islam because Allāh was a greater power than any other spirit endowed with a name and a cult so far known in Arabia, and the problem is not the ease with which they could convert, but the inducement. What was it that Allāh had to offer?

What he had to offer was a programme of Arab state formation and conquest: the creation of an *umma*, the initiation of *jihād*. Muḥammad was a prophet with a political mission, not, as is so often asserted, a prophet who merely happened to become involved with politics. His monotheism amounted to a political programme, as is clear not only from non-Muslim accounts of his career, but also from Ibn Isḥāq.

Thus Ibn Isḥāq informs us that the turning point of Muḥammad's career as a prophet came when he began openly to attack the ancestral gods of Quraysh and to denounce his own ancestors.[36] This was a turning point because in so doing, he attacked the very foundations of his own tribe; and it was for this that he would have been outlawed or killed if his own kinsmen had not heroically continued to protect him—not for the threat that his monotheist preaching allegedly posed to the pagan sanctuary or Meccan trade. He was, after all, no more than a local eccentric at the time, and Quraysh were quite willing to tolerate his oddities, including his minor following, as long as he confined his teaching to abstract truths about this world and the next. But they were not willing to tolerate an attack on their ancestors. By his they were outraged, and quite rightly so: a man who tries to destroy the very foundation of

[35] As Wellhausen argued (*Reste*, pp. 220 f.).

[36] Ibn Hishām, *Leben*, pp. 166 ff.

his own community is commonly known as a traitor. But Muḥammad would scarcely have turned traitor without some vision of an alternative community. In denouncing his own ancestors, he had demonstrated that his God was incompatible with tribal divisions as they existed; and this incompatibility arose from the fact that his God, unlike that of the Christians, was both a monotheist *and* an ancestral deity. Allāh was the one and only God of Abraham, the ancestor of the Arabs; and it was around ancestral deities that tribal groups were traditionally formed. It follows that it was around Allāh, and Allāh alone, that the Arabs should be grouped, all the ancestral deities that sanctioned current divisions being false. If we accept the traditional account of Muḥammad's life, Muḥammad was thus a political agitator already in Mecca, and it was as such that he offered himself to other tribes. "If we give allegiance to you and God gives you victory over your opponents, will we have authority after you?" an ʿĀmirī is supposed to have asked, fully aware that acceptance of Muḥammad was acceptance of a ruler with ambitious plans.[37] It was also as such, not merely as an otherworldly arbitrator, that he was accepted in Medina.[38]

Assuming that Medinese society was rent by feuds, as opposed to united by proto-kings, it is not difficult to explain why the Medinese should have been willing to experiment with Muḥammad's political programme; but given that Arabia had never been politically united before, and was never to be so again, it is certainly extraordinary that he and his successors should have succeeded in bringing this unification into effect. Why did the Arabs in Muḥammad's time find the vision of state structures and unification so attractive?

It is customary to invoke Meccan trade in answer to this question. Quraysh, we are told, had in effect united most of Arabia already, numerous tribes having acquired an interest in the conduct of Meccan trade as well as in the maintenance of the sanctuary; inasmuch as the interests of Mecca and Arabia at large had come to coincide, Muḥammad's conquest of Mecca amounted to a conquest of most of Arabia, though the process of unification was only to be completed on the suppression

[37] *Ibid.*, p. 283.

[38] This is clear from the Constitution of Medina, drawn up on Muḥammad's arrival there. When the date of this document is queried, it is inevitably on the assumption that Muḥammad must have developed into a ruler there rather than arrived as such.

of the *ridda*.[39] But though it is true that the suppression of the *ridda* completed the process, this is not an entirely persuasive explanation. If the interests of Mecca and the Arabs at large had come to coincide, why did the Arabs fail to come to Mecca's assistance during its protracted struggle against Muḥammad? Had they done so, Muḥammad's statelet in Medina could have been nipped in the bud. Conversely, if they were happy to leave Mecca to its own fate, why should they have hastened to convert when it fell? In fact, the idea of Meccan unification of Arabia rests largely on Ibn al-Kalbī's *īlāf*-tradition, a storyteller's yarn. No doubt there was a sense of unity in Arabia, and this is an important point; but the unity was ethnic and cultural, not economic, and it owed nothing to Meccan trade.[40] Muḥammad's success evidently had something to do with the fact that he preached both state formation *and* conquest: without conquest, first in Arabia and next in the Fertile Crescent, the unification of Arabia would not have been achieved.[41] And there is no shred of evidence that commercial interests contributed to the decision, on the part of the ruling elite, to adopt a policy of conquest[42]; on the contrary, the sources present conquest as an alternative to trade, the reward of conquest being an effortless life as rulers of the earth as opposed to one as plodding merchants.[43] Nor is there any evidence that the collapse of Meccan trade caused an "economic recession" that contributed to the enthusiasm with which the tribesmen at large adopted this policy.[44] It is, of course, legitimate to conjecture that trade may have played a role, but there is no need for such conjecture. Tribal states *must* conquer to survive, and the predatory tribesmen who make up their members are in general more inclined to fight than to abstain. "How many a lord and mighty chief have our horses trampled under foot . . . we march forth to war, the ever renewed, whenso it threatens," one pre-

[39] This interpretation is endorsed with particular forcefulness by Shaban, *Islamic History*, I, 6 ff.

[40] Cf. Crone, *Slaves*, pp. 24 f.

[41] Muḥammad's state would soon have disintegrated, as Khazanov rightly notes (A. M. Khazanov, *Nomads and the Outside World*, p. 275).

[42] As argued by Donner, *Conquests*, pp. 270 f.

[43] Cf. Ibn Ḥabīb *Muḥabbar*, p. 479, where Ḥusayn tells Muʿāwiya that if it were not for Islam, he would still be toiling away at his two journeys. For the view that *jizya* was a substitute for Meccan trade, see the references given above, ch. 5 n18.

[44] As argued by Shaban, *Islamic History*, I, 14.

Islamic poet boasts.[45] "We slew in requital for our slain an equal number [of them], and [carried away] an uncountable number of fettered prisoners . . . the days have thus raised us to be foremost with our battles in warfare after warfare; men find in us nothing at which to point their finger of scorn," another brags.[46] "When I thrust in my sword it bends almost double, I kill my opponent with a sharp Mashrafī sword, and I yearn for death like a camel overful with milk," a convert to Islam announced.[47] Given that men of this kind constituted Muḥammad's following, we do not need to postulate any deterioration in the material environment of Arabia to explain why they found a policy of conquest to their taste.[48] Having begun to conquer in their tribal homeland, both they and their leaders were unlikely to stop on reaching the fertile lands: this was, after all, where they could find the resources which they needed to keep going and of which they had availed themselves before. Muḥammad's God endorsed a policy of conquest, instructing his believers to fight against unbelievers wherever they might be found; and if we accept the testimony of non-Muslim sources, he specifically told them to fight the unbelievers in Syria, Syria being the land to which Jews and Arabs had a joint right by virtue of their common Abrahamic descent.[49] In short, Muḥammad had to conquer, his followers liked to conquer, and his deity told him to conquer: do we need any more?

The reason why additional motives are so often adduced is that holy war is assumed to have been a cover for more tangible objectives. It is felt that religious and material interests must have been two quite different things—an eminently Christian notion; and this notion underlies the interminable debate whether the conquerors were motivated more by religious enthusiasm than by material interests, or the other way round. But holy war was not a cover for material interests; on the contrary, it

[45] ʿAbīd b. al-Abraṣ IV, 14: 17, in C. J. Lyall, ed. and tr., *The Dīwāns of ʿAbīd Ibn al-Abraṣ*.

[46] Ṭufayl b. ʿAwf, I, 62, 76 f., in F. Krenkow, ed. and tr, *The Poems of Ṭufail Ibn ʿAwf al-Ghanawī and aṭ-Ṭirimmāḥ Ibn Hakīm aṭ-Ṭāʾyī*. Boasts of this kind are standard ingredients of pre-Islamic poetry.

[47] Ibn Hishām, *Leben*, p. 447 (the translation is Guillaume's).

[48] When the Persian commander at Qādisiyya explained the Arab invasion with reference to material hardship, Mughīra b. Shuʿba correctly pointed out that the Arabs had suffered similar and worse hardship before (Ṭabarī, *Taʾrīkh*, ser. 1, p. 2,352).

[49] Crone and Cook, *Hagarism*, pp. 7 f.

was an open proclamation of them. "God says . . . 'my righteous servants shall inherit the earth'; now this is your inheritance and what your Lord has promised you . . . ," Arab soldiers were told on the eve of the battle of Qādisiyya, with reference to Iraq; "if you hold out . . . then their property, their women, their children, and their country will be yours."[50] God could scarcely have been more explicit. He told the Arabs that they had a right to despoil others of their women, children, and land, or indeed that they had a duty to do so: holy war consisted in obeying. Muḥammad's God thus elevated tribal militance and rapaciousness into supreme religious virtues: the material interests were those inherent in tribal society, and we need not compound the problem by conjecturing that others were at work. It is precisely because the material interests of Allāh and the tribesmen coincided that the latter obeyed him with such enthusiasm.

The fit between Muḥammad's message and tribal interests is, in fact, so close that there is a case for the view that his programme might have succeeded at any point in Arabian history. The potential for Arab state formation and conquest had long been there, and once Muḥammad had had the idea of putting monotheism to political use, it was exploited time and again, if never on the same pan-Arabian scale. Had earlier adherents of Dīn Ibrāhīm seen the political implications of their own beliefs, might they not similarly have united Arabia for conquest? If Muḥammad had not done so, can it be argued that a later prophet might well have taken his role? The conquests, it could be argued, turn on the simple fact that somebody had an idea, and it is largely or wholly accidental that somebody did so in the seventh century rather than the fifth, the tenth, or not at all.[51]

But the fact that it was *only* in the seventh century that the Arabs united for conquest on a pan-Arabian scale suggests that this argument is wrong. If we choose to argue otherwise, we must look for factors which were unique to Arabia at that particular time, not constants such as the feuds of Medina, and which affected the entire peninsula, not just a single city such as Mecca. Given the fit between Muḥammad's message and tribal interests, the factors in question should also be such as to ac-

[50] Ṭabarī, *Ta'rīkh*, ser. 1, p. 2,289; cf. Qur'ān, 21:105; *Psalms*, 37:29.

[51] This is what I have argued myself (Crone, *Slaves*, p. 25), though I no longer believe it to be correct.

centuate the perennial interests of tribal society rather than to undermine them in the style of Meccan trade as conventionally seen. There is only one development which meets all three specifications, and that is the foreign penetration characteristic of sixth- and early seventh-century Arabia.

As mentioned already, the Persians had colonies throughout eastern Arabia, in Najd, and in the Yemen, as well as a general sphere of influence extending from the Syrian desert to the Ḥijāz. The Byzantines had no colonists to the south of Tabūk, but their sphere of influence was felt throughout western Arabia from the Syrian desert where they had client kings to the Yemen where their Ethiopian allies ruled until they were ousted by the Persians.[52] Muḥammad's Arabia had thus been subjected to foreign rule on a scale unparalleled even in modern times: where the Persians had colonists and fire-temples, the British merely had Philby.[53] The scale on which Muḥammad's Arabia exploded is equally unparalleled, the nearest equivalent being that of the Ikhwān. It seems unlikely that the two phenomena were unrelated.

If so, how? One model can be eliminated at once. It is well known that empires tend to generate state structures among their barbarian neighbours thanks to the ideas that they provide, the material sources that they pass on, and the resentment that their dominance engenders; and having generated such state structures, they will usually become targets of conquest, too. This is the pattern known from Central Asia and Europe; but it is not the pattern to which Arabia conforms.[54] There was no incipient growth of state structures at the expense of tribal ties in Arabia, not even in Mecca.[55] Muḥammad's state in Medina was formed by a prophet, not a secular statesman, by recourse to religious authority, not material power, and the conquests were effected by a fusion of tribal

[52] They did have colonies to the north of Tabūk, cf. J. E. Dayton, "A Roman/Byzantine Site in the Hejaz."

[53] Cf. above, ch. 2 n150.

[54] Crone, *Slaves*, ch. 2.

[55] Cf. Wolf, "Social Organization of Mecca," where the Meccan transition to a commercial economy creates a political malaise to which Muḥammad responds by completing the transition to statehood. The objections to this interpretation are much the same as those to Watt's. Mecca is described as a successful society, political conflicts being both rare and speedily settled: statelessness was no problem here. And it was in Medina that Muḥammad was welcomed, the Meccans resisting his innovations until they were conquered (similarly Asward, "Social and Ecological Aspects," p. 420).

society, not by its disintegation. If the imperial powers contributed to the rise of Islam, they must have done so in a different way.

An alternative hypothesis would be that Islam originated as a nativist movement, or in other words as a primitive reaction to alien domination of the same type as those which the Arab conquerors were themselves to provoke in North Africa and Iran, and which European colonists were later to provoke throughout the Third World.[56] If we accept the testimony of the non-Muslim sources on the nature of Muḥammad's teaching, this interpretation fits extremely well.

Nativist movements are primitive in the sense that those who engage in them are people without political organization. Either they are members of societies that never had much political organization, as is true of Muḥammad's Arabia, or they are drawn from these strata of society that lack this organization, as is true of the villagers who provided the syncretic prophets of Iran. They invariably take a religious form. The leaders usually claim to be prophets or God Himself, and they usually formulate their message in the same religious language as that of the foreigners against whom it is directed, but in such a way as to reaffirm their native identity and values.[57] The movements are almost always millenarian, frequently messianic, and they always lead to some political organization and action, however embryonic; the initial action is usually militant, the object of the movement being the expulsion of the foreigners in question. The extent to which Muḥammad's movement conforms to this description can be illustrated with reference to a Maori prophet of the 1860s who practically invented Islam for himself. He reputedly saw himself as a new Moses (as did Muḥammad), pronounced Maoris and Jews to be descended from the same father (as were the Jews and their Ishmaelite brothers), and asserted that Gabriel had taught him a new religion which (like that taught to Muḥammad) combined belief in the supreme God of the foreigners with native elements (sacred dances as opposed to pilgrimage). He proclaimed, or was taken to proclaim, the Day of Judgment to be at hand (as did Muḥammad). On that day, he said or was taken by his followers to say, the British would be expelled from New Zealand (as would the Byzantines from Syria), and

[56] Cf. A. Bel, *La religion musulmane en Berbérie*, I, 170 ff.; G. H. Sadighi, *Les mouvements religieux iraniens au IIe et au IIIe siècles de l'hégire*; V. Lanternari, *The Religions of the Oppressed*.

[57] This feature has been analyzed by A.F.C. Wallace, "Revitalization Movements," and R. Linton, "Nativist Movement."

all the Jews would come to New Zealand to live in peace and harmony with their Maori brothers (as Jews and Arabs expected to do in Syria). This, at least, is how his message was reported by contemporary, if frequently hostile, observers.[58] And though he may in fact have been a pacifist, his followers were not. Unlike the followers of Muḥammad, however, they fought against impossible odds.

Like the Maori prophet, Muḥammad mobilized the Jewish version of monotheism against that of dominant Christianity and used it for the self-assertion, both ideological and military, of his own people. It is odd that what appears to have been the first hostile reaction to alien domination, and certainly the most successful, should have come in an area subject to Byzantine rather than Persian influence, that of the Persians being more extensive. But Jewish-Arab symbiosis in northwest Arabia could perhaps account for this: according to Sebeos, the Byzantine victimization of Jews played a crucial role in the birth of Muḥammad's movement.[59] In any case, Muhammad was not the only prophet in seventh-century Arabia, and two of his competitors, Musaylima and Aswad, were active in areas subject to Persian influence, the Yamāma and the Yemen, respectively, while a third, Sajāḥ, was sponsored by tribes known to have participated in the celebrated battle against the Persians at Dhū Qār.[60] The fact that the resistance to Islam in Arabia was led by imitators of Muḥammad rather than by representatives of traditional paganism is thus unlikely to mean that traditional beliefs and values had

[58] Lanternari, *Religions*, pp. 248 ff., with references to further literature. The more recent work by P. Clark, *"Hauhau," the Pai Marire Search for Maori Identity*, is apologetic. Clark stresses the peaceful intentions of the prophet (on which there seems to be widespread agreement) and refuses to believe that even his followers wished to expel the British. The prophet's identification with Jews is admitted, but not developed, and the millenarian nature of his preaching more or less denied. Clark is of course right that there was an element of cultural adjustment in the cult in that the Maoris were eager for all the secret knowledge of the Europeans (the technological disparity between natives and foreigners is an aspect missing from the Arabian case); but the fact that they wanted European science does not mean that they wanted the Europeans. He adduces such Maori sources as exist, but does not apparently know the work of Vaggioli, an Italian historian who was in New Zealand at the time and who is the main source behind Lanternari's account.

[59] Cf. Crone and Cook, *Hagarism*, pp. 6 f.

[60] Cf. F. M. Donner, "The Bakr b. Wā'il Tribes and Politics in Northeastern Arabia on the Eve of Islam," p. 30. Note also the attempt during the *ridda* to restore the Lakhmid dynasty in the Baḥrayn area (*ibid.*, p. 31; restoring a native dynasty abolished by the Persians obviously was not a pro-Persian move).

lost force in Arabia;[61] on the contrary, Muḥammad would seem to have hit upon a powerful formula for the vindication of those values.[62] And this formula was, of course, likely to be used against Muḥammad himself when he began his subjection of Arabia.[63]

A more serious objection would be that the foreign presence is unlikely to have affected the majority of Arabs very deeply. Unlike the Maoris, who were losing their land to the British, they certainly cannot have felt that their entire way of life was under threat; and unlike the Berbers, they were not exposed to forced conversion. Nor are expressions of dissatisfaction with foreign domination very common in the sources. There is, admittedly, no lack of anti-Persian feeling in the poetry triggered by the battle of Dhū Qār,[64] which the Prophet supposedly described as the first occasion on which the Arabs obtained revenge from the Persians, the conquests (by implication) being the second.[65] But in historical fact this battle may not have represented more than a short-term disagreement between the Persians and their Arab subjects.[66] Still, there were some who felt that "the Arabs were confined between the lions of Persia and Byzantium," as Qatāda said in a passage contrasting the ignominious state of the Arabs in the Jāhiliyya with the grandeur achieved on the coming of Islam.[67] "Other men trampled us beneath their feet while we trampled no one. Then God sent a prophet from among us . . . and one of his promises was that we should conquer and overcome these lands," as Mughīra b. Shuʿba is supposed to have explained to a Persian commander.[68] In general it is acknowledged that

[61] Cf. Wellhausen, *Reste*, p. 221.

[62] Compare the proliferation of prophets in early ʿAbbāsid Iran (Behāfarīd, Sunbādh, Muqanna', Bābak, and so on). There were also several in Maori New Zealand.

[63] That Musaylima's movement should be seen as a nativist (or "revitalist") response has in fact been suggested before; cf. D. F. Eickelman, "Musaylima." Eickelman sees it as a response to pressure from Islam, however, not a response to foreign interference, or to foreign interference *and* Islam.

[64] M. A. Mu'id Khan, ed. and tr., *A Critical Edition of Diwan of Laqīṭ Ibn Yaʿmur*.

[65] See for example Yaʿqūbī, *Taʾrīkh*, I, 246.

[66] Donner, "The Bakr b. Wā'il Tribes," pp. 28 f.

[67] Cf. Kister, "Ḥīra," p. 143 and the references and variants cited there.

[68] Abū Yūsuf Yaʿqūb b. Ibrāhīm, *Kitāb al-kharāj*, p. 39; cited by Rodinson, *Mohammed*, p. 295. But variant versions of this speech omit the protest against foreign domination, or even acknowledge the benefits of Persian government (cf. Ṭabarī, *Taʾrīkh*, ser. I, pp. 2,240 f., 2,276 f., 2,352).

the Arab conquests were nothing if not "an outburst of Arab nationality."[69]

To what extent, if at all, the nativist model can be applied to the rise of Islam is for future research to decide; no doubt there are other ways in which the interaction between Arabs and foreigners could be envisaged. But it is at all events the impact of Byzantium and Persia on Arabia that ought to be at the forefront of research on the rise of the new religion, not Meccan trade. Meccan trade may well turn out to throw some light on the mechanics behind the spread of the new religion; but it cannot explain why a new religion appeared at all in Arabia or why it had such massive political effect.

[69] R. Bell, *The Origin of Islam in Its Christian Environment*, p. 184.

APPENDICES

APPENDIX I

THE PROVENANCE OF CLASSICAL CINNAMON

Cinnamon is an aromatic bark nowadays obtained from two species of the genus *Cinnamomum*, of the family of Lauraceae or laurels, that is, *C. zeylanicum* Nees and *C. cassia* Blume. The former, sometimes identified as "true cinnamon," is native to south India and Ceylon; it is reputed to produce better cinnamon in Ceylon than anywhere else, but it is now widely cultivated in other parts of the old and the new world, as well. The latter is native to south China and does not appear to be much cultivated outside China itself. Numerous other species of *Cinnamomum* with a distribution from India to New Guinea also yield aromatic barks of various kinds, some of them used as cinnamon substitutes, though the so-called "white cinnamon" or canella bark is derived from a completely different genus native to the West Indies (Uphof, *Dictionary*, *s. vv.* Cinnamomum spp. and Canella alba; G. Watt, *The Commercial Products of India*, pp. 310 ff.; I. H. Burkhill, *A Dictionary of the Economic Products of the Malay Peninsula*, I, 543 ff.). Cinnamon is used primarily as a condiment today, but this usage is of fairly recent origin (cf. C. Schumann, *Kritische Untersuchungen über die Zimtländer*, p. 24). In antiquity it was an ingredient in ointments and perfumes, as well as a medicine.

Cinnamon is first attested under this name in the Old Testament, where *qinnᵉmon beśem* is mentioned as an ingredient in the holy oil (Exodus 30:23), and *qinnāmôn* figures as a perfume (Proverbs 7:17; Song of Songs 4:14). Cassia, the inferior form of cinnamon commonly referred to in antiquity, is perhaps also first mentioned under this name here, but only in the plural form of *qᵉṣîʿôt* (Psalms 45:8, *sg.* **qᵉṣîʿâ*; as a singular it occurs only as the name of Job's daughter, Job 42:14). It is, however, also believed to be attested here under the name of *qiddâ* (Exodus 30:24; Ezekiel 27:19).

Greek *kinnamōmum* (later also *kinnamon*, *kinamon*) is first attested in Herodotus, according to whom the Greeks learned the word from the Phoenicians (*History*, III, 111). Herodotus also mentions cassia (*kasia*,

Ionian *kasiē*, III, 110), a word that they presumably also learnt from the Phoenicians and that is attested even before Herodotus in the poetry of Sappho (fragment 44 cited by Müller, *Weihrauch*, col. 708).

Cinnamon is associated with, among other things, myrrh in several of the Biblical passages; cassia is mentioned together with myrrh and frankincense in Sappho, and together with frankincense in Melanippides (fragment 1 cited by Liddell and Scott, *Lexicon*, *s. v.* Kasia) as well as in an account of aromatics used by the Phoenicians (Müller, *Weihrauch*, col. 732). This suggests that the Phoenicians obtained their cinnamon and cassia from the same people who supplied them with myrrh and frankincense, and by the time of Herodotus this was clearly so: Herodotus explicitly says that cinnamon and cassia came from south Arabia (*History* II, 86; III, 107, 111). Herodotus believed the south Arabians to obtain the products, or at least cinnamon, from the nests of large birds: nobody knew where cinnamon actually grew, though the land in which Dionysius was brought up had been proposed (*ibid.*, III, 111; possibly a reference to Ethiopia). But classical authors soon acquired the belief that cinnamon and cassia grew in Arabia itself. This opinion was shared by Theophrastus (*Plants*, IX, 4: 2), Alexander the Great (Arrian, *Anabasis*, VII, 20:2; cf. also Strabo, *Geography*, XV, 1: 22, 25), Eratosthenes (cited by Strabo, *ibid.*, XVI, 4: 4), Agatharchides (§ 97) and, following him, Artemidorus (cited by Strabo, *Geography*, XVI, 4: 19) and Diodorus Siculus (*Bibliotheca*, II, 49: 3); it was also the opinion of Dioscorides (*Materia Medica*, I, 13/12). The belief that cinnamon and cassia were products of south Arabia was thus current in the classical world for almost five-hundred years. Occasionally, it is found in later authors, too (cf. Jacob of Edessa, *Hexameron*, p. 138 = 115; Schumann, *Zimtländer*, p. 21). The usual and indeed only explanation at first sight is that the Arabs imported cinnamon and cassia from India or even further east, and kept the origin of their spices secret in order to preserve their monopoly on the trade (cf. above, ch. 2 nn104 f.). There are no species of *Cinnamomum* in Arabia. The Arabs must have been middlemen in an eastern trade of a very early date (cf. above, ch. 2 n102).

When, then, did the Greeks discover the true origins of cinnamon? According to McCrindle, they knew of the Indian cinnamon tree as early as the fourth century B.C., when Ctesias described it under the name of *karpion* (J. W. McCrindle, tr., *Ancient India as Described by Ktêsias the Knidian*, pp. 29 f. and the note thereto). But this cannot be right. For one thing, Ctesias, who collected this information in Persia, was hardly in a position to reproduce a Tamil word (supposed to be *karuppu* or the like, though I have not been able to verify the existence of such a word); and if *karpion* reproduces Sanskrit *karpūra*, the tree was a source of camphor, not of cinnamon. For another thing, Ctesias says that whereas the Indian name of the tree is *karpion*, its name in Greek is *myroroda*, not *kinnamōmon*. Above all, no species of *Cinnamomum* has leaves like those of a date palm, nor does any such species exude a resin or gum, as did that of Ctesias; the essential oil of *Cinnamomum* is obtained from the leaves, bark, pods, or twigs, invariably by distillation. It follows that Ctesias' tree was neither a cinnamon nor a camphor tree (camphor being derived from a species of *Cinnamomum*, too).

It would appear, though, that the Greeks discovered Indian *Cinnamomum*, possibly *C. zeylanicum*, in connection with Alexander's campaigns. Strabo, at all events, cites Aristobulus as being of the opinion that "the southern land of India . . . bears cinnamon, nard, and other aromatic products" (*Geography*, XV, 1: 22). And by the first century A.D. there were those who held most cassia in the Greco-Roman world to be of Indian origin (*ibid.*, XVI, 4: 25). But those who held as much were also under the impression that the best frankincense came from Persis, so they cannot have been well informed. By the second century A.D. Apuleius also spoke of Indian cinnamon, as did Philostratus in the third (both cited in L. Casson, "Cinnamon and Cassia in the Ancient World," p. 223. I owe my knowledge of this work to Professor G. Bowersock); but such statements were exceptional. What did come from India was *malabathrum*, the "Indian leaf" conventionally (but probably wrongly) said to be derived from *C. tamala* Nees, which is indigenous to India, but which does not yield a bark of much commercial value (cf. Watt, *Commercial Products of India*, pp. 312 f.; Miller, *Spice Trade*, pp. 5 ff., 23 ff., 201; the conventional identification was rejected by B. Laufer, "Malabathron," on grounds that have been ignored rather than countered). But though the Greeks and Romans now visited India themselves, they did not generally return with the impression that India was the land of the spice they knew as cinnamon.

They did discover the true origins of cinnamon in the first century A.D., however, or so they said: it came from East Africa, not from Arabia. Already Aristobulus had noted that south India bore cinnamon "like Arabia and Ethiopia" (Strabo, *Geography*, XV, 1: 22). Artemidorus also knew of cinnamon and "pseudo-cassia" in Africa, presumably on the basis of Agatharchides (*ibid.*, XVI, 4: 14). But it was Pliny who set out to explode the myth of Arabian cinnamon: contrary to what people said, it grew in East Africa, being transported to Arabia from there by raft (*Natural History*, XII, 85 ff.). The *Periplus*, a merchant's guide to African, Arabian, and Indian ports, soberly enumerates the East African ports from which cassia was exported (§§8, 10, 12 f; the word is *kasia* throughout, though Schoff translates it as cinnamon). Dioscorides also knew of cinnamon and cassia from East Africa, more precisely from Mosyllum, a port mentioned by the Periplus (*Materia Medica*, I, 13f./12f.; cf. *Periplus*, § 11). Ptolemy likewise held them be African products (*Geography*, IV, 7:34), as did Philostorgius (*Kirchengeschichte*, III, 6). Isidore of Seville, echoing some earlier source, held them to come from India *and* Ethiopia (Schumann, *Zimtländer*, p. 22, cf. p. 25). But Cosmas, the sixth-century traveller to India, once more omitted India as a source: cassia came from East Africa, being collected in the interior and brought to the coast for export from Adulis (*Topographie*, II, 49). The belief that cinnamon and/or cassia were products of East Africa thus held sway for another five hundred years, and was unshaken in the century before the Muslim conquests.

Against this background, the conventional explanation of the origins of cinnamon looks considerably less convincing than it did at first sight. If cinnamon and cassia actually came from India or the Far East, a mysterious guild of cinnamon dealers must have operated in both Arabia and East Africa, successfully keeping the provenance of their goods, not to mention their own existence, secret for over a thousand years. "So strong was the age-long understanding between Arab and Hindu, that cinnamon . . . was still found by the Romans only at Guardafui and was scrupulously kept from their knowledge in the markets of India" (Schoff, *Periplus*, p. 6). But how could such a secret possibly have been maintained? By the sixth century, Greek merchants had long been familiar with both India and Ceylon; yet they had not noticed that this was where cinnamon actually came from, the belief to the contrary being limited to ill-informed people of the first century A.D. Equally, by the sixth century, Greek merchants had long frequented both Arabian and East African ports, and missionaries had even penetrated the interior; yet nobody had noticed that the reputed cinnamon and cassia trees simply were not there. Some authors stopped talking of cinnamon, mentioning cassia only for reasons that are not clear. (Previous authors had distinguished sharply between cinnamon and cassia, and Pliny explicitly states that both grew in East Africa. Since the *Periplus* similarly distinguishes sharply between different kinds of cassia, I take the change to be purely terminological; differently Sigismund, *Aromata*, pp. 27 ff.) But whatever the label by which they knew the product, they continued to be duped by the age-long understanding between Arabs and Indians. Does it make sense?

It does not, and the argument is reduced to nonsense if we accept that cinnamon and cassia were already known to the ancient Egyptians. According to classical authors, the Egyptians used cinnamon and cassia in mummification and the manufacture of perfumes (cf. A. Lucas, *Ancient Egyptian Materials and Industries*, pp. 86 f., 299; I owe my knowledge of this and most other Egyptological works to Professor J. Baines). The Egyptians themselves knew a substance named *tjšps*, which is generally identified as cinnamon, if only with a question mark (as for example in H. von Deines and H. Grapow, *Wörterbuch der ägyptischen Drogennamen*, pp. 549 f.). The identification of *ḫs'jt/ḫs'jt* or *ḫ'sjt* as cassia is considerably more uncertain (cf. *ibid.*, pp. 319 ff., 417 f.; A. Erman and H. Grapow, *Wörterbuch der Ägyptischen Sprache*, *s.vv.*; J. H. Breasted, *Ancient Records of Egypt*, II, 109, 265. And *qdj/qdt*, identified by Miller as cassia on the basis of Breasted, is more likely to have been a resin, (cf. Erman and Grapow, *Wörterbuch*, *s.v.*). The identifications are uncertain above all because of the fact that spices native to India and the Far East are unlikely to have reached Egypt as early as about 2000 B.C.: it is hard to accept the suggestion that the Arabs transported them from there at this early stage (cf. V. Loret, *La lore pharaonique*, p. 51). But the Egyptian sources merely say that they came from Punt, or in other words East Africa, possibly also Arabia.

If ancient Egyptian, Biblical, and classical evidence all suggests or explicitly asserts that cinnamon and cassia came from Arabia and/or East Africa, it is futile to insist that they did not. What, moreover, are the alternatives? Contrary to what is often stated, they cannot have come from India, China, or Southeast Asia.

They cannot have come from India because the plants from which they were derived were shrubs or small tress, "about three feet high at the most" according to Pliny (*Natural History*, XII, 89; cf. Theophrastus, *Plants*, IX, 5: 1 ff.; Galen in Casson, "Cinnamon and Cassia," p. 232). *C.*

zeylanicum is a large tree in the wild. It does exist as a coppiced bush under cultivation, and Miller adduces this fact in support of the eastern origin of the products (*Spice Trade*, p. 44, though he does not want them to be products of *C. zeylanicum* or to have come from India). Pliny is, however, explicit that the bush known to him was wild ("it flourishes among the thickest of bushes and brambles, and is difficult to gather"; this point is also overlooked by Casson, "Cinnamon and Cassia," p. 238). And *C. zeylanicum* does not appear to have been cultivated commercially in Ceylon until the Portuguese and Dutch conquests; in south India it still had not come to be thus cultivated by the time Watt wrote his *Commercial Products of India* (pp. 313 f.).

Equally, the products cannot have come from China. The view that cinnamon bark was used as a spice, aromatic substance, and medicine in China as early as the third millennium B.C. would appear to be gratuitous (*pace* A. Dietrich, "Dār Ṣīnī"). According to Laufer (*Sino-Iranica*, p. 543), the tree and its products only entered the literature on the Chinese colonization of south China during the Han, that is, between 200 B.C. and 200 A.D. and the first mention of the medicinal use of cinnamon only dates from the fifth or early sixth century A.D. By then, however, it must have come to be exported to the west, for it was known already in Pahlavi as **dār-i čēnik*, "Chinese wood," an appelation that survives as a loan word in Armenian and Arabic, as well as in modern Persian (cf. *ibid.*, p. 541n). The word is attested already in the Talmud (Löw, *Flora der Juden*, II, 112); and Moses of Khoren also knew cinnamon as a Chinese product (cf. Schumann, *Zimtländer*, p. 41). It was Chinese, not Indian cinnamon that came to dominate the market after the Arab conquest of the Middle East (cf. Schumann, *Zimtländer*, p. 42, citing Ibn Khurdādhbih; Dietrich, "Dār Ṣīnī"; Jāḥiẓ, *Tijāra*, p. 33 = § 14). But unless we are willing to grant that the south Arabians sailed all the way to south China in their leather boats even in remote antiquity, it cannot have been "Chinese wood" that circulated in the ancient or classical Near East. Nor is there any reason to believe that Greek *kasia* is derived from Chinese *kwei-shi*, "cinnamon branch," as opposed to from Hebrew *qṣīʿâ*, or rather its Phoenician equivalent, a good Semitic word meaning something cut off (*pace* Schumann, *Zimtländer*, p. 7; Miller, *Spice Trade*, pp. 42 f.; cf. Laufer, *Sino-Iranica*, p. 542n). And Sigismund's explanation of *kinnamōmon* as "Chinese amomum" on a par with "Chinese wood" (*Aromata*, p. 30) is impossible on a number of grounds: China was scarcely known by this name before the Ch'in dynasty; the initial sound could not have been rendered by a "q" or "k" (cf. Laufer, *Sino-Iranica* p. 569); and the proposed word order is wrong, given that the construction is explicitly said to have been borrowed from the Phoenicians. Moreover, *C. cassia* is not a bush, but a tree growing to a height of some forty feet (Hill, *Economic Botany*, p. 468). It is distinguished from other species by its aromatic buds, and of these there is no mention in the classical literature (cf. *ibid.*; Burkhill, *Economic Products*, p. 549; Burkill rightly notes that this cannot possibly have been the cassia of antiquity).

That leaves us with Southeast Asia. According to Miller, Indonesia was the source of cinnamon in the classical world, China supplying cassia only. Cinnamon, he argues, was transported by outrigger canoe from Indonesia to Madagascar and from there to East African ports for sale to Greek and Roman merchants (*Spice Trade*, pp. 153 ff.). This is an imaginative, but not exactly plausible solution. The Malay colonization of East Africa may conceivably go back to the first century A.D., as Miller holds; but it needs to go much further back to account for the early classical and Biblical evidence, and still further back to accommodate the cinnamon that the ancient Egyptians obtained at Punt; and this it clearly cannot. (Miller nonetheless contrives to present the antiquity of imports from East Africa as "a very relevant factor in confirming the existence, in Pliny's day, of a true Far Eastern trade by the East African route," *Spice Trade*, p. 154.) Moreover, the fact that the Malays could cover long distances by canoe does not mean that they could keep up a regular trade between Southeast Asia and East Africa by such means, and the idea that they assiduously plied the oceans to keep the Near East supplied with cinnamon for several thousand years is somewhat unpersuasive (similarly Groom, *Frankincense*, p. 85). Miller manages to find a reference to this trade in Pliny (*Natural History*, XII, 86 ff.). But Pliny here says that cinnamon grew in East Africa, not that it was imported there; the sailors who transport it to Oceolis are Trogodytes, that is, Somalis, not Malays; and their means of transport are boats without rudders, oars, and sails, that is to say rafts, not outrigger canoes (similarly E. W. Gray, review of Miller, p. 222). Five years does seem a long time for them to reach Oceolis, and it was the enormous duration of the journey that impressed Miller; but presumably Pliny simply got it wrong. Naturally, Miller also adduces the view that "cinnamon" is a word of Malay derivation (*Spice Trade*, pp. 45 f.); but for this view there is little justification, as pointed out by Lassen long ago (C. Lassen, *Indische Altertumskunde*, I, 330n).

Cinnamon and cassia thus cannot have come from India, China, or Southeast Asia. Moreover, if they had come from so far afield, the sources would not have been able to describe the plants from which the spices were derived. Yet the ancient Egyptians were familiar with the roots of the *tjšps* or cinnamon tree (von Deines and Grapow, *Wörterbuch*, p. 551); and Theophrastus and Pliny offered descriptions of both the cinnamon and the cassia trees (a point also noted by Groom, *Frankincense*, p. 84), giving information about harvest methods and harvest rituals, as well (*Plants*, IX, 5; *Natural History*, XII, 89 ff.). It must thus be accepted that cinnamon and cassia came from where the sources say they came, that is, Arabia and/or East Africa, as numerous scholars have concluded before (cf. the defenders of East African cinnamon in Schumann, *Zimtländer*, pp. 25 ff.; similarly Sigismund, *Aromata*, pp. 26 ff.; Laufer, *Sino-Iranica*, p. 543; R. Hennig, "*Kinnamōmon* und *Kinnamōphoros Khōra* in der antiken Literatur"; Raschke, "New Studies," pp. 652 ff. [where the case is exceedingly well made]; Groom, *Frankincense*, pp. 84 f.).

The defenders of Arabian and/or African cinnamon are up against the problem that no species of *Cinnamomum* is native to these countries. (A *C. africanum* Lukmanoff was reported in *Index Kewensis*, supplementum sextum, Oxford 1926, with reference to a publication of 1889; but this species is unknown to the literature on East Africa, cf. E. Chiovenda, *Flora Somalia*; P. E. Glover, *A Provisional Check-list of British and Italian Somaliland, Trees, Shrubs and Herbs*; E. Milne-Redhead and others, *Flora of Tropical East Africa*; G. Cudofontis, *Enumeratio Plantarum Aethiopiae*.) Indeed, the entire family of Lauraceae is weakly developed in Africa and apparently not represented in Arabia at all (A. Engler, *Die Pflanzenwelt Afrikas*, III, 1: 219; Blatter, *Flora Arabica* and *Flora of Aden*). This point was stressed and elaborated with impressive learning by Schumann, who also argued that East Africa does not offer the right conditions for *Cinnamomum* at all, thus disposing of the hypothesis that it had been introduced there at some stage (*Zimtländer*, pp. 28 ff.). *Pace* Casson ("Cinnamon and Cassia", p. 235), time has not proved Schumann right. *C. zeylanicum* was cultivated experimentally in East Africa (though more widely in West Africa) at the beginning of the present century (Engler, *Pflanzenwelt*, p. 220); by the 1950s it had been introduced to Ethiopia,

Zanzibar, Tanganyika, and elsewhere (Cudofontis, *Enumeratio*, p. 118); and not only *C. zeylanicum*, but also *C. cassia* and *C. camphora* have been naturalized in Tanganyika (Watt and Breyer-Brandwijk, *Medicinal and Poisonous Plants*, pp. 530 f.). But it would nonetheless be futile to argue that the cinnamon and cassia obtained from East Africa in the ancient world were derived from a species or various species of *Cinnamomum*. No trace of *Cinnamomum* has been found in ancient Egyptian remains (Lucas, *Ancient Egyptian Materials*, pp. 301, 308 f.), and one can confidently predict that none ever will be.

As conjectured by Laufer (*Sino-Iranica*, p. 543), Groom (*Frankincense*, p. 85) and others, including a professional botanist (F. N. Hepper, "On the Transference of Ancient Plant Names," p. 130), the spices known as cinnamon and cassia in antiquity were not the spices known as such today. This point can be established beyond all reasonable doubt on the basis of the descriptions given by Theophrastus (*Plants*, IX, 5) and Pliny (*Natural History*, XII, 89 ff.). Cinnamon was obtained from shrubs that grew in ravines (Theophrastus), among the thickest bushes and brambles, being difficult to gather (Pliny). The shrubs were small (Theophrastus), ranging in height from a mere span to three feet (Pliny), and the whole plant was cut down for harvesting (Theophrastus; differently Pliny). It had a dried-up appearance and a leaf resembling wild marjoram. It liked dry ground, being less fertile in wet weather. It grew in the vicinity of cassia, though the latter was a mountain plant (Pliny). Cassia was also a shrub, but of a coarser kind (both). The colours of the bark were black and white (Theophrastus), light, dark, mottled, and pure white in the case of cinnamon and white, reddish, and black in the case of cassia (Pliny, cf. also Dioscorides, *Materia Medica*, I, 12 f./13 f.; cf. also Casson, "Cinnamon and Cassia," pp. 228 ff., 232).

By no stretch of the imagination can this account be taken to refer to a species of *Cinnamomum*, a genus that flourishes in humid climates, producing large trees with glossy leaves. Modern users of cinnamon will also be surprised by the reference to black, white, and mottled varieties of this spice, though this is not a decisive point (cf. Casson, "Cinnamon and Cassia," pp. 229 f.). What Theophrastus and Pliny describe is a xerophilous shrub of the kind that proliferates in the thorn-woodland of the regions bordering on the Red Sea (cf. Polunin, *Plant Geography*, pp. 442 f.). It leaves no doubt that the plants in question grew where classical authors say they grew (and there is nothing in the description to rule out Arabia). But it does rule out that the spices which these plants produced should be identified with ours.

If classical cinnamon and cassia were different from "Chinese wood," one would expect the sources to say as much once "Chinese wood" had come to be imported. Several sources do, in fact, say precisely that. Thus a Gaonic comment on the Talmudic passage on *darṣīnī* explains that *darṣīnī* is a Chinese plant similar to *qinnamon*, or maybe identical with it (Löw, *Flora der Juden*, II, 112; but the rabbinical "cinnamon" that grew in Palestine, where it was eaten by goats, was clearly an altogether different plant again, cf. *ibid*, pp. 108 f.; *id.*, *Pflanzennamen*, p. 346). A Syriac author of unknown date similarly explains that *qinnāmōn* "is not the substance which they call *qinnāmā* or *darṣīnī*, but a kind of wood which has a pleasant smell" (Budge, *Syriac Medicine*, p. 609 = 724; here too *qinnāmōn* is also the name of an altogether different product, namely, storax). And countless Arabic authors state that *qirfa* is an aromatic substance different from, similar to or maybe identical with *darṣīnī*. *Qirfa* is identified as any bark, including *qirfat al-ṭīb*, by Dīnawarī, who seems still to be ignorant of its associations with "Chinese wood" (*Dictionnaire*, no. 865). But we are soon told elsewhere that "*qirfa* is a species of *dārṣīnī*; it is also said that it is a different species that resembles it" (Khwārizmī, *Mafātīḥ*, p. 172). "*Darṣīnī* . . . is not *qirfa*; I state this because the Egyptians call *qirfa dārṣīnī*" (Maimonides in M. Levey, *Early Arabic Pharmacology*, p. 150; Qurṭubī in Schmucker, *Materia Medica*, p. 342, where the refusal to identify the two is wrongly taken to reflect Qurṭubī's idiosyncratic views). "*Qirfat al-darṣīnī* . . . is much less aromatic than *darṣīnī*; it is also said that it is another species different from *darṣīnī* . . . some is black . . . and some white . . ." (Arrajānī in Bīrūnī, *Pharmacy and Materia Medica*, p. 303 = 265). "*Qirfa* is a bark varying in colour from red to black . . . it resembles *dārṣīnī*" (Rāzī cited *ibid.* p. 303 = 266). "*Qirfa* . . . is much rarer (*aqallu*) than *dārṣīnī*; some people say that it is a species (*jins*) different from *darṣīnī*" (attributed to Dioscorides in Bīrūnī, *Pharmacy and Materia Medica*, p. 304 = 266). *Qirfa*, in other words, was a bark that was sufficiently similar to *darṣīnī* to be confused with it, though it was less aromatic and came in white and black as well as reddish colours (these colours are mentioned by several authorities cited by Bīrūnī and they do not seem to be derived from Dioscorides). It was an Arabian product (this is implied by Dīnawarī, whose plants are Arabian unless otherwise specified); and it had come to be much rarer than its Chinese equivalent. There can thus be little doubt that *qirfa* was the cinnamon and/or cassia of the classical world.

Qirfa was found in East Africa, too. "Ethiopian (*ḥabashī*) *darṣīnī* is *qirfa*" (attributed to Paul of Aegina in Bīrūnī, *Pharmacy and Materia Medica*, p. 190 = 156). "There is East African (*zanjī*) *darṣīnī* which is malodorous and which is adulterated with a species of plants with a weak aroma. There is also a species of plants with a weak aroma which resembles *dārṣīnī* " (*ibid.*, pp. 190 = 156, clearly independent of the classical tradition).

Whether the plants in question can be more precisely identified is for professional botanists to decide. So far they have not succeeded (F. N. Hepper, personal communication); and it is their silence that allows the controversy to continue. For "if it is hard to believe that traders in cinnamon and cassia in the ports of Somalia were able to keep their products a secret from the author of the *Periplus*, it is even harder to believe that Ethiopia and Somalia boasted a tree that at one time supplied a fragrant bark in sufficient quantity to take care of the needs of the whole Roman empire and then disappeared without leaving a trace in the botanical record," as Casson rightly observes ("Cinnamon and Cassia," p. 236; Casson opts for China and mainland Southeast Asia). It is, however, a little premature to assert that it *has* disappeared from the botanical record. How many botanists have worked on the areas in question with the problem of classical cinnamon in mind? And of those who have, how many have looked for a small shrub as opposed to a tree?

But whatever the outcome of the botanical search, there is no doubt that "cinnamon" is a word of Semitic origin on a par with *qirfa* and *qᵉṣīʿâ* (the latter translated into Arabic as *salīkha*, cf. Löw, *Pflanzennamen*, p. 349; Lane, *Lexicon*, *s.v.*). It cannot be derived from the root *qnm* (rightly rejected by Löw, *Flora der Juden*, II, 107). But the first part of the word is presumably "reed" (Arabic *qanāh*, pl. *qināʾ*). *Qinnamōn*, *kin(n)amōmon* (the latter influenced by the false parallel with *amōmon*) would thus mean "the reed" or "reeds" of something; the word with which the reeds are in construct can no longer be identified.

APPENDIX 2

CALAMUS

A reed described as aromatic (*qāneh bōśem*, *qāneh ṭôb*) is mentioned in the Old Testament, where it is always found in the company of at least one Arabian product and where the Phoenicians of Tyre are said to have traded in it (Exodus, 30:23 f.; Jeremiah, 6:20; Ezekiel, 27:19; Song of Songs, 4:14). This suggests an Arabian commodity. An aromatic reed (*kalamos euōdēs; calamus odoratus*) was, in fact, to be found in Arabia, according to Theophrastus and Pliny, both of whom knew it to grow in Syria, too; in particular, it grew by the dried-out lake in the Lebanese valley in which sweet rushes (Arabic *idhkhir*) were also to be found (Theophrastus, *Plants*, IX, 7: 1 f.; Pliny, *Natural History*, XII, 104 ff.). It grew in south Arabia, too, according to Agatharchides (§ 97); and a Mineaean who sold myrrh and calamus in Egypt is attested in an inscription of 264 B.C. (Rhodokanakis, "Sarkophaginschrift von Gizeh," p. 113). *Qlm* is also attested on south Arabian incense bowls (Ryckmans, "Inscriptions sud-arabes," p. 176).

According to Pliny (*Natural History*, XII, 104ff.), calamus also grew in India, and Dioscorides identified it as Indian *tout court* (*Materia Medica*, I, 18/17). "Indian calamus" is mentioned elsewhere, too (Raschke, "New Studies," pp. 651 f.). But "Indian calamus" apparently also grew in East Africa, for Strabo mentions it there (*Geography*, XVI, 4:9); and it was from East Africa that calamus was imported in the sixth century (Cosmas, *Topographie*, II, 49).

Islamic sources identify calamus (*qaṣab al-ṭīb*, *qaṣab al-dharīra*, cf. Löw, *Pflanzennamen*, p. 342.; Lane, *Lexicon*, *s.v.* dharīra) as primarily Iranian. It was imported from Khwārizm, according to Jāḥiẓ (*Tijāra*, p. 36; mistaken for sugarcane in Pellat's translation, § 15), though Qazwīnī held it to be exclusive to Nihāwand (cited in M. Ullmann, *Die Natur- und Geheimwissenschaften im Islam*, p. 93). "The Persian reed is called calamus in Greek" (*al-qaṣab al-fārisī bi'l-rūmiyya qalāmūs*), we are told by Bīrūnī. Bīrūnī knew from both classical and Muslim sources that it also grew in India (*Pharmacy and Materia Medica*, p. 309 = 269 f.).

The plant in question is generally identified as *Acorus calamus*, L., Araceae, a perennial herb with a distribution from Ceylon to northern

Europe and beyond. Its English name is sweet flag, and its rhizomes have been widely used to flavour food and drink, as a source of toothpowder and insecticides, and as a remedy against dysentery and other ailments (Uphof, *Dictionary*, *s.v.*). It does not grow in Syria, Arabia, or East Africa (cf. G. E. Post, *Flora of Syria, Palestine and Sinai*, Blatter, *Flora of Aden* and *Flora Arabica*; Glover, *Provisional Check-list*; Chiovenda, *Check-list*; Watt and Breyer-Brandwij, *Medicinal and Poisonous Plants*, and so forth). If this identification of the plant is accepted, we thus have a problem parallel to that of cinnamon, and a ready-made explanation: the Arabs imported calamus from India or further east and kept its provenance secret in order to preserve their monopoly on the trade; they must have begun to do so already in Pharaonic times (cf. Moldenke and Moldenke, *Plants*, p. 41; Miller, *Spice Trade*, p. 93), and they operated in both Arabia and East Africa, thereby giving rise to the idea that this was where the plant in question grew.

But why go to such elaborate lengths in defense of an implausible identification? If the sources describe a plant as growing in Syria, Arabia, East Africa, Persia, and India, it is willful to identify it as one attested for Persia and India, but not for East Africa, Arabia, or Syria. And if the sources speak about reeds, who are we to say that they actually meant rhizomes? "*Kalamos* and *skhoinos* grow beyond the Libanus between that range and another small range, in the depression thus formed . . . there is a large lake, and they grow near it in the dried-up marshes, covering an extent of more than thirty furlongs. They have no fragrance when they are green, but only when they are dried, and in appearance they do not differ from ordinary reeds and rushes" (Theophrastus, *Plants*, IX, 7: 1; cf. Pliny, *Natural History*, XII, 104 ff.; Hort duly renders the untranslated words as sweet flag and ginger-grass). How could rhizomes imported from India give rise to such a circumstantial and matter-of-fact description? As has been seen, *skhoinos* was not ginger-grass, and we may take it that *kalamos* was not sweet flag, either. Acorin, the substance extracted from *Acorus calamus*, is bitter, and while it may counteract insects, dysentery, and tooth decay, it does not seem to have been used in perfumery (*British Pharmaceutical Codex*, p. 241; Watt, *Commercial Products of India*, p. 24; it is classical sources that lie behind Uphof's information on its supposed use in perfumery). Aromatic reeds used in the manufacture of scents and ointments with a habitat ranging from India to East Africa can most plausibly be identified as members of *Cymbopogon* (formerly *Andropogon*), the genus of scented grasses to which *skhoinos* also belongs. This identification has, indeed, been proposed before (cf. Moldenke and Moldenke, *Plants of the Bible*, p. 40; Miller, *Spice Trade*, p. 93; Schmucker, *Materia Medica*, p. 348). The sources could be referring to one or several species of *Cymbopogon*, or indeed to several genera of scented reeds, under the label of calamus: presumably they were referring to several. As for the plant that bears the name of *Acorus calamus* today, Muslim authors were familiar with it under its Indian name of *wajj* (Schmucker, *Materia Medica*, pp. 528 f.).

The history of the calamus of trade may thus be summarized as follows. Calamus was distributed in Biblical Palestine, possibly also in ancient Egypt, by the Phoenicians along with other Arabian commodities such as myrrh, frankincense, and cinnamon. Their supplies came from south Arabia and/or Syria, both south Arabian and Syrian calamus being attested as early as the third century B.C. Curiously, the south Arabians adopted a Greek word for their scented reed (*qlm* on Sabaean incense bowls, *qlmyt* in the Minaean sarcophagous inscription; compare E. Boisacq, *Dictionnaire étymologique de la langue grecque*, p. 397), while at the same time the Greeks adopted a Semitic word for reeds of their own (*kanna*, cf. *ibid.*, p. 406). Whatever significance one is to attach to this exchange, Syrian and Arabian calamus seems to have dominated the market even in the first century A.D. when Indian varieties of the commodity had come to be known: calamus is absent from the extant tariffs, and its price was low (cf. Miller, *Spice Trade*, p. 94, where this is a problem). African varieties of the commodity were also known, and by the sixth century East Africa had become the main or only supplier to the Greco-Roman world. There is nothing to suggest that Quraysh handled *qaṣab al-ṭīb*, be it for export or local consumption.

APPENDIX 3.

THE ETYMOLOGY AND ORIGINAL MEANING OF *Aloē*

According to Miller, Greek *aloe* in the sense of fragrant wood (lign-aloe or eagle-wood) is derived from Sanskrit *agaru* via intermediaries such as Tamil *akil* and Hebrew *ʾahālôt* (or its Phoenician cognate). *Aloē* in the sense of bitter medicine (aloes) he proposes to derive from Persian *alwā* (*Spice Trade*, pp. 35 f., 65 f.). This cannot be right.

The derivation of Hebrew **ʿāhāl* from Sanskrit *agaru* is uncertain, though generally accepted (cf. Löw, *Pflanzennamen*, p. 295). It is true that *ʿahālôt* sound like a foreign spice in Proverbs, 7:17, Psalms, 45:8, and Song of Songs, 4:14, where they are enumerated together with myrrh, cinnamon, and other aromatics. But in Numbers, 24:6, where they are mentioned in the alternative plural form of *ʾahālîm*, they are trees familiar to Balaam's audience by sight. *ʾahālīm* might, of course, be something different from *ʾahālôt*; but if so, one would assume them to be trees that produced the spice known as *ʾahālôt* rather than trees that happened to bear the same name as a spice imported from India.

Even if we accept that **ʾāhāl* is eagle-wood, however, we cannot derive Greek *aloē* from it. *Aloē* must be a Semitic loan word, as Löw observed (*Flora der Juden*, II, 149), and it must have entered Greek with the sense of bitter medicine. The name of the plant that produced this medicine is written with an *ʿayn* in Aramaic and Syriac (cf. Löw, *Pflanzennamen*, p. 295; *id.*, *Flora der Juden*, II, 149); and Syriac *ʿalway* (attested for example in Budge, *Book of Medicines*, *passim*) provides an almost perfect prototype for Greek *aloē*: the Greek word is a straightforward transcription of a Semitic name. The Greek word was transcribed back into Syriac and Aramaic (cf. Löw, *Pflanzennamen*, p. 295; in Jacob of Edessa, *Hexaemeron*, p. 139, the name of the bitter medicine is *alwā* and *ṣabrā*, the former a Greek and the latter an Arabic loan word). And from Syriac and Aramaic it passed to Arabic and Persian (cf. Löw, *loc. cit.*; Dīnawarī, *Plants*, p. 39, no. 40 (*aluwwa*, *uluwwa*). Persian *alwā* and variants are thus transcriptions of the Greek word, not its source, as was noted long ago (cf. Laufer, *Sino-Iranica*. p. 481).

The original meaning of Greek *aloē*, then, was aloes or bitter medicine. The original word for eagle-wood, on the other hand, was *agallokhon*, a word picked up by the Greeks in India and first attested in Dioscorides (*Materia Medica*, I, 22/21). There is no confusion of the two in Dioscorides or other writers of the first and second centuries A.D. When the *Periplus* (§ 28) mentions *aloē* among the articles exported from the Ḥaḍramawt, it clearly refers to the bitter medicine of Socotra (*pace* Huntingdon, *Periplus*, p. 132; cf. also MacCrindle, *Periplus*, p. 15). When Nicodemus offers myrrh and *aloē* for the embalming of Jesus in John, 19:39, he is offering two bitter substances, myrrh and aloes (as in the Authorized Version). And when Celsus recommends *aloe* as a purgative, it is again the bitter medicine he has in mind (*De Medicina*, I, 3: 26; correctly translated by Spencer). Celsus mentions *aloe* again in other passages, and Spencer takes these passages to refer to eagle-wood. Miller follows suit (*Spice Trade*, p. 35; cf. above, ch. 3 n54). But if Celsus had suddenly understood a completely different substance by the word, one would have expected him to indicate as much: how was his reader to guess that the medicine prescribed here was not identical with that mentioned as a purgative in I, 3: 26? Clearly, Celsus was thinking of bitter aloes throughout, a fact corroborated by the constant association of aloe with myrrh in his recipes.

How then did *aloē* come to mean eagle-wood as well as bitter medicine? Apparently thanks to the Septuagint. The translators of the Old Testament into Greek had trouble with ʾ^{a}*hālîm* and ʾ^{a}*hālôt*. They did not know the identity of the trees referred to in Numbers, 24:6, where the tents of Israel are compared to cedars and ʾ^{a}*hālîm* planted by God; so they read the word as ʾ^{o}*hālîm*, "tents," which is clearly wrong. Apparently they were equally unfamiliar with the nature of the spice elsewhere referred to as ʾ^{a}*hālôt*, for they translated it as *aloē* even though *aloē* only can have meant bitter medicine at the time: presumably they opted for this word on grounds of mere similarity of sound, much as Miller does. But the Biblical passages do, of course, suggest that ʾ^{a}*hālôt* were something sweet-smelling such as, for example, *agalokhon*. If Greek readers of the Bible assumed the Biblical spice to be eagle-wood, they must have inferred from the Septuagint that eagle-wood was known as *aloē* too. This would explain why the confusion between the two substances spread with Christianity. *Aloē* presumably means eagle-wood in the Alexandrian tariff excerpted by Justinian (reproduced in Miller, *Spice Trade*, p. 279), and it certainly does so in Cosmas (*Topographie*, XI, 15). It was also with the double sense of bitter medicine and lign-aloe that the word passed back into Syriac and Arabic. The spice *'ahălôt* having been identified as *aloē* in the sense of Indian eagle-wood, the *'ahălîm* with which Balaam's audience were familiar became so, too: the tents of Israel are "as the trees of lign aloes which the Lord hath planted" in the Authorized Version.

BIBLIOGRAPHY

ʿAbbās b. Mirdās. *Dīwān*. Edited by Y. al-Jubūrī. Baghdad, 1968.

ʿAbd al-Laṭīf al-Baghdādī. *Kitāb al-ifāda waʾl-iʿtibār*. Edited and translated by K. H. Zand and J. A. and I. E. Videan under the title *The Eastern Key*. London, 1965.

ʿAbd al-Razzāq b. Hammām al-Ṣanʿānī. *al-Muṣannaf*. Edited by Ḥ.-R. al-Aʿẓamī. 11 vols. Beirut, 1970-1972.

ʿAbīd b. al-Abraṣ, *see* Lyall.

Abūʾl-Baqāʾ Hibatallāh. *al-Manāqib al-mazyadiyya*. British Library, MS add. 23,296.

Abu Ezzah, A. "The Political Situation in Eastern Arabia at the Advent of Islam." *Proceedings of the Twelfth Seminar for Arabian Studies*. London, 1979, pp. 53-64.

Abū Ḥayyān al-Tawḥīdī, *Kitāb al-imtāʿ waʾl-muʾānasa*. 3 vols. Edited by A. Amīn and A. al-Zayn. Cairo, 1939-1944.

Abū Nuʿaym Aḥmad b. ʿAbdallāh al-Iṣbahānī. *Dalāʾil al-nubuwwa*. Hyderabad, 1950.

Abū Yūsuf Yaʿqūb b. Ibrāhīm. *Kitāb al-kharāj*. Cairo, 1346.

Afghānī, S. al-. *Aswāq al-ʿarab fīʾl-jāhiliyya waʾl-Islām*. 2nd ed. Damascus, 1960.

Aga-Oglu, M. "About a Type of Islamic Incense Burner." *Art Bulletin* 27 (1945), 28-45.

Agatharchides: in Photius, *Bibliothèque*. Vol. 7. Edited and translated by R. Henry. Paris, 1974; in C. Müller, ed. and tr., *Geographi Graeci Minores*. Vol. 1. Paris, 1855; in D. Woelk, tr., *Agatharchides von Knidos über das Rote Meer, Übersetzung und Kommentar*. Bamberg, 1966. Partial translation by J. S. Hutchinson in Groom, *Frankincense*, pp. 68 ff. (§§ 86-103); by Pirenne, *Qatabân*, pp. 82 ff. (§§ 97-103); by Huntingford, *Periplus*, pp. 177-197.

Aghānī, *see* Iṣbahānī.

Ahsan, M. M. *Social Life under the Abbasids*. London, 1979.

Albright, W. F. "The Chaldaean Inscription in Proto-Arabic Script." *Bulletin of the American Schools of Oriental Research*. No. 128. December 1952, pp. 39-41.

———. "The Chronology of Ancient South Arabia in the Light of the First Campaign of Excavation in Qataban." *Bulletin of the American Schools of Oriental Research*. No. 119. October 1950, pp. 5-15.

Ammianus Marcellinus. *Rerum Gestarum Libri*. Edited and translated by J. C. Rolfe. 3 vols. London, 1935-1939.

ʿAmr b. Qamīʾa. *Poems*. Edited and translated by C. Lyall. Cambridge, 1919.

Arrian. *Anabasis Alexandri.* Edited and translated by P. A. Brunt. 2 vols. Cambridge, Mass. and London, 1976-1983.

The Assyrian Dictionary of the Oriental Institute. Chicago and Glückstadt, 21 vols. 1956-1982.

Aswad, B. "Social and Ecological Aspects in the Origin of the Islamic State." *Papers of the Michigan Academy of Science, Arts and Letters* 48 (1963), 419-442.

Atchley, E.G.C.F. *A History of the Use of Incense in Divine Worship.* London, 1909.

Azraqī, Muḥammad b. ʿAbdallāh al-. *Kitāb akhbār Makka.* Edited by F. Wüstenfeld. Leipzig, 1858.

Bailey, H. W. *Zoroastrian Problems in the Ninth-Century Books.* 2nd ed. Oxford, 1971.

Bakrī, Abū ʿUbayd ʿAbdallāh b. ʿAbd al-ʿAzīz al-. *Muʿjam mā istaʿjam.* Edited by F. Wüstenfeld. 2 vols. Göttingen, 1876-1877.

Balādhurī, Aḥmad b. Yaḥyā al-. *Ansāb al-ashrāf.* Süleymaniye (Reisülkuttap) ms 598. Vol. 1, edited by M. Ḥamīdallāh, Cairo, 1959; vol. 2, edited by M. B. al-Maḥmūdī, Beirut, 1974; vol. 4b, edited by M. Schloessinger, Jerusalem, 1938; vol. 11 (= *Anonyme arabische Chronik*), edited by A. Ahlwardt, Greifswald, 1883.

———. *Kitāb futūḥ al-buldān.* Edited by M. J. de Goeje. Leiden, 1866.

Baldry, J. *Textiles in Yemen.* British Museum, occasional paper no. 27. London, 1982.

Balfour, I. B. *Botany of Socotra.* Edinburgh, 1888.

Barthold, W. W. "Der Koran und das Meer." *Zeitschrift der Deutschen Morgenländischen Gesellschaft* 83 (1929), 37-43.

Basham, A. L. "Notes on Seafaring in Ancient India." *Art and Letters, the Journal of the Royal India and Pakistan Society* 23 (1949), 60-70.

———. *The Wonder That Was India.* 3rd ed. London, 1971.

Bayḍāwī, ʿAbdallāh b. ʿUmar al-. *Anwār al-tanzīl wa-asrār al-taʾwīl.* 2 vols. Istanbul, n.d.

Bayhaqī, Aḥmad b. al-Ḥusayn al-. *al-Sunan al-kubrā.* 10 vols. Hyderabad, 1344-1356.

Beek, G. W. van. "Ancient Frankincense-Producing Areas." In R. Le Baron Bowen, Jr., F. P. Albright, and others, *Archaeological Discoveries in South Arabia.* Baltimore, 1958, pp. 139-142.

———. "Frankincense and Myrrh." *The Biblical Archaeologist* 23 (1960), 70-95.

———. "Frankincense and Myrrh in Ancient South Arabia." *Journal of the American Oriental Society* 78 (1958), 141-151.

———. "The Land of Sheba." In J. B. Pritchard, ed., *Solomon and Sheba.* London, 1974, pp. 40-63.

———. "Pre-Islamic South Arabian Shipping in the Indian Ocean—a Surrejoinder." *Journal of the American Oriental Society* 80 (1960), 136-139.

Beek, G. W. van, and A. Jamme. "The Authenticity of the Bethel Stamp Seal." *Bulletin of the American Schools of Oriental Research*. No. 199. October 1970, pp. 59-65.

———. "An Inscribed South Arabian Clay Stamp from Bethel." *Bulletin of the American Schools of Oriental Research*. No. 151. October 1958, pp. 9-16.

Beeston, A.F.L. "Abraha." *Encyclopaedia of Islam*. 2nd ed.

———. "Ḥaḍramawt." *Encyclopaedia of Islam*. 2nd ed.

———. "Ḳatabān." *Encyclopaedia of Islam*. 2nd ed.

———. "Pliny's Gebbanitae." *Proceedings of the Fifth Seminar for Arabian Studies*. London, 1972, pp. 4-8.

———. "Some Observations on Greek and Latin Data Relating to South Arabia." *Bulletin of the School of Oriental and African Studies* 62 (1979), 7-12.

———. "Two South-Arabian Inscriptions: Some Suggestions." *Journal of the Royal Asiatic Society* 1937, pp. 59-78.

———. Review of G.W.B. Huntingford (ed. and tr.), *The Periplus of the Erythraean Sea by an Unknown Author*. In *Bulletin of the School of Oriental and African Studies* 44 (1981), 353-358.

Bel, A. *La religion musulmane en Berbérie*. Vol. 1. Paris, 1938.

Bell, R. *The Origin of Islam in Its Christian Environment*. London, 1926.

Berg, B. "The Letter of Palladius on India." *Byzantion*, 44 (1974), 5-22.

Bevan, A. A. *The Naḳā'iḍ of Jarīr and al-Farazdaḳ*. 3 vols. Leiden, 1905-1912.

Birkeland, H. *The Lord Guideth: Studies on Primitive Islam*. Oslo, 1956.

Bīrūnī, Muḥammad b. Aḥmad al-. *al-Biruni's Book on Pharmacy and Materia Medica*. Edited and translated by H. M. Said. Karachi, 1973.

Blatter, E. *Flora of Aden*. *Records of the Botanical Survey of India*. Vol. 7. Calcutta, 1916.

———. *Flora Arabica*. *Records of the Botanical Survey of India*. Vol. 8. Calcutta and New Delhi, 1921-1936.

Blunt, A. *Bedouin Tribes of the Euphrates*. London, 1879.

Boisacq, A. *Dictionnaire étymologique de la langue grecque*. 4th ed. Heidelberg, 1950.

Boneschi, P. "L'antique inscription sud-arabe d'un supposé cachet provenant de Beytīn (Béthel)." *Rivista degli Studi Orientali* 46 (1971), 149-165.

———. "Les monogrammes sud-arabes de la grande jarre de *Tell El-Ḫeleyfeh* (Ezion-Geber)." *Rivista degli Studi Orientali* 36 (1961), 213-223.

Bor, N. L. *Gramineae* (= K. H. Rechinger, ed., *Flora Iranica*, no. 70). Graz, 1970.

———. *Gramineae* (= C. C. Townsend, E. Guest, and A. al-Rawi, eds., *Flora of Iraq*, vol. 9). Baghdad, 1968.

———. *The Grasses of Burma, Ceylon, India and Pakistan*. Oxford, 1960.

Bousquet, G.-H. "Observations sociologiques sur les origines de l'Islam." *Studia Islamica* 2 (1954), 61-87.

Bowersock, G. W. *Roman Arabia*. Cambridge, Mass. and London, 1983.

Branden, A. van den. *Histoire de Thamoud*. Beirut, 1960.

Brandis, D. *The Forest Flora of North-West and Central India*. London, 1874.

Braun, O., tr. *Ausgewählte Akten persischer Märtyrer*. Kempten, 1915.

Breasted, J. H. *Ancient Records of Egypt*. 5 vols. Chicago, 1906-1907.

Brice, W. B., ed. *An Historical Atlas of Islam*. Leiden, 1981.

The British Pharmaceutical Codex. London, 1934.

Brock, S. "Jacob of Edessa's Discourse on the Myron." *Oriens Christianus* 63 (1979), 20-36.

———. "A Syriac Life of John of Dailam." *Parole de l'Orient* 10 (1981-1982), 123-189.

Brockett, A. "Illustrations of Orientalist Misuse of Qur'ānic Variant Readings." Paper presented at the colloquium on the study of Ḥadīth. Oxford, 1982.

Budge, E.A.W., ed. and tr. *Syrian Anatomy, Pathology and Therapeutics, or "The Book of Medicine."* London, 1913.

Buhl, F. *Das Leben Muhammeds*. Leipzig, 1930.

Bukhārī, Muḥammad b. Ismāʿīl al-. *Le recueil des traditions mahométanes*. Edited by L. Krehl and T. W. Juynboll. 4 vols. Leiden, 1862-1908.

Bulliet, R. W. *The Camel and the Wheel*. Cambridge, Mass., 1975.

Burckhardt, J. L. *Travels in Arabia*. London, 1829.

Burkill, I. H. *A Dictionary of the Economic Products of the Malay Peninsula*. London, 1935.

Burnell, A. C. "On Some Pahlavî Inscriptions in South India." *Indian Antiquary* 3 (1874), 308-316.

Caskel, W. *Ǧamharat an-nasab, das genealogische Werk des Hišām Ibn Muḥammad al-Kalbī*. 2 vols. Leiden, 1966.

Casson, L. "Cinnamon and Cassia in the Ancient World." In Casson, *Ancient Trade and Society*. Detroit, 1984, pp. 225-246.

Celsus. *De Medicina*. Edited and translated by W. G. Spencer. 3 vols. London, 1935-1938.

Chabot, J.-B. *Choix d'inscriptions de Palmyre*. Paris, 1922.

Charlesworth, M. P. *Trade-Routes and Commerce of the Roman Empire*. Cambridge, 1924.

Chiovenda, P. *Flora Somalia*. Vol. 1. Rome, 1929.

Chittick, N. "East African Trade with the Orient." In D. S. Richards, ed., *Islam and the Trade of Asia*. Oxford, 1970, pp. 97-104.

Christensen, A. *L'Iran sous les Sassanides*. 2nd ed. Copenhagen, 1944.

Clark, P. "*Hauhau,*" *the Pai Marire Search for Maori Identity*. Oxford and Auckland, 1975.

Cleveland, R. L. "More on the South Arabian Clay Stamp Found at Beitîn." *Bulletin of the American Schools of Oriental Research*. No. 209, February 1973, pp. 33-36.

Colless, B. E. "Persian Merchants and Missionaries in Medieval Malaya." *Journal of the Malaysian Branch of the Royal Asiatic Society* 42:2 (1969), 10-47.

Cook, M. A. "Economic Developments." In J. Schacht and C. E. Bosworth, eds., *The Legacy of Islam*. 2nd ed. Oxford, 1974, pp. 201-243.

———. *Muhammad*. Oxford, 1983.

Cosmas Indicopleustes. *Topographie chrétienne*. Edited and translated by W. Wolska-Conus. 3 vols. Paris, 1968-1973.

Cowell, E. B., and others, trs. *The Jātaka*. 7 vols. Cambridge, 1895-1913.

Cowley, A., ed. and tr. *Aramaic Papyri of the Fifth Century B.C.* Oxford, 1923.

Crone, P. "Jāhilī and Jewish Law: the *Qasāma*." *Jerusalem Studies in Arabic and Islam* 4 (1984), 153-201.

———. *Slaves on Horses*. Cambridge, 1980.

Crone, P., and M. Cook. *Hagarism*. Cambridge, 1977.

Cudofontis, G. *Enumeratio Plantarum Aethiopiae* (*Bulletin du Jardin Botanique de l'État*, supplement). Brussels, 1954.

Dareste, R., B. Haussoullier, and T. Reinach. *Recueil des inscriptions juridiques grecques*. Paris, 1891-1898.

Dayton, J. E. "A Roman/Byzantine Site in the Hejaz." *Proceedings of the Sixth Seminar for Arabian Studies*. London, 1973, pp. 21-25.

Deines, H. von, and H. Grapow. *Wörterbuch der ägyptischen Drogennamen*. Berlin, 1959.

Desanges, J. "D'Axoum à l'Assam, aux portes de la Chine: le voyage du 'scholasticus de Thèbes' (entre 360 et 500 après J.-C.)." *Historia* 18 (1969), 627-639.

Dietrich, A., "Dār Ṣīnī." *Encyclopaedia of Islam*, 2nd ed., supplement.

Dīnawarī, Abū Ḥanīfa al-. *The Book of Plants (aliph to zā')*. Edited by B. Lewin. Uppsala and Wiesbaden, 1953.

———. *The Book of Plants, Part of the Monograph Section*. Edited by B. Lewin. Wiesbaden, 1974.

———. *Le dictionnaire botanique (de sīn à yā')*. Edited by M. Ḥamīdallāh. Cairo, 1973.

Dio Cassius. *Roman History*. Edited and translated by E. Cary. 9 vols. London and Cambridge, Mass., 1914-1927.

Diodorus Siculus. *Bibliotheca Historica*. Edited and translated by C. H. Oldfather and others. 12 vols. London and Cambridge, Mass., 1933-1967.

Dioscorides. *De Materia Medica*. Edited by M. Wellmann. 3 vols. Berlin, 1906-

1914. Translated by J. Goodyer as *The Greek Herbal of Dioscorides*, edited by R. T. Gunther. Oxford, 1934. References given in the form 1, 15/14 stand for book 1, paragraph 15 of the text, paragraph 14 of the translation.

Doe, B. *Southern Arabia*. London, 1971.

———. "The *WD'B* Formula and the Incense Trade." *Proceedings of the Twelfth Seminar for Arabian Studies*. London, 1979, pp. 40-43.

Donner, F. M. "The Bakr b. Wā'il Tribes and Politics in Northeastern Arabia on the Eve of Islam." *Studia Islamica* 51 (1980), 5-37.

———. *The Early Islamic Conquests*. Princeton, 1981.

———. "Mecca's Food Supplies and Muhammad's Boycott." *Journal of the Economic and Social History of the Orient* 20 (1977), 249-266.

Doughty, C. M. *Travels in Arabia Deserta*. London, 1936.

Dunlop, D. M. "Sources of Gold and Silver according to al-Hamdānī." *Studia Islamica* 8 (1957), 29-49.

Ebeling, E. "Mittelassyrische Rezepte zur Bereitung von wohlreichenden Salben." *Orientalia* 17 (1948), 129-145, 229-313.

Eickelman, D. F. "Musaylima." *Journal of the Economic and Social History of the Orient* 10 (1967), 17-52.

The Encyclopaedia of Islam. 2nd ed. Leiden and London, 1960–.

Engler, A. *Die Pflanzenwelt Afrikas*. Vol. III, part 1. Leipzig, 1915.

Erman, A., and H. Grapow. *Wörterbuch der ägyptischen Sprache*. Leipzig, 1925-1931.

Fahd, T. *La divination arabe*. Leiden, 1966.

———. "Hubal." *Encyclopaedia of Islam*. 2nd ed.

Fāsī, Muḥammad b. Aḥmad al-. *Shifā' al-gharām bi-akhbār al-balad al-ḥarām*. Edited by F. Wüstenfeld. Leipzig, 1859.

Fraenkel, S., *Die aramäischen Fremdwörter im arabischen*, Leiden 1886.

Frye, R. N. "Bahrain under the Sasanians." In D. T. Potts, ed., *Dilmun, New Studies in the Archaeology and History of Bahrain*. Berlin, 1983, pp. 167-70.

Gaudefroy-Demombynes, [M]. *Le pèlerinage à la Mekke*. Paris, 1923.

Gibb, H.A.R. *Islam* (= 2nd ed. of *Mohammedanism*). Oxford, 1975.

Glaser, E. *Skizze der Geschichte und Geographie Arabiens von den ältesten Zeiten bis zum Propheten Muḥammad*. Vol. 2. Berlin, 1890.

Glover, P. E. *A Provisional Check-list of British and Italian Somaliland, Trees, Shrubs and Herbs*. London, 1947.

Glueck, N. "The First Campaign at Tell el-Kheleifeh." *Bulletin of the American Schools of Oriental Research*. No. 71, October 1938, pp. 3-17.

———. *The Other Side of the Jordan*. Cambridge, Mass., 1970.

———. "Tell el-Kheleifeh Inscriptions." In N. Goedicke, ed., *Near Eastern Studies in Honor of William Foxwell Albright*. Baltimore and London, 1971, pp. 225-242.

Goitein, S. D. *A Mediterranean Society*. Vol. 1. Berkeley and Los Angeles, 1967.

Goldziher, I., ed. "Der Dîwân des Ǵarwal b. Aus al-Ḥuṭej'a." *Zeitschrift der Deutschen Morgenländischen Gesellschaft* 46 (1892), 1-53, 173-225, 471-527.

Gray, E. W. Review of J. I. Miller, *The Spice Trade of the Roman Empire*. In *Journal of Roman Studies* 60 (1970), 222-224.

Great Britain. Admiralty. *A Handbook of Arabia*. Vol. 1. London, 1916.

Great Britain. Foreign Office. *Arabia*. London, 1920.

Grohmann, A., ed. and tr. *Arabic Papyri from Ḫirbet el-Mird*. Louvain, 1963.

———. "Makoraba." In Pauly-Wissova, *Realencyclopädie*.

———. *Südarabien als Wirtschaftsgebiet*. Vol. 1. Vienna, 1930.

Groom, N. *Frankincense and Myrrh, a Study of the Arabian Incense Trade*. London, 1981.

Guidi, I., and others, eds. and trs. *Chronica Minora* CSCO, Scriptores Syri, third series. Vol. 4. Louvain, 1903-1907.

Guillaume, A., tr. *The Life of Muhammad*. Oxford, 1955.

Ḥalabī, ʿAlī b. Burhān al-dīn al-. *al-Sīra al-ḥalabiyya*. 2 vols. Cairo, 1349.

Hamdānī, Ḥasan b. Aḥmad al-. *Ṣifat Jazīrat al-ʿarab*. Edited by D. H. Müller. 2 vols. Leiden, 1884-1891.

———. *Kitāb al-jawharatayn*. Edited and translated by C. Tolll. Uppsala, 1968. *See also* Dunlop.

Ḥamīdallāh, M. "Al-īlāf, ou les rapports économico-diplomatiques de la Mecque pré-islamique." *Mélanges Louis Massignon*. Vol. 2. Damascus, 1957, pp. 293-311.

———, ed. *Sīrat Ibn Isḥāq*. Rabat, 1976.

Haran, M. "The Uses of Incense in the Ancient Israelite Ritual." *Vetus Testamentum* 10 (1960), 113-129.

Harding, G. L. *Archaeology in the Aden Protectorates*. London, 1964.

Hasan, H. *A History of Persian Navigation*. London, 1928.

Ḥassān b. Thābit. *Dīwān*. Edited by W. N. ʿArafat, London, 1971; edited by H. Hirschfeld, Leiden and London, 1910. References are to ʿArafat's edition unless otherwise stated.

Hawting, G. R. "The Origin of Jedda and the Problem of al-Shuʿayba." *Arabica* 31 (1984), 318-326.

Hell, J., ed. and tr. *Neue Huḏailiten-Diwane*. 2 vols. Hannover and Leipzig, 1926-1933.

Hennig, R. "Die Einführung der Seidenraupenzucht ins Byzantinerreich." *Byzantinische Zeitschrift* 33 (1933), 295-312.

———. "*Kinnamōmon* und *Kinnamōphoros Khōra* in der antiken Literatur." *Klio* 32 (1939), 325-330.

Hepper, F. N. "Arabian and African Frankincense Trees." *Journal of Egyptian Archaeology* 55 (1969), 66-72.

Hepper, F. N. "On the Transference of Ancient Plant Names." *Palestine Exploration Quarterly* 109 (1977), 129-130.

Herodotus. *History*. Edited and translated by A. D. Godley. 4 vols. London and Cambridge, Mass., 1920-1925.

Hill, A. F. *Economic Botany*. New York and London, 1937.

Hirschfeld, H. *New Researches into the Composition and Exegesis of the Qoran*. London, 1902.

Hirth, F. *China and the Roman Orient*. Leipzig, 1885.

Hitti, P. K. *Capital Cities of Arab Islam*. Minneapolis, 1973.

Hjelt, A. "Pflanzennamen aus dem Hexaëmeron von Jacob's von Edessa." In *Orientalische Studien Theodor Nöldeke*. Edited by C. Bezold. Giessen, 1906.

Hornblower, J. *Hieronymus of Cardia*. Oxford, 1981.

Hourani, G. F. "Ancient South Arabian Voyages to India—Rejoinder to G. W. van Beek." *Journal of the American Oriental Society* 80 (1960), 135-136.

———. *Arab Seafaring in the Indian Ocean in Ancient and Early Medieval Times*. Princeton, 1951.

———. "Did Roman Commercial Competition Ruin South Arabia?" *Journal of Near Eastern Studies* 11 (1952), 291-295.

Howes, F. N. *Vegetable Gums and Resins*. Waltham, Mass., 1949.

Huber, C. *Voyage dans l'Arabie centrale*. Paris, 1885.

Huntingford, G.W.B., tr. *The Periplus of the Erythraean Sea*. London, 1980.

Ibn ʿAbd al-Ḥakam, ʿAbd al-Raḥmān b. ʿAbdallāh. *Futūḥ Miṣr*. Edited by C. C. Torrey. New Haven, 1922.

Ibn Abī'l-Ḥadīd, ʿAbd al-Ḥamīd b. Abī'l-Ḥusayn. *Sharḥ nahj al-balāgha*. 4 vols. Cairo, 1329.

Ibn ʿAsākir, ʿAlī b. al-Ḥusayn. *Tahdhīb taʾrīkh Dimashq al-kabīr*. Edited by ʿA.-Q. Badran and A. ʿUbayd. 7 vols. Damascus, 1911-1932.

———. *Taʾrīkh madīnat Dimashq*. Edited by Ṣ.-D. al-Munajjid and M. A. Dahmān. Damascus, 1951–.

Ibn al-Athīr, ʿAlī b. Muḥammad. *Usd al-ghāba*. 5 vols. Cairo, 1280.

Ibn Bayṭār, ʿAbdallāh b. Aḥmad. *al-Jāmiʿ al-kabīr*. Translated by J. Sontheimer. 2 vols. Stuttgart, 1840-1842.

Ibn Durayd, Muḥammad b. al-Ḥasan. *Kitāb al-ishtiqāq*. Edited by ʿA.-S. M. Hārūn. Baghdad, 1979.

Ibn Ḥabīb, Muḥammad. *Kitāb al-muḥabbar*. Edited by I. Lichtenstädter. Hyderabad, 1942.

———. *Kitāb al-munammaq*. Edited by Kh. A. Fāriq. Hyderabad, 1964.

Ibn Ḥajar al-ʿAsqalānī, Aḥmad b. ʿAlī. *Kitāb al-iṣāba fī tamyīz al-ṣaḥāba*. 8 vols. Cairo, 1323-1325.

———. *Tahdhīb al-tahdhīb*. 12 vols. Hyderabad, 1325-1327.

Ibn Ḥanbal, Aḥmad. *al-ʿIlal*. Vol. 1. Edited by T. Koçyiğit and I. Cerrahoğlu. Ankara, 1963.

———. *al-Musnad*. 6 vols. Cairo, 1895.

Ibn Ḥazm, ʿAlī b. Aḥmad. *Jamharat ansāb al-ʿarab*. Edited by ʿA.-S. M. Hārūn. Cairo, 1962.

Ibn Hishām, ʿAbd al-Malik. *Das Leben Muhammed's nach Muhammed Ibn Ishâk*. Edited by F. Wüstenfeld. 2 vols. Göttingen, 1858-1860. *See also* Guillaume.

———. *al-Sīra al-nabawiyya*. Edited by M. al-Saqqā and others. 2 vols. Cairo, 1955. All references are to Wüstenfeld's edition unless otherwise stated.

Ibn Isḥāq, *see* Ḥamīdallāh; Ibn Hishām.

Ibn al-Kalbī, Hishām b. Muḥammad. *Kitāb al-aṣnām*. Edited by Ahmed Zéki Pacha. Cairo, 1914.

Ibn Kathīr, Ismāʿīl b. ʿUmar. *al-Bidāya waʾl-nihāya*. 14 vols. Cairo, 1932.

———. *Tafsīr al-qurʾān al-ʿaẓīm*. 4 vols. Cairo, n.d.

Ibn Khālawayh, Ḥusayn b. Aḥmad. *Mukhtaṣar fī shawādhdh al-qurʾān*. Edited by G. Bergsträsser. Leipzig, 1934.

Ibn Khurdādhbih, ʿUbaydallāh b. ʿAbdallāh. *Kitāb al-masālik waʾl-mamālik*. Edited and translated by M. J. de Goeje. Leiden, 1889.

Ibn Manẓūr, Muḥammad b. Mukarrim. *Lisān al-ʿarab*. 20 vols. Būlāq, 1300-1307.

Ibn al-Mujāwir, Yūsuf b. Yaʿqūb. *Descriptio Arabiae Meridionalis*. Edited by O. Löfgren. 2 vols. Leiden, 1951-1954.

Ibn Qays al-Ruqayyāt, ʿUbaydallāh. *Dīwān*. Edited and translated by N. Rhodokanakis. Vienna, 1902.

Ibn al-Qaysarānī, Muḥammad b. Ṭāhir. *Kitāb al-ansāb al-muttafiqa*. Edited by P. de Jong. Leiden, 1865.

Ibn Qutayba, ʿAbdallāh b. Muslim. *al-Maʿārif*. Edited by M.I.ʿA. al-Ṣāwī. Beirut, 1970.

———. *Taʾwīl mushkil al-qurʾān*. Edited by A. Ṣaqr. Cairo, 1954.

Ibn Rusta, Aḥmad b. ʿUmar. *Kitāb al-aʿlāq al-nafīsa*. Edited by M. J. de Goeje. Leiden, 1892.

Ibn Saʿd, Muḥammad. *Al-Ṭabaqāt al-kubrā*. 8 vols. Beirut, 1957-1960.

Irvine, A. K. "The Arabs and the Ethiopians." In D. J. Wiseman, ed., *Peoples of the Old Testament Times*. Oxford, 1973, pp. 287-311.

Iṣbahānī, Abūʾl-Faraj ʿAlī b. Ḥusayn al-. *Kitāb al-aghānī*. 24 vols. Cairo, 1927-1974.

al-Iskāfī, Muḥammad b. ʿAbdallāh al-Khaṭīb al-. *Luṭf al-tadbīr*. Edited by A. ʿA. al-Bāqī. Cairo, 1964.

Ivanow, W. *Ismaili Traditions Concerning the Rise of the Fatimids*. Oxford, 1942.

Jacob, G. *Altarabisches Beduinenleben*. 2nd ed. Berlin, 1897.

Jacob of Edessa. *Hexaemeron*. Edited and translated by I.-B. Chabot and A. Vaschalde. CSCO, *Scriptores syri*, vols. 44, 48. Louvain, 1928, 1932.

Jāḥiẓ, ʿAmr b. Baḥr al-. *Rasāʾil*. Edited by Ḥ. al-Sandūbī. Cairo, 1933.

———. *Tria Opuscula*. Edited by G. van Vloten. Leiden, 1903.

——— (attrib.). *Kitāb al-tabaṣṣur bi'l-tijāra*. Edited by H. H. ʿAbd al-Wahhāb. Cairo, 1966. Translated by C. Pellat as "Ǧāḥiẓiana, I. *Le Kitāb al-tabaṣṣur bi'l-tijāra* attribué à Ǧāḥiẓ." *Arabica* 7 (1954), 153-165.

Jamme, A., ed. and tr. *The Al-ʿUqlah Texts* (*Documentations Sud-Arabe*, III). Washington, D.C., 1963.

Jamme, A., and G. W. van Beek. "The South Arabian Clay Stamp from Bethel Again." *Bulletin of the American Schools of Oriental Research*. No. 163, October 1961, pp. 15-18.

Jastrow, M. *A Dictionary of the Targumim, the Talmud Babli and Yerushalmi, and the Midrashic Literature*. 2 vols. New York, 1903.

Jaussen, A. *Coutumes des arabes au pays de Moab*. Paris, 1948.

Jones, A.H.M. "Asian Trade in Antiquity." In D. S. Richards, ed., *Islam and the Trade of Asia*. Oxford, 1970, pp. 1-10.

———. "The Economic Life of the Towns of the Roman Empire." *Recueils de la Société Jean Bodin* 1955 (= *La ville*, part 2), pp. 161-192.

Jones, J.M.B. "The Chronology of the Maghāzī—a Textual Survey." *Bulletin of the School of Oriental and African Studies* 19 (1957), 245-280.

———. "Ibn Isḥāq and al-Wāqidī." *Bulletin of the School of Oriental and African Studies* 22 (1959), 41-51.

———. "*Al-Sīra al-nabawiyya* as a Source for the Economic History of Western Arabia at the Time of the Rise of Islam." *Studies in the History of Arabia*. Proceedings of the First International Symposium on Studies in the History of Arabia, April 1977. Vol. 1, part 1. Riyadh, 1979, pp. 15-23.

Josephus. *Jewish Antiquities*. Edited and translated by H. St. J. Thackeray and others. 6 vols. London, New York, and Cambridge, Mass., 1930-1965.

———. *The Jewish War*. Edited and translated by H. St. J. Thackeray. 2 vols. London and New York, 1927-1928.

Kalāʿī, Sulaymān b. Sālim al-. *Kitāb al-iktifāʾ*. Part 1. Edited by H. Massé. Algiers and Paris, 1931.

Kawar, *see* Shahid.

Kelso, J. L. "A Reply to Yadin's Article on the Finding of the Bethel Seal." *Bulletin of the American Schools of Oriental Research*. No. 199, October 1970, p. 65.

Kennedy, J. "The Early Commerce of Babylon with India." *Journal of the Royal Asiatic Society* 1898, pp. 241-273.

Kennett, F. *History of Perfume*. London, 1975.

Khalīfa b. Khayyāṭ. *Taʾrīkh*. Edited by S. Zakkār. 2 vols. Damascus, 1967-1968.

Khan, A. "The Tanning Cottage Industry in Pre-Islamic Arabia." *Journal of the Pakistan Historical Society* 19 (1971), 85-100.

Khan, M. A. Muʿid, ed. and tr. *A Critical Edition of Diwan of Laqīṭ Ibn Yaʿmur.* Beirut, 1971.

Khazanov, A. M. *Nomads and the Outside World.* Cambridge, 1984.

Khwārizmī, Muḥammad b. Aḥmad al-. *Kitāb mafātīḥ al-ʿulūm.* Edited by G. van Vloten. Leiden, 1895.

King, D. A. "The Practical Interpretation of Qur'ān 2.144: Some Remarks on the Sacred Direction in Islam." Forthcoming in *Proceedings of the Second International Qur'ān Conference, New Delhi 1982.*

Kindī, Muḥammad b. Yūsuf al-. *The Governors and Judges of Egypt.* Edited by R. Guest. Leiden and London, 1912.

Kister, M. J. "The Campaign of Ḥulubān." *Le Muséon* 78 (1965), 425-436.

———. "al-Ḥīra." *Arabica* 15 (1968), 143-169.

———. "Labbayka, Allāhumma, Labbayka. . . . On a Monotheist Aspect of a Jāhiliyya Practice." *Jerusalem Studies in Arabic and Islam* 2 (1980), 33-57.

———. "Mecca and Tamīm (Aspects of Their Relations)." *Journal of the Economic and Social History of the Orient* 8 (1965), 117-163.

———. "On an Early Fragment of the Qur'ān." *Studies in Judaica, Karaitica and Islamica Presented to Leon Nemoy.* Ramat-Gan, 1982, pp. 163-166.

———. "Some Reports Concerning Mecca from Jāhiliyya to Islam." *Journal of the Economic and Social History of the Orient* 15 (1972), 61-91.

Kortenbeutel, H. *Der ägyptische Süd- und Osthandel in der Politik der Ptolemäer und römischen Kaiser.* Berlin and Charlottenburg, 1931.

Kosegarten, J.G.L., ed. *Carmina Hudsailitarum.* London, 1854.

Kraemer, C. J., Jr., ed. and tr. *Excavations at Nessana.* Vol. 3 (Non-Literary Papyri). Princeton, 1958.

Krauss, S. "Talmudische Nachrichten über Arabien." *Zeitschrift der Deutschen Morgenländischen Gesellschaft* 70 (1916), 321-353.

Krenkow, F., ed. and tr. *The Poems of Ṭufail Ibn ʿAuf al-Ghanawī and aṭ-Ṭirimmāḥ Ibn Ḥakīm aṭ-Ṭā'yī.* London, 1927.

Kuthayyir ʿAzza. *Dīwān.* Edited by H. Pérès. Algiers and Paris, 2 vols. 1928-1930.

Labib, S. Y. *Handelsgeschichte Ägyptens im Spätmittelalter.* Wiesbaden, 1965.

Lammens, H. *L'Arabie occidentale avant l'hégire.* Beirut, 1928.

———. *Le berceau de l'Islam.* Rome, 1914.

———. *La cité arabe de Ṭāif à la veille de l'hégire* (reprinted from *Mélanges de l'Université Saint-Joseph,* vol. 8). Beirut, 1922. References are to the original pagination.

———. *Fāṭima et les filles de Mahomet.* Rome, 1912.

Lammens, H. *La Mecque à la veille de l'hégire* (reprinted from *Mélanges de l'Université Saint Joseph*, vol. 9). Beirut, 1924. References are to the original pagination.

———. "La république marchande de la Mecque vers l'an 600 de notre ère." *Bulletin de l'Institut Égyptien* 5th series, 4 (1910), 23-54.

Lampe, G.W.H., ed. *Patristic Greek Lexicon*. Oxford, 1961.

Landau-Tasseron, E. "The 'Sinful Wars', Religious, Social and Historical Aspects of *Hurūb al-Fijār*," forthcoming in *Jerusalem Studies in Arabic and Islam*.

Lane, E. W. *An Arabic-English Lexicon*. London, 1863-1893.

Lanternari, V. *The Religions of the Oppressed*. London, 1963.

Lapidus, I. M. "The Arab Conquests and the Formation of Islamic Society." In G.H.A. Juynboll, ed., *Studies on the First Century of Islamic Society*. Carbondale and Edwardsville, 1982, pp. 49-72.

Lassen, C. *Indische Altertumskunde*. 2nd ed. Vol. 1. London, 1867.

Laufer, B. "Malabathron." *Journal Asiatique* ser. 11, vol. 12 (1918), 5-49.

———. *Sino-Iranica*. Chicago, 1919.

Le Baron Bowen, R. "Ancient Trade Routes in South Arabia." In R. Le Baron Bowen, Jr., F. P. Albright, and others, *Archaeological Discoveries in South Arabia*. Baltimore, 1958, pp. 35-42.

———. "Irrigation in Ancient Qatabân (Beiḥân)." In R. Le Baron Bowen, Jr., F. P. Albright, and others, *Archaeological Discoveries in South Arabia*. Baltimore, 1958, pp. 43-132.

Legge, J., tr. *An Account by the Chinese Monk Fâ-Hien of His Travels in India and Ceylon (A.D. 399-414)*. Oxford, 1886.

Levey, M. *Early Arabic Pharmacology*. Leiden, 1973.

Lewicki, T. "Les premiers commerçants arabes en Chine." *Rocznik Orientalistyczny* 77 (1935), 173-186.

Lewis, B. *The Arabs in History*. 4th ed. London, 1966.

Liddell, H. G., and R. Scott. *A Greek-English Lexicon*. 9th ed. Oxford, 1968.

Linton, R. "Nativist Movements." *American Anthropologist* 45 (1943), 230-240.

Lisān, see Ibn Manẓūr.

Loret, V. *La flore pharaonique*. 2nd ed. Paris, 1892.

Löw, I. *Aramäische Pflanzennamen*. Leipzig, 1881.

———. *Die Flora der Juden*. 4 vols. Vienna and Leipzig, 1924-1928.

Lucas, A. *Ancient Egyptian Materials and Industries*. 2nd ed. Edited by J. R. Harris. London, 1962.

Lüling, G. *Die Wiederentdeckung des Propheten Muhammad*. Erlangen, 1981.

Lyall, C. J., ed. and tr. *The Dīwāns of ʿAbīd Ibn al-Abraṣ, of Asad, and ʿĀmir Ibn aṭ-Ṭufail, of ʿĀmir Ibn Saʿṣaʿa*. London, 1913.

———, ed. and tr. *The Mufaḍḍalīyāt*. 3 vols. Oxford, 1918-1924.

McCrindle, J. W., tr. *Ancient India as Described by Ktêsias the Knidian*. Calcutta, etc., 1882.

———, tr. *The Commerce and Navigation of the Erythraean Sea, being a Translation of the Periplus Maris Erythraei*. Calcutta, etc., 1879.

Malalas. *Chronographia*. Edited by L. Dindorf. Bonn, 1831.

Margoliouth, D. S. *Mohammed and the Rise of Islam*. London, 1906.

———, ed. and tr. *The Table-Talk of a Mesopotamian Judge*. 2 vols. London, 1921-1922.

Maricq, A., ed. and tr. " 'Res Gestae divi Saporis,' " *Syria* 35 (1958), 295-360.

Martius, C. *Versuch einer Monographie der Sennesblätter*. Erlangen, 1857.

Marzūqī, Aḥmad b. Muḥammad al-. *Kitāb al-azmina wa'l-amkina*. 2 vols. Hyderabad, 1332.

Masʿūdī, ʿAlī b. al-Ḥusayn al-. *Kitāb murūj al-dhahab*. Edited and translated by A. C. Barbier de Meynard and A. J.-B. Pavet de Courteille. 7 vols. Paris, 1861-1877.

Māwardī, ʿAlī b. Muḥammad al-. *Aʿlām al-nubuwwa*. Beirut, 1973.

Meeker, M. E. *Literature and Violence in North Arabia*.

Meisner, B. "Bʿdōlaḥ," *Zeitschrift für Assyriologie* 17 (1903), 270-271.

Milani, C., ed. and tr. *Itinerarium Antonini Placentini, un viaggio in Terra Santa del 560-570 d. C.* Milan, 1977.

Milik, J. T. "Inscriptions grecques et nabatéennes de Rawwāfah." Appended to P. J. Parr, G. L. Harding, and J. E. Dayton, "Preliminary Survey in N. W. Arabia, 1968." *Bulletin of the Institute of Archaeology* 10 (1971), 54-58.

Miller, J. I. *The Spice Trade of the Roman Empire*. Oxford, 1969.

Milne-Redhead, E., and others. *Flora of Tropical East Africa*. London, 1952—.

Mingana, A. "The Early Spread of Christianity in India." *Bulletin of the John Rylands Library* 9 (1925), 297-371.

Minorsky, V., tr. *Ḥudūd al-ʿālam*. London, 1937.

Mitchell, T. C. "A South Arabian Tripod Offering Saucer Said To Be from Ur." *Iraq* 31 (1969), 112-114.

Moberg, A. *The Book of the Himyarites*. Lund, 1924.

Moldenke, H. N., and A. L. Moldenke. *Plants of the Bible*. Waltham, Mass., 1952.

Monnot, G. "L'Histoire des religions en Islam, Ibn al-Kalbī et Rāzī." *Revue de l'Histoire des Religions* 188 (1975), 23-34.

Mookerji, R. K. *Indian Shipping. A History of the Sea-borne Trade and Maritime Activity of the Indians from the Earliest Times*. 2nd ed. Bombay, etc., 1957.

Mordtman, J. H. "Dusares bei Epiphanius." *Zeitschrift der Deutschen Morgenländischen Gesellschaft* 29 (1875), 99-106.

Mordtmann, J. H., and D. H. Müller. *Sabäische Denkmäler*. Vienna, 1883.

Mubarrad, Muḥammad b. Yazīd al-. *al-Kāmil*. Edited by W. Wright. Leipzig. 2 vols. 1864-1892.

Müller, W. W. "Das Ende des antiken Königsreichs Ḥaḍramaut. Die Sabäische

Inschrift Schreyer-Geukens = Iryānī 32." In *al-Hudhud, Festschrift Maria Höfner*. Graz, 1981, pp. 225-256.

———. "Notes on the Use of Frankincense in South Arabia." *Proceedings of the Ninth Seminar for Arabian Studies*. London, 1976, pp. 124-136.

———. *Weihrauch. Ein arabisches Produkt und seine Bedeutung in der Antike*. Offprint from Pauly-Wissowa, *Realencyclopädie*, Supplementband 15. Munich, 1978.

Muqaddasī, Muḥammad b. Aḥmad al-. *Descriptio imperii moslemici*. 2nd ed. Edited by M. J. de Goeje. Leiden, 1906.

Muqātil b. Sulaymān. *Tafsīr*. MS Saray, Ahmet III, 74/II.

Murray, G. W. *Sons of Ishmael*. London, 1935.

Muṣʿab b. ʿAbdallāh al-Zubayrī. *Kitāb nasab Quraysh*. Edited by E. Lévi-Provençal. Cairo, 1953.

Musil, A. *The Manners and Customs of the Rwala Bedouins*. New York, 1928.

———. *Northern Neǧd*. New York, 1928.

Muslim b. Ḥajjāj. *al-Ṣaḥīḥ*. Cairo, 18 vols. 1929-1930.

Nābigha al-Dhubyānī. *Dīwān*. Edited and translated by H. Derenbourg. Paris, 1869.

Nallino, C. A. "L'Égypte avait elle des relations directes avec l'Arabie méridionale avant l'âge des Ptolémées?" In his *Raccolta di scritti editi e inediti*. Vol. 3. Rome, 1941, pp. 157-68.

Nicole, J., tr. *Le livre du préfet*. Geneva, 1894. Reprinted in *The Book of the Eparch*. London, 1970.

Nöldeke, T., tr. *Geschichte der Perser und Araber zur Zeit der Sasaniden*. Leiden, 1879.

———. "Der Gott *Mr' Byt'* und die Kaʿba." *Zeitschrift für Assyriologie* 23 (1909), 184-186.

———. *Neue Beiträge zur semitischen Sprachwissenschaft*. Strassburg, 1910.

———. *Sketches from Eastern History*. London and Edinburgh, 1892.

Nonnosus in Photius, *Bibliothèque*. Edited and translated by R. Henry. Paris, 1959. Vol. 1.

Ogino, H. "Frankincense and Myrrh of Ancient South Arabia." *Orient* (Tokyo) 3 (1967), 21-39.

Oppenheim, A. L. "The Seafaring Merchants of Ur." *Journal of the American Oriental Society* 74 (1954) 6-17.

Ozenda, P. *Flore du Sahara*. 2nd ed. Paris, 1977.

Palgrave, W. G. *Narrative of a Year's Journey Through Central and Eastern Arabia (1862-3)*. 2 vols. London, 1865.

Palmer, A. "Sources for the Early History of Qartmin Abbey with Special Reference to the Period A.D. 400-800." D.Phil., Oxford, 1982.

Paret, R. "Les villes de Syrie du sud et les routes commerciales d'Arabie à la fin du vi^e siecle." *Akten des XI. Internationalen Byzantinistenkongresses, München 1958*. Munich, 1960, pp. 438-444.

Parsa, A. *Flore de l'Iran*. Vol. 2. Tehran, 1948.

Pauly-Wissowa = *Pauly's Realencyclopädie der classischen Altertumswissenschaft*. 2nd ed. Edited by G. Wissowa. Stuttgart, 1893–.

Payne Smith, R. *Thesaurus Syriacus*. 2 vols. Oxford, 1879-1901.

Periplus Maris Erythraei. Edited by H. Frisk. Göteborg, 1927. Translated by W. H. Schoff as *The Periplus of the Erythraean Sea*. New York, 1912. *See also* Huntingford; MacCrindle.

Philby, H. St. J. B. *The Heart of Arabia*. London, 1922.

———. *The Queen of Sheba*. London, 1981.

Philostorgius. *Kirchengeschichte*. Edited by J. Bidez. Re-edited by F. Winkelmann. Berlin, 1972. Translated by E. Walford as *The Ecclesiastical History of Philostorgius*. London, 1855.

Pigulewskaja, N. *Byzans auf den Wegen nach Indien*. Berlin and Amsterdam, 1969.

Pirenne, J. "The Incense Port of Moscha (Khor Rori) in Dhofar." *Journal of Oman Studies* 1 (1975), 81-96.

———. *Le royaume sud-arabe de Qatabân et sa datation*. Louvain, 1961.

Pliny. *Natural History*. Edited and translated by A. H. Rackam and others. 10 vols. London and Cambridge, Mass., 1938-1962.

Polunin, N. *Introduction to Plant Geography*. London, 1960.

Polybius. *The Histories*. Edited and translated by W. R. Paton. 6 vols. Cambridge, Mass., 1922-1927.

Posener, G. *La première domination perse en Égypte*. Cairo, 1936.

Post, G. E. *Flora of Syria, Palestine and Sinai*. 2nd ed. Edited by J. Dinsmore. 2 vols. Beirut, 1932-1933.

Powers, D. S. "The Islamic Law of Inheritance Reconsidered: a New Reading of Q. 4:12B." *Studia Islamica* 55 (1982), 61-94.

Procopius. *History of the Wars*. Edited and translated by H. B. Dewing. 5 vols. London, 1914-1928.

Ptolemy. *Geographia*. Edited by C.F.A. Nobbe. 3 vols. Leipzig, 1888-1913.

Qālī, Ismāʿīl b. al-Qāsim al-. *Kitāb dhayl al-amālī waʾl-nawādir*. Cairo, 1926.

Qalqashandī, Abūʾl-ʿAbbās Aḥmad al-. *Ṣubḥ al-aʿshā*. Cairo, 14 vols. 1913-1920.

Qays b. al-Khaṭīm. *Dīwān*. Edited and translated by T. Kowalski. Leipzig, 1914.

Quezel, P., and S. Santa. *Nouvelle flore de l'Algérie*. 2 vols. Paris, 1962-1963.

Qummī, Abūʾl-Ḥasan ʿAlī b. Ibrāhīm al-. *Tafsīr*. Edited by Ṭ. al-Mūsawī al-Jazāʾirī, Najaf, 1386-1387.

Qurṭubī, Muḥammad b. Aḥmad al-. *al-Jāmiʿ li-aḥkām al-qurʾān*. 20 vols. Cairo, 1933-1950.

Rahmani, L. Y. "Palestinian Incense Burners of the Sixth to Eighth Centuries C.E." *Israel Exploration Journal* 30 (1980), 116-122.

Raschke, M. G. "New Studies in Roman Commerce with the East." In H. Temporini and W. Haase, eds., *Aufstieg und Niedergang der römischen Welt*. Part II (*Principat*), vol. 9:2. Berlin and New York, 1978, pp. 604-1378.

Rathjens, C. "Die alten Welthandelstrassen und die Offenbarungsreligionen." *Oriens* 15 (1962), 115-129.

Raven, W. "Some Islamic Traditions on the Negus of Ethiopia." Paper presented at the colloquium on the study of ḥadīth, Oxford, 1982, forthcoming in *Journal of Semitic Studies*.

Rawi, A. al-. *Wild Plants of Iraq with Their Distributions*. Baghdad, 1964.

Rawi, A. al-, and H. L. Chakravarty. *Medicinal Plants of Iraq*. Baghdad, 1964.

Rawlinson, H. G. *Intercourse between India and the Western World from the Earliest Time to the Fall of Rome*. Cambridge, 1916.

Rāzī, Fakhr al-dīn al-. *Mafātīḥ al-ghayb*. 8 vols. Cairo, 1307-1309.

Rechinger, K. H. *Burceraceae* (= K. H. Rechinger, ed., *Flora Iranica*, no. 107). Graz, 1974.

———. *Flora of Lowland Iraq*. New York, 1964.

Repertoire d'Épigraphie Sémitique. Vol. 7. Edited by G. Ryckmans. Paris, 1950.

Rhodokanakis, N. "Die Sarkophaginschrift von Gizeh." *Zeitschrift für Semistik* 2 (1924), 113-133.

Ridley, H. N. *Spices*. London, 1912.

Riedel, W., and W. E. Crum, eds. and trs. *The Canons of Athanasius of Alexandria*. Oxford, 1904.

Rodinson, M. *Islam et capitalisme*. Paris, 1966.

———. *Mohammed*. London, 1971.

Rosmarin, T. W. "Aribi und Arabien in den babylonisch-assyrischen Quellen." *Journal of the Society of Oriental Research* 16 (1932), 1-37.

Ross, A.S.C. *Ginger, A Loan Word Study*. Oxford, 1952.

Rothstein, G. *Die Dynastie der Laḫmiden in al-Ḥîra*. Berlin, 1899.

Rubin, U. "Places of Worship in Mecca." forthcoming in *Jerusalem Studies in Arabic and Islam*.

———. "Ḥanīfiyya and Kaʿba. An Inquiry into the Arabian Pre-Islamic Background of Dīn Ibrāhīm." forthcoming in *Jerusalem Studies in Arabic and Islam*.

Rufinus of Aquileia. *Historia Ecclesiastica*. In J. P. Migne, *Patrologia Graeco-Latina*. Vol. 21. Paris, 1849.

Ryckmans, G. "Un fragment de jarre avec caractères minéens de Tell El-Kheleyfeh." *Revue Biblique* 48 (1939), 247-249.

———. "Inscriptions sud-arabes (troisième série)." *Le Muséon* 48 (1935), 163-187.

———. "Ophir." *Dictionnaire de la Bible*. Supplément, vol. 6. Paris, 1960.

Ryckmans, J. *L'institution monarchique en Arabie méridionale avant l'Islam*. Louvain, 1951.

Sadighi, G. H. *Les mouvements religieux iraniens au IIe et au IIIe siècles de l'hégire*. Paris, 1938.

Schacht, J. "On Mūsā b. ʿUqba's Kitāb al-Maghāzī." *Acta Orientalia* (Copenhagen) 21 (1953), 288-300.

———. "A Revaluation of Islamic Traditions." *Journal of the Royal Asiatic Society* 1949, pp. 143-154.

Scher, A., and others, eds. and trs. "Histoire Nestorienne." In *Patrologia Orientalis*. Edited by R. Graffin and F. Nau. Vol. 4 (1908), 215-313; vol. 5 (1910), 219-344; vol. 7 (1911), 97-203; vol. 13 (1919), 433-639.

Schmucker, W. *Die pflanzliche und mineralische Materia Medica im Firdaus al-Ḥikma des Ṭabarī*. Bonn, 1969.

Schoff, *see Periplus*.

Schröter, R., ed. and tr. "Trostschreiben Jacob's von Sarug an die himjaritischen Christen." *Zeitschrift der Deutschen Morgenländischen Gesellschaft* 31 (1877), 360-405.

Schulthess, F., ed. and tr. *Der Dîwân des arabischen Dichters Ḥâtim Ṭej*. Leipzig, 1897.

Schumann, C. *Kritische Untersuchungen über die Zimtländer*. Gotha, 1883.

Schwarzlose, F. W. *Die Waffen der alten Araber*. Leipzig, 1886.

Sebeos (attrib.). *Histoire d'Héraclius*. Translated by F. Macler. Paris, 1904.

Segal, J. B. "Arabs in Syriac Literature before the Rise of Islam." *Jerusalem Studies in Arabic and Islam* 4 (1984), 89-124.

Serjeant, R. B. "Ḥaram and Ḥawṭah, the Sacred Enclave in Arabia." *Mélanges Taha Husain*. Edited by ʿA.-R. Badawī. Cairo, 1962, pp. 41-58.

———. "Hūd and Other Pre-Islamic Prophets of Ḥaḍramawt." *Le Muséon* 67 (1954), pp. 121-179.

———. *The Saiyids of Ḥaḍramawt*. London, 1957.

Sezgin, F. *Geschichte des arabischen Schrifttums*. Vol. 1. Leiden, 1967.

Shaban, M. A. *Islamic History, A New Interpretation*. Vol. 1. Cambridge, 1971.

Shahid, I. (= I. Kawar). "The Arabs in the Peace Treaty of A.D. 561." *Arabica* 3 (1956), 181-213.

———. *The Martyrs of Najrân*. Brussels, 1971.

———. "Two Qur'ānic Sūras: *al-Fīl* and *Qurayš*." In *Studia Arabica et Islamica, Festschrift for Iḥsān ʿAbbās*. Edited by W. al-Qāḍī. Beirut, 1981, pp. 429-436.

Shaybānī, Muḥammad b. al-Ḥasan al-. *al-Kasb*. Edited by S. Zakkār. Damascus, 1980.

Sigismund, R. *Die Aromata in ihrer Bedeutung für Religion, Sitten, Gebräuche, Handel und Geographie des Alterthums bis zu den ersten Jahrhunderten unserer Zeitrechnung*. Leipzig, 1884.

Simon, R. "Ḥums et īlāf, ou commerce sans guerre." *Acta Orientalia* (Budapest) 23:2 (1970), 205-232.

Smith, S. "Events in Arabia in the 6th Century A.D." *Bulletin of the School of Oriental and African Studies* 16 (1954), 425-468.

Snouck Hurgronje, C. *Mekka in the Latter Part of the 19th Century*. Leiden and London, 1931.

Sozomen. *Kirchengeschichte*. Edited by J. Bidez and G. C. Hansen. Berlin, 1960. Translated by E. Walford as *The Ecclesiastical History of Sozomen*. London, 1855.

Sprenger, A. *Das Leben und die Lehre des Mohammad*. 2nd ed. Vol. 3. Berlin, 1869.

Spuler, B. Review of W. W. Müller, *Weihrauch*. In *Der Islam* 57 (1980), 339.

Steensgaard, N. *Carracks, Caravans and Companies*. Copenhagen, 1973.

Steiner, R. C. *The Case for Fricative-Laterals in Proto-Semitic*. New Haven, 1977.

Strabo. *Geography*. Edited and translated by H. L. Jones. 8 vols. London and Cambridge, Mass., 1917-1932.

Strothmann, W., ed. and tr. *Moses Bar Kepha, Myron-Weihe*. Wiesbaden, 1973.

Suhaylī, ʿAbd al-Raḥmān b. ʿAbdallāh al-. *Kitāb al-rawḍ al-unuf*. 2 vols. Cairo, 1914.

Suyūṭī, Jalāl al-dīn al-. *Kitāb al-durr al-manthūr fīʾl-tafsīr biʾl-maʾthūr*. 8 vols. Beirut, n.d..

Ṭabarānī, Sulaymān b. Aḥmad al-. *al-Muʿjam al-ṣaghīr*. Edited by ʿA.-R. M. ʿUthmān. 2 vols. Medina, 1968.

Ṭabarī, Muḥammad b. Jarīr al-. *Jāmiʿ al-bayān fī tafsīr al-qurʾān*. 30 vols. Būlāq, 1905-1912.

———. *Taʾrīkh al-rusul waʾl-mulūk*. Edited by M. J. de Goeje and others. 3 series. Leiden, 1879-1901.

Talbot, W. A. *The Trees, Shrubs and Woody Climbers of the Bombay Presidency*. 2nd ed. Bombay, 1902.

Tarn, W. W. *The Greeks in Bactria and India*. 2nd ed. Cambridge, 1951.

Tarn, W. W., and G. T. Griffiths. *Hellenistic Civilisation*. London, 1966.

Taylor, J. E. "Notes of the Ruins of Muqeyer." *Journal of the Royal Asiatic Society* 15 (1855), 260-276.

Thaʿālibī, ʿAbd al-Malik b. Muḥammad al-. *The Laṭāʾif al-maʿārif*. Translated C. E. Bosworth. Edinburgh, 1968.

———. *Thimār al-qulūb*. Edited by M. A.-F. Ibrāhīm. Cairo, 1965.

Theodoretus. "In Divini Jeremiae Prophetiam Interpretatio." In J. P. Migne, *Patrologia Graeco-Latina*. Vol. 81. Paris, 1859.

Theophanes. *Chronographia*. Edited by C. de Boor. 2 vols. Leipzig, 1883-1885.

Theophrastus. *Enquiry into Plants*. Edited and translated by A. F. Hort. 2 vols. London and Cambridge, Mass., 1916-26.

Ṭirimmāḥ, *see* Krenkow.

Trimingham, J. Spencer. *Christianity among the Arabs in Pre-Islamic Times*. London, 1979.

Ṭufayl, *see* Krenkow.

Ṭūsī, Muḥammad b. al-Ḥasan al-. *al-Tibyān fī tafsīr al-Qur'ān*. Edited by A. Ḥ. Qaṣīr al-ʿĀmilī and A. Sh. Amīn. 10 vols. Najaf, 1957-1965.

Ullmann, M. *Die Natur- und Geheimwissenschaften im Islam*. Leiden, 1972.

Uphof, J.C.T. *Dictionary of Economic Plants*. 2nd ed. New York, 1968.

Vasiliev, A. A. "Notes on Some Episodes Concerning the Relations between the Arabs and the Byzantine Empire from the Fourth to the Sixth Century." *Dumbarton Oaks Papers* Vols. 9-10 (1955-1956), pp. 306-316.

Vesey-Fitzgerald, D. F. "The Vegetation of Central and Eastern Arabia." *Journal of Ecology* 45 (1957), 779-798.

———. "The Vegetation of the Red Sea Coast North of Jedda, Saudi Arabia." *Journal of Ecology* 45 (1957), 547-562.

———. "Vegetation of the Red Sea Coast South of Jedda, Saudi Arabia." *Journal of Ecology* 43 (1955), 477-489.

Vööbus, A. *Syrische Kanonessammlungen*. Vol. 1a (CSCO, Subsidia, vol. 35). Louvain, 1970.

Wāḥidī, ʿAlī b. Aḥmad al-. *Asbāb al-nuzūl*. Beirut, 1316.

Walker, W. *All the Plants of the Bible*. London, 1958.

Wallace, A.F.C. "Revitalization Movements." *American Anthropologist* 58 (1956), pp. 264-281.

Wansbrough, J. *Quranic Studies*. Oxford, 1977.

Wāqidī, Muḥammad b. ʿUmar al-. *Kitāb al-maghāzī*. Edited by M. Jones. 3 vols. Oxford, 1966.

Warmington, E. H. *The Commerce between the Roman Empire and India*. 2nd ed. London and New York, 1974.

Watt, G. *The Commercial Products of India*. London, 1908.

Watt, J. M., and M. G. Breyer-Brandwijk. *The Medicinal and Poisonous Plants of Southern and Eastern Africa*. 2nd ed. Edinburgh and London, 1962.

Watt, W. M. "The 'High God' in Pre-Islamic Mecca." *Vᵉ Congrès International d'Arabisants et d'Islamisants, Bruxelles 1970, Actes*. Brussels, n.d., pp. 499-505.

———. *Islam and the Integration of Society*. London, 1961.

———. "Ḳuraysh." *Encyclopaedia of Islam*. 2nd ed.

Watt, W. M. "The Materials Used by Ibn Isḥāq." In B. Lewis and P. M. Holt, eds., *Historians of the Middle East*. London, 1962, pp. 23-34.

———. "Muhammad." In P. M. Holt, A.K.S. Lambton, and B. Lewis, eds., *The Cambridge History of Islam*. Vol. 1. Cambridge, 1970, pp. 30-56.

———. *Muhammad at Mecca*. Oxford, 1953.

———. *Muhammad at Medina*. Oxford, 1956.

———. *Muhammad, Prophet and Statesman*. Oxford, 1964.

———. "The Qur'ān and Belief in a 'High God.' " *Proceedings of the Ninth Congress of the Union Européenne des Arabisants et Islamisants*. Leiden, 1981, pp. 327-333.

Wellhausen, J., ed. and tr. "Letzter Teil der Lieder der Hudhailiten." In his *Skizzen und Vorarbeiten*. Vol. 1. Berlin, 1884, pp. 103-175, 3-129.

———. "Medina vor dem Islam." In his *Skizzen und Vorarbeiten*. Vol. 4. Berlin, 1889, pp. 3-64.

———. *Reste arabischen Heidentums*. Berlin, 1887.

Wensinck, A. J. *The Ideas of the Western Semites Concerning the Navel of the Earth*. Amsterdam, 1916.

Wensinck, A. J., and others. *Concordances et indices de la tradition musulmane*. 7 vols. Leiden, 1933-1969.

Wheeler, R. E. M. "Roman Contact with India, Pakistan and Afghanistan." In F. Grimes, ed., *Aspects of Archaeology in Britain and Beyond, Essays Presented to O.G.S. Crawford*. London, 1951, pp. 345-381.

Whitehouse, D., and A. Williamson. "Sasanian Maritime Trade." *Iran* 11 (1973), 29-49.

Wilkinson, J. C. "Arab-Persian Land Relationships in Late Sasānid Oman." *Proceedings of the Sixth Seminar for Arabian Studies*. London, 1973, pp. 40-51.

Wissmann, H. von. "Madiama." In Pauly-Wissowa, *Realencyclopädie*. Supplementband 12.

———. "Makoraba." In Pauly-Wissowa, *Realencyclopädie*. Supplementband 12.

———. *Die Mauer der Sabäerhauptstadt Maryab*. Istanbul, 1976.

———. "Ōphīr und Ḥawīla." In Pauly-Wissowa, *Realencyclopädie*. Supplementband 12.

Woelk, *see* Agatharchides.

Woenig, F. *Die Pflanzen im alten Ägypten*. Leipzig, 1886.

Wohaibi, A. al-. *The Northern Hijaz in the Writings of the Arab Geographers, 800-1150*. Beirut, 1973.

Wolf, E. R. "The Social Organization of Mecca and the Origins of Islam." *Southwestern Journal of Anthropology* 7 (1951), 329-356.

Wörterbuch der klassischen arabischen Sprache. Wiesbaden, 1970–

Yadin, Y. "An Inscribed South-Arabian Clay Stamp from Bethel?" *Bulletin of the American Schools of Oriental Research*. No. 196, December 1969, pp. 37-45.

Ya'qūbī, Aḥmad b. Abī Ya'qūb al-. *Kitāb al-buldān*. Edited by M. J. de Goeje. Leiden, 1892. Translated by G. Wiet as *Les pays*. Cairo, 1937.

———. *Ta'rīkh*. Edited by M. T. Houtsma. 2 vols. Leiden, 1883.

Yāqūt b. 'Abdallāh. *Kitāb mu'jam al-buldān*. Edited by F. Wüstenfeld. 6 vols. Leipzig, 1866-1873.

Zacharias Rhetor. *Historia Ecclesiastica*. Edited and translated by E. W. Brooks (CSCO, Scriptores syri, series tertia, vols. 5, 6). Louvain, 1924.

Zubayr b. Bakkār. *al-Akhbār al-muwaffaqiyyāt*. Edited by S. M. al-'Ānī. Baghdad, 1972.

INDEX

Page references refer to text and notes alike regardless of whether the two are connected or not: the reader should not confine his attention to the note *ad* the word in the text. Separate note references (indicated by superscript) are only given for entries not found in the text. Square brackets indicate that the passage referred to does not use the actual word given in the entry.